RIPPLE
OF CHANGE

Sarah,
Enjoy!
Remember OQA.
OQA Advocate!

Todd R. Otten, M.D.
Joshua J. Judy, Patient

Our Quadruple Aim
Media, LLC

ISBN: 979-8-9873644-0-6 (Softcover)
ISBN: 979-8-9873644-1-3 (Hardcover)
ISBN: 979-8-9873644-2-0 (eBook)

Library of Congress Control Number: 2023908283

Cover and interior design/formatting by Vickie Swisher, Studio 20|20, Toledo, IL.

Printed by Color House Graphics, Inc., in the United States of America.

First printing edition 2023.

www.ourquadrupleaim.com

DEDICATION

To: Angie, Megan, and our children;
without your love and support
this would not have been possible.

To: Linus Silver, M.D.—
may you rest in peace,
and your memory an inspiration to many.

CONTENTS

((1))

Do No Harm

Joshua J. Judy – Patient:

Everything I share here, I share from the patient perspective. I was born in 1981. Life has given me four decades of experience as both a patient under a medical professional's care, and as a patient of life. That passage of time has provided me many hats to wear—sometimes a pill taker, other times a shot taker, now more than ever—a premium, co-pay, and high deductible payer. It wasn't always that way though.

I remember as a child not paying for doctor's visits and scripts were $2. Other times they were free. My father had worked at General Motors and the insurance plans for blue collar workers and their families were actually worth admiring. Not the stuff we have now.

I oscillate somewhere between active insurance company hater and disinclined policy holder. The pharmaceutical companies don't fare much better in my eyes. Sometimes I'm a severe side-effect sufferer, and other times I've felt okay. But I've probably never felt as good as when my own body balanced everything, before ever taking a pill.

I've had many touch points with the healthcare industry, some good, some terrible, and some lifesaving. And with that last one—I've experienced feelings of eternal gratitude. Along the way, I've met many doctors, nurses, and supporting staff. Some individuals have been amazing and left you feeling like you were an immediate family member. Others have been tone deaf, with terrible bed-side manners and massive egos. Some, simply incompetent. As the oft-quoted saying goes, not everyone graduates at the top of their class.

I've watched the changes in the healthcare industry through the years: some painless and inconsequential, some of convenience, some of unyielding frustration and masterful time-wasting. I recall rows and rows of paper records and yellow legal pads, tear-off paper scripts with illegible writing. I remember doctors exclusively wearing a pair of slacks, a dress shirt, and a tie, all visible underneath their trustworthy bright white coats. I remember being impressed as a child by that white coat. I could put my faith in this person. And in a kid's mind back then, only two professions existed in the world: doctors, and lawyers—and as I learned more about the world, maybe a police officer, teacher, or firefighter.

Growing up, if you had a good relationship with your primary care doctor, you didn't always need an office visit. If it was just bronchitis or a sinus infection as you described it over the phone, a script was called in. The weapons of choice: amoxicillin and cough syrup with codeine.

As the years passed, I watched as society dressed more casually, sometimes very casually. So too did medical staff—scrubs and tennis shoes became more the norm. Who wouldn't want to wear their pajamas to work? That's what Megan, my wife, who works in veterinary medicine and enjoys similar fashion, jokingly says.

The long rows of records and manila folders disappeared, moving to unseen or forgotten storage facilities. In their place were computers and tablets. Patient web portals came into existence. I could now see my lab results often before the doctor did. If you geek out about that kind of stuff, this was an exciting new world as a patient. "Dr. Google" became both a blessing and a curse—a know-it-all-resource-I-absolutely-am-convinced-I-have-that-disease, for patients; and, a heard-enough-who's-the-real-doctor-here, for doctors.

I've been through at least four dentists in my life. The first dentist I had for about 30 years, until he finally retired. It was well deserved and I was happy for him. But it brought up an important reflection point: When you find a doctor you love, one of the first selfish thoughts you have is that someday this person is going to retire and I'll have to find someone else. Perhaps this was my first flawed thought: Doctors aren't human, and because of that, they never get sick or need to rest themselves, right?

The next three dentist changes all happened within a matter of maybe a year. I heard none of these young dentists owned the practice or could even begin to think of owning it. But they owed someone—and lots, on their student loans. I would guess in the ballpark of $400k or more.

Apparently another out-of-state retired dentist had worked himself into the "investor class" of society, letting my childhood dentist cash out his practice and retire himself. I wondered if the revolving door of young dentists I was experiencing had anything to do with how they were starting out so deep in the hole after dental school—moving to where they could get the best pay, cheapest housing, and shortest commute.

To a lesser degree, I felt I could relate. It took me and my wife ten years to pay off our respective student loans. Our first apartment together was a loft in an old converted wool mill factory that once made blankets for Army soldiers during WWII. It was barely 400 square feet. We used to be able to reach the TV controls from our couch with our toes because our "living room" was that narrow. Changing the stations by toe is a fun game, if not a bit embarrassingly silly.

I've only had two family doctors in my life, so a bit more stable than my rolodex of dentists. My first family doctor was

Linus Silver, M.D. He was there when I was born by cesarean. He weighed me and scribbled it on a yellow legal pad. He once proudly showed me his handwritten record of it decades later. 6 lbs 9 oz. It was a small gesture, but touching and it stuck with me. It felt personal.

My mother told me this same family doctor would make her eat liver because her iron was low. Not her favorite dish, but you do what you have to do. I don't think prenatal vitamins were a thing back then. When I broke up with my first serious girlfriend in college, he prescribed some sleeping pills for a short time period. It helped get me through.

Dr. Silver eventually retired from his practice and moved on to become the director of the town's urgent care. He reduced his hours but still got to practice medicine. He once told me his hours were in the mid- to high-twenties most weeks and that was plenty enough. I later heard policy changes by hospital administrators kept happening and he was displeased. When I attended his memorial service years later, I remembered some of these random things. His wife told those in attendance that he spent all day caring for others, but he often privately wondered who cared about him.

The news of his passing was equally shocking and confusing. I was sitting in my hometown barber's shop, uncertain chatter swirling around–how he had been in a motorcycle accident a few towns over. I knew he rode. While it sounded plausible, it felt abrupt and heart-breaking. Nevertheless, some doubts had formed in my mind and lingered.

Dr. Silver was an experienced rider. He knew his way around dangerous machines that went blazingly fast. Beyond motorcycles, I recalled the pictures of him drag racing on the walls of his office. Wouldn't we have seen something this significant in the local papers? Among family and friends, we quietly debated what added up, and what did not.

Quite some time later the truth was revealed and it was ugly. He had died by suicide and the manner in which it occurred was shocking. My naïvety on display, I only knew the world of medicine to heal, not destroy—and never the healers themselves. Oh, what I would learn in time... How could the signs of burnout be missed?

'Why' is always one of the first questions you ask. But to simply ask doesn't mean there's a simple answer. It was depressing and seemed wholly unnecessary. It is strange when someone you know passes, let alone tragically. Even when you don't think you know them on a deeply personal level, all these little innocent interactions, seemingly forgotten, come flooding back. It's like your brain has been covertly tucking these moments away–until the finality of the situation shatters your ability to hide behind the noise of the day. What's left are only memory reels on center stage—to replay over and over. You realize you knew this person better than you thought.

Someone, I don't recall who, had slipped some information to me...something along the lines of my doctor deciding to go about this day like any other. He planned to golf with his sons and he did. He was in his car when it happened. He pulled over somewhere and catastrophically exited the stage.

He was highly respected in the area by his patients—more than he ever knew. I was told the motorcycle accident was concocted to save his reputation and legacy. It was a believable cover story initially, that quickly fell away to reveal at least one simple answer—he didn't deserve this.

Even though he had pulled back his commitments significantly, the system kept asking for more. He had internalized too many of the stresses and failures of this system. From 1977 to 2017 he personified Family Practice. He was only 65.

My second primary care doctor, Todd R. Otten, M.D., served in the Navy. I have watched how he has grown from the military environment to family care, his bed-side manner softening to his patients' appreciation. And now he is overbooked with patients, with more that want to see him than possibly can. Again, I find myself selfishly wondering when he retires if I'll be able to find another doctor I truly like and respect.

This is the system we're all cogs in.

I share these true-life stories from not just a patient's perspective, but also as a father, husband, son, and brother. My hope is that these collective experiences help others learn, and importantly, find some healing if you're in search of it. But most importantly, I would like people to realize that we're all human. And our shared humanity, need for mutual respect, and ability to relate to one another is bigger than any system we think we're cogs in. After all, I think we all just want to be cared for.

With sincere regards,
Joshua J. Judy

((2))

History of Present Illness

"The people who are crazy enough to think they can change the world are the ones who do."

— STEVE JOBS

Todd R. Otten, M.D.:

The desk is covered in heart-shaped glitter, balloons decorate the wall, and a rainbow unicorn hangs in the corner. Opposite the desk, other treasures lie—a vintage wooden case proudly displaying Lego figures, a Spider-Man pillow lying on an antique coffee table. A piece of petrified wood as a bookend and a globe with push pins signifying places I have been, the red on the pins fading over the years.

I suppose my office does look like something of an antique store, or maybe a flea market. The red folder of death sitting on my desk beckons me, but I set it aside for the moment. Having just returned from a week's vacation with my family, I feel rejuvenated. I am in a productive mood and happy to be here, in our family practice clinic. I honestly looked forward to returning. The nurse practitioners (NP) hung the unicorn in my absence. It speaks to the office culture and the joy we regularly experience.

A wry smile forms. As I began reviewing messages, I checked the post-mortem section. One of my long-time patients lost her battle with lung cancer. I remember the day I had a minor fender bender driving into work. Nothing serious, but I was rattled. She was the first patient I saw that day, and gave me a hug when I explained my tardiness. The hugs continued over the years. She always had compassion and empathy toward me, even while she was fighting for her life. This speaks to the doctor-patient, and patient-staff relationship in our office. Serendipitously, shortly after her death I had a follow up with her husband and was able to share this paragraph with him. Powerful and cathartic for both of us.

Work hasn't always been this way. I used to dread returning from vacation, often with over 500 messages to review or respond to. It often took me a week to catch up. Now it typically takes a day or two. And what about the patients waiting for my input? What changed to prompt my difference in perspective? Everything.

((NOTES TO THE READER))

"What is your favorite vegetable?"

– TODD R. OTTEN, M.D.

"Sausage."

– 4 YEAR OLD PATIENT

Before we begin, a comment on the jokes sprinkled throughout. For the past 13 years I have been jotting down humorous things patients have said, and many are hoping to see them in print. In fact, many patients specifically requested their inclusion. No names will be attached—the jokes will simply be labeled as *my patient*, unless consent was obtained. Even then, how many Gary's are in the world? Please note, I have a dry sense of humor—akin to the Sahara on a 120 degree day. Please enjoy, no offense intended.

A few other introductory comments are warranted. As my vision evolved into words, it became clear that opportunities arose for a greater audience, far beyond physicians. I see *Ripple of Change* as an opportunity on innumerable levels, energizing many, regardless of profession. Think of a compass that points towards answers or solutions. I am writing this book as a broad commentary, an inquisition regarding the dysfunction that exists in healthcare and beyond, and hopefully it will be an inspiration for change. As the final product took shape, the metamorphosis of the target audience became: **the American healthcare consumer.**

Ripple of Change is laid out in a particular sequence, weaving Joshua's story with mine (and occasionally, others). We were very intentional with the chronicity of the chapters, and encourage you to follow doctor's orders, as the themes will build along with our prescription for change. As such, we will annotate any change in authorship, similar to the beginning of this chapter. I will occasionally offer explanations (for the layperson) regarding the medical jargon that is intuitive for me. Other times, I will leave that investigation to the reader.

There is a litany of acronyms as well, all available for reference. We intentionally do not include a glossary, but one term is worth a short digression. Silo. Many think of a farm or perhaps missiles. But, silo (s) or siloing in healthcare is frequently used to describe when systems, departments, processes, information, data or more are isolated from one another. For example: patient information from one hospital to another is often siloed, creating many issues for those of us trying to provide appropriate care. Undoubtedly, this term applies to many industries.

There are stories that involve patients, colleagues, administrators, friends, and family. Out of respect for confidentiality I have replaced names with pseudonyms, unless given permission. Countless people contributed: friends, family, colleagues, physicians, NPs, nurses, administrators, medical assistants (MA), patients, pharmaceutical representatives, architects, professional athletes, Ph.D.s, teachers, business leaders, lawyers, writers, chief executive officers (CEO), military officers, and more. The outpouring of ideas was incredible and eventually we had to limit the topics. But, we are all affected by healthcare—hence the multitude of viewpoints.

There will be discussion of evidence-based medicine, research, editorials, and recent news. Humor and poetry are included, as are inspiring quotes, and some chapters are closer to a collection of essays. There are a few profane words, a product of serving in the military. But emotions run high in medicine and I wanted to be true to the moment. Perhaps those who may be offended should refrain from continuing. My hope is that all of us reconsider our views of, or roles in, healthcare. Certainly I have.

Would I do medicine again? I believe I would, but I am not sure I would encourage my children. This would have been an easy answer 10 years ago. An emphatic—yes. But things have changed. Clerical duties for physicians are greater than ever and priorities often misaligned. Costs are spiraling out of control, and life expectancy in America is decreasing. I would have to give it considerable thought. And depending on the day, I might even say no. For someone who has dedicated over 20 years of their life in making a difference to others this is a sad commentary on the current state.

The joy of seeing patients is hard to put into words—euphoric at times. Sharing in positive outcomes, an improved mood, a defeated cancer. These moments are blessings I share with my patients. One of my patients with schizophrenia recently told me I was the only person she could count on; immediately goose flesh appeared on my arms. But, medicine has become increasingly convoluted, with profits often prioritized over people. That is not what I signed up for. Perhaps I was naive. I believe most healthcare workers are in it for the right reasons. Our system needs to stop extracting maximum value from workers and patients. Our healthcare system needs to reassess what the priorities are, and it needs to put patients and providers at the forefront, with quality outcomes over filling coffers.

((INSPIRATION))

"Just keep me alive—so I can get an autographed copy."

– MIKE RANVILLE, AUTHOR, FRIEND, AND FORMER PATIENT

So what inspires a 45-year-old physician on the verge of retirement to write a book? The answer would probably constitute an entire chapter itself—but would it be entertaining? I have long considered authoring a book, and my thoughts return to the topic I know best...medicine. I pondered what works well in healthcare and what does not. I suppose my altruism even extends to fulfilling an item on my bucket list.

What I found fascinating was that the book started to write itself. Having been through burnout and watching my colleagues grow increasingly frustrated with the current climate of healthcare—writing became cathartic. At some points, I could not get my thoughts down fast enough as the ideas flowed freely into my finger tips. The amount of information available regarding the current issues in healthcare is immense and even overwhelming. And suggestions for improvement are increasingly available. Unfortunately, healthcare as a collective is far from ideal.

((MEDICINE IS A WORLD OF GRAY...))

As I reflect on over 20 years of practicing medicine,
I wonder, how did we get here?
How did the profession I love become so black and white?

I am despondent with the clerical burdens.
I am saddened by the box clicking.
I am disheartened when it's just one more form.

I am discouraged when I hear prior auth.
I feel desolate.

Black or white?

I feel happy seeing patients.
I feel fulfilled teaching students and APP's.
I feel content making a difference.

Black or white?

Lest we forget the patient...
Access, insurance, polypharmacy, mental health...
Providers staring at a screen.
Does data make the dying feel better?

Is this the balance we want?

I question if I am truly making a difference?
How many burned-out providers does it take?
Will this crisis in medicine end?
Perhaps when healthcare leaders actually hear the voices of physicians and patients, and listen.

Too often, issues in healthcare
are assumed to be black and white...
medicine is a world of gray.

– TODD R. OTTEN, M.D., 2021

This short poem reviews my 20-year career and how it has been impacted by issues that plague healthcare in the United States. I wrote this two years after surviving burnout. Two years have passed, and that part of my career was still haunting me. As I sat listening to Father Mark Martin's homily at our local parish, inspiration hit me like a ton of bricks. Why not write a book about my experiences with Our Quadruple Aim (OQA)?

Why not share the successes my patients, colleagues, and I have experienced when we emphasized OQA? I believe, if effectively implemented, Our Quadruple Aim can transform our current healthcare delivery system into one where all stakeholders thrive.

Good physicians really do make a difference, despite the dysfunctional system that has been built around us.

As healthcare has morphed more and more into a business model, the drivers are often finance, legal, information technology (IT), and infrastructure, among others. Unfortunately, clinical leaders often play second fiddle. This has led to increasing burdens on the people actually delivering care and, as a result, burnout rates are at unacceptable levels. Unless there is a culture shift at the highest levels, this will not improve. Is there hope? Absolutely, and I believe it starts with:

(("OUR" QUADRUPLE AIM))

"In the overhaul of healthcare, we all have our role to play."

– JOHN HAMMERGREN, *SKIN IN THE GAME*[1]

Before we move forward and learn of Joshua J. Judy's healthcare journey thus far, I would like to formally introduce the concept of "Our" Quadruple Aim. "Our" Quadruple Aim is an evolution of the Quadruple Aim, which was preceded by the Triple Aim. Both the Triple Aim and the Quadruple Aim are unified goals in delivering healthcare. Confused? Don't fret, it will all make sense shortly.

So why add the "Our"? Doesn't the Quadruple Aim sound logical enough? Can it stand alone? Absolutely. However, the Quadruple Aim doesn't imply a sense of ownership. Who is responsible for delivering? We all utilize healthcare, shouldn't we all be accountable? Absolutely. Adding "Our" strengthens the phrase. The "Our" emphatically states that we all are responsible.

A revolution or an evolution then? Some may consider this nebulous, but **medicine is a world of gray**. Going forward, we will lose the quotation marks. As Joshua and I begin to weave our stories—Our Quadruple Aim is born.

OUR QUADRUPLE AIM

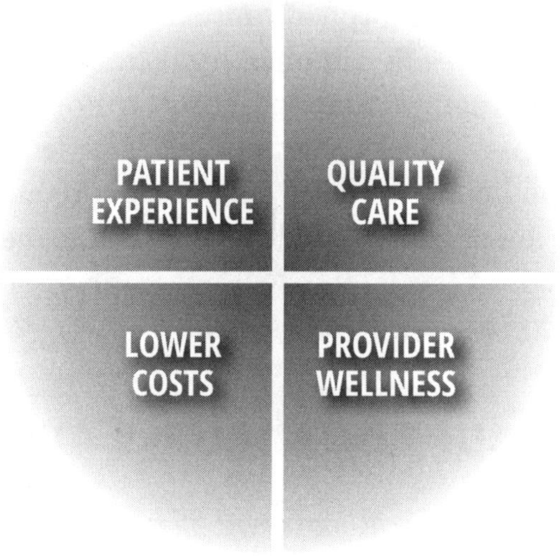

1. **Patient Experience**
2. **Quality Care**
3. **Lower Costs**
4. **Provider Wellness**

Sanguinely, as more individuals take ownership of our healthcare system (under the auspices of Our Quadruple Aim), the more things will improve—not only in healthcare, but beyond. Beyond? Our Quadruple Aim is ubiquitous, and the four principles can easily be applied to just about any environment. Think of OQA as a light guiding you home in the darkest of nights.

For example, consider how OQA might apply if you owned a restaurant. Think of Patient Experience as customer satisfaction,

Quality Care replaced by a wonderful meal, Lower Costs as fair pricing, and Provider Wellness as employee wellness. What about a local brewery, such as Dimes in Dimondale, Michigan—Dimes' Quadruple Aim. Or how does Our Quadruple Aim translate to our educational system?

Our Quadruple Aim	Education's Quadruple Aim
1. Patient Experience	Student learning/experience
2. Quality Care	Quality pedagogy for all
3. Lower Costs	Reasonable tuition
4. Provider Wellness	Teacher wellbeing

As this example in education illustrates, the opportunities are endless; Our Quadruple Aim can be crafted or molded as warranted. Like your fingerprint, every patient is unique. So too, every situation. The American healthcare consumer has plenty of skin in the game; more like an appendage (for many)—given our exorbitant spending. Patients and providers are drowning in a sea of dysfunction, as dollars are disproportionately allocated to the surrounding sharks.

Our Quadruple Aim offers powerful insight, inspiration and courage to reimagine yourself, the workplace, and our healthcare system. In his discussion of aligned incentives, Benjamin Schwartz, M.D. discusses a ground-up approach to overhaul American medicine. He suggests current stakeholders have disparate goals and misaligned incentives.[2] I agree, but if enough voices join Our Quadruple Aim, they will be difficult to ignore. Having all stakeholders transparently working towards common goals is fundamental to OQA. Joshua and I believe the four components of Our Quadruple Aim masterfully blend aligned incentives into a bare bones approach. Concepts that are easily grasped and implemented, allowing you to contribute to our *Ripple of Change*.

Joshua J. Judy – Patient:

Dr. Otten is spot on. **Medicine is a world of gray**. That makes it hard to know who or what to trust. And if you don't know who to trust, it may seem easier to default to trusting nobody. It's a lonely path and unquestionably dark.

"Trust dies but mistrust blossoms."

– SOPHOCLES

Many would raise their hands if asked, "Is trust the bedrock of any relationship?" But what does it mean in the context of wellness? I offer that trust is what binds together every interaction between you (as a patient) and your doctor, you and insurance, you and the pharmacy, doctors and their staff, doctors and pharmaceutical representatives, doctors and administrators, and even you and your body.

In my ongoing health care journey, many days I wondered if I could trust my body to do the right thing, let alone trust others. I wondered if some of my doctors had my back and trusted what I told them about my concerns. Similarly, did I have my doctors' backs by being completely up front with them about my expectations? While this describes doctor-patient interactions, haven't you asked yourself similar questions in your own relationships?

When you do, it becomes obvious: Trust isn't something you can set and forget. It must be owned and maintained—continually fostered, in every exchange. It means not purposely omitting information. It means considering how your actions will not only impact yourself, but others too. It means doing the right thing without being asked or forced. Trust is earned and grows over time—one wrong move can quickly sweep it away. Trust is hard to build and it won't last without effort.

Absent trust, how can a physician and a healthcare administrator optimize Patient Experience, Quality Care, Lower Costs, or

Provider Wellness? In short, they won't. Unfortunately, there's a lot of mistrust in the healthcare system. Mistrust has blossomed while trust has died. We owe it to ourselves to explore why, and stake a claim in our healthcare system—Our Quadruple Aim.

Dr. Otten's and my hope is that our joint journey will light a path to rebuild trust in healthcare. We hope our transparency enables you to realize the potential of your own wellness journey. And, in turn, help you discover how each of us can contribute to building a more equitable healthcare system. It can't just be mine or Dr. Otten's system, or 'Aim,' because we all own the system's success or failure. This requires reestablishing trust in a healthcare system that cares about you, and you about it. The key is to find that happy balance—think Yin and Yang—by highlighting what still works in addition to what Dr. Otten states, having the courage to challenge the status quo.

((DOCTORS ARE PEOPLE TOO))

Todd R. Otten, M.D.:

As I struggle with the current state of healthcare, I remind myself, "Why did I go into medicine?" My thoughts typically drift back to successes with patients. Whether it was making a difficult diagnosis, helping transition a dying patient into hospice, or reducing polypharmacy (multiple medications), these are the things that provide me joy. However, the current burdens that exist often outweigh the positives of delivering care and can drown a provider. I am not alone in this sentiment, and it can be very disheartening. Sara Berg cites Rush University Medical Center's Chief Wellness Officer Bryant Adibe, M.D., in a recent American Medical Seminar (AMA) webinar. Dr. Adibe eloquently summarizes the macro and institutional contributors to burnout:[3]

"The primary driver of burnout is macroeconomics, spanning the entire U.S. health system. But there are also secondary drivers, typically at the organization-level; such administrative barriers and burdens or operational inefficiencies that significantly contribute and make it worse. Additionally, there are also tertiary drivers," he added. "These include the realities of trying to balance a professional career with a family and other personal life challenges. It is the confluence of these factors that ultimately drives burnout— not one individual piece, but all of these together. Our role as organizational leaders is to acknowledge and address those drivers over which we have control and attempt to provide solutions that will be impactful."[4]

Coincidently, as I started writing I precipitated a tension headache, thinking about all of the flaws in healthcare. The irony. So before I get into the heart of the matter, I think it's important the reader knows a little more of who I am and why I am writing this book. So let's go back in time and meet a young man...

My formative years were filled with trials and tribulations. A bright and fearless child proved a volatile combination. As a middle school student I wasn't challenged enough, and boredom got me in trouble. I recall arguing with a math teacher about why I didn't need to show my work (if the answer was correct). This led to some passive aggressive behavior that ultimately got me suspended. Can you imagine the frustration of the teacher?

Bullying was another major challenge during my youth, as I often overreacted with other students (as children like to tease), and was bullied relentlessly. The bullying led to fighting with other students and more than one suspension from school; and over time contributed to some significant depression. I distinctly remember staring at the bathroom mirror in grade school—contemplating suicide. Looking back on these developmental years, it certainly explains my frustrations with how healthcare has evolved. And, I will not be bullied.

I share these struggles of my adolescence to convey some of the deficiencies that existed in healthcare some 30 years ago, and yet still remain. But it still serves to question, how well do we deal with mental health in the U.S.? Unfortunately, many, including myself, would say this is a horribly underfunded specialty. In a letter to the United States House of Representatives on February 2, 2022, the American Hospital Association writes: “Our healthcare system is underfunded and understaffed to meet Americans’ behavioral health needs.” The AHA reports that over 25% of patients admitted to a hospital have a concomitant behavioral health disorder and over 100 million Americans live in areas with a shortage of psychiatrists.[5]

Fortunately, my high school years were better. The depression resolved, and I excelled both athletically and academically. I had the fortune of winning a state championship in soccer and was an all-state track and field athlete. These accomplishments allowed me to get an academic scholarship and run Division I track at the University of Detroit Mercy. College was an amazing experience. I worked extremely hard and ultimately graduated as valedictorian in 1997 (in three and a half years). My athletic success continued, earning three varsity letters in track and field as a sprinter and long jumper. Most importantly, I met my best friend—my wife, Angie. We married in 2001 and have four wonderful children (Joshua, Brandon, Daniel, and Natalie).

Why do I write about my developmental years? Historically, physicians are held to a higher standard. However, we are human beings—not machines. We have feelings, emotions, families, worries, hobbies, faith, losses. The list goes on and on. Being able to compartmentalize is essential, but witnessing death or telling someone they are dying can only happen so many times before it wears on you. I tell patients, “...everyone has a bucket that they can pour stress into, some people have big buckets and some small; but when the bucket starts to overflow—problems develop.” I am a person, just like you.

((GOOD FORTUNE))

After graduating from the University of Detroit Mercy, I went on to medical school at Wayne State University in Detroit. It didn't take long to realize I belonged. I was 16-years old when I decided to dedicate my life to the practice of medicine. However, I was a little naive about the process and fortunate to be accepted the first year I applied. I know many brilliant physicians who took two or three years to be accepted.

Nervous and alone, fate was on my side. While waiting for my interview, I ran into a colleague with whom I had attended high school. He was a third-year medical student at the time and we had previously run track together. He asked who I was interviewing with. I told him the name and he offered, "Dr. Blessing loves the DMC, whatever you do—mention the DMC." The following is a brief excerpt from my interview.

Mild-mannered pediatrician: "So, why do you want to go to medical school?"

Me: "Honestly, I love science and I want to make a difference in the world."

Mild-mannered pediatrician: "So what do you like most about Wayne State?"

Me: "Well, I really love the DMC!"

At that point he spoke for 20 minutes about the DMC, how great it was, the learning and the opportunities that availed. It was during these passionate 20 minutes I learned what the DMC was—the Detroit Medical Center. Oops. Inside I laughed, as fortune smiled on me. Green behind the ears, that interview still felt right. The good Lord had plans for me and I was accepted into medical school a few months later.

((DO YOU HAVE THE COURAGE FOR CHANGE?))

"Change will not come if we wait for some other person,
or if we wait for some other time.
We are the ones we've been waiting for.
We are the change that we seek."

– BARACK OBAMA

My wife, family, and friends will tell you: I always need to be challenged. Rarely am I satisfied with the status quo. Perhaps that is the impetus to write this book. It breaks my heart to see the level of malfunction in healthcare. I occasionally tear up when a colleague conveys their frustrations and experience with burnout. A little part of me dies every time a patient tells me about the struggles they endure, and obstacles to overcome trying to obtain care. Quality healthcare should be accessible and affordable for everyone. The healthcare experience should be positive for both patients and providers. Profits should not be the primary driver.

I do not have all of the answers. But I do have the courage to ask questions. I have the courage to challenge the status quo. I have the courage to stand up for what I believe. I believe in Our Quadruple Aim. Think of OQA as the lighthouse guiding your ship on a stormy night, or better yet, a mindset or framework for evaluating existing problems. I pray this book encourages you to ask questions and stand up for what you believe. Healthcare in the U.S. won't fix itself, but an army of patients and providers just might. If enough of us make an effort we just might move the needle.

Joshua J. Judy and I first met over a decade ago, as fate would have it—our lives forever intertwined. What started as a doctor-patient relationship has evolved to a friendship through a common bond and healing process. Our journeys overlap in a myriad of ways. This relationship has been a driving force to create *Ripple of Change*, and we consider it our first stone to be cast. We hope it's as powerful for you as it has been for us.

As we co-authored the book, there certainly is a Yin and Yang. For clarity, we will annotate whose words you are enjoying with our name prior. For example: Joshua wrote the first chapter, his name preceding his thoughts. Any time the author changes—the appropriate name will appear. There will be an evolution of Joshua's adoption of the Our Quadruple Aim as we progress. We will toggle back and forth, with subtle interplays. The themes are intended to challenge you, be thought-provoking, and occasionally uncomfortable—as change is rarely easy.

((3))

Journey Beyond the Triple Aim

"I don't like to put chemicals in my body."
– PATIENT, REGARDING MEDICATIONS

"Yet, you smoke."
– TODD R. OTTEN, M.D.

((THE TRIPLE AIM))

Todd R. Otten, M.D.:

Our Quadruple Aim builds on the work of many health care professionals over the past 20 years who have suggested new approaches to delivering and lowering the cost of care.

Prior to the Triple Aim, the priority of healthcare was often limited to quality of care as outlined in the Institute of Medicine's (2001) publication, *Crossing the Quality Chasm: A New Health System for the 21st Century*. The book outlined six aims for improving quality in healthcare:

1. Safe
2. Effective
3. Patient-centered
4. Timely
5. Efficient
6. Equitable[6]

The executive summary eloquently conveys numerous concerns regarding quality in healthcare, going so far as to describe *"Between the health care we have and the care we could have lies not just a gap, but a chasm."*[7] *Crossing the Quality Chasm* offers numerous areas for improvement and ideas for facilitation in healthcare. The text presents a discussion of evidence-based medicine, technology, transparency, information flow, and more. An illuminating introductory quote from the text echoes that many of the concerns addressed (over 20 years ago) are still problematic today.

> *"The frustration levels of both patients and clinicians have probably never been higher. Yet the problems remain. Health care today harms too frequently and routinely fails to deliver its potential benefits."*[8]

To fully appreciate the Quadruple Aim (and evolution to Our Quadruple Aim), let's pause to review the history of the Triple Aim. The Triple Aim originated with John Wittington and Tom Nolan in 2006 at the Institute for Healthcare Improvement in Cambridge, Massachusetts. The Triple Aim advocates for a systemic approach to improving our healthcare system. It attempts to align the primary drivers of our healthcare system with the needs of society. "It's like a compass that helps us define success" says Don Berwick M.D., President Emeritus and Senior Fellow at the Institute for Healthcare Improvement.[9]

The model they introduced, the Triple Aim, seeks to identify the primary goals for our healthcare system from a societal point of view using three simply stated, easy-to-understand principles:

1. Improved patient experience of care (including quality and satisfaction)
2. Improved health for populations
3. Lower per capita cost of delivering care[10]

In an attempt to return the focus back to the three original goals, the Institute for Healthcare Improvement published a follow-up article in 2014, *A Primer on Defining the Triple Aim*. It's a wonderful article that reiterates the premise of the Triple Aim (the simultaneous pursuit of improving patient experience, improving health of populations, and reducing per capita costs). The reader is reminded that the Triple Aim is a single aim with three goals and the pursuit is extremely ambitious. Ultimately, meaningful and sustained change won't be achieved with minor modifications to the status quo.[11] Rather, a dramatic reset of the system is needed to achieve a new model that works better for all of us.

It seems pretty logical when you think about it. Who wouldn't want higher quality and a better experience at a lower cost? I do, and I think most Americans agree. At its core, I believe the Triple Aim is brilliant. If stakeholders can let go of their own insular desires and resistance to change, aligning systemic improvements based on the simple principles contained in the Triple Aim will lead to significant, beneficial, and lasting change. However, in 20 years of practicing medicine, I would argue we are further behind than when I first cut into a cadaver in medical school.

In hindsight, it seems The Institute of Medicine recognized the enormity of the challenge and presented powerful insight, with an agenda for crossing the quality chasm. The authors even allude to the fourth component of the Quadruple Aim: *"Such a system would also be better for clinicians and others who would experience the satisfaction of providing care that was more reliable, more responsive to patients, and more coordinated than is the case today."*[12]

As a primary care provider (PCP), I am in a unique position to pursue the Triple Aim. I have the privilege to care for patients, families, and friends for extended periods. I frequently make choices that save our healthcare system money, and are balanced with providing high-quality care and a solid patient experience. But medicine is a complicated world of gray. Just as every human being is unique, so to—every provider and deliverer of health care. As a result, it's not surprising that over time the simplicity and genius of the Triple Aim model has been lost, as stakeholder groups develop their own interpretations and versions—often self-serving. For human beings, drastic change is difficult.

My first leadership experience with the Triple Aim was in 2016 while serving as the Medical Director for the Rural Southern Michigan Accountable Care Organization (ACO). At the time, ACOs were in their formative years and this was a new experience for many, including myself.

> *"Accountable Care Organizations (ACOs) are groups of doctors, hospitals, and other health care providers, who come together voluntarily to give coordinated high quality care to the Medicare patients they serve. Coordinated care helps ensure that patients, especially the chronically ill, get the right care at the right time, with the goal of avoiding unnecessary duplication of services and preventing medical errors. When an ACO succeeds in both delivering high-quality care and spending health care dollars more wisely, it will share in the savings it achieves for the Medicare program."*[13]

The learning curve was steep. However, their fundamental values were aligned with the Triple Aim and I recognized the potential. In my six years as an ACO medical director, I had a tendency to simplify this framework to better patient experience, improved quality, and lower cost.

Our ACO accounted for approximately 10,000 Medicare patients, and the overarching goal was to lower overall cost (per patient) by delivering high quality care. I was charged with engaging physician leaders within our hospital network (under the umbrella of the ACO) to help drive change. I spoke with numerous physicians regarding the Triple Aim model and how to disseminate the concepts of value-based reimbursement, shared savings, and risk coding to their colleagues. The notion of being compensated for delivering lower cost, quality care resonated with them, mirroring the altruistic reasons many of us went into healthcare in the first place.

I believe Centers for Medicare and Medicaid Services, or CMS, is onto something with its ACO model. In essence, all parties started to have skin in the game: patients, payers, caregivers, hospitals, and various stakeholders. The premise is ingenious, if the incentives are aligned. Unfortunately, and speaking from experience, this is not always what occurs. Hospital systems often see the dollars from value-based reimbursement as new revenue. They used "creative accounting" strategies to justify not distributing dollars from shared savings (i.e. value-based reimbursement) with other stakeholders. This corrupts the model and ensures failure. It's the antithesis of aligned incentives. And as a result, engagement from stakeholders deteriorates, then evaporates.

((EARLY PIVOT))

"The Triple Aim does indeed need to morph to the Quadruple Aim."

– PATIENT

Concurrent with the introduction of the Triple Aim, concerns were also growing over provider burnout and the detrimental ripples it creates. As deleterious effects of burnout continued to be elucidated, the negative impact of burnout on achieving the Triple Aim was significant. In retrospect, the Triple Aim did not adequately address provider wellbeing.

In 2014, Thomas Bodenheimer, M.D. and Christine Sinsky, M.D. authored an article suggesting adding a fourth goal to the Triple Aim, addressing provider wellness. The article, "From Triple to Quadruple Aim: Care of the Patient Requires Care of the Provider," was published in *The Annals of Family Medicine*.[14]

This landmark article eloquently articulates the notion that, for healthcare to operate at the highest level, all parties need skin in the game. In other words, the goals of all stakeholders need to be aligned. Their poignant question marks the origin of the Quadruple Aim:

> *"In visiting primary care practices around the country, the authors have repeatedly heard statements such as, 'We have adopted the Triple Aim as our framework, but the stressful work life of our clinicians and staff impacts our ability to achieve the 3 aims.' These sentiments made us wonder, might there be a fourth aim—improving the work life of health care clinicians and staff—that, like the patient experience and cost reduction aims, must be achieved in order to succeed in improving population health? Should the Triple Aim become the Quadruple Aim?"*[15]

This question is layered with complexity, so let's simplify. I unequivocally believe the Triple Aim should become the Quadruple Aim. I am not alone in this sentiment. Here are some similar statements regarding this much needed transition:

- "If all you focus on is the old Triple Aim: Cost, Quality, and Population Health...the only thing you are guaranteed is an epidemic of physician burnout" – Dike Drummond, M.D.[16]
- "Approaches that neglect or fail to include the fourth dimension ultimately fail."[17] as cited on www.csuitesolutions.com

- "As value-based care becomes more prevalent, the quality of care that is provided becomes essential, and it all starts with the provider. The pressure that is put on caregivers is immense, leading to unwanted outcomes that can negatively affect the quality of care provided...lower patient satisfaction, reduced health outcomes, and higher costs-which goes directly against the Triple Aim."[18] as cited on www.privishealth.com

I too, believe the Triple Aim has created numerous unintended consequences for physicians and front-line providers, depending on how the Triple Aim was interpreted or implemented. Surely examples exist of the Triple Aim succeeding, but as a collective our healthcare system is far from optimal. The lack of transparency has contributed to an epidemic of issues, including lack of ownership. Going forward, we all need to advocate for, and take ownership of, healthcare at both the individual and population level. This is our healthcare system, and pointing fingers isn't acceptable. Every stakeholder needs an equitable amount of skin in the game and wellness should be an essential part of our care delivery system.

((CURRENT STATE))

"Addressing the failures of the health care system will require uncomfortable reflection and bold action."

– ERIC REINHART, M.D.[19]

As this endeavor evolved, I queried numerous individuals for their thoughts regarding healthcare and particularly Our Quadruple Aim. Commonly, a quizzical or perplexed look was returned (from patients, administrators, and even physicians). Disappointed, I would take a cleansing breath and give a short explanation of the origins of the Triple Aim and why I think transformation to OQA is paramount. I would suggest OQA is a toolkit or toolbox for evaluating the many failures in healthcare, perhaps a template for corporate America; and why not a mindset for business, wellness, and life? Conversations would morph into the individual expressing existing concerns, and wishing me well to inspire change. But interest was evident, and desire for positive change—universal.

It would have been an intriguing experiment to see how many people knew what Our Quadruple Aim was when I asked. Perhaps I will. It will be fascinating to see what ripples of change are created. Regardless, the interest was omnipresent. Concerns, abundant. Worries, apparent. The need for multifaceted drivers leading the way in healthcare (in lieu of finances), long overdue. People (particularly patients) are desperate for our current healthcare system to listen to sounding alarms and wake up.

Satire is the use of humor, irony, exaggeration, or ridicule to expose and criticize stupidity or vices, particularly in the context of contemporary politics and other topical issues. And humor is considered a mature defense mechanism, which I often employ in my daily routine. Pondering the following comments, I could not think of a better word to summarize them. Satire. These scathing remarks are from a well-educated and articulate patient of mine, regarding a local institution and Our Quadruple Aim.

1. "Improved patient experience? Hospital X wouldn't know this, even if metaphorically it was a snake and hospital X was bitten in the nose."

2. "Improving the health of the overall population? Ann Landers used to say 'no improvement unless the patient wants to get better.' 40% of the U.S. population doesn't care."

3. "Lower costs??? Ha, Ha. Charge what the market will bear."

4. "Care team wellbeing to prevent provider burnout? Hospital X is maniacally driven to fatten the bottom line.

Richer = new buildings = more demands on providers = higher prices = less patient satisfaction."

Ouch. A lot to unpack in his comments. Regardless, they are not flattering. The comments regarding financial drivers are laced with the poison of a satirical bite. But they eloquently set the stage for process improvement. Is Our Quadruple Aim the antivenom? Absolutely. OQA can help peel back the layers of dysfunction, unwind the rampant fraud, waste, and abuse, and start to heal the moral injury that exists. "But as clinicians, we are increasingly forced to consider the demands of other stakeholders—the electronic medical record (EMR), the insurers, the hospital, the health care system, even our own financial security—before the needs of our patients. Every time we are forced to make a decision that contravenes our patients' best interests, we feel a sting of moral injustice. Over time, these repetitive insults amass into moral injury."[20]

AthenaHealth looked at the growth of administration compared to physicians since the late 1970s. Despite the data being a few years old, it captures a very salient point: the growth of administrative positions has outpaced that of physicians over 20-fold from 1975 to 2010.[21] This parallels the clerical burdens today's physicians and frontline workers have to endure. As a result, more and more time is spent on data collection and paperwork, rather than direct patient care. Bureaucratic burdens (charting and paperwork) are cited as the top cause of burnout for physicians in the United States (across three age groups: millennials, Gen Xers and baby boomers).[22] Barring improvement, I anticipate burnout will continue to rise among physicians and every cohort of front-line workers in the healthcare arena.

The physician shortage is another concern in danger of acceleration in the coming years. Focusforhealth.org projects a shortage of 121,000 physicians by 2032. Daunting. The study identified many reasons for the shortage: a growing and aging population, physician retirements, physician morale, and burnout.[23] Primary care is of particular concern, as high student debt often propels medical students into specialties that have greater earnings power. These issues have led many of my colleagues to pursue other opportunities. I know one friend who retired at 45, another in his 40s who no longer practices. Worrisome. And I know many others who plan to reduce direct patient care and many more who would retire if possible. What does that reveal about our healthcare system when physicians in the prime of their career walk away?

Elisabeth Rosenthal, M.D. in her book, *An American Sickness: How Healthcare Became Big Business and How You Can Take It Back*, discusses medicine as a business and the financial strain it has taken on the American people. While reviewing the commercialization of a physician's practice, she refers to Dr. Robert Brown (a family physician in Bronx, New York). "He never invested in labs or scans or sold his practice to a hospital to add facility fees." Dr. Rosenthal adds, "If medicine continues on its current trajectory, the kinds of doctors whom Americans say they value and want could very well become, in his words, like 'dinosaurs.'"[24]

Ironically, while researching the Triple Aim on my cell phone, an article from *Medscape* popped up entitled, "'I've had it with medicine!': 16 options for second careers." (See Below).[25] When this article presented itself, I had already made the decision that 2022 would be my last year seeing patients full-time. Why? Despite my love caring for patients, teaching NPs, and making a difference, the other "stuff" is overwhelming. Little did I know my trajectory would change.

Serendipitously, I had started an investment club and began writing (two items on my so-called "bucket list"). Despite the challenges with both endeavors, they are enjoyable and rewarding. Perhaps I found my second career in a blend of #8 and #13 on Medscape's list of potential second careers, under the heading:

((WHAT IF CLINICAL MEDICINE IS NO LONGER REWARDING?))

1. Move Into Hospital Administration
2. Become a Physician Advisor at Your Hospital
3. Start a Practice Management Consultancy
4. Become a Career Coach
5. Work With Computer Technology
6. Review Insurance Claims
7. Work at a Management Consulting Firm
8. **Become a Financial Planner**
9. Work for a Venture Capital Company
10. Get Involved in Retail or Manufacturing
11. Get a Job in the Pharma Sector
12. Become a Physician Recruiter
13. **Become a Freelance Writer**
14. Produce CME Presentations
15. Become a Teacher
16. Start an 'Encore Career'[26]

Before we explore how Our Quadruple Aim can create a lasting *Ripple of Change*, I feel compelled to reiterate this book is a blend of personal experience, humor, patient experiences, evidence-based medicine, and much, much more. OQA is like a Swiss army knife, a tool to transform just about any workplace. But OQA is not a magic wand and certainly not a plug and play solution. The ideas, concepts, solutions are intended to facilitate a grassroots approach, create lasting change, and recognize that every voice counts. Our ultimate goal is to facilitate increasing conversations around, and subsequent adoption of Our Quadruple Aim—as standard operating procedure.

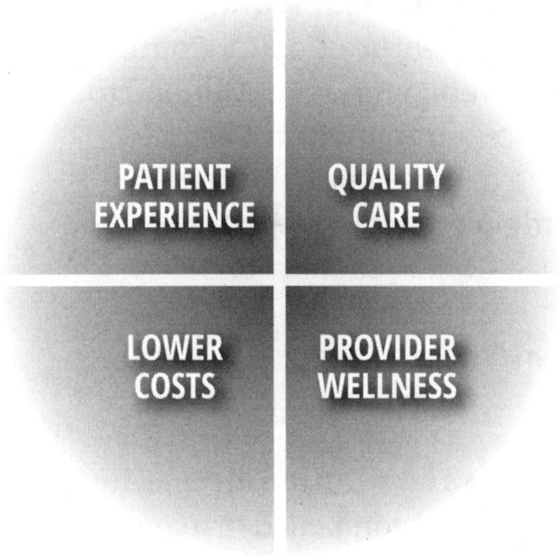
PATIENT EXPERIENCE
QUALITY CARE
LOWER COSTS
PROVIDER WELLNESS

((4))

"Losing the Blueprint"

((THE YIN AND THE YANG))

Todd R. Otten, M.D.:

Yin and Yang is an ancient Chinese philosophy that revolves around the concept of competing and complementary forces. Typically the elements come in pairs—the moon and the sun, hot and cold. The balance of Yin and Yang is essential. The symbol is a circle divided into two halves by a s-curved line. One half is black, the other white. A dot of opposing color is situated near the center—representing a small seed of the opposite side.[27]

The tenet of Yin and Yang beautifully highlights the doctor-patient relationship. Patients provide information and doctors (in turn) assimilate and formulate treatment plans. The delicate interaction between doctor and patient can be wonderful, magical.

But balance is required. Without it, an appointment can be disappointing for one or even both parties. Certainly, Yin and Yang can be extrapolated to many aspects in healthcare and beyond.

When Joshua and I first met regarding the book, we discussed a Yin and Yang approach. This meeting sparked the idea of weaving his unique history throughout. As you will come to learn, the devastating response to 60 mg of duloxetine Joshua has endured is the exact opposite of my experience; 60 mg of duloxetine solved my two year battle with crippling headaches. In some ways it seems as though duloxetine represents the small dots of opposing color in our Yin and Yang.

Our collaboration offers a delicate balancing act between his perspective and my views, that creates a powerful conversation regarding issues that exist and opportunities for change. In his work, *Losing the Blueprint (LTB)*, Joshua shares his medical journey. Triumphs and tribulations. Raw detail from the patient perspective. As such, Joshua's story will be woven into the fabric of Our Quadruple Aim.

((BEGINNING OF THE END))

Joshua J. Judy – Patient:

patient ***noun***

pa· tient | \ ˈpā-shənt From the Latin "patiens," from "patior," to suffer or bear[28]

My health was about to take a turn for the worst. Things went down hill shortly before I turned 30. And where I thought I would find answers within easy reach stretched into a long road with an untold destination. Over a decade later, I'm 40 as I write this, and it's a road I'm still traveling.

I began taking duloxetine at 30 mg once daily on March 27, 2014.

I never imagined this medication would be the beginning of the end of the old me. Unfortunately, my patient story encapsulates much of the current dysfunction in healthcare. It will be complex, at times maddening. Just don't expect me to dilute what I say. You'll read about curious blood work results and learn obscure scientific facts. There will be details I can't prove, just report and share. It's acceptable to feel incredulous and still show empathy.

I explained to Dr. Otten the reason why I go so deep into my story is because I felt many doctors never wanted a complicated case. Like they were saying, "Please let this be another cookie cutter one so I can plow to the next one." I knew I needed to take ownership of my health if I was to get better. Sure, that's part of it. But it's a larger reflection of trying to counter the frustration I felt. As in, I'll show you (provider) by running circles around your medical knowledge. I will 'out doctor' you. Of course, I didn't know the other side of it. How overwhelmed and swamped providers are with their own frustrations. Coming to terms with this, I understand it's not *you* (provider), it's *us* (provider and patient).

Gradually, I began to realize doctors were just like me, distracted and working their 'own cases'. They were consumed with surviving the daily frustrations of a broken system. We're not adversaries. If we all take a minute, we would see we're rowing the same boat. Opening my mind freed me to stop seeing an appointment as just a transaction. In many ways, when the doctor enters the room, they are also a patient.

A major principle of Our Quadruple Aim is to maximize the health provider's wellness, allowing them to provide the best possible care for their patients. Call it *mutual empowerment.* This is an idea we will deeply explore.

If you're a patient, especially one unwell or burnt out, I hope my story helps you in your own health journey. If you're a doctor facing similar struggles, the same still applies. I attempt to break things down into understandable pieces. To take something unbridled or unwieldy and grow it into a sphere of control for you.

((RISKY IRONY))

Early in my career, I had moved into a new role at work: risk analyst. While I won't bore you with every detail of corporate life, here is a glimpse: Bosses asking for updates every day and hour doesn't necessarily produce results faster-in fact, often the opposite because of the steady interruptions. The report out becomes the job rather than the job being the job. It's like when your computer starts bogging down, rather than allowing processing time, you just keep clicking the mouse more and more feverishly. Before you know it, crash! Screen of death. Like some form of computer burnout.

My predecessor had left behind countless filenames, half-completed process steps, and system clicks of the job hastily hand-scribbled across dozens of sticky notes. The notes were strewn across my desk. However, many of them were linked together with tape and several feet long like demented avant-garde Christmas lights, each note representing a different colored bulb in the string. My boss gruffly said those notes were all the on-the-job training I could reasonably expect. Was this guy joking?

Like many corporate jobs, you find yourself swimming in ambiguity and mostly on your own to navigate. Many times, you're told the answer isn't known, just that your answer isn't the correct one. In other words, it's a way to criticize without offering something constructive. Not exactly morale building. My boss had a great saying for when this happened: *"Sure, it's different, but is it better?"* Most of the time, those seven words ended the debate.

To my surprise, at month and quarter's end, my boss stayed with me until late into the night to help unravel how to run archaic reports and verify the numbers. He would buy me dinner. Turns out, the joke was on me—behind that gruff exterior my boss had a soft side. I found the camaraderie of an experienced leader who wouldn't ask anything of an employee he wouldn't do himself. Secure in his mind and position. It was comforting to know I wasn't alone. Early in my professional career, I received a lesson in grace.

I made my living as a corporate risk analyst, which made me an expert in assessing corporate risks. But, looking back, it didn't put me any further ahead in assessing health risks. Because I didn't have a clue about the medical uncertainties ahead. An irony not lost on me.

((PASSED AROUND))

The sticky notes, starting to collect dust and coffee stains as the months went by, decorated what otherwise was a typical nondescript office cubicle. Nearby were a couple family pictures sparsely adorning my limited space. I made it a priority to turn these (barely) sticky notes into something more usable—a standard operating desk procedure to leave for the next person. Later, my boss said it was my "golden ticket"—if I wanted a promotion.

My company didn't spare any expense when it came to purchasing high quality office furniture. I had two monitors, a keyboard, and an ergonomic chair with a L-shaped desk. Each cubicle was thousands of dollars and the chairs alone approached a grand. At higher pay grades, your consolation prize was a door and partial walls almost high enough for some privacy. These special arrangements, while nice, were essentially expensive cubicles.

In 2012, when I hurt myself, it was just another day dedicated to spreadsheets, emails, and reports. It was a very innocent movement I had done countless times. Swiveling in my chair gently, I turned to reach and grab a report. Immediate, searing pain–any further movement arrested. I held my breath. Something had popped inside my neck. I felt it, heard it. I had experienced back and neck pain before—but this was undeniably different.

As the week progressed, I was relegated to my head being cranked to one side, locked in position. Too agonized to drive myself, I would have to carpool with my future best man.

First stop, a chiropractor. Whenever I had felt my neck or back out of place, a quick trip there would help release the tension and put me back into alignment. Not this time. Despite treatments, the damage inside was causing continued pain. I felt tingling and numbness in my fingertips. My quality of life diminished. Because it's so close to your head, neck pain is such a distraction—constant, focal and unrelenting. I didn't know at the time, but "continued pain" meant another six years. The price I would have to pay for the pain to disappear was something I never could have foreseen.

Next stop, my primary care doctor. He was open to my concerns and supportive. First, we could try simpler solutions—NSAIDs (non-steroidal anti-inflammatory drugs, from acetaminophen or ibuprofen to naproxen), but any perceived relief was short-lived. As each failed, one by one, they were set aside. Muscle relaxers like cyclobenzaprine were another volley that missed its target and only served to put me to sleep.

Third stop, a specialist. One who focuses on Physical Medicine & Rehabilitation and Interventional Pain Management. She would perform nerve conduction tests (for my doctor friends, an electromyography, or EMG). This involved placing tiny pins into my skin to measure how well the nerves conducted their signals. The results were curious. The latency, or time it took for the nerve signal to travel compared to the expected target, was borderline abnormal. However, we were no closer to a treatment plan.

Along the way, there was Magnetic Resonance Imaging (MRI). They wanted to see if there were blown discs or nerve impingement—a mechanical reason for the severe pain. I was told that much like the earlier nerve conduction tests, while there was some disc compression and bulging in the C4-C5 region, I *shouldn't* be experiencing that much pain.

Megan (my then fiancée), recalls how I burst into our apartment, upset after a recent MRI exam, "They can't see it! They can't see anything!" Without hesitating, her reply was, "Of course they can't. You're laying down. You always tell me it feels better in the morning but as the day wears on, your fingers are tingling or numb."

One conversation with a specialist who reviewed my MRI results stood above the rest. I was going to do my damndest to reconcile what I was being told and what I *actually* felt. I replayed in my mind a scene from the 1996 movie Jerry Maguire. It's the part where the little boy's character whose name is Ray blurts, "Did you know that the human head weighs 8 pounds?" I knew laying flat drew a false picture—did the provider? I felt ready to pounce, as coiled as my neck.

A big bowling ball, known as our head, sits atop our neck. As the day drags on the discs compress, naturally. Of course, nothing would look pinched in an unsprung position. To bolster my conviction, I usually felt better after resting or sleeping. Whatever was being pressed upon was temporarily uncoiled. Ray's innocuous question set the stage to challenge the doctor, "Why are all the MRI machines configured so the patient is lying flat? Isn't that when the neck would be the least compressed?"

I wasn't ready for the doctor's answer, recalling his words, "It's funny you say that. At an industry conference, we discussed this. But I never found an answer as to why MRIs lay flat. There may have been upright MRIs, but they never caught on. I'm not sure why. What you're saying makes perfect sense." Now there was some real logic.

If these mystical upright MRIs existed, they didn't exist in my neck of the woods (pun intended). Interestingly, as I write this, a quick search shows they exist(ed). A write-up published at the National Institute of Health titled, "Open stand-up MRI: a new instrument for positional neuroimaging" and dated April 2006, paraphrased here:

> *We present a 40-year-old man, referred with complaints of neck pain, left arm pain, headaches, pins and needles in the index and middle fingers, with numbness. Conventional (flat) magnetic resonance imaging (MRI) shows small protrusion at C5-C6 that did not correlate with his symptoms. He underwent an upright, weight bearing MRI that revealed a disc at C6-C7 protrusion. The protrusion was causing an impingement that correlated with his symptoms. With this new information, we were able to offer a targeted epidural block.*[29]

Fifth, sixth, seventh stops—I lost count. More doctors, more attempts to find solutions. Later came facet joint injections. I had to miss work because they would put me under. Unlike the man in the April 2006 upright MRI study, there would be no targeted treatment—leaving much desired. While more precise than a swallowed pill, the injections weren't targeted enough.

With facet joint injections losing the pain war came the chance to deploy a new weapon—a nerve burn (rhizotomy). At our first visit, the specialist shared that he preferred a nerve burn because the results were meant to last longer. But without two additional injections (and anesthetics), denial of coverage was guaranteed. What a waste of resources and time. An early clue of a powerful, deciding force overseeing Patient Experience, Quality Care, Costs, and Provider Wellness. I played the game, and in turn, received a nerve burn.

The specialist was correct. A nerve burn performed better than injections, partially dulling my neck pain for a year. When the year passed however, the pain returned, at even greater intensity.

I had been living under false pretenses. Temporarily masked by the treatment, my neck had further degraded over time.

Days turned into months. Months turned into years. Frustration and desperation grew commensurate with the pain. The pain-signaling continued to fire away. Fortunately, two things remained as equally constant but equally opposing to the pain—Megan and my parent's support. Without it, I don't think I would be here to write this.

I was referred to a doctor that focused on gentle spinal manipulations, which provided some relief before fading. This same doctor (many years later) would help us with our baby daughter, who wasn't even close to a twinkle in our eyes at the time. Fortunately, our daughter's treatments would work splendidly under her care.

Another referral—to another doctor who focused on traction. This meant being placed in a machine hooked to a computer that would gently pull and stretch the neck at various timed intervals. The idea was to decompress any impingement. It would take many visits to know if it was a workable treatment. Huge roadblock: I didn't have *many* visits. I was allowed a handful, nothing more. I was being rationed a third of the recommended amount for proper treatment. A pattern of exasperation soon formed and it felt like sabotage. Clearly a patient's ability to follow their doctor's plan of treatment is often governed by an ***unseen hand***, a financial cap that lies upstream. What the insurance company wants—the insurance company gets. What the patient needs and the doctor prefers, forget it.

What does this mean? It means if your doctor clearly tells you it will take 16 treatments before knowing if the plan works but the insurance predetermines under no circumstances will you be allowed more than six paid treatments, the patient and doctor's plan is doomed to failure. Just checking boxes and going through motions. In this example, the doctor didn't come up with 16 treatments arbitrarily. They know it takes that much based on studies and real-life clinical experience.

Who is winning here? I'll give you three guesses, and the first two of doctor and patient don't count. Had I been able to do all 16 treatments, would the story have a different ending? We'll never know. I am starting to wonder if doctors and patients amount to proxy employees for the insurance company—far from equal stakeholders.

I felt passed around, eventually landing in the office of a neurosurgeon. I had been daydreaming of finding a large knife and flaying open my own neck, to somehow cut out the pain. I'm not a surgeon, so rather than a fool-hearted attempt, I decided I would talk to an expert in cutting.

A cervical fusion might be in the cards. I would probably lose some mobility in my neck. People said treatment might only work for a few years, if at all. Apparently, fusing cervical discs places pressure on the other discs above and below the fused area, leading to similar wear and similar problems. Knowing I had more than one disc bulging, this option was unlikely to be a success. There was a good chance I would need more and more fusions. For whatever reason, I envisioned a hyper-elongated neck stacked in rings like you see some tribal cultures practicing on the pages of National Geographic.

Equally unsettling was that it might not even work, leaving behind or making the pain worse. It felt like such a gamble.

(("WHAT WOULD YOU DO?"))

This office encounter with the neurosurgeon started like any other. I was already in the room. White coat enters the room and asks me to repeat what I told the nurse earlier. White coat does it in a way to control and guide the conversation. As the clock ticked, a sense of déjà vu came over me. I assumed I would be walking out like I walked in—without new answers, frustrated, my pocketbook a bit lighter, and my depression a bit heavier. I was becoming bitter.

As the reader, you may be wondering why I'm referring to

a person as "white coat." I'll soon explain. As I sensed myself drawing a foregone conclusion, a voice in my head said: *Stop! Try something different.*

"Doctor, if you were in my shoes, what would you do?"

Reflecting back, I made an astoundingly simple choice: I decided to recognize my doctor as a fellow human being. The doctor, likewise, also made a simple choice: He decided to recognize his patient as a fellow human being. The titles and protocols melted away. The baggage was left at the door. The exam room walls seemed further away, and the three feet that separated us seemed closer. We were just two people talking. We were better for it and it felt surprisingly healthy.

"It's funny you should ask. It wasn't long ago that I was in your shoes. You know, I would hear patients describing their pain. I couldn't see it, their imaging didn't match the symptoms. I would hear it but it was difficult to relate. Was it real? It was real to the patient, maybe, but what to do? Until one day, I started having terrible pain in my neck. Over time, I became desperate. At first, I considered a fusion but weighed the same concerns you share," he openly revealed.

"What about disc replacement?" I questioned. The doctor replied, "See these tiny pieces of titanium?"

He pulled out two small, shiny metal plates. One plate had a raised ball and the other with its matching socket, "I could do it for you. It would cost about $5,000 out of pocket. Europe is about 20 years ahead of us in widely performing and accepting the procedure. However, I've only done about 12 of these surgeries. Besides, I can only offer a 50/50 chance at best that it will help. Not great odds. You would be out a lot of money and potentially still in pain. Then what?"

"Did you get a disc replacement yourself?" I asked.

"No, but I very seriously considered it. What I did is go to physical therapy weekly for a year—a full year! And it eventually worked. Look, I realize as a doctor, I'm in a position that offers financial and schedule flexibility. Even if insurance wasn't going to cover it, I could swing it. Not everyone could do what I did. But it worked." I nodded as he continued, "You should keep your money. I won't take it from you knowing the odds. You should try everything else you can first."

It was a completely new experience! In some ways it felt like it was back to the drawing board. On the other hand, while I didn't have a definitive solution to my problem, I left the visit knowing what to eliminate. Disc replacement was out. Fusion too, for now.

TL;DR (Too Long; Didn't Read)—lessons for OQA:

***Sometimes, knowing what treatment <u>not</u> to do can be just as helpful.* Sadly, this type of encounter and candid doctor-patient interaction still feels rare to this day. Looking back at my numerous medical interactions over the years, I know it's rare.**

I learned just how important honest and unpresumptuous communication on a similar playing field was for progress. What I gained is a renewed effort to keep searching for answers and a new appreciation to not presume. In order to move forward together, we have to collectively let our guards down.

Both doctor and patient had to become vulnerable: Egos have no place in treatment plans. The only fear we should have is the fear of a missed opportunity.

Reflecting, I realize a powerful truth: *We don't spend enough time talking between patient and doctor. We're not afforded the time to do it.*

Why can't doctors find the time and patience to actually converse with patients beyond the surface? Why can't patients always feel comfortable speaking to doctors like real people or trusted partners? Why was this visit so different? What did I mean by "white coat"?

Yes, doctors wear white coats–that's the literal interpretation. It's their uniform. They've wholly earned that privilege, a symbol of professionalism and integrity. There is even a historical context behind it, dating back to the late 19th century. It's worn for easy recognition by colleagues and patients. However, my mind started seeing the doctor not as a person, but just another step or cog in an overall poor process.

I went into the visit (falsely) thinking this would be another check-the-box exercise, and to emphasize how disconnected I was feeling as a patient by this point. I had preconceived thoughts in my mind, driven by frustration and pain; *I'm being bounced around. I had to just go through the motions.* Sometimes, all of it just felt like theater, and we were actors in a play. How sad is it that today's healthcare design is making patients feel that it's just an empty walking coat rather than a real person.

But here was a doctor who had personally shared a similar experience! Had I not thought to ask the question, "what would you do?"—another missed opportunity. Moreover, had the doctor not been feeling transparent, he wouldn't have shared. Somebody had to make the first move to engage in a genuine way. It's not the doctor's fault, but not necessarily the patient's either.

How do we teach each other to have meaningful, impactful interactions? My interaction with the neurosurgeon had a greater impact on my health than any procedure or treatment. I think it speaks to how so many of us are feeling disenfranchised—doctors and patients alike. Yet, we're often like strangers despite being two sides of the same healthcare coin. How did we ever get here?

((HONEYMOON))

Have you ever heard of Sleeping Bear Dunes National Lakeshore in northern Michigan? It's a unique and picturesque enclave with high bluffs and miles of coastline juxtaposed with the near limitless freshwater body of Lake Michigan. It was voted the 'most beautiful place' in the United States by Good Morning America in 2011. There are so many enchanting and inviting places to visit around the world, but it wouldn't be a huge stretch to believe the results of their contest.

A stately wall of sand greets you as you pull into the parking lot of the Dunes. I wondered what kind of invitation this was. Not everyone thinks of sand as beautiful. I didn't either, initially. I distinctly recall how daunting that first hill looked, and intrigued by what possibly lay on the other side. Perhaps that's where most beauty hides, anyway—in the possibilities of what comes next.

In August 2013, Megan and I made it one of several stops on our honeymoon. We headed to the visitor center. The ranger said, "You sure you want to go? It's supposed to be 90 degrees today and I'm not sure I'd recommend it. But if you do, take plenty of water."

We obliged. With extra water in hand, we locked the car and gazed at the stubborn wall of sand ahead. Looking at each other with a smile, either of exciting adventure or naïve silliness, we started hiking towards the nascent hill. There were a hundred people, maybe more, in various stages of climbing. I was certain some had miscalculated the arduous gradient, the muscles in their thighs and calves soon blazing from the exertion. Upon waking the next day, their muscles would still be smoldering from the prior day's activities, a reminder of their fleeting conquest.

We noticed many hikers who overtook this first peak—also made it their last. Upon reaching the summit, they basked in their achievement for a brief moment before turning back to their vehicles. An environment of air-conditioned coddling awaited to provide celebrated relief.

But pampering wasn't what we came for. My wife and I kept throwing one leg in front of the other, stomping upward and watching the loosely packed sand give way with each step. We decided barefoot was the only way to go and felt the fine grains chaff between our toes.

We did this until our leading foot took the step that ultimately propelled us onto the summit of the first dune. We paused and looked back. My black Camaro was somewhere out there in the many rows of reflective steel and precipitously heating rubber. Our sunglasses provided just enough of a darkened world to not squint.

Beyond the hillcrest, a glint of shimmering water pierced our vision—its presence simultaneously appealing and intimidating. Somewhere down this path in front of us, over many mounds, was Lake Michigan. I figured there was a vigorous tide but if so, it remained inaudible and altogether swallowed up by the vast expanse beyond.

Many medium-sized to small dunes stood between us and the reach of the horizon. Mangy-looking plant life and brush dotted the hills. As I examined the shrubs, each seemed unsure whether to remain seated or give up the ghost. I don't recall seeing much wildlife save for a few birds. We were unsure—could we trust our depth perception as the heat rays of the sun bounced off the sand unabatedly? Our imaginations began to tease us. Would the surf be wonderfully cool and energizing as we hoped for?

We went up one dune and down the next. While each still demanded effort, none were as steep as the first. Still, I wasn't sure if the water was getting closer with each step or if each receding wave pulled the earth further out into the lake. I thought of a mirage but trusted we were making progress—not that I didn't swat away an occasional nibbling doubt. Doubts can be like that, swarming like bothersome gnats that keep you off kilter.

Gradually, the overlapping dunes gave way to a gentler slope and the lakeshore. The lake's frothy waves no longer retreated towards the horizon but galloped toward us. No longer did the water remain hushed. Instead, it crashed and hissed, spraying mist that the wind picked up and delicately feathered against our hair and cheeks. Our persistence had rewarded us.

There were a few people in the water. After rolling up our pant legs, we headed straight for the waves and walked in. Even in the

August heat, the massive, deep and unsalted water preserved a revitalizing coolness. We noticed a young woman taking pictures of friends while wading through the shallow breaks. We hoped she wouldn't accidentally drop her expensive looking tablet, which she was using as a camera. It certainly didn't look waterproof, shallow breaks or not.

Ouch. *Ouch. OUCH!*

We quickly forgot about the woman with the high-priced gadget. Invisible to us beneath the turbulent and foamy currents were stones picked up by each wave to smash into our shins. The lakebed was rocky—and for us, completely foreign. Every Lake Michigan beach we had visited had a sandy lake bottom.

Nevertheless, what remained was uniquely beautiful and worthwhile. After a short rest on the beach in which we rehydrated with our water bottles, our stomachs reminded us of the approaching lunch hour. By now, we were feeling mostly rejuvenated but subsistence wasn't going to come all the way out here. If we wanted food, we were going to have to go find it back in town.

Starting earlier in the day was a sensible choice. But it wasn't long before the sun pinpointed us. Initially barefoot, we put on our sandals for tracing our path back as the hurriedly warming sand began burning our feet.

Our honeymoon was in August 2013. Over the previous couple years, I had been prescribed a smorgasbord of medications. But during our trip, I didn't really think much of them. Unaware, the first hints of fatigue from the medications were creeping in. It was way more convenient to chalk it up to our half-day canoe ride down the river, or playing on the beach. Even if it wasn't the medications, perhaps my body was fatiguing from the ever-present pain.

I've come to contemplate that trek to the waters of Lake Michigan as a metaphor for life and being a patient in today's healthcare system. What you expect to be perfect will have flaws, but it doesn't always mean it's less rewarding—sometimes it just means it's different. Yet, at certain times, you have to accept the bitter with the sweet. Today, what Megan and I remember about that hike is our curiosity and desire to keep going. The destination became an afterthought.

((5))

Our Quadruple Aim

"The fear of death follows from the fear of life.
A man who lives fully is prepared to die at any time."
– MARK TWAIN

Todd R. Otten, M.D.:

The year is 2010, I have been practicing in my new office for approximately three months, fresh out of residency. Pristine white coat, neatly pressed dress shirt, and tie. Nervous, but confident. My seasoned MA expressed concerns about Mark, age 92. He was recently diagnosed with diabetes; despite being active, eating healthy, and maintaining a good weight. I reviewed his (paper) chart and walked into the room.

"Hello Mark, my name is Dr. Otten. How are you?"

"Pleasure to meet you," he replied. His broad smile, warm demeanor, and soft tone had a calming effect. Immediately we connected.

"Can we start by reviewing your health history," I inquired.

"Certainly."

We reviewed his health history, including: surgeries, medications, allergies, smoking history, and more. We discussed his blood sugar readings and insulin regimen. The review was brief, but thorough. I found it peculiar in his transition from a newly diagnosed diabetic to requiring insulin in less than six months. This does happen on occasion, but I would certainly not put Mark in the category of routine.

"How have you been feeling," I queried.

"A little tired...can't run on the treadmill like I used to."

"I suppose some things change at 92," I replied. We shared a laugh. I continued, "Any other new symptoms?"

"I'm having a hard time maintaining my weight and get full pretty easily," Mark answered.

Red flags are popping up in my mind, like warning signs on a road. Danger ahead! For the non-medical reader, a red flag is as serious as it sounds—a warning of potentially life-threatening issues. Oftentimes an ominous sign.

"Can I examine you?"

"Of course," said Mark. That infectious smile beaming—assuaging my nerves.

What happened next fortunately does not occur with regularity in primary care. Shocked. I listened to Mark's heart and lungs, examined for lymph nodes and then moved towards his abdomen, the area of grave concern. Mark was a thin man, his abdomen ideal for an examination. Typically, if a specific concern exists regarding the abdomen, I will examine it last (as the exam may cause discomfort and mask pertinent findings). So I examined Mark's epigastric area last (upper portion of the abdomen where the stomach and pancreas reside). Horrified. A firm, easily palpable mass was felt, at least 10 centimeters in size. My expression changed—as if I had seen a ghastly monster.

"What's wrong," Mark probed.

When I began my career in medicine, I quickly learned that people appreciate transparency. The vast majority of the time people want the truth. Patients want to know the physician's thoughts. They want your opinion—good or bad. Certainly, there are exceptions. But, people usually trust their doctor and prefer honesty.

"Mark, I feel a mass." I had to fight back tears. I had only known Mark for 15 minutes; yet, it felt like a lifetime.

"It's ok doc, we'll figure it out," Mark reassured. Here I am, telling a patient that I can feel a mass in his abdomen...pancreas no less—and he is consoling me. I regained my composure and explained the plan of action. I ordered some lab work and a CT scan (pictures seeing inside a person). I explained everything and we made a follow-up appointment for a week later.

During the subsequent interval I received Mark's test results. His labs revealed minor abnormalities, but the major concern was with his CT scan. My fears were realized. I felt as though I had been punched in the gut. Mark had a large tumor in his pancreas with metastasis to several locations, including his liver. On my second visit with Mark—I would have to tell a man he was dying.

Prior to his follow-up visit, my MA ensured that a family member would accompany him. Mark's daughter escorted him into the exam room, I followed, concerned how the office visit would go. What happened next was one of the most amazing encounters I have ever experienced.

"Hi Mark," I asked upon entering the room, full of trepidation.

"Hi Dr. Otten, this is my daughter," he smiled.

"How are you feeling," I blurted out, my poor attempt at small talk.

"Tired, but pretty good. How were my tests?" he asked. Straight to the point, dang.

I took a deep breath, suddenly my mouth felt as though I had just chewed a cotton ball. I reverted to my training, compartmentalizing Mark's grave prognosis. I reviewed the lab work, explaining the subtle abnormalities. I then explained the CT scan: "Mark, you have a mass in your pancreas that appears to have spread to multiple areas."

"Is it bad?"

"Yes, I believe you have metastatic pancreatic cancer."

No point in mincing my words. Mark was a man of character and deserved the truth. The radiology report left no illusion: "metastatic pancreatic cancer." A death sentence. I went on to explain the radiologist's readings of the film. We talked about potential treatment options, including: surgical procedures and oncology referrals. We talked about the pros and cons of attempting treatment at his age. Again, I struggled with my emotions, and had to fight back tears. I remember his next question like it was yesterday. "What would you do?"

As if all of the air had been taken out of the room, taking a breath seemed extraordinarily difficult, tears were welling up in my eyes, words struggled to reach my lips. Thoughts of his diagnosis, potential treatment, his age—all swirling in my mind. The moment was surreal. I took a deep breath: "I would spend time with my family."

Mark was quiet for a moment, contemplating my answer. It seemed like an eternity. "Can I still exercise?"

It was as if God was smiling down and guided us to that moment. The tension quickly lifted and I replied, "Of course you can still exercise." His daughter was crying, and thanked me for being kind and honest. Mark wanted to consider his options.

A few days later, Mark replied with his decision. He conveyed that he had a good life and did not want to pursue treatment. He wanted to continue to exercise and enjoy time with his family. Eventually, the exercise stopped. I treated his pain, and the visits ceased. Mark was enrolled in hospice and passed away peacefully at home, just three months after we met. I attended his wake and gave my condolences to his daughter. I felt numb after leaving the wake. I sat in my car and wept.

((MARK'S QUADRUPLE AIM))

Mark's story beautifully introduces the magic of Our Quadruple Aim. OQA is an overarching guide for healthcare that denotes we are all responsible for the outcomes, as interactions between patients and providers are a two-way street. His case highlights the simplicity of Our Quadruple Aim and, when used routinely, yields balanced outcomes for all stakeholders. Before we formally introduce the four tenets of OQA, first a synopsis of Mark's case under its purview.

1. **Patient Experience**—Mark and his daughter were engaged in the decision-making process, his wishes followed, allowing him to die peacefully at home with family by his side.
2. **Quality Care**—The correct diagnosis was made and the patient was involved in determining the treatment path. Lest we forget, quality is both subjective and objective.
3. **Lower Costs**—The hospital still generated revenue by billing for the appropriate ancillary testing, CT scan, and office visits. But treatment that was unlikely to prolong Mark's life (and likely full of complications and expense) was avoided.
4. **Provider Wellness**—I shared many laughs and smiles with Mark despite our short relationship. I remember his story, and hopefully it resonates with many. This is how medicine should be.

OUR QUADRUPLE AIM

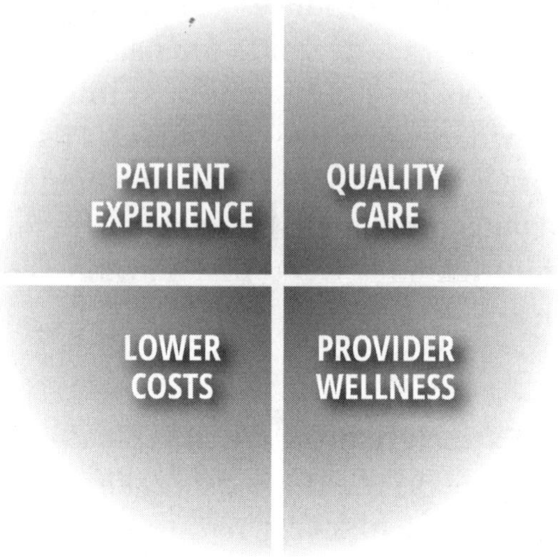

1. **Patient Experience**
2. **Quality Care**
3. **Lower Costs**
4. **Provider Wellness**

((PATIENT EXPERIENCE))

"Again, you make what you measure. If we measure the right things, we may have a chance to pull people together."

– ANDREW YANG, *FORWARD*[30]

The first pillar of Our Quadruple Aim is Patient Experience. This should be at the heart of every decision in healthcare. Patients are the customers and deserve our best. Best does not always mean the most expensive or doing more, but rather doing something outstanding or desirable. I would argue the majority of people in healthcare want what is optimal for patients. This speaks to the altruism that drew many into medicine, including myself. Making the correct diagnosis, limiting unneeded tests, or simply providing empathy can brighten an otherwise gray day. Balance. But, as with every rule, there are exceptions: fraud, waste, and abuse are all too pervasive. Patient experience in OQA demands we provide superlative, affordable care to everyone. Without exception.

Despite the major financial issues in healthcare, there are many providing world-class care, going above and beyond. Caregivers are often called to particular aspects of medicine, and routinely give more than they are ever asked. Hospice nurses are one such example. The empathy and instant connection a hospice nurse routinely makes with a dying patient is incredible. So how do we measure selfless love? Surveying someone on their deathbed is uncouth.

Or the emergency room physician who enjoys the adrenaline surge saving a life threatened by major trauma—a family forever grateful their loved one returned home. I went into medicine for many reasons, but helping others and wanting to make a difference definitely top the list. And I am not alone. The desire to do what is right for patients is prevalent. Yet there are so many obstacles, burdens, and silos that impede us. You will see this paradoxical theme throughout the second half of *Ripple of Change*. Competing forces exist to detract from Our Quadruple Aim, making patient experience secondary. Fascinating, for without patients, many of us would be unemployed.

I remember taking the Hippocratic Oath during the white coat ceremony at the beginning of medical school: "First, do no harm." I was ill prepared for the occasion. Dressed rather casually in shorts and polo shirt—I had forgotten my white coat. Most of my peers were well dressed, wearing dress pants, ties, dresses. Perhaps a bit naïve, or maybe forward-looking? I have long stopped wearing a tie or white coat. Maybe if the office is cold or if I am doing a procedure, the white coat will make a guest appearance. Scrubs or even jeans and a polo are my uniform of choice. Full circle? Patients don't seem to mind, as long as I listen to them and try my best.

Certainly, I have had difficult interactions over the years. Fortunately, as a family physician, you know the majority of patients very well and interactions are routinely positive. In fact, several of my patients have become very good friends. Others are like family. People are intuitive—they sense when you care and know when you listen. When this occurs, medicine is a magical profession.

In my current practice, I constantly remind my staff to try their best, despite the mountain of obstacles. This is a big reason why my office manager and I work so hard to develop a warm, relaxed, and team-oriented approach. These efforts have paid off tremendously (see Chapter 15, "Office Utopia"). Patients want to be treated as people—not numbers. They want to be respected and cared for in a loving, compassionate manner. No surprise that our feedback is typically full of kudos.

Below are some patient comments I have received over the years. I include these to illustrate the difficulty in capturing these sentiments on a survey or via data analysis.

- "We just want to say thank you for saving our son's life. If it hadn't been for you, his tumor may not have been discovered until it was too late."
- "Thank you for making me feel like an actual person, and not another number."
- "Before she became your patient she was so dizzy, she spent most of her time in bed. Because of you, she lived the remainder of her life with some quality. She was able to enjoy evening rides with our father again and even go to the casino."
- "I just wanted the doctor to listen."—A patient who passed away, and (in my opinion) the healthcare system failed to catch her recurrent metastatic breast cancer.

The challenge with patient experience is that it is inherently subjective. What is a positive experience for one may be a disaster for another. So many factors influence a patient experience. Whether the emergency room or inpatient or outpatient world, the number of potential factors affecting patients are infinite. This extends to every corner of our lives and every corner of a hospital. So the challenge becomes: how do we measure patient experience in a meaningful fashion? Furthermore, how do we use this data to improve the existing dysfunction of the healthcare delivery system in America?

In a world where anything less than 5 stars or 10/10 is often deemed a failure, results need to be instantaneous, and costs minimal; healthcare has set itself up to fail.

The following excerpt comes from *The Permanente Journal* looking at the relationship of a physician's well-being to interactions with patients.

> *Dr Smith said, "I had a patient last week who said to me, 'Dr Smith, I've been thinking about coming in so many times since last year. When I would feel bad and be worried—think maybe I'm dying—and I'd say to myself, "You just think about Dr Smith," and I would feel better.'"*
>
> *Dr Smith said, "That blew my mind. I've always known for myself that feeling that I've got a great doctor, who's there for me even if I don't see them, gives me a sense of physical well-being. I can't explain that, but I experienced that. And when that patient said that to me, that just knocked my socks off. 'I just visualize you,' he said, 'and I feel better.'" (General Internist)*[31]

This is a wonderful example of the power of a healthy physician-patient relationship. It speaks to many fundamentals of practicing good medicine. Empathy, listening, and teaching—to name a few. However, how do we translate this specific example into objective data?

Ironically, I began this section after hearing about a conference call to create a business model that supported hiring a psychiatrist for a health system. Unfortunately, I can't make this stuff up. In a world where mental health is underserved and people are struggling with the global COVID-19 pandemic, it is incomprehensible this isn't an automatic yes. Yet, three physicians and two administrators were trying to justify why a psychiatrist is needed for a physician group of over 300. This highlights the bureaucratic inefficiencies that plague many healthcare systems. I suggested to my colleague they use the cost of one physician not leaving as justification.

Unfortunately, when the C (executive) suite is not aligned with caregivers, these are the kinds of dilemmas that occur.

Another colleague described quality initiatives that were disseminated to their primary care physician group. Quality initiatives are designed to monitor providers, facilitate improvement, and result in better patient outcomes. These initiatives are often tied to compensation. Included in the initiatives was a survey for patients to grade how well a medication reconciliation was performed. Medication reconciliation is used to confirm what medication a patient is actually taking, ideally matching their chart. This is critical to minimize errors.

Unfortunately, some patients have no idea what medications they take, despite the best efforts of medical assistants, nurses, doctors, and other medical professionals. I cannot even tell you how many times a patient has said something to the effect of: "I take the little white pill." Yet, some are surveying the same patients regarding medication reconciliation and tying that to compensation. I would make the case there are inherent flaws with this methodology. Perhaps we should invest that time, effort, and funding into appropriate staffing to assist with educating patients. This request would likely be received with resistance at many institutions, with a question of: "What is the ROI (return on investment)?"

I find it extremely concerning that medical staff's compensation is potentially tied to patients' perception of the effectiveness of medication reconciliation via a survey. Does it make sense for a patient who is verbally abusive to medical staff, to then receive a survey tied to compensation? This is a dangerous slippery slope. Medicine is not black and white.

Patient experience is a critical part of care delivery; as a system, we must work on our methodology of measuring this. For sure, not one size fits all. However, the financial wins will follow happy patients.

((QUALITY CARE))

"As value based care becomes more widespread, the provision of quality care becomes essential. The point of departure is the provider. The pressure brought to bear on clinicians is immense and leads to negative outcomes that can adversely impact the quality of care provided to the patient."[32]

In 2020, the World Health Organization (WHO) defined quality care: "Quality of care is the degree to which health services for individuals and populations increase the likelihood of desired health outcomes and are consistent with evidence-based professional knowledge." As with many components of healthcare there are both subjective and objective components to quality care as perceived by every stakeholder. The WHO further suggests several elements to be considered when providing quality care: effective, safe, people-centered, timely, equitable, integrated, and efficient. The overarching aim of the WHO is for all people to receive high quality care without financial hardship. [33]

Improved health for populations is often shortened to population health, and quality care is essential regardless of the terminology. Another shade of gray? Absolutely. As with many components of medicine, numerous interpretations exist for population health, but ultimately the goal is: to improve the health of a larger cohort (see Chapter 20). Depending on the size of the cohort, this task can be daunting. The psychosocial components of medicine make this task complex. Factor in the current financial landscape and it may seem impossible. But there is hope. Think of OQA as a template to providing quality care for individuals and entire populations. When you ingrain Our Quadruple Aim into your vision of healthcare delivery, the path to delivering quality care becomes clearer.

I have been blessed as both a clinician and as a physician leader to work on numerous quality and population health initiatives. Whether it was my role as a family physician or a medical director of an ACO with over 150,000 patients—the principals and goals were ultimately the same. To deliver high quality, cost effective care to all.

In 2003, David Kindig M.D., Ph.D. and Greg Stoddart Ph.D. conceptualized the modern concept of population health in the *American Journal of Public Health.* They define population health as "the health outcome of a group of individuals, including the distribution of such outcomes within the group." In their review of the literature they cited the following from The Health Promotion and Programs Branch of Health Canada, "...the overall goal of a population health approach is to maintain and improve the health of the entire population and to reduce inequalities in health between population groups."[34]

As a physician, I appreciate this statement. It's poignant, brilliant. It speaks to the overarching goal of improved health of an entire population. There are definitely success stories, but these efforts are often isolated, siloed, and not extrapolated to the greater good. Furthermore, if you ask 100 physicians "who is responsible for population health at a macro level," you are likely to get 100 different answers. So who has skin in the game? Let me remind you: we all do. So let's simplify.

In re-working this section I texted Joshua regarding quality care. He suggested that maybe I was overthinking it, and asked about examples of high-quality outcomes for individual patients. I replied affirmatively, but wanted simplicity. He suggested I look ahead to one of his chapters, stating he already wrote about the highest quality care he ever received. Joshua writes: "Earlier in my journey, I'm reminded of when we were trying different solutions, Dr. Otten wrote to me in the patient portal, 'I'll help you anyway that I can.' Ever a servant leader, the good doctor offered the perfect example of saying: 'I'm here for you.'"

Medicine has enough complexity. Part of Our Quadruple Aim is to provide easily understood principles that are actionable by everyone. Hence, the reasoning behind "Our" replacing "The." I would like to simplify even further. Clearly, I am an advocate of improved health for populations or population health, but the complexity of prior endeavors seemingly has stalled many efforts. If those trying to implement improvement struggle to grasp the concept, is it doomed to fail? I am proposing simplicity. Every patient wants and deserves quality care. Instead of convoluted plans, let's slow down, focus on the patient in front of us and provide Quality Care.

((LOWER COSTS))

"Unless you have been asleep for the last 20 years, you will agree that everything in the US healthcare marketplace is distorted and US prices are far different from global prices."

– VINAYAK K. PRASAD, M.D., *MALIGNANT*[35]

The Triple Aim's tenets are lowering costs, while delivering high quality care with an improved patient experience. Simple and profound in its premise. Unfortunately, this isn't what routinely happens in the U.S. Capitalism is extracting maximum profits while front line workers are burned out, their wages have stagnated, and many are leaving their profession. In recent years we have spent 18-20% of our Gross Domestic Product (GDP) on healthcare. One of every five dollars perpetuates the problem. U.S. healthcare expenditures are spiraling out of control as evidenced by a total expenditure of $4.3 trillion dollars in 2021.[36]

There is an old adage: "you get what you pay for." But are we, when it comes to healthcare spending? To elucidate an answer I researched U.S. healthcare expenditures compared with life expectancy—over time. Without a doubt the COVID-19 pandemic impacted these numbers. But the trends preceded 2020 with the life expectancy curve flattening and even turning negative.[37] Graph after graph resulted in the same conclusion: the United States has failed to improve life expectancy commensurate with other developed nations despite our exorbitant per capita cost expenditures. The U.S. continues to be an outlier.

I realize change takes time, however our life expectancy data seems to be regressing, not improving. A multitude of reasons has contributed, including COVID-19 and the opiate crisis (to name a few). Additionally, our years of fee-for-service reimbursement, fraud, waste, and abuse have created a financial nightmare for many Americans. Our capitalist society is extracting profits at an alarming rate. Suffice it to say, when finances are the primary driver for a healthcare system, these disappointing results seem inevitable.

Marty Makary, M.D. writes about this in his book *The Price We Pay: What Broke American Health Care—And How to Fix It*. This eye-opening book is a must read for anyone interested in lowering healthcare costs. Dr. Makary dives into numerous issues that contribute to the financial strain. Unneeded procedures being performed to line physicians' pockets. Predatory billing and garnishing wages. Lack of transparency and surprise billing—all in a game to maximize profits.[38] This is contrary to Our Quadruple Aim, and as a fellow physician I applaud Dr. Makary for his work. I was horrified at the exploitation that is unveiled and motivated even more to play my part for change.

Is there hope? Absolutely. Many are working towards affordable care for every American—but we need a legion of disruptors. Isolated examples are far from sufficient. Until our outcomes improve, life expectancy increases, and costs are contained—it is not enough.

I have witnessed a high-functioning organization achieve lower costs when OQA was the driving force. I'll offer an example of work I contributed to while working on the ACO model of care delivery. I served as an ACO Medical director for several years in conjunction with Caravan Health, and in 2018 the Southern Michigan ACO was Caravan Health's ACO of the Year. In 2018, we achieved 9.5% in savings, a reduction in spending of several million dollars for a population of approximately 10,000 patients.[39] Those are staggering results if you think about it. The following year we were absorbed into a larger ACO, and continued to succeed with cost containment. There are many reasons why our ACO was successful, but aligned incentives were the driving force. Having payors, providers, and administrators moving towards common goals is invaluable and can lead to many wins for not only patients, but every stakeholder.

Interestingly, it was through my work as a medical director with Caravan Health that I first learned about The Quadruple Aim (the predecessor to Our Quadruple Aim). This concept seemed intuitive to me and I quickly adopted it into my vernacular. I don't think I went to a single meeting without bringing up the Quadruple Aim. My anecdotal evidence supporting this approach is immense. The contributions to this book from friends, colleagues, administrators, physicians, and family in forming OQA are some of my evidence.

Despite this microcosm of success, there is unlikely to be a simple answer to the financial complexities of U.S. healthcare. Hopefully, I am wrong. Instead of offering an oversimplified answer to achieving lower costs, I hope to inspire many to play their part in moving the financial needle using Our Quadruple Aim as a guide. As we move forward, we will discuss the importance of transparency, aligned incentives, free markets, and more when working towards the collective goal of lower healthcare costs for the American healthcare consumer.

((PROVIDER WELLNESS))

"The Quadruple Aim brings the health care endeavor more full-circle, making the practice of medicine a better experience for the patient and hopefully a better experience for the healthcare provider. Approaches that neglect or fail to include the fourth dimension ultimately fail. Forward thinking strategies that embrace the needs of the healthcare providers will energize the healthcare enterprise."[40]

As **medicine is a world of gray**, the fourth component of Our Quadruple Aim has the potential for many interpretations. Even I inadvertently use provider well-being and wellness interchangeably now and again. *Pas de probleme* if the end result is a happy, healthy, and productive workforce. Few would argue against it. The fourth component of OQA in its simplest and purest form, and my preference is...Provider Wellness. Provider being someone who serves or provides something. And wellness connotes good health, particularly in the context of a pursued goal. Isn't that what healthcare and practicing medicine are all about—providing health to others?

Defining provider wellness is the easy part, however implementation can become exceedingly complex, particularly for physicians. Jina L. Sinskey, M.D. writes that physician well-being is a wicked problem without a clear-cut solution in her article *"The Wicked Problem of Physician Well-Being."* Her work reviews the history of wellness in medicine, defines historical barriers, existing failures, and offers opportunities to "unwind" systemic flaws. The historical mantra of increasing resilience and superficial well-being initiatives can paradoxically worsen burnout and reduce trust, when systemic issues are not addressed.[41] Wellness is not a plug and play component of healthcare. In fact, it requires buy-in at every level of our system.

Without provider wellness, the Triple Aim is doomed.

Unfortunately, adoption of the provider wellness component of OQA has been slow and in many cases non-existent. Barriers to adoption are everywhere. Excuses are easy to make and all too commonplace. Often the finances of wellness adoption create barriers. "What is the ROI on a wellness committee?" As the great resignation has made its way into healthcare, I hope Our Quadruple Aim facilitates an S-shaped curve of adoption to provider wellness. This doesn't just apply to physicians, but everyone in healthcare. To stem the tide of strikes, resignations, retirements, suicides, provider wellness demands not only attention—but action.

The modus operandi has to change. I would contend, what is the cost of NOT having a wellness officer or better yet—a wellness team? The cost of hiring a new physician is estimated to be between $500,000 to $1 million. What is the cost to the system of a provider who commits suicide? What is the cost of a provider who struggles with substance abuse? Are these costs our system can continue to "afford?"

What's more amazing with the lack of adoption is the mounting evidence in favor of preventing burnout or adopting a wellness program. In 2017, Tait Shanafelt, M.D. wrote an amazing article entitled "The Business Case for Investing in Physician Well-Being." Dr. Shanafelt even presents a potential ROI calculator for investing in preventing physician burnout, as well as a model outlining the typical journey for an organization on this path[42]. For any system debating if they should address burnout and wellness, this is a must read. For example, Dr. Shanafelt writes:

"The business case to address physician burnout is multifaceted and includes costs associated with turnover and lost revenue associated with decreased productivity, as well as financial risk and threats to the organization's long-term viability due to the relationship between burnout and lower quality of care, decreased patient satisfaction, and problems with patient safety."[43]

Our existing healthcare infrastructure and incentive model has created a multitude of issues for physicians, nurses, and other healthcare providers. As we enter 2023, the headlines highlighting the existing failures are fast and furious. The current trajectory is not sustainable. As I write this text, my story through burnout and moral injury is a microcosm, highlighting many systemic flaws.

As the issues of provider burnout and well-being have become common buzzwords, many have offered ideas for improvement, including the National Academy of Medicine in 2019: *"Taking Action Against Clinician Burnout: A Systems Approach to Professional Well-Being."* Their goals for eliminating clinician burnout and enhancing professional well-being are a fantastic starting point. The endeavor introduces the following six goals: "1) create positive work environments, 2) create positive learning environments, 3) reduce administrative burdens, 4) enable technology solutions, 5) provide support to clinicians and learners, and 6) invest in research."[44]

Fortunately, OQA offers hope and opportunity. We will explore how emphasizing provider wellness will naturally enhance patient experience through quality care and lower costs. And remember, this principle doesn't just apply to frontline workers and physicians. Wellness applies to everyone involved in our healthcare system: administrators, dietary workers, custodial workers. EVERYONE. Wellness requires cultural change. Wellness mandates a top-down approach, commitment and effort. Whether at a local, system or national level, this component of Our Quadruple Aim is mandatory. We need an army of people to create a *Ripple of Change* when it comes to provider wellness, so grab your pebble and find a pond.

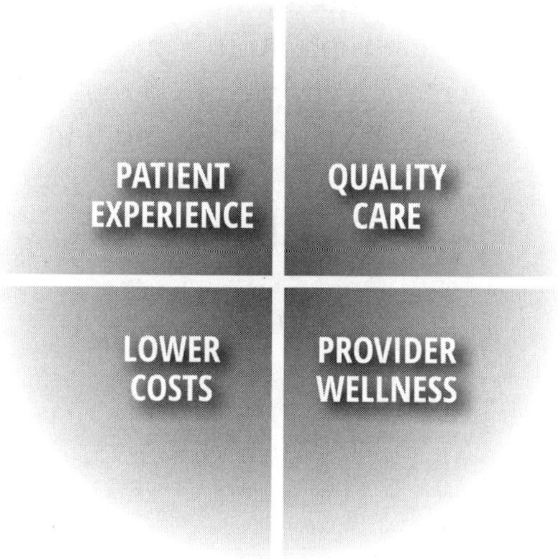
PATIENT EXPERIENCE
QUALITY CARE
LOWER COSTS
PROVIDER WELLNESS

((6))

Anatomy of Burnout

"Burnout is a state of emotional, physical, and mental exhaustion caused by excessive and prolonged stress. It occurs when you feel overwhelmed, emotionally drained, and unable to meet constant demands."[45]

Todd R. Otten, M.D.:

When patients see their physicians, it is expected that we are at our best. Not just some of the time, but 100%. I can attest: Being a physician is a demanding job and I doubt many would argue. Over time, the stress can lead to numerous issues—mental health problems, substance abuse, burnout, moral injury, even suicide. For those physicians that paid the ultimate price, what was gained?

Recent statistics offered by the Mayo Clinic, Becker's Healthcare, and the AMA regarding burnout among U.S. physicians are scary. Forty two percent of physicians in the U.S. experienced burnout in 2021, and things are getting worse. Mayo Clinic Proceedings show that 63% of physicians surveyed reported at least one symptom of burnout at the end of 2021 (and beginning of 2022), a big jump from 44% in 2017 and 46%

in 2011. Sixty percent of physicians agreed—there are too many bureaucratic tasks. Furthermore, projected physician shortages for the U.S. are alarming, with estimated vacancies upwards of 122,000 by 2023, as one in five physicians plans to reduce their work hours due to a multitude of reasons.[46, 47, 48]

And how can I forget my dear friend and colleague—Dr. Linus Silver. Suicide rates are much higher among physicians than the general population. Physicians commit suicide at rates of 28 to 40 per 100,000, more than double the rate of average Americans. Suicide rates among female physicians are even higher than their male counterparts, and 4x more likely to commit suicide compared to their counterparts in other industries.[49, 50, 51] Simon G. Talbot, M.D. and Wendy Dean, M.D., in reviewing moral injury, suggest that: "Physicians are the canaries in the healthcare coalmine, and they are killing themselves at alarming rates (twice that of active duty service members) signaling something is desperately wrong with the system."[52]

These alarming statistics go beyond physicians and touch every corner of healthcare. Recent data suggests half of registered nurses are considering leaving the profession. The cost of burnout to the healthcare system is estimated to be as high as $6.3 billion annually, and 16-18% of physicians and nurses report Post-traumatic stress disorder (PTSD).[53] Hiring support staff has become increasingly difficult, with competition from private industry and work-from-home opportunities contributing to shortages. Inadequate staffing has a massive impact on our ability to deliver quality care.[54]

We are currently in the midst of the great resignation. Employees are leaving in droves due to job dissatisfaction and poor work-life balance. People blame the COVID-19 pandemic, but many of these problems have been going on for years. I think the pandemic was the accelerant for a fire that started long before, particularly in healthcare. Doing more with less. Stagnant pay and inappropriate staffing levels desperately need addressing, particularly for nursing. Christina Maslach offers:

"Burnout...an erosion of the soul caused by a deterioration of one's values, dignity, spirit and will." Dike Drummond, M.D. in *Stop Physician Burnout* suggests the full expression of Maslach Burnout Inventory (MBI) includes: exhaustion, cynicism, sarcasm, compassion fatigue, and apathy.[55] Whereas moral injury is a collapse of resilience from "death by a thousand cuts" leading to the inability to provide high quality healthcare.[56]

My copyeditor is an English professor and reminds me that the issues of job dissatisfaction and burnout are an increasing concern in many occupations, particularly service professions like teaching. Fortunately, the components of OQA can easily be extrapolated. What executive would not want to deliver a high-quality product at a low cost? With satisfied customers and fulfilled employees? Finding balance is key. Incorporating the components of Our Quadruple Aim into strategic planning and day-to-day operations has tremendous potential.

Our Quadruple Aim	Retail/Service/Etc.
1. Patient Experience	Consumer experience
2. Quality Care	High quality product
3. Lower Costs	Low (or fair) cost
4. Provider Wellness	Employee wellbeing

When I began writing this book, I was 45-years-old and debating retirement. I had survived burnout and was working in a near-ideal medical practice. I absolutely loved seeing patients and teaching the NPs. The joy of helping others is why I went into medicine. The smiles and gratitude provide fulfillment that exceeds any paycheck. So why did I commit to 2022 as my last year practicing full-time? How did I get to the point of walking away from medicine after successfully navigating burnout? How did the delivery of healthcare become so dysfunctional and perpetuate moral injury? Is there hope?

Undoubtedly—it starts with Our Quadruple Aim. Think of the four pillars of Our Quadruple Aim as a framework or foundation. A strategy to implement when questions arise or challenges are presented. A guide for culture and process improvement. We will explore different components of the worsening crisis in healthcare throughout. More importantly, we delve into solutions, experiences, and paths forward—not only for healthcare, but beyond.

As we progress through opportunities and ideas for improvement, it is important to dissect how the medical community has gotten to this point. As a part of this analysis, I am sharing my journey up to and through burnout. Perhaps I have a unique qualification in this regard, having lived through burnout and emerging as a better physician, leader, and human being. However, the emotions and memory of burnout still haunt me today.

((THE BACKGROUND))

"Insanity is doing the same thing over and over and expecting different results."

- ALBERT EINSTEIN

Historically, medical training has preordained medical students, interns, residents, and attending physicians for the inevitability of burnout. Imagine making life and death decisions for people when you haven't slept in 36 hours. I remember hearing at our medical student indoctrination ceremony, "Medical school is like standing in front of a fire hydrant... open your mouth, and try to swallow as much as you can."

The year was 2002, and I was a surgical intern at Portsmouth Naval Hospital. At the time, I wanted to be a trauma surgeon. Foreshadowing some 17 years, it was during this year that I first experienced symptoms of burnout. Thank goodness I have a very loving and supportive wife. Without Angie, the year would have been even harder, with potentially disastrous consequences.

2002 was the final year before work hour restrictions were imposed on residents and their training program, a mere 80 hours per week. The rules regarding work hour restrictions were passed in 2003 by the Accreditation Council for Graduate Medical Education. My intern year started with a grueling string of four monthly rotations: general surgery, general surgery, trauma surgery, and general surgery again. Don't get me wrong—I learned a tremendous amount of medicine. However, my intern year hinted at the burnout that was to come.

A typical day started with me getting to the hospital between 4 and 5 a.m., to "round." Rounds consist of seeing patients, writing daily progress notes, writing orders (the old fashioned way—pen and paper), and presenting cases to the senior resident and again to the attending physician. We would then work on the floor, write additional orders, evaluate patients, see clinic appointments, attend lectures, and operate. Mentally and emotionally exhausted, the day would end around 6 p.m. Then add on being "on call" every two to three days. I was a walking zombie.

Sleep deprivation was extreme. I would rather sleep than do just about anything. Intercourse for a newlywed was minimal... I lived at the hospital. Angie often recalls, "I was glad your first year of residency was our second year of marriage."

My record for being in the hospital during a one-week period was 126 hours. There are only 168 hours in a week.

That left 42 hours to sleep, exercise, go to church, and recharge my batteries. Study? Survival instincts had taken over.

The most difficult month was my trauma surgery rotation at a local level one trauma center. We had a Q2 call schedule: two (surgical) trauma teams, on call every other day. Each team consisted of three interns, a junior resident, and a senior surgical resident. The month went like this: our surgical team would arrive at 8 a.m. to round with the other surgical team.

Team rounds would last two or three hours, with the oncoming team apprised of new patients and events of the last 24 hours. Then more rounding on our patients, performing surgery, and responding to any trauma alerts in the emergency room (ER). Routinely our census was 40-50 patients, including another 10-15 in the Intensive Care Unit (ICU). Sleep was a precious commodity. We essentially got half of the required sleep for the month, and made life and death decisions on a daily basis.

Despite the exhaustion, it was exhilarating. I successfully cardioverted a patient in atrial fibrillation. Atrial fibrillation is an uncoordinated quivering of the top chambers of the heart, instead of the normal rhythmic contraction that moves blood forward. Atrial fibrillation can cause low blood pressure and strokes. Essentially, I shocked the patient and converted them to a normal rhythm. The picture in your mind is likely correct—pretty much what you might see in a movie.

The learning was non-stop—lectures, rounding, surgery, procedures. I inserted numerous chest tubes (literally a tube into a patient's chest), central lines (essentially a large IV), and operated on some amazing cases. ***Cases.*** As I edited this section, I realized, 20 years later, I referred to patients as cases. My mind quickly places me at the hospital—white, sterile, illuminated, cold. I cannot even recall how many lives I witnessed fade and then extinguish, despite our best efforts.

One memorable case involved a gunshot wound, or what we call a "GSW," to the chest. We couldn't normalize the patient's blood pressure despite numerous fluid boluses (a large amount of fluid given intravenously). Our senior resident performed an ultrasound which revealed cardiac tamponade (fluid around the heart causing significant dysfunction). We sprinted to the operating room, while the attending physician raced to the hospital. A medium sternotomy (splitting the chest open with a saw) revealed the still beating heart with a punctured ventricle (a chamber of the heart).

"Todd, stop the bleeding."

I automatically responded to the senior resident's directives by putting my finger in the bullet wound, while preparations were made to close the defect. Without my finger, the cascade of blood was impressive—a red spray rhythmically showered the sky blue surgical field. We saved that man's life, and yet a simple thank you was never uttered before he was discharged home. Ungrateful. I started to doubt my plans to become a trauma surgeon.

I became increasingly short-tempered. Patience with family, friends, coworkers, and patients began to diminish. During a dental exam, I fell asleep. I lost 15 pounds, from 165 to 150. I began to experience symptoms of depression. When I did get a chance to relax and have a drink, it was occasionally too much. I argued with Angie, who was only trying her best to support me. My work-life balance was far from healthy.

The pinnacle of my frustrations came at an informal meeting with 30 other physicians (surgical residents and interns, and various rotating interns). My fourth month of training—general surgery again. I was certainly/definitely/obviously becoming a more seasoned intern, and I was turning out to be very good at my job. I was learning a tremendous amount, making significantly improved decisions regarding patient care, and I was given increasingly more responsibility. However, most interns were rotating through general surgery for their first, and for many their only time. As an intern you learn a good amount of medicine, but the clinical experience is limited and can (at times) lead to less than ideal decision-making.

Surgical residency can be brutal—yelling and shouting often ingrained into the teaching. M and M (morbidity and mortality) conferences consist of residents getting interrogated in a theater setting, with an audience of their peers and senior physicians, over cases with adverse outcomes. It's far from a nurturing environment. Later, I sat quietly in my living room wondering how many physicians have died by suicide over honest mistakes.

It was at this informal meeting (not M and M) that my frustrations boiled over. Indeed, I was getting burned out—

four months into training. The chief resident imparted some information (something about gallbladder surgery), then proceeded to scream at everyone regarding mistakes. The same simple blunders by interns rotating through general surgery. I was getting yelled at again for the mistakes of others. Mistakes that, at this point, seemed obvious. Don't get me wrong, I made my fair share of errors. However, I quickly learned from my misgivings and was becoming an efficient intern. After the chief's tirade, he left, and someone asked if anyone else had anything to add. I did.

I quickly stood up and proceeded to what could only be described as: lose my mind. I started to scream at my colleagues, maybe 30 other intern physicians! This went on for two to three minutes. I yelled at everyone. One excerpt: "I am sick and tired of getting f**king yelled at because you are f**king morons." Can you imagine? Burnout at its finest. The looks on peoples' faces were priceless. I had become what I abhorred.

I am not proud of that moment. But, ironically, after venting I felt much better. My friends (other surgical interns who knew me well) laughed at the outburst and we moved on. I am pretty sure the other interns thought I was insane. The rest of the year was less intense, and my disposition gradually improved. I survived the year, but realized being a surgeon was not for me. After nearly a decade of training, I was full of knowledge and uncertainty.

Astonishingly, at the year-end awards ceremony I received the lion's share of recognition. There were approximately 70 interns at Portsmouth Naval Hospital that year and I was recognized as general surgery intern of the year, emergency medicine intern of the year, and overall intern of the year (shared with a colleague). I received a Navy and Marine Corps Commendation medal. I also won a mock award: "most likely to kill a colleague." My buddy (a former Navy SEAL), was jealous. Many present at my outburst wondered, "How in the hell did he win all of those awards?" My friends and mentors knew...more importantly, so did the patients I cared for. Fortunately, I can look back on those moments with pride and laugh (for the most part). However, the seeds of burnout had been planted.

The following is an abstract from Medical Student and *Resident Burnout: A Review of Causes, Effects, and Prevention* in the *Journal of Family Medicine and Disease Prevention*. The article was printed in 2018 and is profound—giving me chills the first time I read it. The authors encapsulate burnout and its subsequent impact:

> *"Professional burnout is a multi-dimensional phenomenon, which may result from prolonged unhealthy occupational stress. Symptoms in burnout cluster in three domains: emotional exhaustion, feeling isolated, and low work satisfaction. Medical students and residents are at particular risk because of their dual student pressures and in-training clinical care responsibilities. Common sources of personal and professional stressors include lack of time for leisure activities, inordinate workloads and sleep deprivation, emotional drain stemming from sick and dying patients, and training coinciding with major events of life. Symptoms of burnout include distress and depression, anxiety/worry, dropping out, substance abuse, and suicidality. If not managed appropriately, burnout can result in a lowered quality of life, negative impacts on patient care, and in extreme cases, professional impairment."*[57]

((THE INTERLUDE))

"So this Shingles shot, will it help me finish my roof?"

– PATIENT

Over the next 14-15 years, my career was full of many more highs than lows. From Portsmouth, VA, Angie and I traveled to Pensacola, FL—training to become a Naval flight surgeon. Training was intense. I learned to egress from an upside-down helicopter in a pool. A submerged helicopter flips due to the weight of the engine on the top. Recovering from a spin (in flight) is terrifying. A spin is when the aircraft is stalled (losing all lift) and spins toward the ground out of control. Imagine pulling up on the stick, as you race toward the ground, and recovering the aircraft to avoid certain death. After nine months of learning aerospace pathology and physiology, weather, aerodynamics, and learning to fly a plane, I received my wings in 2004. I was one of approximately 5,000 individuals who achieved the flight surgeon designation for the U.S. Navy.

The following three and a half years I served as the flight surgeon for Patrol Squadron Ten (VP-10) in Brunswick, Maine. Flight surgeon is a bit of a misnomer. People would ask, "Does that mean you performed surgery on a plane?" I politely explain: a flight surgeon is essentially a primary care physician for the squadron. I loved my job, and joked it was like being a physician in a fraternity. Work was a joy, and I enjoyed a great deal of autonomy while honing my leadership skills. It would take 30 minutes or more to get a cup of coffee from the mess hall—I was constantly met with inquiries, conversations, and "hey, doc...."

I relished teaching my corpsmen medicine and triaging patients. A corpsman is an enlisted service member who receives basic medical training. They are often the first to administer first aid (during combat) for the Navy and Marine Corps, saving countless lives. A good corpsman can make a physician's life much easier. As such, I treated my corpsmen like gold and taught them as much as I could. In return, they were very devoted to me and the mission of keeping our squadron healthy. Years later, one called to thank me.

Life was balanced, I was at peace, and I knew family medicine was my calling. I loved the camaraderie, continuity, and managing the entire patient. The squadron became part of my family, and caring for them shaped my decision to become a family physician.

After the Navy, I went to St. John's Hospital in Detroit, Michigan to complete a residency in family medicine. Residency had its usual challenges. Lack of sleep, studying, 80-hour work weeks, and trying to balance family life. But I had wonderful attending physicians and my prior Naval experience allowed me to excel. I had been responsible for every component of my squadron's health for nearly four years. Five years of clinical and leadership experience made time management a breeze, and the two and a half years of residency flew by. A stressful period for many, I acclimated quickly and thrived.

Interestingly, I did avoid using the Electronic Medical Record (EMR) in the outpatient setting—cumbersome and far from user-friendly. (Cerner for the interested reader). The EMR detracted from the patient interaction in my opinion. Imagine a physician who stares at the computer screen, never looking up, never making eye contact. Cold, detached. So I went to the clinic that still utilized paper charts, limiting my exposure to a common contributor to burnout.

As I started my job search during residency, I reflected upon past experiences. A former Boy Scout ("Be Prepared") and Naval flight surgeon, I appreciate being prepared in advance. And yes, I have some obsessive compulsive tendencies, as many physicians do. So I started my job search 18 months prior to finishing residency.

The search occurred primarily online and, ultimately, I interviewed with five hospitals. In my first interview, Angie and I sat in front of several administrators and answered questions. It is common for spouses to accompany segments of these extended interviews, in part, to determine fit. A little daunting. However, 20 minutes into the interview I realized it wasn't them interviewing me—I was interviewing them. Immediately, I knew looking for a job was going to be a fun process and I enjoyed every moment. We stayed in lovely hotels or bed and breakfasts and had wonderful meals. But I took it very seriously, making pros and cons lists for each place as we learned and were entertained.

Eventually I narrowed down the list and made a decision. I chose Hayes Green Beach Hospital in Charlotte, Michigan—a small rural, critical access hospital. Honestly, a large part of the decision came down to my prior CEO, Matt Rush. A strategic thinker—he had a vision, and I wanted to be a part of that vision. I wanted to see patients and have opportunities as a leader. As we walked out of the interview, I told Angie, "I think this is the place." Thirteen years later, I still work there. And yes, Matt and I are good friends. There is something to be said for trusting your instincts.

((THE BUILD UP))

"Physician dissatisfaction, therefore, is an early warning sign of a health care system creating barriers to high quality practice."

– THOMAS BODENHEIMER, M.D. AND CHRISTINE A. SINSKY M.D.[58]

In January 2010, Hayes Green Beach Hospital became my home for practicing medicine. I joined Linus Silver, M.D., an icon in the community; his patients loved him, having been in Charlotte since the late 1970s. Completing paper charts, dictating office notes, I was soon seeing 25 patients a day. My first MA was amazing—doing enough work for two MAs for years. My practice grew quickly, soon seeing 30 patients per day and working with two MAs. My vision of being one of the busiest offices in the area came to fruition. Patients appreciated that we truly cared for them.

The office continued to grow and additional NPs were added. It was only 18 months into my tenure that I started to take on administrative roles. I was asked by my CEO to join a project development team—tasked to work on our small hospital joining a larger hospital system. Imagine a young, clean-shaven physician sitting with two Chief Financial Officers (CFO), two COO's, a Chief Medical Officer (CMO), and another executive physician leader? Trial by fire. However, I definitely added value to that process albeit at a smaller level. In retrospect, this was my initial experience with how disconnected administration can be with providers, and the subsequent problems.

Over the years, I took on many administrative roles—it's common at smaller hospitals for physician leaders to wear many "hats." I won't bore you with all of the details. However, as the pressures built, I became Chief of Staff, a Medical Director of an ACO, a member of formative committees for a clinically integrated network, a supervisor for two NPs, and the Chief Clinical Officer at Hayes Green Beach, seeing 6,000 patients per year. Reflecting upon these experiences, warning signs abounded regarding burnout as I was trying to save the world.

The clerical burdens increased,
my leadership roles were maxed,
EMRs were the norm,
RUVs (relative value units) drove our salaries;
the sparks of burnout were starting to ignite.

I saw a billboard in Chicago that read: "No one goes to medical school to get good at paperwork." In reflecting on the billboard, I estimated the number of clicks it took to burn me out.

17 years

47 weeks per year

4.5 days per week

25 patients per day

5000 clicks per day

17,977,500 total clicks

Fortunately, I had developed some mature coping skills over the years and incorporated them into my regular routine—both in the office and leading meetings. Trying to stave off the burnout, I constantly worked on mindset and wellness. I think it's important to include a few examples.

Word of the day. Every Friday I would present the office staff with a word to define, typically something very esoteric (like esoteric), and they would offer a definition. I kept a tally with the winner receiving a prize (a well-versed MA was the winner). One Friday, I presented: capitulate. One of the MAs didn't know the answer, saying, "I just give up." When I explained what the word meant, a good-hearted laugh was shared by all. I started to let my staff take something from my treasure box, vestiges from my antiquing and flea marketing forays. I would buy the staff lunch. I started to focus on myself—incorporating relaxation techniques, exercising, and better sleep.

In regard to the meetings I led, I would always talk about and incorporate Our Quadruple Aim. I believe in leading by example and tried to weave wellness into my leadership style. We played board games at a medical staff meeting. I presented a lecture entitled, “Burnout to Wellness.” I shared something humorous from patients (anonymously) at the start of meetings. At one meeting, everyone shared something special about a family member. Powerful. Over time, the culture had changed; increased engagement at meetings, more physician volunteers, people were smiling and talking. The board of the hospital was thrilled with my leadership style.

I realized the fourth component of Our Quadruple Aim (Provider Wellness) wasn’t something that was easily measured, but it was something that had to be embedded into the culture and lived.

Despite all of the wonderful things that were happening with my leadership roles, participation in the board meetings, and the ACO accolades, the signs of burnout were starting to show. In addition to work, I was president and coach at a local soccer club, raising four children, and invested in many hobbies. I was burning the candle at both ends. I held meetings on the phone while driving to and from work, rarely had a dedicated lunch hour, and felt a building anger toward the EMR. When I asked Angie if I should consider a different hobby, she looked at me like I had four heads.

In addition, there wasn’t a dedicated office manager in one location I worked at. Instead, several managers shared responsibilities—creating a lack of clarity when issues arose. It was a cluster. Ambiguity prevailed. Patients would show up late and be seen anyways—creating a cascading effect on the day. There was significant siloing going on in the office, with staff and providers working independently of one another. Siloing in healthcare is a major issue, far from a team-oriented approach. Providers wouldn’t cover each other’s messages while on vacation. Toxic.

((HEADACHES BEFORE THE STORM))

Then, more accelerant on the smoldering embers, I developed cluster headaches in January of 2016. These are nicknamed "suicide headaches" because the pain is severe, unrelenting, and very refractory to treatment. Unfortunately, many whose cluster headaches persist do die by suicide—hence the nickname. While present, I would inhale high-flow oxygen between seeing patients, as this was the only modality that provided relief. Imagine seeing 30 patients a day, with minimal respite from pain. Thankfully, my cluster headaches only lasted three weeks (and only one recurrence of similar duration since).

Unfortunately, I sustained a concussion playing soccer a few weeks later. This changed my headache constellation forever. I developed scalp allodynia, a hypersensitivity of the scalp which is interpreted by the brain as pain. Overnight, my glasses were painful to wear. Headaches daily and essentially nonstop, with numerous triggers such as stress, lack of sleep, and anything touching my head. This lasted for the better part of two years. Desperate, I had Lasik surgery, an attempt at relief. The neurologist said I had one of the most complicated headache presentations she had ever seen: a combination of migraine, tension, cluster, post-concussive, and rebound headaches. There were many days filled with tears, and patients knew when I was in pain. I was miserable for nearly two years.

A short Yin and Yang is fundamental. Please forgive my short digression. After several modalities and medications were exhausted, in an effort at pain relief for my headaches, I started taking duloxetine. First 30 mg and then 60 mg. After two years of daily headaches, this medication provided the pain relief I so desperately craved. I recall my headache journal and the first day I had no headaches in some 800 days. Duloxetine. Abatement.

Back to burnout… Everything was amassing, and then a red flag. The day was going okay at the office, but suddenly I had a big gap in my schedule, so I caught up on some notes and messages.

Then a patient was roomed for a physical 30 minutes after their appointment time. This particular patient has cognitive delay, communication issues, and English was the patient's second language. Immediately, I was put over an hour behind, and it had little to do with my efficiency. A culmination of issues building—I was furious. I did the physical, followed by another difficult patient encounter. I was ready to explode with frustration.

I walked over to my MA and said, "I'm leaving."

She was shocked, "Where are you going?"

"I don't know, figure it out." I walked out of the office to speak with the VP of physicians' practices. We had a good chat, and I was able to vent. After about an hour, I went back to the office and finished up the day. The whole experience was surreal. The office improved (for a while), as it always did, but eventually the same bullshit started again. Problems with flow in the office, no control over my schedule, more demands from administration, lack of accountability, more productivity, more patients, more, more, more. And frankly, I was no longer coping well with any of it. I was burned out. Then it happened.

((THE MOMENT))

"Your principles mean more than any money or success."

FORTUNE COOKIE I GOT IN COLLEGE (AND STILL HAVE)

At the time, our physician contracts were predominantly productivity-based, with a withhold for citizenship, meeting attendance, quality, etc. Relative Value Units (RVUs) are a way to assign a numeric value for work performed. Simply put, my salary was based on the number of patients I saw, and if you followed "the rules," you received your "bonus" pay at the end of the year. I believe these types of contracts are inherently flawed with waves of negative effects.

During the contract development, I attempted to decouple productivity and quality, but failed. I was emphatic as we migrated from a fee-for-service reimbursement model to a value-based reimbursement model—there should be a natural transition of pay from one bucket to the other. For example, a provider's pay from value-based reimbursement should go up and pay from fee-for-service reimbursement should go down. I was convinced if you aligned the incentives correctly, a huge opportunity existed to further Our Quadruple Aim. Unfortunately if quality and productivity are tethered, your pay is predominantly determined by how many widgets are generated. Disappointingly, I was unable to win the debate.

Regarding citizenship, if a physician's charts were incomplete on the day of reckoning, they did not receive that component of pay. The intent of this rule was to prevent physicians from having an excessive amount of incomplete charts. But this contractual component was interpreted as black or white, two open charts were equivalent to 100. Ensuring charts are complete two days out of the year wasn't the intent; rather, having a financial disincentive for repeat offenders was.

On the day of chart reconciliation, I had two incomplete charts. The charts were incomplete because a MA had to check a box. Two incomplete charts as a result of two unchecked boxes. Because of this, the administration withheld my citizenship component of pay (roughly $3,000). It wasn't the money for me: it was the principle. I felt like I had been punched in the stomach. Gasoline had just been poured on the already smoldering cinders of burnout. Over the coming weeks, the "shit hit the fan."

My frustrations with work hit an all-time high. I realized my days of trying to save the world were coming to an end. I appealed the decision, but to no avail. Essentially everything at work angered and frustrated me, and worse yet, my family and patients were not getting the best version of myself. I contemplated quitting. I cut back on patient visits. I asked for a meeting with two of the administrators regarding the decision. I had been a model physician for over a decade. No malpractice suits, only one patient complaint in 10 years, and rarely an open chart. Despite my pleading, the decision had been made and the explanation left me wanting.

I looked them straight in the eyes, "I am already thinking about quitting. This may be one of the worst f**king decisions you ever make."

"What are you going to do," was the reply.

"Anything I f**king want. I can get a job tomorrow."

((FAMILY AND FRIEND RESPONSES))

"This chapter was hard for me to read, it was like reliving it."

– ANGIE

"I just remember you were mad and angry at the office."

– DANIEL, MY SON, AGE 10

"Instead of having a temper tantrum,
why don't you go see the patient in room 2."

– DONNA, FRONT OFFICE STAFF MEMBER

"Watching Dr. Otten go through burnout was heartbreaking. He was always in a meeting, never had a break, and was overwhelmed with paperwork and buttons to click. Between cluster headaches he would sit in his office with an oxygen mask on, often in tears. We tried everything to prevent him from getting frustrated. After his sabbatical, he seemed distant; he wasn't the same strong confident doctor we knew—broken. Perhaps worse, his colleagues turned on him. Bitter, hateful, and cruel at times."

– CARI, MA

"Burnout is a real thing. I never understood how real until I witnessed it right in front of me and it was heartbreaking. I worked with Dr. Otten for five years. It was wonderful. When I first started, we were seeing lots of patients, the day

always full of physicals, small procedures, checkups, and new patients. We had a very busy schedule, but the days always went smoothly. He brought a positive atmosphere to the office. Always open-minded, lots of smiles, loved to teach us, and was a great listener. He truly cared for his patients and still does. He was and still is an exceptional physician.

It was in the last year that I worked with him that I noticed things weren't as great as what they used to be. I realized that he was having more bad days than good. There didn't seem to be enough time in the day anymore and he was struggling. He was having daily headaches. He was not smiling as much and just seemed like life was slowly being sucked out of him. I would do the best I could to help make things easier for him, but there was always something. The schedule was overbooked, patients were late, paperwork and the messages were never-ending. It was hard to see him that way, seeing him dread being there—doing what he loved.

There were many times I thought I wasn't doing enough for him; that I could do more, but I didn't know what. I didn't understand why he was feeling the way he was, and it was a terrible feeling. After a while, I came to realize it was not me. He was burnt out. Just as real as it sounds. Overwhelmed with the reality of healthcare. So much paperwork, buttons to click to satisfy this, boxes to be checked to satisfy that, and so on. All he wanted to do was see his patients and treat them. Plain as that. Not have to play a game with insurance to see what medication is covered or what hoops patients had to jump through before ordering an MRI. For many years we were the "A" team and I cherished those days."

– JESSICA, FORMER MA

((THE FALLOUT))

"When we hold on to our anger, it is like poisoning ourselves but expecting the other person to die."

– BUDDHA

Over the following weeks, dominoes started to fall, and fast. A week later I resigned as Chief of Staff, and never attended another Medical Executive meeting. Suddenly, I had less tension headaches. Another week passed and I resigned as Chief Clinical Officer. Both positions had a modest stipend attached. I declined another paid position in a formative Clinically Integrated (CI) Network, a leadership position designed to improve outcomes and lower costs. I reduced patient visits. I struggled mentoring a new NP in our office. Despite my best efforts, my coping skills were failing me. I was the epitome of a burned out physician.

I tried to take some time off—a guy's weekend golfing. But, my mind constantly went back to work, and I played terribly. Tears were shed with one of my best friends, an emergency room physician, with whom I attended medical school. I had vacation time with my family. Every hiatus led to short-term improvement, but everything changed with that moment. I was different. Hurt. I wanted to quit and start over.

The following is a letter I read to a medical executive committee:

> *"Given the events of the past few weeks I feel I owe the HGB community and the board an explanation. I once received a fortune cookie that said your principles mean more than any money or success. As a physician, I feel blessed to have had the opportunity to have touched thousands of lives. And as a prior naval officer I took an oath of honor, courage, and commitment.*

> *The events of the past two weeks have shaken me to the core. Never before have I had so much doubt...on so many levels. I feel as though I have failed as a leader, my integrity has been questioned, and I don't know where this leaves me. I have a lot of soul-searching to do, and at this point I'm not sure what my future career path has in store. For now I plan to focus on patient care and limit my leadership responsibilities. For those I have let down, I am sorry."*

The letter held many truths. I wish a colleague had asked how I was doing. I left that meeting in tears. In retrospect, I realize the person I failed the most was: myself. I was not the same. I hated work. Interactions with patients suffered, and I was short tempered with the staff. Medicine was no longer fun.

A few days later, I had a conversation about taking a month off with my physician partner, who was very supportive. I decided to take a month off, regardless of the consequences. I sent a passive aggressive email to the CEO and CFO stating that I wanted to take a month off—without pay. I was notified that I was going to have an impromptu meeting with my CEO at noon. My patient schedule gradually melted away for that afternoon. I remember the last patient I saw prior to that meeting. He is still a patient of mine today.

Noon arrived, and so did my CEO. I immediately tried to justify why I was so upset. My CEO politely but firmly asked me to just listen. The following insert is from Matt Rush, my former CEO:

"As I look back over my career as a healthcare executive, if there is one thing I wish I would have learned earlier from my experiences with physicians, it would be to understand that they are people. While all are necessarily strong and talented, they also have fears and vulnerabilities. Fortunately, I have been blessed to have known

a few very special physicians later in my career that afforded me the wisdom to deal with one of them on an urgent basis.

It was no surprise (after reflecting on Dr. Otten's downward spiral in performance over the past few months), that I received an email about his desire to leave the practice for a time. As the hastily arranged meeting ensued thereafter, he began with his justification for the request. In typical 'administrator' fashion, I was about to reiterate our commitment to redouble our efforts to improve the work environment...when the gift (of the aforementioned wisdom) materialized and I knew an 'intervention' as a person was in order.

After sharing my decision to impose a leave of absence, and requirements for return with Dr. Otten, I initiated transitional operational plans with the team and went back to my office. Immersed in the somber moment, I felt compelled to share the story with a former colleague, to let him know how much I appreciated him for doing the same for me (once upon a time). To that end, I will also forever be grateful to those special physicians and to Dr. Otten (who is now among them), who remind me that we are all connected by our humanity. While this centering of humanity is a seemingly simple solution to the complex issue of physician burnout—it is one worth remembering."

After the meeting, I informed my MAs I was leaving, and that I would return. I was given three months off, required to start counseling, and completely detach from work. No charts, no email, nothing. I walked over to another physician practice—the moment was surreal. I felt as though the weight of the world had been lifted, and yet my world was crashing around me. It was as if the channel had been changed from a violent movie to a channel with static. I was numb. After a short meeting with a colleague (who was happy for me), I called my wife and drove home.

"Those that can master the art of medicine are special, and often followed by patients—no matter how far the distance."

– TODD R. OTTEN, M.D.

Joshua J. Judy – Patient:

No matter how far the distance–is Dr. Otten exaggerating? Long out of the military, his daily mission had been replaced with serving his many patients. Yet, Dr. Otten was missing in action. And nobody knew if he was ever coming back. I didn't know why. I just knew that I was without a provider and I didn't know him then like I do now. Now what? I didn't even know how to reach him, other than calling the office (and maybe that was awkward). I wasn't sure where to go, so I decided to see if he was on Facebook.

Facebook Message
9/2/2019, 8:53 PM

Hello Dr. Otten,
I hope all is well. We see you're out of the office for an extended period and we are all worried about your wellbeing (Megan, James, me, and my parents!). Will you be returning? It's not our place to ask what happened but we would like to know if you are coming back? If not, do you plan to move to another health system within driving distance? We do not want to have to find a new family doctor. We all like you as our doctor and

the relationship built over the last decade matters! We would prefer to transfer and stay with you, wherever you land. Or should we be honestly concerning ourselves with trying to find a new family doctor? We really hope that isn't the case but it takes time and if we need to start looking, we would appreciate knowing. Thank you and we send our well wishes. – The Judy's

Todd R. Otten, M.D.:

I will be back, thanks for the kind words.

Joshua J. Judy – Patient:

I may have nonchalantly said something about staying "within driving distance" but with him being a poker aficionado, I was hoping he didn't call my bluff. It didn't really matter though. No bluff was needed for the most obvious point: I was seeing one of the real world impacts of provider burnout unfold. Doctor had become patient and was taking time to heal. No matter what happened next, there was comfort in him knowing our gratitude.

Todd R. Otten – M.D.:

((THE WAVES))

"Senior doctors whose knowledge and skills transcend the next business cycle should be treated with loyalty and not as a replaceable, depreciating asset."

– SIMON G. TALBOT, M.D. AND WENDY DEAN, M.D.[59]

As years have passed, the magnitude of those months in 2019 grows larger in my mind. I knew my journey through burnout impacted many people, but the repercussions are far greater than I realized. Interestingly, when a physician (provider, nurse or just about anyone) is struggling, there can be a perception that they are whining, or not tough enough, or don't have enough coping mechanisms, or enough resilience. When a patient has a preventable adverse outcome, there is often a root cause analysis.

It is time we work on a root cause analysis for the multitude of burned out providers, and do something to reverse this trend.

What I failed to appreciate (at the time) was how my struggle was impacting others. Whether it was: patients who didn't get my best; my family, who dealt with my anger and frustrations; my staff, who dealt with a short-tempered, frustrated physician; colleagues who didn't know how bad my burnout was; administrators who took the brunt of my complaints. Many people were hurt by my actions and words. I am not proud of this, and have done my best to heal those wounds. But many of the wounds run deep and need more time, and some may never heal...

And we haven't even touched on the financial impact. Fortunately, I had a good grasp of the practice finances and I estimate the following losses:

- $120,000 – salary paid to retain me
- $180,000 – lost revenue in patient visits
- $250,000 – lost revenue in ancillary and preventative studies
- $50,000 – lost revenue in referrals
- $100,000 – work hours, of those picking up the mess I left behind

Speechless as I write this, many tumultuous emotions swirling through my mind. A negative $700,000 impact to a small hospital due to a preventable event. Root cause analysis: burnout at its finest.

((THE SABBATICAL))

"I prefer to be true to myself,
even at the hazard of incurring the ridicule of others,
rather than to be false, and to incur my own abhorrence."
– FREDERICK DOUGLASS

Writing this section was an arduous task. Perhaps that relates to the fact that since high school, I had been driven from one challenge to the next. Becoming a physician, then a flight surgeon, then a family doctor, and then a medical leader. And then? Now what?

Initially I was worried about occupying my time; days were filled with random tasks: weeding, fixing items, yard work, preparing the kids for school, exercising. But as time passed, I healed. My sabbatical became a journey of learning how to adapt to the disarray that awaited, upon my return.

After a week, I got into a routine. I would get up early, have a cup of coffee (or several), and get the kids ready for school. I cherished this time. We would have breakfast and I made their lunches. I would always tell them I loved them and give them a lasting hug. Previously, Angie handled the morning shuffle, but I treasured these moments. I realized the balance had been gone—priorities had become distorted, and work had been eating me alive.

The routine evolved. After the kids went off to school, I spent more time on hobbies. Heading to the basement, sorting and pricing comic books became a staple of my morning. It's amazing how a simple task can return you to your youth. Often *ESPN Sportscenter* or *Get Up* was playing on the television. It was a wonderful time to reflect on how I had gotten to this point and where I wanted to go. What had become crystal clear: I needed to ensure happiness at work was a priority. I learned that I could not save the world and I was suboptimal to my patients, my family, my friends, and myself while burned out.

I vowed to never get burned out again.

Part of my sabbatical was formal counseling. Initially, I was nervous and trepidatious. I didn't know what to expect. I knew the value of counseling, and had referred hundreds, if not, thousands of patients over the years. However, I had never experienced it first-hand. The first meeting started a little awkward, as I was used to leading these conversations. But it wasn't long into the appointment that I appreciated the value. My frustrations with work were being heard—not solved, but heard. It felt cathartic, to release the pressure that had been building. Perhaps counseling should be a standard part of medical training—an opportunity for learning and healing.

As time passed, I looked forward to counseling. Conversations about work, family, life, and religion. We talked about comic book sales. Mark would affirm the positive things I was trying to accomplish at work, but also helped me learn to set boundaries. Energy was spent discussing my return to work and what that would look like—I talked and he listened. Mark didn't have all the answers, yet he had wonderful insight and would offer me things to consider. Counseling was instrumental in helping me climb out of the pit of despair that is burnout.

The days turned into weeks, and weeks into months. I started to read books for pleasure; I hadn't done that in years. I attended all of my children's sporting events. Not as a coach or a board member, but as Dad. I started to find the balance that had been missing. I was enjoying my time off and understood why my boss had given me the opportunity. Matt did it because it was the right thing to do. He did it because he didn't want a good physician to leave the hospital. He did it because he was my friend...and remains so to this day. I am forever grateful to Matt for the decision he made. The decision wasn't without ramifications—good and bad. It saved my career, helped me find balance again, and become a better human being. Perhaps more of us should "pay it forward."

((THE RETURN))

"What is your Dad's favorite fruit?"

– TODD R. OTTEN, M.D.

"Chocolate."

– THREE-YEAR-OLD PATIENT

My first day back in the office was a tangle of emotions—nervous, excited, relieved, fearful. Another surreal experience in a matter of months. Seeing patients was the easy part; relearning the EMR was frustrating. Fortunately, muscle memory returned and the staff was extremely supportive (especially my MA, Cari). During my time off, one of my MAs decided to take another position. Disappointing, but I understood. I encouraged her to do what was best for her and her family.

Before and after the sabbatical, I split time between two clinics. Upon my return, much had changed...unfortunately more had not. My office space at one clinic remained—used, but essentially as I had left it. At the other office, my belongings were in a box tucked away in the storage room. That broke my heart. I always tried to do the right thing, and that small decision frustrated and angered me. I realized many emotions that contributed to my burnout were still smoldering. Suppressed frustration soon returned as I was immersed in a frenzied dysfunction. Many of the same issues still existed and some had even gotten worse. The respite was short-lived.

> *"Whether you take a long weekend, an extended vacation, a full-on sabbatical, or go to a conference or a retreat in an effort to recharge those batteries, you will find your energy is only temporarily improved. You will be back in the exhaustion of survival mode very soon upon your return. It cannot be any other way. To remain in a positive balance in your energy accounts, you must change the actions that drained you in the first place. Lower your stress levels, increase your ability to recharge, or both."*
>
> – DIKE DRUMMOND, M.D., *STOP PHYSICIAN BURNOUT*[60]

Fortunately, I realized what was going on. I knew I had to adjust my routine at work to avoid burnout—again. I cut back on my number of visits. I upped the ante regarding my coping skills and mindset. Additionally, I tried to make work fun again, and for several months, the joy of medicine returned.

((THE TRANSFORMATION))

"In order to see the way through, you must step out of your programming and make a 180-degree shift in your awareness. Move from avoiding the things you don't want ...
...to figuring out what you really want ...
...and going to get it."

– DIKE DRUMMOND, M.D., *STOP PHYSICIAN BURNOUT*[61]

Most of my career, days have flown by, as I loved to see patients and make a difference in others' lives. When I returned from my sabbatical, the difference between the two clinics I worked was remarkable. One clinic had a friendly, team-oriented approach, a joy to work with the NP and staff. The office flow was ideal and I looked forward to my time there. Unfortunately, the other office's silos had gotten worse and the office flow was a disaster. It's amazing what culture can do for a work environment and people's dispositions.

There were many reasons for problems and some of them were my fault. Many of the chronic pain patients (I had inherited from my predecessor) were a dividing force. The opiate crisis was in the spotlight and several of my colleagues wanted nothing to do with pain management. Some physicians refuse to write for opiates despite medicine being a world of gray. These patients were forced on them during my sabbatical, much as they had been forced on me years before. I recognized this wasn't going to last and that I needed a change.

Auspiciously, an opportunity presented itself in early 2020, just before the COVID-19 pandemic exploded. Matt and another administrator presented an opportunity to take over a clinic with a new practice model that I could help develop and mold. A fresh start. The existing provider was relocating and the hospital system envisioned a model with one physician and two NPs. With plans for a rural health clinic designation, renovations were planned and the clinic could be ready in months. Intriguing. An invitation to put my stamp on an ideal practice. I could gather an all-star team (of staff and providers) and enjoy medicine again.

After some negotiations, my contract was signed. In retrospect, I am not sure the administrators truly understood what they were taking on (with me signing). I was not going to be strong-armed into excessive clerical burdens, unrealistic RVU expectations, and other bureaucratic aspects of medicine. I was going to develop a high-functioning practice where patients wanted to visit, and providers and staff were happy at work. Our Quadruple Aim would be prioritized.

Over the next few months, several key pieces to the puzzle were placed. My MA, who hates change, agreed to follow me. She recently celebrated working with me for nine years—an all-star and a rock for the office. Cari is an example of how culture and relationships contribute to developing an amazing employee.

I told the administration I wanted three NPs and potentially a fourth. I preferred new graduates and was asked if I was crazy. I replied, "time would tell." I wanted new grads who were excited to learn, and who didn't come with bad habits, or were jaded. I wanted to be able to mold them into solid practitioners. Teach them to finish charting at work, not at home. See a patient and finish the note. It takes discipline for sure. I wanted to teach them how to live the joy of medicine.

As we developed our team, the office manager spot was open. Even though I had been presented with a few options, I just wasn't sure if any of these individuals were the best choice. Then it happened. While working at the frustrating office, a patient was scheduled to see me that I had discharged from the practice years ago. Why does this happen? What am I supposed to do? The person who was covering for the current manager had expressed some interest in the position. This dilemma presented an ideal opportunity to see her management skills. I asked her to deal with it—and she did. The matter was handled in a professional and expeditious manner. I was so impressed that I asked her to meet me at lunch. We talked about the new office and I asked if she would consider applying. She did and our paths are forever intertwined.

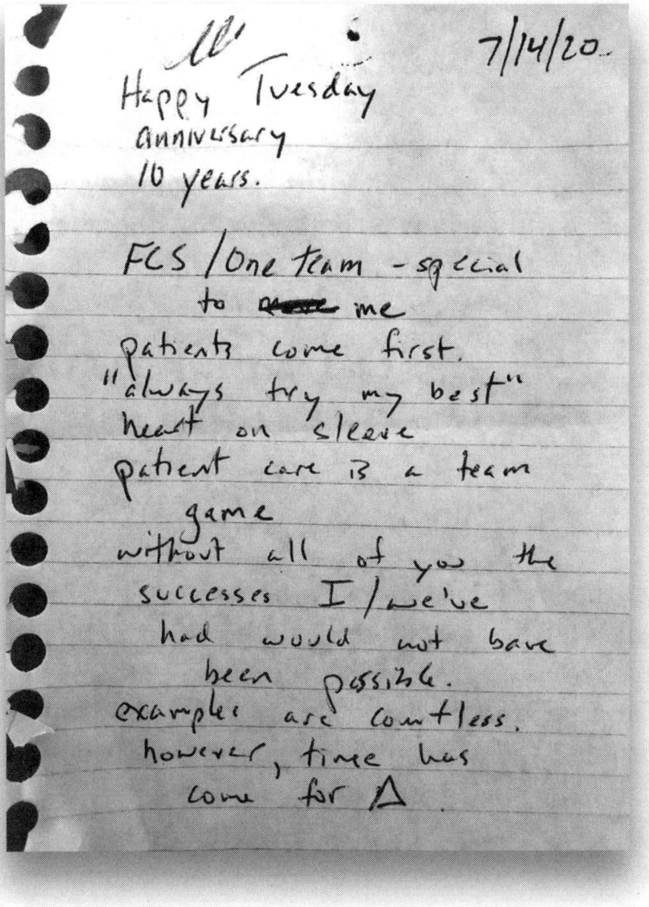
7/14/20

Happy Tuesday
anniversary
10 years.

FCS / One team - special
to me
patients come first.
"always try my best"
heart on sleeve
patient care is a team
game
without all of you the
successes I/we've
had would not have
been possible.
examples are countless.
however, time has
come for Δ.

After several months of recruiting, rumors started to swirl, and I decided to notify my staff I would be leaving. In July, I informed the staff with a short speech that reminisced, offered thanks, and discussed opportunities. I included my notes for the speech here. Over the years I have kept folders of messages from staff and patients, hundreds of thank yous and mementos. They are hung on a cork board and help remind me of how important patient care is. At year-end, I clean off the board and start anew.

On November 16, 2020, we opened the clinic with mixed emotions. With fresh paint, new carpet and masks in place, we saw our first patients. I started taking on patients from the previous providers, and opened to new patients (I had been closed to new patients for almost five years). The clinic was busy from day one. Despite working with a skeleton crew in the middle of a pandemic, I was determined to make the clinic a success and a place people wanted to work. I was committed to share my happiness and never get burned out again. My mindset was firmly focused on the fourth component of Our Quadruple Aim: Provider Wellness.

((LIVING OUR QUADRUPLE AIM))

"I jokingly say to other providers,
'I am working in my own little utopia.'"

– TODD R. OTTEN, M.D.

I started the book just over two years after returning from sabbatical. During that interval, there were definitely bumps in the road. However, I currently would rate my practice at a 9/10 on a self-fulfillment score. It took two years to recover from burnout. Two years to get my emotional well-being fully restored, and feel balanced.

The office has three highly functioning NPs and we have a fantastic working relationship that is full of teaching, comradery, laughter, and empathy. I have an open-door policy and it is a joy to watch them hone their skills. I am proud of their development and look forward to their successes. Fully staffed, we have taken on over 1,000 new patients since opening, in addition to my very full panel of existing patients. We are designed as a PCMH (Patient Centered Medical Home) and just recently named a rural health clinic as well. Both of these designations lead to increased revenue streams, but also create more clerical burdens. Another

Yin and Yang. There is laughter nearly every day, people step up to help one another and, importantly, there are no silos.

This didn't happen overnight. There were definitely moments where I wondered if I had made the right decision. However, my office manager and I had a vision, and we are definitely on the same page. We back one another up and occasionally I tell administrators "no, we aren't going to do that." She is an amazing nurse, who constantly goes above and beyond. During the COVID-19 pandemic when we were short staffed, she filled in the front office, as an MA, in addition to her role as manager.

My schedule involves seeing approximately 20 patients per day. It gives me time to teach and review cases with the NPs, while still generating 4700 RVUs (near the mean of productivity for a family physician). I am not running around like a chicken with my head cut off. The providers cover for one another while on vacation and Friday afternoons (three providers are off), and have evening hours four days per week. We have fun, but take patient care very seriously.

The balance I craved has been achieved. When challenges arise, the staff rolls with the punches and makes the best out of it. I occasionally buy lunch for the entire staff. Recently, we had fun-fact Friday. Each member of the staff wrote an interesting fact about themselves and I read them aloud. The team guessed who authored the fact and the winner got their lunch paid for. I bring in treasures for the staff to choose from. And recently, we had a lovely holiday party. What is the driving force for my personal transformation and the success of the office? Provider Wellness allows Our Quadruple Aim to flourish.

I believe focusing on Our Quadruple Aim
can not only create successful micro environments,
but can be translated to entire systems;
and my hope is that it can alleviate the dysfunction
that exists in healthcare and beyond.

((7))

Rarity and Grace

Joshua J. Judy – Patient:

What allows Dr. Otten to jokingly say he is working in his, “own little utopia?” Utopia is an environment with near perfect qualities for its members. Care, balance, stability and grace come to mind. Now consider the opposite. If you immediately declared dystopia, you would be technically correct. But you could easily substitute other words that describe healthcare—dismissiveness, dysfunction, frustration, burnout.

I think back over the years to phrases I’ve often heard as a patient. These are much further from utopia:

"You're just stressed."

"You're just depressed."

"Never heard of that." (a common euphemism to imply not interested either)

"...But that's rare!" (which means you can't possibly have it)

The last statement especially bothers me. If you're a doctor, do you ask what if "rare" is sitting in front of you today? What if it's simply that you, as a doctor, haven't seen a case like this yet? A rare diagnosis is quite different from the uninitiated white coat.

When I reached school age, it became crystal clear that I had a vision problem. I always gravitated towards the front row, despite the unwritten rule that you would become cooler to your peers the further back you sat. It wasn't to be the teacher's pet. Rather I couldn't read the black board or overhead projector (no white boards in those days). Even in the front row, I struggled.

A pattern formed. I would fail the school's eye exam. My parents would be informed, and off to the optometrist we would go. I would get a new script for glasses. Rinse and repeat. There was something more to this but nobody knew—the answer was always another script for glasses.

Seven pairs of glasses and an equal number of eye doctors later, I landed in the seat of a retina specialist. To this point, the focus had been on the front of my eyes. Now it was on the inside, at the back. My retina specialist was a relatively short man of German descent, with a warm demeanor—Dr. Penman. He was inquisitive and open-minded. Dr. Penman had the innate ability to do what others couldn't to this point.

It's not that the other doctors I saw were unwilling to help. The difference was Dr. Penman had the confidence to admit he didn't know the diagnosis, but could send me to someone who might. Recognizing he didn't know everything, he said, "I can see something but I'm going to refer you out to be sure." His humility (and strong hunch) allowed a more experienced specialist to confirm his initial diagnosis.

I'm quickly reminded of my first sit down with Dr. Otten regarding this book. He was carrying a notebook for ideas and he scribbled the words that said it's okay for a doctor to say: **"I don't know."** It was simple and powerful.

Let's set something straight. I don't pass fault or judgment on not recognizing every disease that comes through the door. It's impossible to know what you don't know. Patients don't always have the words to describe exactly what they're feeling. They might feel embarrassed or intimidated. They might be gaslighting themselves, meaning second-guessing their own experience.

Some doctors might be having a bad day or, at the very least, are overworked and overbooked. Not every doctor likes a know-it-all or strong-willed patient just like patients don't always appreciate a know-it-all or strong-willed doctor. Egos might be creating tunnel vision, for both parties.

If both doctor and patient are demoralized, either by the overbearing healthcare system or their illness, meaningful conversation can take a back seat. Both enter the conversation already tired, even defeated. How can anyone articulate their case when at their weakest? It feels like a pre-emptive barrier to transparency.

TL;DR—lessons for OQA:

I'm not suggesting for a doctor to suddenly give up and keep bouncing the patient to the next appointment (optimizes the patient experience by offering clear communication and limiting inconvenience). I think it's important to exhaust their own knowledge first because it can take months to get into a specialist (lowers costs by minimizing unnecessary visits).

However, when hitting a wall, or a limiting factor, it's time to try something completely different. Physicians, when you don't know, say so. Ask for help from another colleague, like Dr. Penman did (supports provider wellness by balancing workload). Confer, then refer out (provides quality care by sending the patient to someone who can properly treat). Impressively, while I highlight the primary component of Our Quadruple Aim in each of the preceding scenarios, all four concurrently apply.

((NORTH STAR))

I used to daydream about what 20/20 vision must look like. Sometimes, to this day, I will stare at something in the distance, take a mental image, then raise my glasses to see the world without them. I take another mental image. Then I drop my glasses back into place and figure it's a bit like that distinctive jump from blurry to slightly less blurry. But the leap to perfect is unimaginable.

Poor vision has led to bad posture, a likely contributor to my neck issues. One disease feeds the other. They gang up on you. Over the years, I've had many people ask why I sit so close to the computer screen. My answer back is always the same, "To see." In many ways, working from home since March 2020 because of the COVID-19 pandemic has been a blessing. I can sit as close as I want—without being questioned. Head and neck injuries die hard, if they ever do—an important footnote that will come up later.

One of the best parts of working from home has been my 6-year-old son yelling out, "Do good on your calls, Daddy!" before heading down to my home office each morning. I always yell back, "You too, buddy!" before he jumps onto his own Zoom call for class. Our son had attended in-person school until multiple COVID-19 quarantine events forced our hand. Megan and I would home school our son for kindergarten and reconsider in-person school next fall. Beyond the disruption to his education, we wanted him safe and we had a newborn in the house. Our decision provided care, balance, stability, and grace for family life—Our Quadruple Aim provided the navigation.

((BLUE LIGHT SPECIAL))

Dr. Penman referred me to the University of Michigan – Kellogg Eye Center, to see Dr. Paul Sieving, M.D., Ph.D. It was early 1991 and I was nine years old. While waiting for my appointment, Dr. Penman warned, "No jumping." There was concern I might have detached retinas and until that could be ruled out, no bouncing around—a tall order for a 9-year old boy. If you've ever wondered why it's called the Kellogg Eye Center:

> *In 1934, cereal magnate William Keith Kellogg donated more than $66 million in Kellogg Cereal Company stock and other investments to the W. K. Kellogg Trust (equivalent to $1 billion in 2019 dollars) revealing the sizable fortune he had amassed from success in the cereal industry, in spite of the Great Depression. As with other endowments, the yearly dividend income from this trust funds the foundation.*
>
> *W.K. Kellogg, blinded by glaucoma for the last 10 years of his life, once said: "I would give all my money just to see the sun and green grass again."*[62]

Dr. Sieving was considered the country's foremost expert on my eye disease. Amazingly, if you look up Dr. Sieving today, he still is. He went on to be the director of the National Eye Institute, part of the U.S. National Institutes of Health, before retiring in 2019. He currently is Professor of Ophthalmology at the University of California – Davis. As for Dr. Penman—he retired in 2014 after 44 years of service. I remember being at the Kellogg Eye Center most of the day with my parents. With vividness, I recall in-depth color tests—who knew there were that many shades of green, among other colors. I had to put them in order from dark to light. They all looked very close in tint, but surprisingly, I got them right. That ruled out a problem with my color vision.

I was instructed to hold up a card at a distance where I normally would read from. I moved it within a few inches to proudly show I could mostly make out the 20/20 line (even if a person with healthy vision held it 12-14 inches away). As a quick aside, 20/20 means having normal vision–enjoying the visual acuity to see what one should normally see at a 20 foot distance. I was then instructed to read a chart on the wall. My distance vision was anywhere between 20/50 and 20/60. My left eye is slightly stronger. By correcting a slight astigmatism in both of my eyes, the best corrected acuity is 20/40. Simply put, a person with healthy eyes can see clearly at 40 feet what I need to be at 20 feet to see. But it's an imperfect measurement–often, I need to be even closer.

I distinctly remember a specialized contact lens apparatus with electrodes placed onto my eye, then flashing strobes. Known as an electroretinogram (ERG), this is used to gauge function of retinal nerve tissue.

A day filled with extensive testing—my eyes grew tired from constant probing, and the strain of reading tiny print. As a 9-year-old boy, I felt incredibly small in a big world. Hours on end, until the results unmasked an official diagnosis: Juvenile X-linked Retinoschisis.

Retinoschisis literally means "splitting of the retina into two layers." This eye disease causes cysts to form in the cells of the retina. Normal retinas make a particular protein called retinoschisin, which in layman terms essentially acts like a cell glue. I too make this protein in my retina cells, but an abnormal form of it. As a result, the cysts form because the layers of cells are not being held together correctly. Think of a pastry crust, or breakfast Danish—the light, flakey layers of crust separate, forming little pockets.

Because the disease is "X-linked recessive," it means it is heredity and passed down from the mother's side and only to boys. A single defective gene, identified as RS1 on my X chromosomes, has a mutation. In the 1990s, it was Dr. Sieving along with other colleagues who helped discover this gene as the culprit.[63, 64, 65]

Growing up, the last name of Judy and glasses made for a solid icebreaker with peers—"Hey you, four eyes with the girl's last name...." But it did little to inspire confidence. One of the more discouraging times of my early life came in searching for that first job outside of the house; with someone who wasn't a family friend—you know, one that had an official W2 form attached to it. I couldn't buy that first job.

I remember applying to my local K-mart, McDonald's, Burger King and all the others in between. I couldn't figure out why I wasn't getting a return call. My parents always emphasized that they're not going to beat your door down—you have to pursue them. It was an early lesson in mindset. So, I called K-mart, my first prospect, and thoughtfully asked to speak with the hiring manager.

> *"Good morning. My name is Joshua Judy. I was wondering if you might have reviewed my application."*
>
> *The reply: "Yeah, it's here in the trash. We need someone who can work all hours." *Click**

So much for a surprise blue light special. When filling out the applications, they asked for my hours of availability. I was only granted a day-time driver's license by the State of Michigan, due to my lowered visual acuity. I finally figured out my limiting factor. The entire experience definitely injured my self-assurance. When you first get your driver's license, it's a chance for independence and freedom. It was time to try something different.

In a small town, there weren't a ton of employment options for a 16-year-old. My last shot was the Carter's Plus grocery store. Grocery bagging, sorting bottle returns, picking up cigarette butts and cleaning toilets was about to become my new profession. Sometimes, I would carry groceries out for the elderly and load their vehicles. There still existed a human touch to the shopping experience. I sat down with the hiring manager. Her name was Wendy.

Before she could shoot me down, I pounced, "I just want to put this out there. I'm not leaving the store until I get this job, so you might as well make it easy on yourself and hire me."

Wendy, a bit surprised, blinked and said, "I'll be right back." She got up from the table and walked into an office where her superior sat. After exchanging a few words, she came back and said, "I spoke with my boss. I told him how much I liked your attitude (mindset). When can you start?"

I felt it was okay to come clean about my driver's license limitation at this point, "You know I can't work when it's dark out, right?"

"Well, we will just work around that," she replied without thinking twice.

For the next couple of years, I worked hard for Wendy and she worked hard for me. She always went out of her way to accommodate my daytime schedule. Perhaps unknowingly, Wendy practiced what the best physicians do for their patients every day (substitute a patient with an employee). She created a great employee experience by being supportive and transparent. By being caring, she succeeded in efficiently filling the job vacancy, and in a quality manner. She lowered costs for our employer by keeping turnover low. In turn, she made her job as a supervisor easy because loyalty remained high (provider wellness). Wendy, if you're out there, thanks for your grace.

((A LABOR OF LOVE))

I was the 13th known retinoschisis case in Michigan. What my eye specialists explained:

> *"If you can make it through your teen years without degradation, you'll probably be stable into your middle age years."*

There is no known cure for degenerative forms of retinoschisis. Some with the disease have 20/200 vision, or worse. For the latter, seeing the big "E" on the standard eye chart is out of the question—legally blind. In the end, I'm one of the very lucky ones—my vision has stayed relatively stable. While I've had intermittent blurriness due to thyroid dysfunction, it isn't all due to retinoschisis.

The thoroughness and thoughtfulness Dr. Sieving brought to my care was exemplary. I include the following letters from Dr. Sieving to Dr. Penman and my then-family doctor, my parents and my teachers so you can read for yourself what I mean. I mentioned these letters to Dr. Otten and one of his staff members kindly secured them out of storage after weeks of searching. "I bet they're better than what we're afforded to write these days," mused Dr. Otten–sir, I think the odds are overwhelmingly in your favor.

The University of Michigan
W.K. Kellogg Eye Center

1000 Wall Street
Ann Arbor, Michigan 48105
Clinic: (313) 763-5906
Office: (313) 763-8097

Paul A. Sieving, M.D., Ph.D.

January 25, 1991

[redacted]

[redacted] P [redacted] MD
[redacted]

Re: JUDY, Joshua J.
Reg: [redacted]

Dear Drs. [redacted] and P[redacted]

I had the pleasure of seeing your patient 9-year-old Joshua Judy at the Kellogg Eye Center for a second opinion regarding juvenile X-linked retinoschisis. I concur with Dr. P[redacted] in this diagnosis. I have sent the parents a letter which contains other information regarding this case. We performed several tests of vision in the office to firm up the diagnosis and to gain a sense of the overall retinal function. A copy of these test results is enclosed for your records. Fortunately, the fields were full, color vision is normal, and the electroretinogram is of good amplitude, although it does reveal classical signs of juvenile X-linked retinoschisis.

Sincerely,

Paul A. Sieving, MD, PhD
Associate Professor of Ophthalmology
Retinal Degeneration/ERG Consultations

PAS:lh
Encl: Visual Fields
ERG Waveforms
Color Vision
Letter to Parents
School Letter

The University of Michigan
W.K. Kellogg Eye Center

1000 Wall Street
Ann Arbor, Michigan 48105
Clinic: (313) 763-5906
Office: (313) 763-8097

Paul A. Sieving, M.D., Ph.D.

January 25, 1991

Mr. & Mrs. [redacted] Judy
[redacted]

Re: JUDY, Joshua J.
Reg: [redacted]

Dear Mr. & Mrs. Judy:

This letter is a follow-up of your son Joshua's evaluation with me at the Kellogg Eye Center on referral from [redacted]. Joshua had previously seen Dr. [redacted] P[redacted] who had made a diagnosis of juvenile X-linked retinoschisis. I concur in this diagnosis. Your son shows classical schisis cavities in the fovea of both eyes. My retinal examination of the periphery shows no evidence of schisis. This is the best news, since the peripheral schisis can be the most troublesome in this condition.

The two features of juvenile X-linked retinoschisis are that the central vision for reading is usually decreased to a level of 20/40 - 20/80. It is uncommon to have vision of either better or worse that these values. Second, the peripheral retina can show deterioration during life and lead to a detachment. For this reason, I would recommend yearly examination by a retinal specialist, such as Dr. P[redacted] or myself.

In my office, I performed several tests to get a sense of the overall quality of retinal function at this time. These test results showed the following:

Color Vision: Although the central vision is decreased to 20/50 in both eyes, the color vision tested normal on the Farnsworth D-15 test. This indicates that the photoreceptor function remains intact, as is expected in retinoschisis.

Peripheral Vision: His side vision showed no losses. This compliments my looking at the peripheral retina, since any peripheral schisis would show up as a missing part of peripheral vision.

Electroretinogram: An ERG shows an exaggerated a-wave from the photoreptors and a slightly diminished b-wave. These are classical findings in juvenile retinoschisis, although in your son's case, the changes are relatively mild. There are no other reductions of amplitudes which would warrant concern.

CLINICAL IMPRESSION: In other words, my impression is that overall, Josh had good retinal function and that there is a good probability that the vision he currently has is what he will keep in his future.

Page Two
Mr. & Mrs. [redacted] Judy
January 25, 1991

Re: JUDY, Joshua J.
Reg: [redacted]

As part of a molecular genetics study, during the past three years we have seen a large number of cases of retinoschisis from seven families in the State of Michigan. The average acuity was on the order of 20/40 - 20/80. My impression was that the vision a child had by age 7 - 15 years old was probably what he would keep throughout his lifetime until a later age of 60 or older.

Young children have very plastic ability to accomodate and do not need special reading glasses, even with vision of 20/50. Reading glasses may become helpful after age 14 or 16 years.

No special vision precautions need to be taken other than a yearly examination. I would not recommend repeating all of the test that were done here on this visit, since it is highly unlikely that any changes will be seen in the next decade or so.

As Dr. [redacted] explained, juvenile X-linked retinoschsis is inherited as a male only disease. Females carry the genetic trait and pass it to their sons. Sons do not pass it directly to any of their male children, but their daughters must inherit the gene and thereby start the chain over again. This means that any sons Josh has will <u>not</u> have retinoschsis, but <u>all</u> of his daughters must carry the gene and thereby pass it to his grandsons at 50% risk factor. Any sons Mrs. Judy has will each be at 50% risk for retinoschisis. Any daughters of Mrs. Judy will have 50% chance of being a carrier. Thus, Joshua's sisters (by his same mother) may have sons with retinoschisis.

Unfortunately, there are no treatments known to be affective in this condition.

You asked about organizations which are supporting research in the area. The best is the National Retinitis Pigmentosa Foundation at the following address:

National Retinitis Pigmentosa Foundation
Fighting Blindness, Inc.
1401 Mt. Royal Avenue, 4th Floor
Baltimore, Maryland 21217
Phone: 1-800-638-2300

Please be aware that Joshua does not have retinitis pigmentosa which is a progressively blinding eye disease. However, retinitis pigmentosa is the term loosely used to described genetically inherited retinal or macular dystrophis, including retinoschisis.

I am enclosing a paper recently published on genetic studies of juvenile retinoschsis.

The University of Michigan
W.K. Kellogg Eye Center

1000 Wall Street
Ann Arbor, Michigan 48105
Clinic: (313) 763-5906
Office: (313) 763-8097

Paul A. Sieving, M.D., Ph.D.

January 25, 1991

Re: Joshua J. Judy
DOB: 11/20/81

To the Teachers of Joshua Judy

I am sending this letter to Mr. & Mrs. Judy to provide to his school teachers. Joshua has a condition called "juvenile X-linked retinoschisis." This causes a modest reduction of the central vision for reading or seeing the chalkboard. There is no impairment of color vision, ability to see in dim light, or peripheral vision. We performed tests of these functions on Joshua and find that he performs normally in all regards except for visual acuity.

Retinoschisis causes a congenital splitting of the retina directly at the focal point of vision (the fovea). Fortunately, this is usually not significantly progressive.

Since the changes are in the retina, they cannot be corrected by glasses. Glasses are optional for Joshua because he shows only a mild refractive change.

I recommended to the parents that Joshua be encouraged to sit at the front of the classroom. Further, he can hold a book as close as convenient to his face without straining his eyes or without needing separate bifocals or other reading glasses. In all other regards, it would be best to consider his vision to be normal, since this is the case.

I understand that Joshua is dealing quite well with school work. I would expect that this will continue in the future, at least as regards his vision. I did recommend periodic examinations by a retinal specialist and his parents will be arranging this on their own.

Sincerely,

Paul A. Sieving, MD, PhD
Associate Professor of Ophthalmology
Retinal Degeneration/ERG Consultations

PAS:lh
cc: [redacted] P[redacted], MD
[redacted]

Rarity had walked through the door, illustrated by the rarity of my disease and the uniqueness of Dr. Sieving's response. The same could be said of my old supervisor Wendy's hiring approach. And of Dr. Otten's and his staff's willingness to find these old records. Grace, understanding, and thoroughness were the primary tools deployed. Not disbelief or aloofness. Not patronizing or smug. Not the attitude of "do it as quickly and cheaply as possible." Instead, there was openness. Care. A mindset of curiosity. A desire and freedom to pull on the string.

It begs a question: If the initial doctor-patient interaction is soured, if the long shadow of dismissiveness sets precedent, will the patient downplay their symptoms going forward? Will a wedge of mistrust form? That means more frustration, more time wasted, and more unnecessary visits leading to more unnecessary costs. It means going in circles. It's a downward spiral.

((MISTAKEN IDENTITY))

I can recall one time driving home around 10 pm after a very long work day. My boss and I just wrapped the quarter end. I pulled into the gas station in my town. I just wanted to fill-up and get home. It was warm enough that my driver's side window was down. Before I could get out, a police officer quietly slipped up to the window and somewhat nervously asked for my license and registration. I produced them and then asked, "What's wrong?"

"Your car looks a lot like the descriptions of the sniper who is causing havoc along the highway corridors." There had been reports of a sniper traveling a main east-west highway in Michigan. (In 2014, the perpetrator was charged with terrorism, based on 23 shootings that occurred in Livingston, Oakland, Ingham, and Shiawassee counties over three days in October 2012).[66, 67]

"Oh, we just got a company-wide email today telling employees to avoid the highways like I-94 and I-96 for safety reasons," I replied. At the time I was driving a black, four-door 1998

Oldsmobile Intrigue. I was its second owner, the first being my father. I purchased the car from him after a generous father-son discount.

"Officer, what kind of car is it?" I asked, somewhat knowingly.

"It's a black Oldsmobile Alero," she replied.

I gently answered, "My car only comes in the four-door variety. They look similar but mine's an Intrigue. An Alero may have two doors."

The officer, now somewhat embarrassed, sheepishly said, "I'm sorry for bothering you. What I can tell you is that you drove very well the last 10 miles." I wished her good luck and said there was no need to apologize. I said I wanted the maniac off the roads too. Anything I could do to help was fine by me.

Yikes, I was no deranged shooter! Moving past the name of my car, Intrigue, it felt like enough mystery for one night. Archaic accounting reports at 10 p.m. and scribbled on Post-It notes suddenly seemed comforting, even welcoming.

As I wearily headed home to our small apartment loft, I reflected on the officer's grace. Swap white coats for blue uniforms. Maybe we wrap our identities up too much in the uniforms we wear, and not enough in how we treat each other while wearing them. Mutual respect goes a long way and Our Quadruple Aim reaches far beyond human healthcare.

((OUR QUADRUPLE AIM FOR FUR BABIES))

Megan often shares stories with me from her life as a Licensed Veterinary Technician (L.V.T.). A client brought her dog in to be seen. The pet had been stirring in the night with a cough, causing the owners to stir. In the veterinary world, this typically is what triggers an owner to take action—a disturbance to the owner's normal routine. Because "furry people" cannot explain, they have to find other ways to tell their owners of a problem. The client's pet needed annual blood work, which was run in-house.

The testing revealed the dog had heartworms.

Because the dog had developed a persistent cough, it meant the parasite was already in the heart tissue causing damage. Fluid buildup starts in the lungs. Coughing is the body's natural reaction to try and clear the fluid. But as the heart fails over time, fluid builds up throughout the body.

The clinic Megan once worked at is not owned by a corporation. Unlike the medical system for humans, the "unseen hand" of insurance is nowhere around. The clinic is structured to have "floating" technicians who were not assigned to a specific job—on a given day, they would not have pre-scheduled appointments or surgery. That way, when emergent needs came up, they could attend to them. This is not the case in all veterinary clinics.

Some clinics only use their technicians as lab technicians, so they see no patients of their own and do no exams. Some veterinarian doctors don't empower their technicians to care for the patients other than performing basic tasks (e.g. bloodwork or paperwork). Other clinics can only afford one technician and they must attend appointments while wearing many other hats.

The client was informed the dog was heartworm-positive, and that the condition could be very serious. A cough meant there was already damage. The owner became very anxious, and rightfully so. She had many questions. But at this point, the doctor was delayed to her next appointment—in fact, it pushed the schedule at least two appointments behind. The doctor had to make a decision: end the appointment and push the client out or take extra time to put her at ease however long it took.

As the assigned floating technician that day, Megan immediately stepped in. She asked the doctor if it was okay if she stayed with the client to answer her questions and allay her fears. Due to the COVID-19 pandemic, Megan met with the client outside in the parking lot. She remembers the day clearly. It was late fall and a bit cold out. For the next hour, they talked and built a treatment plan for what the entire next year would look like, including:

- estimates for each treatment
- explanation for all medications, including side effects
- explanation of the disease process itself
- answering all follow-up questions
- explaining the outcome without treatment
- scheduled follow-up appointments
- printed instructions to take home
- multiple (at least five) reassurances her pet would be okay

In other words, all options and potential outcomes were covered to the client's satisfaction.

As an "active listener," Megan was able to ease the client's mind. Each time the client had a question, Megan repeated it back to confirm her understanding before redirecting focus back to the plan of care. "Yes, some damage was done but the disease could be stopped from progressing." Every time the client asked, "Will my pet die?" Megan answered, "No, I'm here to help so nothing like that happens." Megan's active listening skills and sincere interest de-escalated the situation.

Providing quality medical care takes time, and time is so often a luxury. But Our Quadruple Aim teaches this: Invest the time now, or invest much more later. Had someone not been ready and willing to make that time investment, the client would have been a walking timebomb. It takes administrators who are willing to free up compassionate, properly trained resources to defuse the bomb.

At this point in the story, I asked Megan if this is standard protocol everywhere for vet clinics. She replied, "No, but I enjoy educating clients." For practice managers (administrators) out there, take note: In addition to the ingredients listed above, find employees who are passionate about patient education and see if they want to weave it into their role. More importantly, help enable that level of engagement and allow breathing room so they can.

The alternative to investing this upfront time is the client very likely would have called the clinic the next day. She would be asking many questions not of a technician or doctor, but placing a huge burden on the receptionist who is not trained to answer medical questions. The situation would crumble from there. Nevertheless, there was a callback the next day. It was the client thanking staff for pulling her off the proverbial cliff. Grave concern had been transformed into gratefulness.

This raises a critical question: Are we giving our doctors, nurses and staff enough time to be caring? Care is now corporatized more than ever. Optics and reports are often the job instead of the job being the job. Forms for the sake of forms. Meetings for the sake of meetings. Here is the disconnect. Our Quadruple Aim on its face says, if you take care of the doctor and supporting staff, they in turn can take care of their patient. They can educate. They can listen. They can guide.

On what planet would we want our caretakers so buried in non-value-added B.S. (wasting time) that they are deprived of caring for themselves, meaning there's nothing left to give to patients? Isn't that the highest order of paradox?

As for what happened to the dog, you ask? We're happy to share that the dog's cough, while chronic, has significantly improved. Quality of life certainly improved. Things are manageable and both client and dog are enjoying life together.

Again, an exception had walked in the door. How will the medical professional greet it—with grace or dismissiveness? With curiosity to educate (or be educated), or disinterest? If time and energy constantly feels short between doctor and patient, the wrong operating structure is in place. Consider Our Quadruple Aim a conducive antidote.

TL;DR—lessons for OQA:

Everyone, I present the following question, *"Do you handle exceptions and rarity with grace, or dismissiveness?"*

Next time you have the chance in a situation, ask yourself: See if it changes the value proposition you walk away with, for everyone involved. Were you able to find your own little utopia?

Megan M. Judy – L.V.T., Patient:

Our Quadruple Aim	Veterinarian's Quadruple Aim
1. Patient Experience	Patient-Client experience
2. Quality Care	Quality Care
3. Lower Costs	Lower Costs
4. Provider Wellness	Provider Wellness

While you mostly come to know my story through Joshua's writing, I'm honored to contribute to *Ripple of Change*. For 10 years, until taking a step away to care for my family, I cared for animals as a Licensed Veterinary Technician. While still holding my license, what I write here comes from my time as an active care provider.

Our Quadruple Aim in veterinary medicine is largely similar to that of human medicine, with one subtle difference—the change of patient experience to patient-client experience. Human medicine has a doctor-patient relationship, which becomes the doctor-client-patient relationship in the animal world. This is a similar situation to pediatrics and neonatal care, where there is a non-speaking patient under the care of an adult. A little trickier, yes?

In order to know the patient experience, we have to first know the client experience. The range of clients' expectations is extreme. Some call at the first sign of a cough or wheeze, while others will not call in until the coughing has started keeping them awake through the night. Then deem it an emergency.

At my clinic, we placed calls to owners (callbacks) at the seven day mark after seeing a patient, regardless of their ailment. The purpose was brilliantly simple: To check on the patient's treatment plan. If the pet was doing better, the interaction concluded. If worse, it was time for a re-check. A critical step to quality care *before* a callback was pulling the patient record and reviewing. First, a verification that the patient had not passed, and that the owner had not recently called. Failing to do so could result in an awkward, or painful call. Perhaps human medicine could widely adopt and make the patient record pre-check and callback a standard practice. For those already doing it; awesome, as it is a huge step towards a positive patient (client) experience.

Animal care specialists, veterinarians, and veterinary technicians have to rely on the client, the animal's owner, to give the best care to the patient. This comes with many challenges. Animals cannot speak for themselves as to what hurts or doesn't feel good. Signs of illness or injury are sometimes hard to notice. Further complicating matters, some animals, like cats, will practically let themselves die before showing any signs of weakness. The best we have is the client knowing their pet very well and catching on that something is wrong.

It's worth reiterating—quality care in veterinary medicine boils down to education and communication. Providers need the time to explain the 'whys' behind a diagnosis to the pet's owner. Without it, treatment plans are poorly followed, or not at all—steps are judged optional, or skipped. When care providers and clients are aligned, the animal wins.

In veterinary medicine, prevention equals lower costs: vaccines, annual care (exams, diagnostic testing, blood work, dental cleanings), and preventative medications such as flea and tick control and heartworm medication. Much like with human care, annual exams and blood work help the doctor note changing trends over time. Even if values are in range, an intervention can start early–before sickness even occurs.

Let me outline different tools of preventative care. First, vaccines play a role in stopping sickness before it starts. A puppy's traditional series of vaccines come as a bundled package like an infant's first sets of vaccines. Vaccines give the body a standing army to fight an infection of that particular disease.

Next consider annual blood work such as monitoring kidney health. There are several biomarkers to examine kidney function. A kidney can continue to perform properly until it has lost 70% of its usable tissue, after which certain biomarkers rise. Scientists recently discovered a biomarker which identifies kidney function changes much sooner. This allows care changes to be made earlier—a form of prevention that slows injury to the kidneys.

Now on to fleas. They cause their own set of problems without preventative measures. Aside from an itchy bite, some animals are highly allergic to the flea's saliva. This allergy causes severely inflamed skin, hair loss, and allows for other bacterial and fungal skin infections–leaving the patient extremely uncomfortable. Treatment for these conditions can add up quickly, in both costs and complexity. Remedies used in this situation include antibiotics, antifungals, steroids, shampoos, skin sprays, and usually the infamous "cone of shame"—the plastic collar around the head used to prevent self-harm. Using medication against fleas monthly helps keep the fleas off the animal in the first place.

Like flea medication, tick control is used monthly and prevents disease by killing the tick on contact, or by repelling them from the animal. Ticks carry several diseases that are transmissible to humans and animals alike. Many people have heard of Lyme disease. And yes, animals can get it too. Although, our furry friends do not usually present with that famous target shaped lesion.

Lastly, heartworm disease can impact a client and patient severely, but it does not have to. Just like previous parasite preventions, there is one for heartworms too. A patient can get heartworms from a mosquito bite. If there are any follow up concerns or questions on these topics, talk to your veterinarian! Ultimately, preventing disease is better than having to treat, lessening the cost burden on the client in order to keep their animal healthy.

In my 10 years as a L.V.T., I collected lab samples (blood, urine, feces), completed the tests on said samples, provided restraint, placed IV and urinary catheters, administered medications and monitored anesthesia, prepared and assisted in surgery, took radiographs, performed ultrasounds, cared for hospitalized and recovering patients, administered vaccines, educated clients, and provided a shoulder for grieving pet parents. All usually on the same day.

Compassion fatigue and burnout are heavily discussed in the veterinary world due to the heavy burdens we carry. There is usually a dedicated set of courses during all continued education conferences. During my career, I helped deliver puppies during an emergency c-section—and held those same paws as they said goodbye in their senior years. During an animal care provider's career, we will see the entire life of most of our patients and we bond and love them like our own. It is as hard for us to say goodbye to them as it is for their owners. We grieve hard, and then have to bottle it up (compartmentalize) and move on to the next client-patient.

This type of emotional jumping leads many animal care providers to leave medicine, or leave the world by their own hands. Ponder the following sobering information from a 2019 study in the Journal of the American Veterinary Medical Association titled, *"Suicide among veterinarians in the United States from 1979 through 2015"*:

"From 1979 through 2015, male and female US veterinarians had higher than expected proportionate mortality ratios for suicide, compared with the general US population. Female veterinarians in clinical and nonclinical roles were 3.4 and 5.0 times as likely to die by suicide as the general population, respectively. Additionally, 154 of 398 (39%) deaths by suicide among veterinarians over the 36-year study period were the result of pharmaceutical poisoning, a rate nearly 2.5 times that for individuals among the general US population who died by suicide in 2016."[68]

The last statement on high rates of pharmaceutical poisoning sadly validates that providers dispatch tools within easy reach to end their suffering. Tools used one day for caring, and another day for self-harm.

There are days when technicians will be covered in scratch marks, sweat, urine, drool, feces, or any other bodily fluid you can think of. And maybe some you can't, just in the name of toe nail trims. I can't speak for nurses in human medicine and if they can say the same. But for us, it's a typical Tuesday at 9 a.m. Also, I don't think most human patients attempt to bite their caretakers. Our patients do—a lot. When the Veterinarian's Quadruple Aim thrives, so do providers, owners, and their pets.

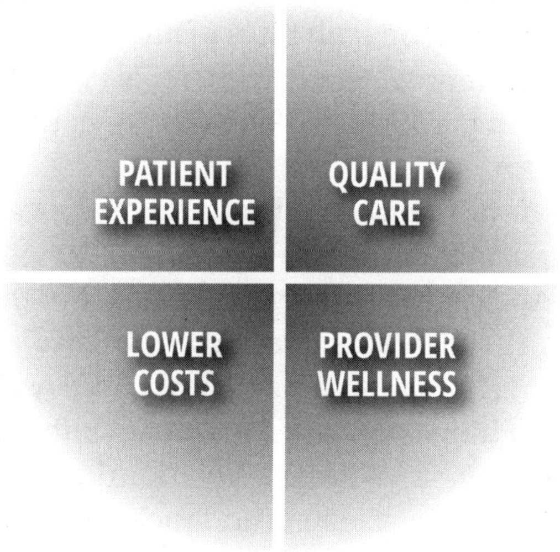
PATIENT EXPERIENCE
QUALITY CARE
LOWER COSTS
PROVIDER WELLNESS

((8))

It's Bigger Than Me

Joshua J. Judy – Patient:

By 2017, Megan and I were headed to a crossroads with our health. My wife's patient story began on a nondescript day in March. A little bored, we drove a couple towns over for a late lunch, or if you will, an early dinner. Our son, James, who had just turned one, rode securely in his car seat. Our meal was casual—opting for the salad bar. It was at a homestyle diner in a small village in Michigan with a satisfying chicken noodle soup. There's often comfort in the stable and familiar.

The stable and familiar made the moment misleadingly serene. Truly, the only hint of something astray was that my wife was feeling a little under the weather—mostly tired. Storm clouds were gathering, just not in the literal sense. I recall her being a bit quiet on the ride. She rested with her eyes closed as the hum of the road gently blanketed the cabin of our Chevy Traverse. Our son, who to this day exposes deft abilities to snooze as a passenger, followed suit.

Later that evening, James was in bed. Megan and I sat in the living room relaxing, sipping on hot tea. I occupied the love seat and she sat kitty-corner on our sectional, crocheting. Netflix recently added the entire original "Unsolved Mysteries" series hosted by the late and well-regarded Robert Stack. We started a binge.

What better way to revisit childhood memories and still be terrified decades later by the distinctly ominous opening theme? Fittingly, in music theory, the tritone whole notes heard in the theme song are called, "The Devil's Interval." If you were a kid in the 1980s, you in no uncertain terms slept restlessly after watching the show with the blanket pulled noticeably higher. It often served as fuel for nightmares.

...Struggling to drift off to sleep, suddenly you are on a dead-end gravel road rutted with mud from an earlier rain. Alone, swallowed by the night. No traffic or lights, leaving it hushed enough to hear the breath you exhaled. The air, chilled and dank, easily skirted through the light jacket that drooped across your child-framed shoulders. The pockets of your faded blue jeans were empty. You wished you had planned better. Why hadn't you at least grabbed a couple quarters? If you stumbled across a payphone in some random empty parking lot, you'd be asking the operator for help—a collect call, hoping for an answer. Or maybe some things are beyond our control and can't be planned for.

A silvery fog hung low to the ground, wisps occasionally sliding over the tops of your loosely tied sneakers. Loose enough that if you had to run, they would surely fall off. The remaining fog hugged the road's shoulder, uncertain whether to slink across the uneven surface or hold back and tip-toe along the nearby tree line.

The moon was unable to penetrate the oily blackness that bore down. The quiet was broken with the subtle crunching of footsteps—a rhythmic scuffling that was coming ever closer to you. The steps grew louder. Your instincts screaming out that whatever was walking toward you was not friendly and wished grave harm. You prayed you were mistaken. Indeed, a terrible nightmare, the Devil couldn't be far...

My thoughts came back to the present. Watching TV, Megan and I would make occasional banter with one another, as partners often do. I don't remember exactly what I said, but I know it was a sassy comment. Megan shot back, "Does this face look amused?" Alarmingly, she then said, "That's odd, I can't really feel my face..."

Her voice trailed off and her head fell back and to the left. An audible, sickly popping sound. My wife convulsed and drooped. Her head and body were shaking and I thought she had somehow snapped her neck. I panicked.

The air in the room was suddenly replaced with a thick gelatin that made inhaling laborious and impractical. I jumped off the couch. But I felt direly weak and was unable to move fluidly. Many fears slammed my brain at once—heart attack, stroke, aneurysm, approaching death. Oh no, our son—my wife was a very young mother. Trembling, I only felt fear.

I remember screaming, *"Dear, I'm going to get you help! I will get you help!"* I doubt any of it sounded confident. I tried to feel for a pulse but my hands were damn near worthless. I felt like I was sinking into a huge tub of wet cement that was quickly setting. My brain kicked into gear for a lucid moment. Dial those digits! 9–1–1. Why was something so elementary so immediately incapacitating? I clumsily got my cell phone unlocked and dialed.

A female operator answered. I spewed words breathlessly, a stream of consciousness draining out of me and into the operator's ear.

Me: "My wife, she's having some kind of episode! Please send an ambulance!"

Operator: "Is she breathing?"

Me: "Yes, I think so—but I need help!"

Operator: "Make sure she's on her side. I will stay with you until the ambulance comes."

Much like the barrage of words I expelled into the 911 operator's ear, the blood had left my face and my hands were freezing cold. I felt tingly and must have said as much.

Operator: "Sir, are you okay? Would you like for us to send help for you too?"

As the operator finished verifying if two stretchers were needed instead of one, my wife groaned and mumbled, "What's going on?"

Operator: "Sir, is that her speaking?"

Me: "Yes, it was! She's coming out of it!"

But I didn't know what "it" was.

I thanked the 911 operator and disconnected. Just outside our living room picture window, long shadows dashed along our walkway and up the stairs of our porch—a subtle, rhythmic scuffling closing in. Friend or foe? Thankfully, the paramedics arrived. Letting them in, I awkwardly apologized for having to navigate around strewn baby toys.

My wife had regained consciousness but revealed significant disorientation at the appearance of strangers brusquely invading our living room. Instinctively, there was some alarm in her eyes. Her brain had gone completely offline and she lost several minutes. *"Wait, who....?"* Her voice trailed off—tenuous and groggy.

Outwardly calm now, I told her she had suffered some kind of medical episode, that help was here and she would be okay. I tried to be reassuring, but I wondered if I believed the last part myself. The paramedics were incredibly supportive and gracious. "I know, it's very scary, isn't it?" one gently asked me with empathy and compassion. Putting my wife on a stretcher, they wheeled her out of the house. They were taking her to the local hospital. Moments later, they came back into the house and told me they had decided on a larger hospital in Lansing, 20 miles away, because there was a neurological unit there.

The sirens weren't on because her vitals were stable. Still, the paramedics' change of plans had me tentative. The ambulance pulled away and I was left behind with only my thoughts—and our sleeping baby down the hall, whom we had tucked in earlier. Tears welled in my eyes. I was distraught and felt remarkably alone. Like a childhood nightmare, except now I was living it.

((OUT OF MY HANDS))

After the ambulance pulled away, I called each set of our parents and packed up our son. I also called my sister and my wife's brothers to let them know what happened. They would meet me later at the hospital. I headed north in the direction the ambulance had just traversed. As I navigated the darkened streets, the glow of the dashboard and occasional street lamp reflected erratically across my glasses, mirroring the considerations in my mind. I thought about our baby son in the back; would he still have a mommy to come to know and love? What about the woman I had fallen in love with? Would she be the same? What greater tragedy in this life than a child having no memories of his mother? I needed to put these jumbled thoughts at bay.

Once I arrived at the hospital, I was given directions to my wife's room. Things had settled down, but we had little in the way of answers. Megan had turned on the TV and was flipping through the channels. Her older brother was in the room and we all were chatting. He was holding our son. Then it happened again.

Mid-sentence, without warning, my wife started convulsing, her face contorting into distressing and peculiar shapes. She was making odd groaning sounds, once again completely gone. Oh God, why? I ran into the hall and down to the nurse's station.

"My wife! I need help please! It's happening again! Come quick!"

First there were three people. Soon, the number was closer to 10. They fanned around her. One injected something into her IV. A doctor walked in and looked toward me, "We have to do a spinal tap, sir. But given possible risks and the fact your wife cannot consent, we need your permission."

I pressed the doctor to find out how many spinal taps she had performed. *"Several dozen,"* she affirmed. Ever an issue? *"No."* I pressed on about possible risks—headaches, infection, or uncontrollable bleeding. They would be looking for infections in the brain such as meningitis. Without the tap, there was no other way to tell.

I made her promise, *"You'll do it right, won't you? No mistakes."* The doctor nodded, *"Yes, I will do my best."* My line of questioning spoke for itself. I was already in an early stage of distrusting healthcare because now my wife was the patient.

TL;DR—lessons for OQA:

Patients: it's always okay to ask a doctor to tell you the risks behind a recommendation they make.

Everyone: it's okay to be scared sometimes. It's how you channel your fear that matters.

((BIG SIS))

The clock ground to a standstill. Stress, staff coming and going, waiting and more waiting—it all blurred in my frazzled mind. Minutes became hours and I lost track. I don't remember how, but I was back in the waiting area. My sister had shown up, keeping me company and helping to feed our son some formula. She seemed to appear out of nowhere, instantaneously, as if a hole opened in the sky and plunked her next to me. Clearly my brain wasn't following events well.

There would be tests, and more tests. Pacing. Hand-wringing. There would be no discharge in the immediate future. We wanted answers, clear ones. Having been up all night, everything was becoming fuzzy. At some point that morning, I went home briefly to freshen up and grab more supplies. My sister had followed me to help clean and tidy things up, emptying the sink and loading the dishwasher. And that was my big sis, doing what she did out of love, which is how most ripples are started. After checking that I was okay, she went home to her family. I headed back to what had become my second home—the hospital.

((FLUKE))

By the following day, Megan was in a new room in the neurology services ward. The department provides treatment for head trauma and neurological disorders, stroke diagnosis and treatment, spinal and brain surgery, and among other things—epilepsy. Scanning the list of services made me feel nervous and raw. I could only feign confidence to the outside world that all would be fine.

Doctor after doctor paraded in, along with an occasional nurse. Over the following year, I would be reconciling bills, as each provider charged a little bit differently. After such major health events, the process to recovery and some semblance of closure comes excruciatingly slow.

Megan received a litany of tests: MRIs, CT scans, and neurological tests with questions that covered the basics like your name and birthday, the calendar date, who is the current U.S. president, reflex and physical strength tests, and so on.

After all of those tests, we didn't get a verdict. *"It's all a fluke,"* they said, like some hung jury unable to reach unanimity. When there's a single seizure event, it's not yet considered epilepsy. After some paperwork and final checks, we were finally discharged home. Megan was given immediate-release levetiracetam. We headed home uneasy, with more questions than answers.

What about that appalling popping sound I had heard on the couch? During the seizure, the force of the muscles tightened so harshly that my wife partially dislocated her left shoulder. In front of her were many sessions of physical therapy. To this day, she considers it her bum arm. It's still weaker than the other one. Curiously, the topic never came up during the hospital stay and no pain treatment was provided. Probably forgotten in the organized chaos of patient care.

Several months later, when picking up our son to hug him, Megan's shoulder partially dislocated again. Instant pain. I feared another seizure as she rapidly contorted and shook. She saw the alarm in my eyes, impressively shimmying without dropping our son. But there wasn't time to explain. She was too occupied putting her arm back in its socket. It scared us both.

TL;DR—lessons for OQA:

Everyone, go hug your significant other, your parents if they're still with you, your kids if you're blessed to have them. Call up a friend and thank them for being able to make you laugh or brighten your day.

Also, it's not recommended to dislocate a limb in the process.

((SOME LUCK BETTER THAN NO LUCK))

By fall 2017, my wife had been on levetiracetam for six months. I noticed she preferred sleep over most things. Very subdued. Quiet. Somewhere else. I knew she wasn't her old self, but I failed to appreciate and comprehend the extent to which she suffered.

She was becoming hollowed out, much like a once-solid tree that's been maliciously struck by lightning. The rapid, withering heat incinerates away much of the healthy tissue. And any trunk left behind is for the termites to eat from the inside out. Even though it's what we most needed, time to talk things out was limited by our mutual fatigue. We were working full time, raising our young son, and mutually combating our own bodies.

For her ongoing treatment plan, Megan was initially sent to a nearby university's neurology department. There, we met with a young resident neurologist. Briefly, the resident was shadowed by a significantly older doctor. Based on his laconic nature, he seemed content letting the younger physician practice. As she suggested an approach, he was in and then out of the room, parting with a stoic, *"Fine. Let's do that."* It was as if he was a trial lawyer resting his case. No further witnesses.

The resident wanted to know if we planned on having more children. Yes, we hoped. Our plan was always two, if so felicitous. For its purported reproductive safety profile, the resident offered lamotrigine. What about risks and birth defects like cleft lip or cleft palate? They would not be dramatically elevated. But if we palpably recall anything about this meeting, it was about the rash. That's right, the rash. By contrast, the resident never asked about any side effects from Megan's current treatment.

We spent more than half our appointment discussing how lamotrigine can lead to a skin condition. We were told to be on high alert and keep a mindful eye out. If we saw it, we were to reach out immediately. Why the urgent warnings? According to a 2014 review of existing studies, lamotrigine-related skin rash occurs in about 10% of patients.[69]

The rash can lead to Stevens-Johnson syndrome (SJS). According to the Mayo Clinic, SJS is a "serious disorder of the skin and mucous membranes" that can be caused by a reaction to medication. Or more severely, it can lead to toxic epidermal necrolysis, which may present as peeling blisters, sepsis, and multiple organ failure leading up to and including death.[70]

When transitioning between epilepsy medications, the patient must remain on their current prescription to provide stabilization. They then titrate or ramp up the new medication, and once at a therapeutic level, taper down, and drop the original. So, for a while, the patient 'double dips,' which can bring on its own set of predicaments. But one element persists—don't make rash moves with epilepsy drugs unless told otherwise. I assume if an easier way existed, we'd already be doing it.

Megan started the lamotrigine on the weekend. On Wednesday, red hives appeared on her chest. As directed, she called the neurologist's office. No answer—a message left for the doctor. Thursday, there was no return call despite multiple messages. By Friday morning, Megan spoke with the office staff emphatically declaring, *"Get someone, anyone!"* By the afternoon, someone called but not her doctor. "You can stop taking the new med. Stick with the levetiracetam. Goodbye."

After this demoralizing trial, we asked Dr. Otten if he would consider sending us to the state's other major university adult neurology center. Our trust in the system was rapidly waning, making our relationship with Dr. Otten paramount. There was nobody else to turn to. Dr. Otten replied he was less familiar with the doctors there, but recognizing our frustrations, he would make it happen—and he did. Once there, we met with Megan's new neurologists. We shared our recent conundrums, including how poorly levetiracetam made Megan feel. The fatigue was overwhelming and Megan shared how she didn't feel safe providing care to our little son or her patients at work. Restraining scared and sick animals requires a razor-sharp focus to keep the animal and providers safe.

One doctor keenly asked, *"Have you ever considered the extended-release version?"*

"Our first time hearing of it." Armed with this new information, the trip paid for itself. However, we wished we had been told about different options sooner. A lesson became obvious: Don't fall in the trap of supposing that your provider will give you all the information or formulations available. Megan transitioned to extended-release levetiracetam where she stayed for years–until life again forced a change. We had only been trying to keep our heads above water, relying on the experts to educate us on side effects—and drug alternatives.

How does the extended-release version work? It gradually releases the medication into the bloodstream, mildly lessening the harsh fatigue that Megan experienced with the immediate-release version. She was on a dosage of 1500 mg, originally filled with two 750 mg extended-release pills. Our prescription plan requires home delivery after the first three fills from a local pharmacy. The main problem—the home delivery pharmacy carried only the immediate-release. The sole pharmacy that offered the extended-release was inconvenient and in a hospital (the last place we wanted to be). Logistical barriers were not just frustrating and time-consuming, they also started to contribute to more medical problems.

In time, Megan would become pregnant. Levetiracetam was increased to 2000 mg to maintain a therapeutic dose, while pregnancy increased her blood volume. A woman's blood supply will increase by 50% during pregnancy, diluting the concentration of medication. Simple math tells you that the easiest way to hit this amount was by adding one 500 mg pill to the existing 1500 mg total. Adding this one pill at that time would have been ideal because refills would track on the same timeline as refills for the original 1500 mg script. Unfortunately, the pharmacy pushed back on filling it, because the insurance pushed back. That delayed the filling of the second prescription and the refill schedules were no longer in sync. Again the healthcare system was steadily throwing up more hurdles to good patient care.

We were stuck managing two different scripts, doubling the number of trips to a brick-and-mortar pharmacy every month. Equally frustrating, the prescription plan service (known as a Pharmacy Benefit Manager, they act as a middleman between insurance and drug companies) started a parade of emails and letters telling us to sign up for home delivery (even though home-delivery didn't stock the extended-release version Megan needed). If we declined, they would start charging significantly more for using the in-person pharmacy. But, for us, there was no choice. Either the home-delivery pharmacy needed to start carrying Megan's particular formulation or, for valid medical reasons, we'd have to stay with in-person scripts. We made many phone calls to our insurance, prescription plan service, and in-person pharmacy. We never got a satisfactory resolution to the dilemma they created for us. Around and around we went.

To cut down on trips to the pharmacy, we called the neurologist's office and asked them to place a new script order for the 500 mg pill so it could be filled on the same schedule as our original script. But, our insurance balked. Too close to the original script's fill date, they said.

By luck (or brilliance), Megan's doctor caught wind of the rigmarole we were enduring. She called in an entirely new single script of 4 x 500 mg pills to the hospital pharmacy to eliminate the original 2 x 750 mg script. We were now under one script. *(Notice, the insurance company didn't offer this as a possible solution, nor did the pharmacy, nor the script service—that means it's up to you and your doctor to advocate!)* It was just one of many games played by the stakeholders that make life as a patient terrifyingly difficult.

Even with that solved, we still faced the problem with the home-delivery mandate. We continued to have to fill the 500 mg script at the inconvenient hospital pharmacy in the months to follow. Eventually, after more months of fighting the insurance company, someone from the script service who we hadn't spoken to before called us.

Finally, a rich discussion with a real person! She said they would now offer the 500s in extended-release for home delivery. Why someone was suddenly cooperative and understanding, we'll probably never know. The battle had worn down a lot of people. Oh, the things we do for fun. As for cost under home delivery, that went from $180 to $131 every three months, and $19 once our $3,000 annual deductible is met. A nice touch. So why? Why all the wasted time and effort for the correct result? To think, ours is just one story. Is the healthcare system so big that simple common sense and good customer service can't rule?

TL;DR—lessons for OQA:

Patients, never be afraid to do your own homework and ask your providers questions. You'll learn something new, and, perhaps, they will, too. Find out about every form and dosage of your medication that exists. If you feel terrible on one formulation, don't be shy: ask if there's an alternative. But, like any good investigator, try to already know some of the answers before you ask.

It's experiences like I've described here that lead people to "Dr. Google." Like many situations in life, if you don't already know, don't expect others to tell you. Sadly, instead of going the extra mile, people often take the path of least resistance. Such lazy approaches can lead to poor quality.

Also, health care providers aren't mind readers. Don't expect them to know everything. And, unknown to you, they might have their own problems distracting them. In a family practice, thousands of patients may be under the care of a single provider. But they might be in a position to help if you ask.

((BLIND FAITH))

All the while we were fighting the bureaucracy to get good care for Megan, my neck pain was getting worse. Far from being over, it amplified, deafeningly on most days. Nothing worked. I went back to Dr. Otten who suggested increasing my duloxetine from 30 mg to 60 mg. Unlike other drugs in the SSRI (Selective Serotonin Reuptake Inhibitor)/SNRI (Serotonin and Norepinephrine Reuptake Inhibitor) family, duloxetine is approved for pain control.

The side effects at 30 mg remained minimal so I saw little harm. Oh, little chemical, how deceptive you are. Up to this point, if my doctor prescribed something, I never questioned it. You don't have a preconceived reason to, so you don't. When you've never been harmed, it's a natural default position.

I wanted the pain to go away. I was over it. I said, okay. In October 2017, I filled my script and swallowed my first 60 mg pill.

((BIGGEST MISTAKE OF MY LIFE))

It was too late—I couldn't take it back. After a single capsule, I felt my mind shutting down. Some kind of internal door was slamming closed. Feelings started to blunt. Emotional excitement sifted away, much like a handful of sand running through one's fingers. I felt them falling away but my grip was helpless to arrest the tiny, fleeing granules.

If 30 mg of duloxetine had amped me up, 60 mg overloaded the circuits and blew a fuse. The world around me was dimming. Sex drive and associated thoughts practically disappeared. Overnight—chemical castration.

I don't know why but I didn't fully connect the medication to what was happening. I think on some level, I simply thought there was another adjustment period. There often is with medications, especially SSRIs or SNRIs. I had never been truly hurt by a medication before, making it truly unforeseen. Nevertheless, my wife and I now shared similar realities. As time elapsed and the chemical assault continued, we further slipped away. In the rubble, two people with two broken brains—we felt like walking corpses, only reflexively breathing.

A major realization dawned: This is just as much my patient story as Megan's. Eventually, in writing this book, I accepted the story was also my doctor's, my family's, and every patient in this sputtering automaton we call healthcare. The scope had grown extensively—way beyond me.

TL;DR—lessons for OQA:

Everyone, things can always be worse. It's not just some polite cliche designed to give a false sense of security. Seriously. Keep your perspective in check and cherish every moment that you feel well.

Sometimes, you get shorted earlier in life, sometimes later. The only certainty is this: Those well moments won't always be there.

((9))

Ripple of Change

"Just as ripples spread out
when a single pebble is dropped into water,
the actions of individuals
can have far-reaching effects."

– DALAI LAMA

Todd R. Otten, M.D.:

In April 2007, I had committed to join St. John Hospital in Detroit, Michigan to continue my medical training in family medicine. It was a beautiful spring day in Grosse Pointe, Michigan. Angie and I were escorted by our real estate agent searching for the perfect home, prior to starting residency. Weather conditions were ideal, about 60 degrees, with a gentle breeze and an endless baby blue sky. A solitary kite painted the sky with its vibrant colors and rhythmic tail. The flowers and trees were starting to bloom—landscapes bursting with life. People were out walking or running after emerging from their winter abodes. It was as if the heavens were smiling down.

Having viewed a few homes so far, none stood out. Fortunately, my mom was watching our two young boys, allowing us to focus on the matter at hand. As our search continued, we found ourselves traveling north on Jefferson Ave (a continuation of Lakeshore Dr). As one might imagine—a lovely road just off of Lake Saint Clair. Million dollar homes dot the eastern side of the road adjacent to the lakeshore. Angie and I sat in the back seat, looking out of the window, while our real estate agent chauffeured.

The promise of the months to come filled my mind. In July, I would become a resident in family medicine. The challenges—a reality. Memories of my year as a surgical resident replayed in my mind—good and bad. My beautiful wife next to me, and my two young boys at home playing with Grandma Ruth. I felt at peace.

"Todd, Todd!" Angie said urgently.

"What?" Coming out of my trance.

"I think we should stop!"

Angie was the first to see the commotion. I looked out of the front window as we arrived at the scene of an accident. It was soon clear the collision had happened in the preceding moments. An SUV was stopped in the middle of the road, with damage to its front end. A motorcycle laid on its side with gas pouring out of its mangled tank. The translucent fluid pooling on the warm pavement. The twisted metal was a stark contrast to prior serenity. As I looked to the right, a middle-aged woman had been thrown against a fence with a few good Samaritans trying to assist. She was lying supine—her left leg amputated just above the knee.

"We should stop," Angie repeated, an increasing urgency in her voice.

I jumped out of the car, and sprinted toward the woman. Time seemed to slow down—as if we were in a movie. I ran past her severed limb, her torn jeans revealing the severed flesh and broken bone. The scene is crystal clear in my mind to this day, images moving frame by frame. As I approached, the woman's eyes were closed. She appeared lifeless. The bystanders were attempting to apply a tourniquet as blood soaked her tattered jeans. The 'golden hour' of trauma had started. Fully knowing if care is delayed beyond 60 minutes—mortality increases.

I knelt beside the woman and quickly assessed her airway and pulse; she was barely conscious, but alive. I evaluated her wound. Despite the bystanders' best efforts, blood was pouring profusely out of her leg. I told the good Samaritans I was a physician, and they gladly let me take over. They backed up and allowed me to manage the tourniquet (as blood loss threatened her life). I grabbed a stick to twist the belt (now transformed into a tourniquet), attempting to increase the pressure. The blood flow began to slow. Then, the stick broke. The snap seemed unusually loud, like the starting gun at a track meet. The race was on, the clock was ticking.

Additional medical professionals arrived to help: a trauma nurse, a neurosurgeon, and several others. In addition, Angie was an ICU nurse. Nearly an entire trauma team had volunteered. But, the most pressing matter was in my hands, literally.

The scene: surreal and controlled chaos. Someone had called 911. The woman's blood covered my hands. The warm, red life-sustaining fluid glistened in the midday sun. I was not deterred.

As the stick broke, instincts kicked in. I grabbed the belt with my bare hands and started to twist. I twisted and twisted as hard as I could. What seemed like an eternity, happened in seconds. My hands were white with pressure from my determined grip. The blood streaming from her leg, first slowed to a trickle, then stopped. I breathed a sigh of relief and waited for reinforcements. Others were helping any way they could, including comforting the woman. The selflessness of so many strangers—compelling.

EMS arrived and were quick to work on transporting the woman to the hospital. As they assessed the situation, one of the paramedics asked, "Do you want to let up on that tourniquet?"

I glared incredulously, "What are you worried about? That she is going to lose her leg?"

"He is a physician," someone said.

Needless to say, I did not let up on the tourniquet. A stretcher was brought out and a more substantial tourniquet applied. An EMT placed an IV and the woman was taken to St. John Hospital. I stood up and looked around. Sweat covered my brow in the hot sun, my hands covered in blood. Our real estate agent was pale and looked like he was going to vomit. I glanced at Angie and she was near tears. A few people thanked us for stopping.

Time suddenly sped up. I walked to a nearby home and asked if I could wash the blood off of my hands. I can only imagine what went through the homeowner's mind. They obliged, and I stood at the white porcelain sink and filled the bowl with bloody water. I looked into the mirror, wondering if I was in a dream.

As we returned to the accident scene, I asked for the woman's name...Mrs. Lining. We climbed into the car, but the remainder of our home search seemed secondary. Our real estate agent was rattled. Priorities shifted. We squeezed our children tightly upon seeing them.

The following morning our agent conveyed he had little sleep from the previous day's crisis. Despite the prior day's impromptu trauma team intervention, we persevered and found a beautiful house. A quaint home, gray paint, brick accents—perfect for our family of four. We made an offer that was accepted. The following days were a blur, with my mind reliving the preceding events. An emotional roller coaster. Mission accomplished, and we returned to Maine to finish our time in the Navy.

But that moment had changed something in me. I wasn't sure what at the time, but a stone had been thrown into the pond.

A few months passed and we returned to Grosse Pointe Woods, where we had purchased our lovely new abode. Built in 1925, our home boasted hardwood floors, French doors, and two stained glass windows. A steep staircase made mattresses very difficult to maneuver and we even had to cut a box spring in half for the ascent. It was the end of June, and I was preparing for residency. I was taking an Advanced Cardiac Life Support

(ACLS) course at St. John Hospital for the fifth time (a two year recertification process). For many of the interns, it was their first experience.

We completed a day of training. I was walking out of the hospital and had a moment of pause. I wondered if Mrs. Lining had survived, and whether she was still in the hospital. I turned around and walked back into the building, at which I was soon to spend countless hours and sleepless nights. I approached the reception desk and made my inquiry, "Is Mrs. Lining still a patient here?"

"Yes, she is in room 527," the receptionist politely replied.

I started to walk out of the hospital, a smile on my face, overjoyed that she had survived. I stopped cold in my tracks. Frozen. Chills ran down my spine. I realized I may never get another chance like this. I turned around and trudged back into the hospital. Hesitating at the elevator, the numbers stared at me, almost daring me; I slowly pushed the button for floor #5. As I made my way towards room 527, time slowed. Approaching the room, I paused, took a deep breath, and entered.

Mrs. Lining sat propped up, reading a book, brilliant sunshine streaming through the partially drawn shades, her left lower leg glaringly absent. As I approached, she set down her book and gave me a quizzical look. "Mrs. Lining, you don't know me, but my name is Todd Otten. I was there the day of your accident." Tears started to well up in my eyes.

"Hello," said Mrs. Lining as she navigated the controls on her hospital bed to sit up more. Wincing some in pain with the subtle adjustment. Her facial expression quickly changed, her guard let down. Her demeanor softened.

I explained that I was taking a class and getting ready to start residency. By chance I asked if she was still in the hospital. I expressed my joy that she was alive and recovering. As I stumbled through introducing myself, I explained that I was the one who put the tourniquet on her leg. Her words bring tears to my eyes every time I share this story.

"I never thought I would meet the man who saved my life."

We both started to cry. I could barely speak. The ensuing silence didn't bother either of us. After composing myself, we chatted for a few minutes, mostly small talk as the words really didn't matter at this point. A circle had been completed. As I left, she simply said, "thank you." The interaction was over in the blink of an eye, the memory permanent and high fidelity. I smiled and hastened to my car, tears streaming down my face.

Why tell this story? Many reasons. Some of them are personal, some to help remember, some to help heal. But, for many individuals present at the accident, it represents a moment in time that would forever change their lives. Mrs. Lining's life was permanently changed, and so was mine. Her misfortune had impacted Angie, our real estate agent, numerous bystanders, and me. This story is one of many in medicine that has touched my life and helped shape me into the physician I am today. I always wanted to make a difference in people's lives, and still do. Moments like this helped inspire me to write this book.

((TROJAN HORSES))

Joshua J. Judy – Patient:

Surely, you've skipped stones before. You've watched them skim the water, breaking the surface tension and sluice tiny ripples as they go. This past summer, I watched Megan do the same at a small city park in Michigan's Upper Peninsula. The park included a mostly empty beach, so she had free reign to really wind up her arm. She threw one stone after another. Nice one—that was seven skips, maybe eight.

It's not that there weren't people around. They were all occupying the sidewalk on a small bluff above us, waiting in anticipation of the fireworks show that would soon light up the sky over the bay. I watched Megan for the next 10 minutes until I noticed some company. One by one, a person got up out of their chair or lifted themselves off the ground and joined her on the beach. They looked for the flattest stones, wound up their pitching arm and let them rip. Before long, there were at least ten people skipping stones.

We looked at each other and laughed. I teased Megan, accusing her of being a social influencer. Little changes have a way of adding up over time. Sometimes, the change doesn't have to be dramatic. Other times, change is tremendous—as Mrs. Lining's story reveals. Rarely will change seem easy.

I remember another change in my life. For my 31st birthday, Megan decided to surprise me with a trip to Frankenmuth, Michigan, a little town that celebrates Christmas year-round. It was early November 2012. Neither of us had been there before but going feels like a rite of passage if you reside in the 'mitten state'—similar to inimitable destinations like Mackinac Island.

Frankenmuth—known as Little Bavaria—traces its origin back to German settlers who came to Michigan in 1845. From its roots, the town displays architecture similar to the timber-framed buildings found in the Franconia region of Germany. It's a small Midwest town of about 5,500 residents.

When asked about Little Bavaria, most folks will mention one of three places: Zehnder's, Bavarian Inn, and Bronner's Christmas Wonderland—the first two are restaurants while the latter declares itself the largest Christmas-themed store in the world. Both restaurants serve a renowned fried chicken dinner, with sides that crowd the table. On the first day of our trip, figuring either restaurant was equally charming, we chose one quickly as we were eager to enjoy our meal.

The environment was fun. Staff wore Bavarian-style folk clothing—lederhosen for the men, which consists of knee-length leather shorts with suspenders, and traditional German dirndl dresses for women, which consists of a bodice with a low neckline worn over top of a blouse, a wide high-waisted skirt and an apron. I recall weaving through room after room until we were abruptly told to park. The food started coming. Any accusations of stingy portions grew unreasonable. Dish after dish—rolls, vegetables, salad and finally the illustrious star arrived—heaps of golden fried chicken. A most impressive spread, but with undoubtedly a most uncanny flavor winner: the coleslaw beat out all contenders in the race for taste, in our humble opinion. Still, the only loser in this contest was our waistline.

Like most days and most trips, my neck pain was ever present. However, you make every effort count because quality time with loved ones remains finite. Duloxetine loomed some years off and my wife had yet to develop epilepsy or take levetiracetam. To help, my family doctor had just started me on tramadol.

Among other mechanisms of action, tramadol is a serotonin norepinephrine reuptake inhibitor (SNRI). Interesting—some overlap with duloxetine. Much later, I learned that. At the time, I only knew it was a pain medication. Like many, you trust what you're prescribed and hope for the best.

The following day, I remember feeling very nauseous as I walked around Bronner's. The store's impressive dimensions bore no weight on my queasy disposition. My stomach was empty and I located an apple. I wolfed it down and felt slightly better. Part of me wondered if certain medications work by distracting you with another feeling, so you forget about what first bothered you.

I continued taking the pills as days rolled by. Weeks turned into months and the nausea slowly subsided as my body adjusted. As long as I took a pill every 4-6 hours, the neck pain dulled to a manageable nuisance. Some days were better and some days worse. This became my routine—my life for the next two years.

TL;DR—lessons for OQA:

You don't always get to pick when a change is going to happen. Sometimes you do. Make sure you speak with your provider about when it's appropriate to make a medication change. If you have an event coming up, ask if you need to start now or if it can wait.

To that end, starting a new medication on a vacation never seems wise. I don't recommend it.

((CHANGE))

"I alone cannot change the world,
but I can cast a stone across the waters to create many ripples."

– MOTHER TERESA

Todd R. Otten, M.D.:

My experience with Mrs. Lining taught me numerous lessons—many about change. Life can change in an instant. Those moments shape who we are. These experiences can define a person; and foster determination, fortitude, perseverance. They can give us the courage to fight for positive change, to try and make a difference. Perhaps Mrs. Lining was the stone creating the ripple in the pond for Our Quadruple Aim.

If change were easy, everyone would do it, or at least consider it. If the COVID-19 pandemic has taught us nothing else: change is inevitable. Most physicians are accustomed to telehealth and video visits now. That was not the case for many providers in 2019, before the pandemic. Interestingly, these visits are now being paid for by health insurers. There is definitely value in having the ability to provide care virtually that is fairly compensated. Historically, these visits have not been routinely covered by insurance, and hammers home the point regarding change.

While I was initially reticent about virtual visits, they are now an integral part of my practice and absolutely align with OQA. I can virtually accomplish a vast majority of an office visit—in a fraction of the time and cost. Logistical roadblocks are removed for both patient and provider. I would advocate for this change to be even more expansive in healthcare, and appropriately valued. Clinicians, insurers, administrators, and policymakers need to appropriately align the incentive structure of virtual health to support Our Quadruple Aim.

Ironically, the concept of virtual visits was suggested over 20 years ago in the Institute of Medicine's, *Crossing the Quality Chasm: A New Health System for the 21st Century*, yet it took a pandemic to facilitate this change at scale. This speaks to the myriad of obstacles and difficulty of facilitating change for our current healthcare landscape.

"...access to care should be provided over the Internet, by telephone, and by other means in addition to face-to-face visits."[71]

At the time of this writing, in 2021, I am currently doing a majority of my patient visits via telehealth and video due to the COVID-19 pandemic. During these visits I mirror my approach from an in office visit, reviewing salient history, probing with questions, and listening. Obviously, the physical exam is severely limited (or absent via telephone), but even obtaining vitals is possible with the right tools. What's more is these visits are very efficient, no bottlenecks in a waiting or exam room. A fascinating transition. Initially skeptical, I have embraced and learned to enjoy these visits. Maybe this is the stone you have been looking for...

I even made a tentative diagnosis of vertebral osteomyelitis over the phone. Simply put, a vertebrae is bone in your spinal column and osteomyelitis is an infection in the bone. This is a relatively rare condition and not easily diagnosed. My ER colleague actually called me with kudos after the diagnosis was confirmed. OQA captured in a phone call.

So why does change in healthcare, (particularly advocating for provider wellness) meet so much resistance? I recently sent a YouTube video (from ZDogMD) to several administrators regarding current concerns in healthcare.[72] The video was intended to be thought-provoking. My intent was to inspire questions about how our health system could improve, particularly with regard to wellness. I even prefaced the video with thoughts regarding Our Quadruple Aim.

Unfortunately, there was a mixed response. Some were even offended. Yes, Dr. Zuban Damanian was a bit crass at times, but most points were valid nonetheless. I wondered why a leader would be so offended regarding an invitation to consider positive change? Many reasons I suppose. Maybe the truth hurts. However, great leaders are able to accept constructive criticism, have critical conversations, and ask why? Instead, I received rebuttals.

Change is a regular and needed part of healthcare, yet the resistance to transform the Triple Aim to Our Quadruple Aim can be fierce.

Not surprising that a disconnected, siloed corporate structure wouldn't embrace ideas for change from a physician in the prime of their career. Why listen to those providing care for patients? Frustrating. Opportunities for change should be embraced or at least entertained. Even more perplexing: those in the corporate silos expect providers to accept change routinely. Demands for more documentation, coding, billing, EMR (ours is Epic), quality metrics, formularies, insurance requirements, and evidence has resulted in a perpetual cycle of change for providers. A never-ending rotation of hoops to jump through. What is needed for healthcare to improve and thrive are systems and institutions where communication flows in both directions (between and among providers and administrators).

((BARRIERS TO CHANGE))

"Perfection is not attainable,
but if we chase perfection we can catch excellence."
— VINCE LOMBARDI

I recently had a phone conference with Dike Drummond, M.D., CEO of thehappyMD.com, about healthcare. I have a lot of respect for Dike, who has made himself a champion for addressing physician burnout and helped countless colleagues over the years. I wish I had read his book, *Stop Physician Burnout*, five years ago. The book has powerful insight, coping mechanisms, and ideas for improving mindset and negotiating transformation.

Dike asked me one simple question that became central to our conversation: "What is your target audience, leadership or front-line workers?"

It took me a few seconds to fully appreciate and answer this question. "Both," I said. What was immediately clear from each of our perspectives is how often a huge chasm exists between healthcare leadership and front-line workers. We disagreed on where the energy should be spent to facilitate change within our current system. But we certainly agreed healthcare is on a concerning trajectory.

As *Ripple of Change* evolved and Our Quadruple Aim was created, my answer to Dike's question morphed and the target audience grew exponentially. Ultimate success of Our Quadruple Aim will require buy-in at every level. We all need to contribute to improving healthcare. So who is our target audience? **The American healthcare consumer.**

Sadly, barriers to change are everywhere. Learning to navigate these barriers is critical as we explore areas of opportunity for change. How change impacts key stakeholders is paramount. The presentation and subsequent implementation of change are just as important. I include a brief example from *"Resolving Barriers to Change in Healthcare and Physicians / 2021 Guide"* as a primer. The guide identifies six key areas where resistance is encountered and, more importantly, ways to overcome it:

Individuals
Departments/Groups
Organization/leadership
Change Managers
Technology
3rd Party Support[73]

"In fact there are many barriers to change in healthcare organizations that cause projects to stall, completely fail, or fall short of their objectives. These barriers can be coming from people, leadership, technology, or any number of other areas."[74]

I believe change is required at every level of the U.S. healthcare system. This will require the work of not only hospital administrators and providers, but also insurers, policymakers, lobbyists, researchers, pharmaceutical companies, patients—**EVERYONE.** There is no one simple solution to unwind the decades of dysfunction. However, change has to start somewhere. Whether it's fraud, waste, abuse, bureaucracy, clerical burdens, or burnout, the current state of healthcare in the U.S. is broken and desperately needs repair.

((INSPIRATION TO CHANGE))

"No matter what people will tell you,
words and ideas can change the world."

– ROBIN WILLIAMS

The change being attempted might be aimed at reducing symptoms of physician burnout, working towards an improved office culture, introducing the concept of wellness or Our Quadruple

Aim to a health system, or perhaps even more ambitious. Regardless of the aim, inspiration and courage are required.

What inspires patients?

Your office staff?

Your supervisor?

A healthcare system?

You?

What was my inspiration? Was it Mrs. Lining? Linus Silver? The thousands of patients I have seen over the years? My family? Or the altruism that lured me into medicine? Perhaps, the pain of burnout and lingering moral injury? Ultimately, there is no one answer to this question. As with many things in life, the answer is multifactorial.

Change is no longer just an option in healthcare; it is happening at breakneck speed. The major question is, do we just sit back and let it happen, or do we embrace it and guide it—actually improving the system? Re-inventing the management and delivery of medical care is required. It will require many people and many conversations. It will take years, if not decades. My dream is: this book offers the hope, insight, ideas and courage to start the ripple of change—for not only healthcare, but for individuals and beyond.

**I want Our Quadruple Aim
to be the gold standard of modern healthcare delivery...
and I am not alone.**

((IMPLEMENTING CHANGE))

"You will succeed if you are fearless of failure."

– NATALIE GOLDBERG

As a physician leader, I have participated in thousands of meetings, discussions, training evolutions, educational sessions, and leadership courses, in addition to my medical training and naval service. Implementing change is often met with resistance, concern, fear, and uncertainty. These are normal emotions as people are comfortable and worry how change will affect them. It's human nature to ask, "What's the W-I-F-M?" What's in it for me? But we mustn't be deterred from moving forward with OQA. Patients are desperate for fair pricing and high quality care that leads to optimal outcomes. All patients and providers deserve a positive experience, regardless of socioeconomic standing.

When you implement change we encourage you to use Our Quadruple Aim as the template. These principals naturally incorporate key stakeholders and mandate alignment of incentives (to the greatest extent possible). Balance is essential in facilitating change. If a decision rewards one group and negatively impacts others, issues will arise. Minimizing negative impact is essential. There is nothing wrong with change, even disruptions, if the end goal nets positive change for the majority—not the few.

I think it is important to share some examples of change and how the interactions between providers and leadership affected the process, both good and bad. The results are dramatically different when providers and leaders are in sync, versus those moments when they are not. I'll share two examples of leadership responding to requests for change from "disruptive" physicians (and front-line workers). I played my part in both of these stories, both good and bad, but I stand by my actions in advocating for patients and providers. Out of respect for anonymity and in the spirit of confidentiality, I will use aliases.

Story #1 – Ineffective listening and threats?

"I hope to upset the people around me occasionally,
to rattle them from time to time,
to challenge them in ways that make them feel uneasy."

– MATTHEW KELLY, *PERFECTLY YOURSELF*[75]

As our new office excelled, a meeting ensued to review the current state of operations and potential opportunities for improvement. The staff and I met with several key administrators. The conversation started well—open, honest, collaborative. There were many insightful questions, and a solid discussion of potential improvements and how the pilot model could be expanded systemwide. Stories of comradery and wellness were shared with the leadership team. We conveyed some limitations, particularly the lack of exam rooms. In an attempt to begin succession planning, I was very transparent about my timeline to practicing part-time and further explained I was considering retirement.

To facilitate the discussion, I created a small bullet point document (which I shared). I offered some key statistics regarding our clinic (only open for 10 months). The office accepted over 800 new patients in the preceding eight months, between myself and two NPs. We had 50.5 hours available each week for patient appointments, and evening hours Monday through Thursday. The projected (annualized) visits and revenue totals were impressive, in my humble opinion. Most administrators would be thrilled with the pilot office—certainly I was. We operated like a team, were extremely productive, fully staffed, and enjoyed our work.

But as a type "A" personality, I am rarely satisfied, always striving to do better. As a result, I detoured the remainder of the conversation down an unexpected path. I offered concerns regarding our local healthcare system: (lack of) aligned incentives, clerical burdens, provider recruitment, and retention. I am honest to a fault at times and transparent—I can even be perceived as blunt or aggressive. As we spoke, each concern was summarily dismissed in favor of "systemness." I felt as though I wasn't being listened to—administrators with eyes glazed over. Just another whiny physician.

My mind drifted to being a patient whose doctor isn't listening. I imagined sitting naked in a hospital gown—exposed and ignored. I wanted them to listen, so I raised the stakes. I paused, and then questioned if the system was driven by clinical outcomes or by IT, legal, and finance. Crickets.

Not getting any traction, I decided to go "all in." I pulled out some reports related to Hierarchical Condition Category (HCC) coding and risk stratification, which are instrumental to value-based reimbursement. I asked if they knew what the documents were. More blank stares. They clearly wanted to stick to their agenda, not mine. Undeterred, I pressed on. I reminded them of my six years on the front lines of change as a medical director of an ACO. I made it clear what the documents were for.

"Do you know what I do with these after a horrible day," I said, holding the stack of documents defiantly in the air.

"No."

"I shred them," I replied, a wry smile forming on my face, fully knowing I don't actually shred them.

I succeeded in injecting some life into the meeting. I thought one of the upper level administrators was going to jump out of their chair. Faces were red, frustration evident. I had gotten their attention.

"That's in your contract," came an exasperated reply.

I laughed nervously and explained that their point was not explicitly written in my contract. I reiterated my understanding and importance of the forms. I made it explicitly clear I appreciated value-based reimbursement and that it was a fool's errand if incentives aren't aligned.

"You get a paycheck from the hospital!" A frustrated executive stated demonstratively.

"I DON'T CARE," I replied triumphantly. Silence. A moment of calm ensued. As if oxygen had been returned to the room, red faces slowly returned to their native state.

I went on to explain that I don't actually shred the forms. I was making a point, and in full transparency, I filled the forms out after the meeting. However, I had shared my worries. Needless to say, the response from the administrator was less than "ideal."

Little response offered over most of my concerns, but raising the potential for a negative financial impact—look out. The meeting was an opportunity for learning, process improvement, engagement, collaboration and much, much more. Disappointed, it was painfully obvious leadership had their agenda, and input from physicians on the front lines was irrelevant and not welcome. I found the whole experience frustrating; it felt like my interest in engaging in a conversation that might improve the system was flat-out rejected. Denied.

Story #2 – Critical Conversation

The year – 2017. I was newly elected as Chief of Staff. Issues with recruitment and retention were growing. Several outpatient clinics were struggling with staffing, particularly with MAs, and the hospital was strained due to nursing turnover. I had the fortune of very little turnover with MAs, only two in the preceding five years. However, in a short period of time, two MAs in the office were transitioning to other careers (better pay and lower stress driving the change). The search for replacements had been futile.

Worse, the hospital nursing staff was in crisis mode. Nursing managers were overworked and overwhelmed. Nursing and physician relationships were strained due to a lack of staffing as the inpatient census increased, and issues in the ER exacerbated the problem. The nursing shortages created less than ideal staffing ratios. Our Chief Nursing Officer had recently retired. These worries were raised regularly at medical executive meetings. Change was desperately needed.

Concern was ubiquitous. Unfortunately, transitions in healthcare are often slow and getting slower as bureaucracy worsens. Many within the hospital were worried and vehemently wanted to improve the staffing issues. Many discussions—but little progress. My frustrations grew as patient care was being negatively impacted. Isn't that the job of a leader—to facilitate positive change?

Concurrently, I led a monthly meeting called the Physician Advisory Council. I genuinely enjoyed these meetings as they were a collaborative think tank—a good mix of administrators and providers in a collegial open forum. Ideas for change and strategy. It was the ideal setting to present my concerns and offer transformative ideas regarding the staffing issues, but how would they be received?

I requested an agenda item regarding staffing recruitment and retention. We covered the usual items, but reserved time to discuss our growing crisis. I presented my concerns and ideas for transformation. People listened intently. We discussed the issues associated with turnover, and how it affected productivity, quality, and OQA. I spoke of additional training for nurses, opportunity for advancement, and programs to help retain our most valuable asset—people. The most contentious issue was an upward pay adjustment for the MAs.

In the ensuing discussion, participants offered concerns on many levels. Understandably so. But small hospitals often operate on narrow margins and the concepts I presented were associated with additional expense. Our hospital was financially solvent and as we got further into the discussion, tempers flared. In particular, the CEO of the hospital and I did not agree on a pay adjustment for the MAs. I had my point of view, as did he. The conversation had hit the point of being critical. Tense.

Fortunately, everyone in the room had a lot of respect for each other and cooler heads prevailed. We agreed to disagree on several items, but ideas and solutions had been discussed. Seeds for change had been planted. Tempers calmed and the meeting ended on a positive note. Agreement was reached on several action items to be explored.

We respected due process. But ultimately, the hospital implemented change as the fruit of that critical, but initially difficult, conversation. The newly appointed Chief Nursing Officer developed a nursing education program, along with goals for recruitment and retention. Over time, nursing and physician relations improved. In regards to the outpatient staffing issue, salaries were adjusted for the MAs and a floating MA pool was created, which would help address coverage issues. These new MAs (in the pool) were rotated through offices, which allowed current staff to meet them and help determine long-term fit. New connections were made with MA schools for recruitment.

Despite temperatures rising at the meeting, both sides knew change was necessary. Both sides had respect for one another, were willing to compromise, and work towards a better future. With the passage of time, the staffing issues resolved and a positive culture developed. Patient volumes increased, hospital quality numbers improved (particularly HCAHPS, Hospital Consumer Assessment of Healthcare Providers and Systems), staffing tensions abated, and wellness was a focus throughout the organization.

((RESULTS OF CHANGE))

"I looked up cat scratch fever and Ted Nugent came up."

– PATIENT

From 2017 to early 2019 at Hayes Green Beach Hospital; we (anecdotally) achieved Our Quadruple Aim. I consider this one of my greatest successes as a physician leader. Having numerous leadership roles positioned me to pursue an agenda of wellness beyond the office setting. I was a committee of one for many months. Undeterred, I mentioned the fourth aim constantly and wellness gained traction. Ripples formed in our small pond. The word "wellness" was heard on a regular basis—at board meetings, leadership meetings, and in the office. People genuinely made an effort and change occurred.

In 2018, our hospital sent three providers and two administrators to the first-ever American Academy of Family Physicians (AAFP) Wellness Convention in Naples, Florida. This was the first time I ever did yoga and enjoyed it; and helped my headache melt away. We returned invigorated, full of ideas—not only for preventing burnout, but to further advance OQA at our institution and hopefully beyond.

It was clear that buy-in needs to be universal, involving both providers and administration. Lip service is not enough. Sending out an engagement survey is not enough. Time, talent, and treasure are all required. What do I mean? Dedicated time needs to be devoted to wellness. Protected (and compensated) time for wellness should be considered, and better yet, mandated. And sabbaticals should be considered to improve retention and the quality of care provided, and to decrease costs longitudinally.

At the risk of being perceived as sophomoric, we played board games at a medical staff meeting. Initially, some thought I was crazy, but it was well-received and very enjoyable. Everyone let their guard down and we enjoyed the moment. Talented individuals need to lead and participate in the process; time and effort need to be acknowledged. Money needs to be allocated and appropriately utilized. Without these components, a wellness program is less likely to succeed. As we focused on wellness, both objective and subjective evidence confirmed that the other three components of OQA followed suit. Some evidence:

HCAHPS scores improved
Ancillary testing increased
Cancer screening increased
Number of covered medicare lives increased
Wellness was ubiquitous
Staffing retention improved
Strong financials
Strategic planning included wellness
New physician leaders emerged
Problems in the ER lessened
High patient satisfaction
Our hospital was part of ACO of the year for Caravan Health
The joy of practicing medicine returned for many

((WHAT'S NEXT?))

"With Great Power, comes great responsibility."
– STAN LEE

"I am inevitable."
– THANOS, MARVEL UNIVERSE

As my staff, board members, CEO, administrators, colleagues, patients, and family will tell you—I enjoy comic books. As a child I was encouraged to read, and comics were my chosen avenue. Recently, I re-kindled my passion for collecting, and some comics can be pretty pricey. Ironically, that passion has turned into an investment club with some of my closest friends, most of whom knew nothing of comic books four years ago.

My favorite character is Peter Parker, i.e. Spider-Man. I relate to the kid who was bullied and a teen whose self-esteem was lacking. I can relate to the adult who is trying to save the world. Perhaps that's why he is one of the most loved comic book characters of all time—people can relate to him.

So what does this have to do with Our Quadruple Aim? Everything. It has to do with change. The comic collection was an integral part of my healing from burnout. The business that resulted was a lifelong dream. The subsequent opportunities are difficult to encapsulate in just a few paragraphs. However, this hobby (turned business, then investing club) helped me to achieve balance. It helped motivate me to pursue another lifelong goal, which is to write this book. The comics weren't the only thing that led to this point; my family, faith, and friends were essential. But, surely a stone was thrown in the pond.

I included the Thanos quote (from the Marvel Universe) for a few reasons. While Thanos is the villain in the Marvel Universe, I see change as something positive and still inevitable. His perception encapsulates what is required from our current healthcare system...change. Too often, finances are the primary focus in healthcare, often to the detriment of its most important resource—people. We must return wellness to healthcare, not just to patients, physicians, nurses, or frontline workers—but to everyone. Wellness should start at the very top and trickle all the way down the chain. I want wellness to include CEOs, board members, administrators, janitors, dietary, IT, legal—everyone. More importantly, at this point (unless you have been sleep reading) I believe change is possible by incorporating Our Quadruple Aim into every part of our healthcare vernacular. It's time we all lead by example.

Change is up to you, change is up to us.

((10))

The Tapers and the Abyss

Joshua J. Judy – Patient:

Through the rest of 2017 and 2018, I continued taking the duloxetine at 60 mg combined with tramadol. Looking back now, I see how my body continued to shut down. I was sinking further in a wormhole of numbness. By late 2018, I knew I needed a vast change—and fast. I was feeling dreadful, so fatigued that I would get winded tying my shoes. Is this what a 36-year-old feels like?

No—this was unacceptable. I started researching male health and entered a new world. There had to be answers to why I felt this way, somewhere. There was a lot of refuse and snake oil. For the inquisitive, there were also many helpful forums and resources.[76] At this point, what were my symptoms?

- Fatigue
- Reduced motivation
- Partial emotional blunting
- Diminished sex drive
- Manifesting erectile dysfunction

But the worst was to come.

((LINUS SILVER))

Fast forward. It's now April 2018. Our son is just shy of two years old. Megan and I had planned an excursion to Arizona as both a vacation and a visit to extended family on Megan's side. Megan's neurologist at the time (piled onto the list of ones we've since left behind), had ordered a two-hour Electroencephalogram (EEG). The neurologist, based on her review of the MRIs and reports, found little reason to stay on levetiracetam. "Once you return from your trip, go ahead and start the two-month taper process. For the first month, remove one of the two 750 mg pills. After the second month, drop to zero." By now we had learned—make major changes *after* vacationing. **Continuing, the doctor explicitly said, "If I see any abnormalities on your EEG, I will make sure to call you and have you stop tapering immediately." Easy words. Simple instructions. No ambiguity.**

Regarding my condition, I asked myself: Could I possibly reverse what I was experiencing? Maybe I could power through and beat back the stifling effects of the duloxetine. I wanted to see what my body could still achieve naturally, so I started exercising—and vigorously. My warm-up routine grew to 200 push-ups. Then came heavy weights and cardio. I was four straight months into my routine. Going into the trip, I was in great physical shape. In terms of medicine and pharmacology, however, I was still very much naïve.

Our getaway started in the saguaro cactus-lined city of Tucson (where I once briefly lived and worked in the aerospace industry years before). Departing the airport at the south end of the city and driving north towards Oro Valley, Megan witnessed mountains and their majestic allure for the first time. Then a few days in, it was onto a short tourist adventure into the old west at Tombstone. There, we listened intently to our tour guide as she recounted lurid tales of saloon girls and gun-slinging poker games at the infamous Bird Cage Theatre. Sometime after midnight, we observed the faint outlines of javelinas slinking along the town's darkened alleyways. Also known as skunk pigs, these creatures' stench will invade your nose long before meeting your eyes. Next, we hung up our proverbial six-shooters and headed further north, to the gorgeous red rock backdrop of Sedona. Our retreat rounded out with the Grand Canyon and back to Phoenix for the flight home.

For all its boundless splendor, our trip also became an enigma. Both Megan and I felt the best we had since being zapped by levetiracetam and duloxetine, respectively. Yet, we were perplexed. In my research, some people and online forums refer to these moments as 'windows.' Sometimes, for whatever reason(s), prior baselines temporarily and, if you're lucky, significantly return. The returns are often so pronounced, that the patient can effortlessly discount any conceivable placebo effect. By returns, I mean a striking restoration of emotions, cognitive clarity, and the ability to feel pleasure. But because these phenomena are under-researched, technical references of 'windows' beyond online communities remain scarce.

One might be misled to think, oh, you'd just been under the spell of generalized depression. You just needed a break from the bustle of daily life. You were stressed. Behind the scenes, we wondered what else it could be (cortisol perhaps). While I have no hard data to share, we felt wholly different and about 80% of our old selves.

Regrettably, the window for us was transient. Within a couple weeks of returning from the trip, we fell back into our sinkholes of despair. Our bodies would not or could not compensate or climb out. That's often a common grievance—windows are short-lived but aptly named.

As directed, a few days upon returning, Megan implemented her doctor's orders. My wife followed her levetiracetam taper protocol to a T. Two weeks after being off the drug completely, on June 25, 2018, she began her day like any other. She got up, got dressed, packed our son up for daycare school and headed first to drop him off before completing the short jog from there to her employer. She did this all with aplomb. With our son securely in the infant room, the last thing my wife recalls is walking out of the double-doors of the school building. After that, emptiness.

She managed to get in her car, start it, and head down the little diagonal side street a couple blocks away. There's a train crossing, and one commonly runs around 8 a.m.—about the time she'd be passing through on her way to work.

I, on the other hand, had the morning off. I had been oblivious and missed the initial call from the EMS. The seizure activity had caused her leg to lock out, flooring the accelerator. Her car had bounced violently between the street curbs and surrounding objects, similar to a bowling ball slamming between two bumper rails, strewing a trajectory of parts across the asphalt. Pieces of her totaled Chevy Malibu could be traced a quarter mile up the road. The prior breadcrumb trail of automobile fragments revealed a path of destruction—a path that, thank God, avoided any trains. I was told my wife had slammed head-on into a utility pole, snapping it half. What if both she and my son.... I refused to finish my thought.

I listened to the voicemail left by the EMS, and once again panic-stricken, I raced to the area hospital. In the emergency room, the attending doctor sought an explanation. I unfolded the details of the recent two-month taper process and how we faithfully followed the neurologist's instructions. She then placed a call to my wife's neurologist, the one who had ordered the prior 2-hour EEG. The look on the attending physician's face said it all. Her words confirmed it. I could tell she was embarrassed, telling our neurologist, "Clearly, there was some kind of miscommunication..."

The neurologist told the ER doctor that Megan's EEG was abnormal. No one from her office had thought to call us. "Miscommunication?" No, it was a complete failure to communicate. Megan's accident was 100% preventable.

Meanwhile, my work phone was blowing up. Earlier, I had kept my manager abreast of what had happened. It didn't matter. There was pressure coming down on him from above. A new department head was asking a lot of trivial questions, putting extreme pressure on my boss to order me to come to work. Nothing on my desk was even due for at least three weeks. There was no way I was leaving my wife at the hospital alone.

After hours of observation, Megan was released. Once back home, she was on the phone with *her* boss explaining everything. Sending well wishes and offering time as needed, Megan's boss was the type of person who places empathy above optics. Not surprising when you own a thriving vet clinic that cares for other living, vulnerable things that can't fully speak on their own.

I looked down at my watch—it was getting late. We needed to pick up our son from daycare. I went to bring the car around and backed it out of the garage. My wife was a few minutes behind me, still on the phone chatting. I watched her place her hand on the passenger door and pull it open. The engine was running so I could barely make out her boss still talking to her on the phone. What was she waiting for? Please, get in. We would miss the school's cutoff time. We needed to go.

Things took on a trance-like pace. My wife was no longer reciprocating the conversation with her manager. Momentarily frozen, her eyes were fixated straight ahead. This lasted mere seconds. I then watched as she crumpled, slinking back along the door's outer frame and disappearing out of sight. I jumped out of the car and ran to the other side. There was my wife, in an unbridled heap on our driveway concrete, shaking and convulsing. My neighbor, a gregarious gentleman who always offers a hand, was in his yard working. He came sprinting over, "What can I do?"

"Please stay with her and try to keep her comfortable!" I dialed 911 and bounded into the house to get my wife a pillow for her head. In her fall to the ground, she suffered further scrapes compounding the injuries of the day's earlier car accident.

The ambulance arrived. Back to the local hospital. We were sick of the place. Some people consider hospitals to be one step above the morgue. What an unholy twist, on one hand a place brimming with doctors and nurses where everyone should feel safest and cared for. On the other hand, a place where only the illest are admitted and a tangible reminder of our mortality. It's a dichotomy only the confounding experience of healthcare can offer.

Into the night we went. Many hours passed and Megan hadn't eaten anything yet. I left and ran to the nearby Walmart. It was the one place still open at midnight worth checking. I returned with a sandwich and soup for her. If we were going to be stuck here, we might as well make it a date night. I held Megan's hand—admittedly not our most romantic outing, but we were together. Perhaps from the outside in, our situation looked disheartening. Still, I believed a resilient mindset could shield us from the worst of it.

The local hospital decided my wife needed access to the resources and specialized care of a larger facility. Once more, by ambulance, Megan was transferred north to the neurological services department, where she could draw on their extended capabilities. There, she was kept overnight for observation. This time there would be a baseline 30-minute EEG. More exams. More deliberations. Pacing and hand wringing. A hem here, a haw there. Questions racing through my mind. *After the car accident, why didn't the hospital offer to put her back on levetiracetam knowing she was fully off and vulnerable? Why didn't the neurologist try to redeem herself, even in a minuscule way, and ask the emergency room attending physician to put her back on?* In a moment of anger, as the mistakes piled up, I vented to Megan, "Don't details f**king matter?" How could things not be screamingly evident?

Eventually, these surplus efforts produced a diagnosis: Idiopathic epilepsy. It's a form of epilepsy, in the most basic terms, that results from abnormal electrical activity in the brain even though the patient has no abnormalities, structure or function-wise, other than the seizures themselves. Put simply, it shouldn't occur. But it does.

When you're not given the 'whys' behind something, how does it leave you feeling? Why my wife's seizure activity started 14 months postpartum, and as she entered her 30s, is the mystery of idiopathic epilepsy. Generally, an epilepsy diagnosis requires at least two episodes in a greater than 24-hour period. My wife had experienced four seizures in less than two years. For her, they always occurred in pairs. However, her doctors considered each pair a single episode since they happened all within 24 hours. Therefore, the first time she experienced seizure activity they considered it an anomaly ("fluke") and not epilepsy, yet.

While on the rarer side, several different forms of epilepsy exist and affect about 3.4 million people in the U.S.[77] It's common enough that you probably know someone in your circle of family, friends or acquaintances affected by it. In 2015, epilepsy resulted in nearly 125,000 deaths globally.[78] And seizures are not always controllable by medication.

I thought of my friend whose sister had experienced Sudden Unexpected Death in Epilepsy (SUDEP) and tragically passed away while at work. It's a poorly understood condition where you go into a seizure that possibly leads to suffocation, abnormal heart rhythm changes, cardiac arrest, or some combination thereof.[79] She had gone into the restroom and that's where they found her.

I also recalled a former employee of mine, an incredibly hard working single mother. Her young daughter had a very refractory form of epilepsy. Sadly, she was born that way. The poor girl had to take a cocktail of antiepileptic drugs, levetiracetam included, to only partially control the seizures. She would experience what's colloquially known by patients as 'kepprage'—excessive anger induced by the drug. The devastation was real and my heart ached for them.

Because her seizure activity happened while driving, my wife's license was revoked. During this arduous period, I was the family's sole driver. To date, Megan had enjoyed her driving privileges for nearly 15 years. To be so young and lose them intensified the depression she felt daily. With my childhood diagnosis of retinoschisis, I knew how precariously close I had been to never receiving a full-time driver's license. After Megan's accident, I appreciated mine more than ever—our family's survival depended on it.

Our routine consisted of me driving the opposite way from my work location to the next town over, then reversing direction and passing back through our town and south to my office. After my shift, I would leave to go get them, and then we needed to backtrack half of the same path back to arrive home. It transformed my daily one hour commute into just under two and a half hours, roundtrip.

However inconvenient, a silver lining emerged—I saw my family off at the start of each day. It was time nobody was taking from us and invaluable. Our son was only this little once in his life.

TL;DR—lessons for OQA:

Healthcare Providers, this disaster could have all been avoided with a simple phone call. A follow-through on a promise. If you're too busy to make or keep them, please make a change.

Patients, you choose how you want to internalize a setback. Sometimes what seems like only a detriment and cost is a net gain in the long-run. Sometimes, that net gain is invaluable.

((AN APOLOGY GOES A LONG WAY))

Never in my life have I thought of retaining a lawyer. I don't see myself as overly litigious but when you're wronged, you're wronged. I next found myself reaching out to a well-deemed and seasoned attorney in the area. His office indicated he was on vacation, but upon his return, he would respond.

To legally practice medicine, all doctors require a valid standing medical license. Having worked in the regulatory space, I was familiar with my state's Licensing and Regulatory Affairs (LARA) division. I searched her name. There it was, the neurologist's license. I sat there for a long while, staring at the 10-digit number. I pushed my mind to produce something, anything exculpatory—a wholly unproductive exercise.

At a minimum, I could file a formal complaint against the physician using the Michigan Professional Licensing User System. A week or so later, I received a letter followed up with a call from the attorney.

ME: "Hey, there was clear negligence here."

ATTORNEY: "It looks like it. I understand you're frustrated. I would be too. The problem is this: Years back, Michigan changed its laws on medical malpractice. Unlike most other states, the burden is to now show not just negligence, but also damages. Before, only negligence was necessary."

ME: "So, what can we do?"

ATTORNEY: "Look, here's my advice. Let it go. You're capped at $500,000. You truly don't want to be in the position where you would get more. For that to happen, your wife would have to be a complete vegetable. Nobody wants that. Hang onto all your records though because if she goes downhill, we come back to this conversation."

That meant any burden was now on me, and I faced a fork in my path. I needed to get this right. I gazed inward. I could choose vengeance or grace. I could behave similarly to how we had been treated by others during this ordeal, or lead a better way.

As difficult as it was to accept, the lawyer had already "beat the case." Grace was the correct answer. For inner peace, I had to let it go. Even though it was still an available option, there would be no formal complaint. There would be no proceedings. If anybody thinks all counsels are stereotypical ambulance chasers, not this one. I respected him for the advice he offered. In time, I too would forgive the upper brass at work and their lack of patronage during a trying moment.

For a while, echoes of Megan's depleting experience remained in our lives. All we wanted was an apology from the neurologist. But it never arrived. Beyond that, we knew we never would feel comfortable working with this physician again. So we placed a call to the office pleading to be placed with another provider, "Sorry, the doctor will have to decide to release Megan." Several front desk calls yielded no change. How much clearer could I make it? We had a terrible experience. Now pursuant to multiple supervisor escalations, the account was finally noted. We were free.

Some days after the accident, Megan went out to check the mail. There was an envelope from the local utility company—a bill for $9,997. If you ever wondered how much a single car pole accident runs, it's about 10 grand these days. Everything was listed, line by line, down to the literal bolts and nuts. Replacement involves a fair amount of labor and materials for the utility crews. Megan's heart jumped into her throat, and then it plummeted to her feet. Thankfully, in relatively small print, the notice said a copy of the bill had already been sent to our auto insurance company. This was a copy for our records. Without Our Quadruple Aim to shine a light, straightforward medical billing remains in the shadows.

We waited for the motor vehicle division to summon us (Secretary of State in Michigan). And we waited some more. It would be nine months before reinstatement. However, we were told Megan needed to pass a road test. How bizarre—she didn't forget how to drive in those nine months. On the scheduled day of the test, we went to meet the state's driver assessment manager. He reassured Megan, "Don't worry. This is the same test I give to the elderly so you should be fine." By the following year, the interaction had changed. He said:

> *"I don't need to see you anymore. We have enough appointments as is. Why does the doctor's office keep checking this box requiring a road test? If it's checked, by law, I have to perform the road test. Next year, please tell them not to check this. This is the same test I give drivers in cognitive decline and the very young and irresponsible due to substance abuse. Not a straight-laced 34-year-old with epilepsy. "*

If that's any indication, year three of this process should be a breeze!

TL;DR—lessons for OQA:

Everyone, please realize that when you're in the deepest chasms of your life, always attempt to place at the forefront what you have that's irreplaceable. There, you will find reprieve.

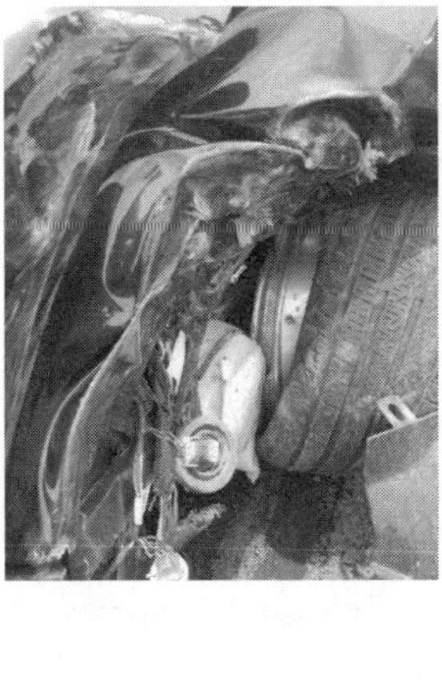

((SWISS CHEESE))

*"Most physicians got into medicine to help people,
but they are limited by the system within which they work.
There are many, many systemic factors
that influence the risk of errors occurring."*

– BRANDON FRANCIS, M.D.

Todd R. Otten – M.D.:

One skill I learned as a naval flight surgeon was mishap investigation. When an aircraft has an accident (meeting a certain dollar threshold for damage) or a life is lost—a mishap investigation is mandatory. A flight surgeon leads these investigations. Thankfully, I was only involved in two of the endeavors during my time in active duty, and neither involved a fatality.

During our training, we discussed the "swiss cheese" model. Think of a series of thinly sliced pieces of swiss cheese, standing in a row, vertical. If the pieces of cheese are aligned just right you can draw a straight line from one end of the row to the other. An analogy to lining up flaws for errors to occur.

And so it goes with medical errors; and in Megan's case, an accident. Preventable—certainly. There is a lot to unpack in Megan's story. Stories like hers underscore how the principles contained in Our Quadruple Aim could have prevented this. We hope to explore many of these lessons in the future in a full version of *Losing The Blueprint*. I'll review just a few from the providers' perspective.

Medical informatics can be a complete nightmare for providers. Imagine several poorly coordinated in-boxes, faxes, paper documents, and electronic records. All expected to be reviewed with a fine-tooth comb. Hundreds of pages of information to review on a daily basis (while seeing patients).

The amount of superfluous information is incredible. Pages upon pages must be scoured, just to try to find that one key sentence buried in the report. Combine that with the fact a provider relies on their staff to label and sort this information in a timely fashion. What if the fax machine breaks? The amount of holes in the swiss cheese start to add up rather quickly. Certainly I am not excusing the error from the neurologist. But in today's medical circus, I can see how it happens.

Box-checking. The term itself is a trigger for me. Some 20 million clicks into my career, I had a t-shirt made: M.D.= professional box-checker. Sad, but true. The clerical burdens placed on providers are out of control and the trajectory is unsustainable. Excessive paperwork and documentation lead to clerical errors. Many physicians routinely spend more time charting than with their patients. I imagine the clerical overload contributed to the box being checked for Megan to have a road test in consecutive years. This is not an excuse—this is reality.

((SEPARATE WAYS))

Joshua J. Judy – Patient:

By June 1, 2019. I started tapering off duloxetine.

I couldn't keep going on like this. The side effects weren't resolving. Desperation set in. I went to see Dr. Otten.

DR. OTTEN: "So, are you thinking you want to come off duloxetine? Josh, I don't know. You've been on for quite a while." *I sensed he was weighing something possibly imperative but I wasn't sure.*

ME: "Yes, I would like to. I'm just not feeling that good anymore."

I don't think a final decision was made that day. There would be many more conversations after this. I remember one in particular that stayed with me for a long time.

ME: "How should I taper?"

DR. OTTEN: "What are you doing this weekend? People come off all the time. You might feel off for a couple days. Headache. Just do it."

Outwardly, I gave a quiet, unassuming acknowledgement. On the inside, it was a different story. I remember leaving and coming home upset that day. Megan confirms it. I felt unheard. A bit disregarded and a bit hurt. I looked up to him. Why was he being so cavalier? Wasn't there any specific guidance?

It was the first time as a patient I decided I was going to go off script, so to say. It felt like cheating but I went to "Dr. Google." I would follow my own taper schedule—based on what I had discovered from others' hardships trying to wean off SSRIs and SNRIs. I discovered there are some tight-knit online communities of others in the same quandary. People who have been hurt not by just serotonin-affecting drugs, but two others considered by some exceedingly risky, finasteride and isotretinoin, the latter of which is used for severe acne.

Isotretinoin, with SSRIs/SNRIs, and finasteride, make up the trifecta, with many saying you're playing Russian Roulette. And I had been exposed to two of the three in my life. Due to poor complexion, I had even considered isotretinoin in my teenage years. My parents talked me out of it, thankfully. They had heard of suicides in the news and the vitamin-A derived drug was suspected.

Eventually, I outgrew my acne with minimal scarring to show. With only one bullet dodged and two out of three others checked off, I suppose it was my turn looking down the barrel. It seemed like a manifestation of another tritone of the Devil's interval.

Interestingly, the smallest duloxetine dosage available is 20 mg, making graduated step downs difficult. There have been quite a few lawsuits against the maker of the brand name of this drug due to alleged attributable suicides (a characteristic also documented with other SSRIs) and severe withdrawal upon discontinuation. Many can't just jump off.[80]

**Looking back to that day's visit,
whether or not anybody realized it then,
what I perceived as disenfranchisement was probably
an early sign of Dr. Otten's emerging burnout.
Plus, I realize he likely had no
specific guidance to offer and I couldn't fault him—
conjointly, we were in uncharted waters.
Whether I liked it or not, some of this voyage
would need to be on my own.**

((COUNTING BEADS))

I started a spreadsheet to chronicle my taper plan. This journal turned into my tracker for capturing any health protocol changes. When you have a complicated case, I highly recommend it. Since you don't see your doctor every day, you can capture important moments in-between the visits and have it ready for when you go. I never really thought I'd ever have reasons to go back through the early parts of this file years later–but here I am.

I have to admit, writing this part feels a bit like a confessional. I know Dr. Otten will read this part of my story, eventually. I never meant to be a little surreptitious. As a patient and now close friend—Dr. Otten, I'm sorry. Darkening your door were too many of me, and not enough of you. There was never enough time or energy to talk about everything. It's years later and we're co-authoring a book together, something I never thought possible. Guess some things are meant to be and serve as a powerful reminder to what Winston Churchill once said: "Difficulties mastered are opportunities won."

The plan was to taper over the next six months. How? Inside the generic duloxetine capsules are little white beads, each one 5 mg. I would remove one of these beads and put the capsule back together. I would stay on that dosage for approximately 3-4 weeks at a time before removing another bead, giving my body and brain time to adjust. 55 mg, 50 mg, 45 mg, and so on. After enough time passed, I reached zero. There, it was over, or so I thought.

For the first couple days after completely tapering, I was okay. It was mystifying. I couldn't explain it. Certain memories suddenly came flooding back that I realized must have been suppressed from the duloxetine. Things I had forgotten about re-entered my mind as if they never left but I knew they had been missing for years. For some odd reason, I arbitrarily remembered the name of a movie from ages ago I wanted to watch but never got around to—*The Abyss*. I played it and there was a scene towards the end that made me tear up.

It dawned on me. By and large, I hadn't felt meaningful emotions, about a single thing, ever since upping my duloxetine dosage. I realized my head had been held under water for at least a year. But after only a few days completely off the medication, any ability and freedom to inhale was horribly short-lived. Just like a filament in an old lightbulb under a terse electrical surge. It was followed by a brilliant flash before flaming out and eclipsing everything in absolute darkness. I reached for my old blueprint and realized it was gone.

Deleted.

((11))

Of Little Faith

"So also faith by itself,
if it does not have works (actions),
is dead."

– BOOK OF JAMES 2:17

Joshua J. Judy – Patient:

Without its original reference points, my body and mind were lost. The earlier detachment that appeared after a 60 mg pill of duloxetine, while considerable, had yet to extinguish life's remaining embers. What ensued next was acute and total obliteration—a nuclear winter had arrived. Others call it a "crash." Would my misery be without an end?

Humans struggle with the concept of infinity. Why wouldn't we? Everything else we encounter as a species has a distinct endpoint. Meals begin and end. Movies begin and end. Life's no different—from a newborn's first breath until the last gasp before death. Beyond that ineffable understanding exists only faith.

To many, space symbolizes infinity and when an astronaut conducts a spacewalk, it's an act of faith. As an astronaut leaves their space vehicle, they wear a specialized suit. A tether, or essentially a rope, holds them close to their spaceship. In that tether, they place their faith because what if that tether snaps? The suit they wear might have two tanks each holding up to eight hours of oxygen to sustain life. They have one last contingent, a backpack to give one last hurrah and propel back to safety. After that, into nothingness. From that void, there's no return.

Oxygen continues to deplete until they're crushed from asphyxia. Takes about two minutes. Or they lose pressure and their bodies boil. It's an unfathomable place, the astronaut watching the Earth shrink to a singular azure dot, then a snuff out of view. Poof.[81]

And what if their suits have enough oxygen to last them five years or more while still taking in nutrients—staying heated, pressurized, and avoiding radiation? They continue to exist. But at what appeal? Rather, are they now adrift, aimlessly floating, ripped away from everything that sincerely matters? It's a provoking thought, the fragility of that rope—a razor thin 'insurance policy' standing between the life you know and the ether.

When thinking about my health journey, I often felt like the astronaut I describe...floating in search of answers nowhere in sight. Instead, for my years of affliction, I was left with only a cruel mystery—whatever nerve signaling had been causing my neck pain was suddenly gone. Fled without a trace. All this time, I had loudly fought my neck troubles to leave. I would have expected a similarly raucous performance from them to stay. In their place now, a silent and painful irony. As for the rest, I was no longer in a stable place. I no longer felt human. If you can't feel emotions (as basic as love), then are you still alive?

After the crash, the most devastating part came next. For the next six months, I would pick up my young son, who I cherish more than anything, and I couldn't feel anything. I knew I was supposed to. I wanted to—desperately. But I simply couldn't. Same towards Megan. Same with our cat. Driftwood. Every living thing felt like driftwood, and I, like the untethered astronaut, drifted further away. My thoughts towards myself had precipitously become gray. Then treacherously black. They were unforgiving and inescapable. This was no place to be anymore. Maybe it was time to leave it all behind.

((GOODWILL))

Later, Dr. Otten came to know about my misery. How could I possibly re-tether myself? Our conversations continued in the coming years.

ME: "Well, at least we cured my neck pain."

DR. OTTEN: "But at what cost? What about all those important things that make us human?"

I couldn't agree more. I knew I didn't have all the answers, and I had to accept—neither did my doctor. During this time, I noticed Dr. Otten opened up more about his own health issues. Years earlier, he sustained concussions while playing soccer. From there, he unfortunately suffered allodynia (scalp pain), crippling post-concussive headaches, along with bouts of cluster headaches. Though I never dreamed he was on oxygen between appointments.

As I mentioned earlier about diseases—they gang up on you. I had taken a severe fall in 11th grade. Throughout the rest of my time in high school and into college, I too experienced headaches and allodynia. In college, I was rear-ended at a stop light. The explosive impact of the fall and car accident, I was certain, added wear on my neck.

I came to learn my doctor was also on duloxetine for pain management. It took me by surprise. We could relate, more than we realized. He first began at 30 mg, but over time, his pain broke through. So he moved up to 60 mg. I felt obligated. I warned him.

ME: *"You be careful. Your body might still be cruising along just fine at 60 mg but who knows what your built-in threshold is. It might be 90 mg or 120 mg, and then it's all over."*

At that moment, I recognized something vital. For the first time ever, I was significantly worried about my doctor—not just myself, but him as the patient. I also now accepted why he prescribed duloxetine at 60 mg to me. Because it helped him in his own health battles, he wanted nothing else but to help. I internalized his intentions and accepted his goodwill—his works (actions). The weight of this turning point cannot be understated. I had cared enough to care. However small, it was a first glimmer of healing.

((12))

Provider Wellness

"Professionally fulfilled physicians...are better equipped not only to practice the art and science of clinical care, but also to lead...improvements to our systems of care."

– BRYAN BOHMAN, M.D. et al.[82]

Todd R. Otten, M.D.:

Wellness = Balance = Thriving

Three simple words. So simple, yet so elusive for many. Later today I am meeting to discuss my transition out of full-time practice. Serendipity? Perhaps, but I have never felt more at peace and excited on my way into work. I have found the joy of medicine again, which had been missing for years. It is a privilege to love my job. How long will I see patients? Obviously, no one can tell the future, but I have a feeling I will have a hard time fully letting go of patient care. Why write this? Think beyond for a moment. Regardless of your profession, I believe with the right framework, the right leadership, the right mindset—this could be you. Well, balanced, and thriving.

As an ACO medical director I presented a webinar, *"Burnout to wellness, Where are you?"* While developing my lecture, Angie created this picture, symbolizing a continuum. Stop. Think about how this could be applied to yourself, your office or workplace, or even our healthcare system. Endless opportunities. But do an introspective search, first, to determine your starting point. Where are you on this barometer? This is essential prior to moving the needle on a larger scale as your ability to help others depends on your wellbeing.

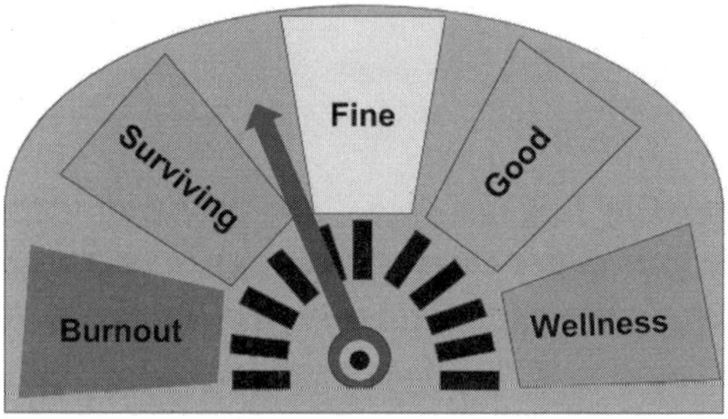

Wellness – *noun*

The quality or state of being healthy in body and mind, especially as the result of deliberate effort.

An approach to healthcare that emphasizes preventing illness and prolonging life, as opposed to emphasizing treating diseases.[83]

So where to begin? How do you peel back the layers of emotional or moral injury? The frustration, sadness, hurt, or even anger. Historically, those in healthcare have been taught to compartmentalize things. We have been taught resilience. At times, even a bit of bravado. We have been taught that the patient is first. But at what cost have we allowed for this? What price have we paid? How many colleagues have we lost?

Believe it or not, in my 20 years as a physician, I have known three colleagues who have died by suicide. A fellow when I was in residency. An ER physician when I was in a medical leadership role. Most painfully, my partner for three years. May you rest in peace, Linus. How was I so oblivious to the desperation for each of these human beings? Each had their story, their own demons. How much does our medical training contribute or perpetuate the problem (as this dark side of medicine lingers)?

I bring these individuals up because provider suicide rates are unacceptable and must improve. I implore anyone who is struggling to ask for help. Reach out! Talk with a colleague. Call a friend or family member. Call a suicide hotline. You are loved, you are valuable, you are needed.

When I struggled with burnout, I hung the serenity prayer above my desk—and it has been present ever since.

**"God, grant me the serenity
to accept the things I cannot change,
courage to change the things I can,
and wisdom to know the difference."**

Wellness is not one size fits all—it is different for everyone. In 2018, when I was advocating for Our Quadruple Aim, in retrospect, I can see I was advocating for myself. I was struggling and was looking for ways to achieve balance and improve my wellbeing. Ironically, this is when I presented, *"Burnout to Wellness, Where are you?"* As part of that lecture I incorporated many ideas, including the eight dimensions of wellness.[81] We will review each of these dimensions and present coping skills and tools to build or augment your wellness toolkit.

But before we dive into ideas for your journey to wellness, a brief pause—what is holding you back? Today is the first day of the rest of your life. Is today the day you toss a stone into your wellness pond and create some ripples?

((MINDSET))

"Once your mindset changes,
everything on the outside will change along with it."
– STEVE MARABOLI

Mindset is the established set of attitudes you hold. And, if you are struggling with burnout, you must first evaluate your mindset. Reflect on what fulfills you, what makes you happy, what recharges your batteries. Assess what has a positive impact on your mindset, and conversely a negative impact. Undoubtedly, not everything is in our sphere of control, but mindset is. You must learn to combat the negative thoughts that infiltrate your mind. You can learn to incorporate hope, determination, motivation, and confidence. Your mindset is where this healing begins.

((YOU ARE WHAT YOU BELIEVE))

Joshua J. Judy – Patient:

Above, my primary care doctor mentions mindset. I've often called it attitude. First attributed to Henry Ford circa 1947, a well-known, slightly paraphrased quote reads, "Whether you think you can or you think you can't—you're right." In other words, your mindset will determine what results come next, good or bad.

As you come to learn more about my patient journey, you'll find I was often fighting my own body. I was battling hormonal imbalances, the culmination of medication side-effects from what I had taken for my neck pain nightmare four years earlier. It wasn't the only thing I was fighting—I was fighting the call on whether to double down on a mindset of healing.

During a December 2020 visit with Dr. Otten, I had brought along Megan and a book on thyroid function. She was there for emotional support, and the book for helping me defend my current mindset with my doctor. I was on a singular track, a freight train that was going to barrel through anything in my path. I had done hundreds of hours of research to find out why I felt horrible–countless National Institute of Health articles and studies. There was even a consultation with the author of the thyroid book, who had suffered for decades himself.

At this particular visit, Dr. Otten told me, "You can over test. You can over analyze. Pick up your guitar. Play with the kids. Write your thoughts down. Work on coping skills."

Behind my mask worn due to the COVID-19 pandemic, I was fighting anger. I doubt the mask concealed it. I don't think my doctor knew I could barely keep my head up. I was dizzy and fatigued. I had brain fog and brain zaps. I was having panic attacks. My entire fight-or-flight system was completely out-of-whack. I felt odd adrenaline-like surges, especially when driving or early in the morning, jolting me awake. I was feeling very sick, mentally, physically, and emotionally. None of it was in my control and every moment was unpredictable.

Didn't he understand? I didn't have the energy to do all those things. Those are the things you do when you feel well; not when you are completely burned out.

We continued to talk. Dr. Otten said, "You need to give yourself more time. Perhaps talk with a counselor. You know, I've found it helped me with my own problems and demons. It's helped me cope."

No. I wanted more testing. I wanted answers—now. Megan began to cry, I got defensive and Dr. Otten broke the tension by assuring us he wasn't trying to cause an argument. I believed he meant well, but I didn't have the mental clarity to process everything. I simply didn't have the energy to fight back. All my energy to this point had been spent fighting something I couldn't control: accepting that there wasn't an immediate answer to my problem. No amount of research or upset thoughts were going to tell me exactly when I would begin feeling better. At this point, I had to consent to an unknown time frame.

Before leaving the room, Dr. Otten told me, **"I believe you will get better—but you have to believe too."**

Not only did he say it out loud, I subsequently noticed he wrote it on the print out of my visit summary. He had typed it into the patient portal and it became part of my record. He might not have known exactly when I would read those words, but he knew I would eventually–when the time was right.

Clearly, my doctor was telling me: when in a hole, stop digging. Though, it was far from clear then. However, I discovered that when you're so busy chasing your own tail, the only person you end up biting is yourself. My doctor wanted me to lay down the 'shovel' and give my body the time it needed to sort things out. This is where the healing process began for me.

Megan and I later talked. She helped reframe my thoughts by saying, "I think he was trying to tell you about his own battles. I think you were so deep in your own hole that you might have been hearing him, but you weren't ready to listen."

It's now early 2022 and guess what? We're listening a bit better these days. We're coping a bit better these days. I'm writing my thoughts down. So is my doctor. You are reading them. I could have stopped believing I would get better. I could still be digging that hole and be clear to the other side of nowhere. Instead, I'm here and I'm healing. Am I 100% yet? No, but my attitude has changed dramatically. Just know, for every minute spent in the negative is another minute taking you further and opposite from where you need to be.

I forced myself to pick up my guitar and play. I forced myself to sit down for family game night even when my head and body felt like it weighed 1,000 lbs. I took the time to seek out a counselor. All of these were deposits, not withdrawals, to my 'well-being account'.

Eventually, I found I wasn't quite forcing myself as much anymore. In the months and year ahead, my body had started balancing some to the thyroid medication after finding a dosage better suited to *my* therapeutic range. I had to advocate for the particular dosage I'm currently on with my endocrinologist, but I got it.

Each one of these things was something I *could* control. Individually, they were very small actions; but collectively, they created a sphere of control that previously didn't exist. As I built this growing sphere, time passed. It was exactly what my body needed to heal, enabled by my new mindset.

"I dreamt I was a muffler last night, and I woke up exhausted."

– PATIENT

Todd R. Otten, M.D.:

When I first read this excerpt from Joshua, I was sitting in my pajamas in a hotel lobby coffee shop in Nashville, Tennessee. My family was with me, dreary-eyed, awoken by a fire alarm in our hotel and the need to evacuate. As we walked out of the hotel, sirens blaring, I decided this was a good moment to work on mindset. Not only for the benefit of myself, but my family as well. I congratulated a woman who had brought a fresh cup of coffee with her. She smiled. Another woman commented this was a terrible start to the morning and I replied, "Amen." She laughed.

Half awake, with a slight headache—I read Joshua's excerpt. The layers to this short piece are plentiful. Peeling them back will take some time. I texted Joshua how much I liked the section and that there was a lot to unpack. A pivot point.

Let's start with the sphere of control I had with Joshua (at that visit) and he with me. I knew Joshua was struggling and the medicine I had prescribed had contributed. Duloxetine had rocked his world and I didn't know how to fix the problem. Even worse, my abilities to refer to appropriate providers or prescribe different medications were constrained by insurance limitations. I felt horrible. My sphere of control on Joshua's health was miniscule at this point.

Considering all the limitations and clerical burdens imposed on physicians, the sphere of control that Joshua had on me was constrained. Microscopic. This wasn't his fault, nor mine. Unfortunately, this is the reality of healthcare. The financial drivers have contributed to this mess—to the detriment of our interactions.

So a 20-minute interaction was all that was allotted to cover an exceedingly complex case. Twenty minutes. Furthermore, I did not know exactly what was wrong with Joshua. But I knew I needed to try my best. Words of encouragement and hope is what I offered that day. Although my sphere of influence was small, I am glad to know my efforts made a difference.

Fast forward to January 2022. Joshua was making some headway with his hormonal treatments. Much of the progress was due to his research and effort. We communicated via the patient portal and often his knowledge base regarding hormones exceeded mine. I am proud of his efforts and conveyed as much. I explained thc evolution of the Triple Aim to Our Quadruple Aim and asked if he was interested. It was a calculated risk to tell Joshua about this book, but I sensed the potential for a much deeper connection. I trusted my instincts. When he asked how he could contribute—I was full of hope. "Just write," I said. In retrospect, I wanted his sphere of influence on me to grow. I never envisioned what synergy we would come to have. Becoming friends, challenging one another, teasing out the very best in our writing. Healing.

At our first meeting regarding the book, it was apparent our visions aligned. We both thirsted for a creative outlet and wanted to make an impact on a larger scale. We spoke for nearly three hours. The energy was palpable. Ideas flowed back and forth naturally. The conversation was pleasant and passionate. What had begun as a doctor-patient relationship was now evolving. Joshua introduced Yin and Yang to our blossoming friendship. Our spheres were growing, and a little seed planted.

As the world of healthcare has become more chaotic, many who struggle with burnout do not even know where to start. It can be a daunting task. I know. Dr. Dike Drummand's previously mentioned *Stop Physician Burnout* is a fantastic read for those who are struggling, I highly encourage it. I wish I had read this five years ago. I purchased numerous copies and shared with my colleagues who are exhibiting signs of burnout, and other copies for those in administration. Why? My hope was to create a ripple in the pond, starting with mindset.

In his book, Dr. Drummond talks about headtrash. This chapter is particularly insightful in improving mindset. "You must take out the trash before you have any chance of living on purpose," writes Dr. Drummond. He discusses dealing with your inner critic, burnout as a dilemma, doing a mindflip, and celebrating wins. He talks about your energy account, as well as the squeegee breath (a mindset technique to recenter yourself).[85] These are all excellent tools to grow and mature your mindset into a healthy space. The book is geared towards physicians, but there is valuable insight regardless of your role in healthcare. Ultimately, we are all working towards the same goal: Our Quadruple Aim.

For some, this transformation will be easier than others. I tend to be optimistic, a glass half-full person, which has facilitated shaping my current mindset. However, mindset is something that has to be continually worked on and cultivated. Like a garden, mindset needs tending. The weeds must be pulled, the headtrash expunged. Perhaps a few primers to help get you started.

"Every person has the power to change their fate if they are brave enough to fight for what they desire more than anything."

– STEPHANIE GARBER

((10 TRICKS FOR DEVELOPING A GREAT MINDSET))

1. Only use positive words when talking.
2. Push out negative thoughts and feelings.
3. Use words that evoke strength and success.
4. Practice positive affirmation.
5. Direct your thoughts.
6. Believe you will succeed.
7. Analyze what went wrong.
8. Give yourself credit.
9. Forgive yourself.
10. Learn from the past.[86]

Catherine Florio Pipas, M.D. highlights in her book, *A Doctor's Dozen*, why a positive mindset is critical for healthcare providers and their patients: "Just as burnout in healthcare providers negatively affects providers and patients, mindfulness training of medical students, residents, nurses, and physicians has been shown to improve their personal well-being, patient care skills, and clinical competence." Dr. Pipas further explains: "Providers with improved mindfulness report reduced burnout; reduced emotional exhaustion and depersonalization; and improved mood, personal well-being, sense of accomplishment, and empathy to their patients' emotional and social lives."[87]

Ideas supporting a positive mindset are everywhere—if you look. Filtering out the negativity can be exhausting, but practice makes perfect. My family and I regularly attend Catholic Mass. Without a doubt I have heard some amazing ideas for mindset over the years while sitting in a pew. I once heard a homily that suggested we visualize others as if they were Jesus Christ, particularly if the interaction is less than ideal. I will implement this technique during frustrating days at work, and it works quite well. Imagine the angry, frustrated patient as though Jesus Christ was sitting in front of you. A potent example of mindset.

((BALANCE))

"I've learned you can't have everything and do everything at the same time."

– OPRAH WINFREY

"How are you doing?"

"Fantastic," is my usual reply. I am surprised how often this query is asked by my patients. Simple and refreshing, yet full of opportunity. A chance to relate on a human level. Someone cares about—me. Not just the doctor caring for my patients. Not just a white coat. Yin and Yang. But the question can open Pandora's box. Depending on the day, it can lead down a number of paths. Praising our children and their successes, or deliberating their shortcomings. Extolling my loving wife. A chat about my favorite football club—Arsenal. Occasionally a discussion of religion or politics. Perhaps even a mini-lesson on the value of the blockchain or cryptocurrency.

Regularly, I will share my thoughts on Our Quadruple Aim. Areas for engagement and positive change within the healthcare system. Some portions of this book are a result of those discussions. Many patients want to help, with ideas both good and bad. Many perceptions. But mostly—patients want to be heard and not treated as a number.

My patients knew when I was struggling in 2019. They knew something was wrong. They knew I wasn't at my best. What changed?

I learned the importance of balance.

My sabbatical taught me how valuable balance is. I became aware how unbalanced my scale had been. As I tried to "save the world," my work-life balance spiraled out of control; as a result, everything in my life was on the verge of imploding.

Fortunately, I learned the art of saying, "NO." What a simple, invaluable lesson. Many struggle with this. I struggled with this.

It is empowering to say no. We don't have the capacity to say yes to every request or challenge that comes our way. Empathy is important, but a skill that needs cultivating. Physicians are not trained to say no, just work harder; this surely contributes to the epidemic of burnout and moral injury that exists.

We only have so much emotional energy. Energy to help others and problem solve. Energy to treat our patients and staff with love and respect. Energy to complete our daily tasks. Mental energy to help the 90-year-old patient with multiple comorbidities, who simply wants to enjoy time with their great-grandchildren.

As physicians we are taught to be resilient and to compartmentalize. Without a doubt, these tools are imperative. We are taught to work harder and to put the patient first. The best physicians pour their heart and souls into their work. I do the same. But unless your world is truly balanced—there may come a time when being more resilient, compartmentalizing, and working harder will no longer work. Whatever your occupation, balance is essential to wellness. Balance is essential to thriving.

So how do you find balance? As with many sections in this chapter, there is not one set answer, but rather a series of probing questions. Some introspection is essential. Take a step back and assess what is important in your life. Family, friends, faith, work, hobbies? What makes you happy? What allows you to stay in the moment? What allows you to be your best? What fills your emotional tank? I will simply offer a series of thoughts, comments, and questions for consideration on your journey to balance.

1. Take a step back and assess your situation.
2. Prioritize what is important in your life.
3. Ask yourself, "what are my goals?"
4. Learn to say NO.
5. Develop your guidelines to achieve balance.
6. Stick to your plan.

((JOURNALING))

"Writing is medicine. It is an appropriate antidote to injury. It is an appropriate companion for any difficult change."

– JULIA CAMERON

It is quiet in my office, and all the staff have gone home—7 p.m. Another tough day filled with a roller coaster of emotions, even some tears, and I am trying to finish charting. Healthcare. I pull a folder out of my desk drawer, and inside are a few sheets of paper. Listed on those pages are names of patients for whom I had the privilege of caring for, and who had since passed away. Most of the names were anticipated and I helped their transition to peace in a dignified manner. Some were unexpected. Over the years, hundreds of names have been added.

Why do I write those names? I write the names to remember. To celebrate their lives. I write the names to help keep myself centered. Every time I look at those pages, I am filled with many emotions, as memories permeate my mind. But ultimately, when I read those names, I feel at peace. I know I did my best, and in the end we all have the same fate. Life is a gift, and how we share that gift and honor it can make all the difference in the world.

In researching burnout and writing about Our Quadruple Aim, I realized writing has become a form of therapy—helping my mindset and disposition tremendously. Journaling can be cathartic. Something magical about picking up a thesaurus to find the perfect word. An opportunity to pour out your emotions, thoughts, ideas. A chance to reflect on both the good and bad. A safe place to vent. To celebrate. Journaling is a protected space to express your deepest thoughts, emotions or fears. A process to heal.

There is no set method. No right or wrong. Journaling is a blank canvas that can serve many purposes. I bring it up in the context of wellness because I highly recommend it as a tool for well-being. Please consider these topics as primers.

((IDEAS FOR YOUR JOURNAL TO WELLNESS))

- COVID-19
- Gratitude
- Forgiveness
- Memories
- Joy
- Quotes
- Prayer
- Inspiration
- Love
- Tell a story
- Family
- Patients
- Coworkers
- Death
- Learning
- Areas to improve
- Aspirations
- Frustrations

Clearly this list is not all-inclusive, but is a good starting point. What started out as a poem about healthcare has turned into a book that I hope will inspire many. I pray this effort will help many navigate their way out of burnout and inspire many conversations regarding change. I suspect this book will empower leaders to incorporate wellness in their workspace. If my journaling helps just one person, then I have succeeded.

"I can shake off everything as I write;
my sorrows disappear, my courage is reborn."

– ANNE FRANK

Amazingly, while I was cleaning out some old paperwork and journal articles I came across an essay I had written in high school—*"The Bird."* Cleaning and sorting are not my favorite chores, just ask Angie. I am not sure what inspired me to go through the paperwork. Although it was placed in an obvious spot—perhaps a clue. Fate? Regardless, I had been looking for a copy of that essay for several years. I think it may have been the only "A" I received on an essay in high school. My teacher (also the track coach) denied my request to get out of the honors

English curriculum—wisdom in his guidance. I am sure Mr. Knoll is smiling down on me as I write this.

After reading the essay, written 30 years ago, I realized I had been journaling about my feelings. Memories and emotions immediately returned. The sadness. The essay provided me with catharsis during that moment in my adolescence. I am including the essay here, unabridged. A small component certainly speaks to Our Quadruple Aim.

((THE BIRD))

When I was younger, a simple stroll through the woods shooting at birds with a b-b gun seemed like an African safari. Derrick, my friend, was extremely intrigued by the outdoors and all its splendor. Derrick expressed this passion in his enjoyment of hunting "big game" in the woods with his gun. Like Derrick, hunting was fun for me, but my aim wasn't as true. Then one day Derrick bought a new scope, which we thought would make our hunts all the more exciting. With this new toy we decided to go to the woods. The hunt began.

As we walked, we came across a group of black birds and made them our initial targets for destruction. Derrick, being the "pro" hunter, shot first. He aimed and fired. Wwwuummp! The air gun sounded as it propelled a small copper ball towards the helpless bird. A direct hit! I couldn't believe my eyes, we had never hit a bird before. With Derrick's hit the bird flew, its wing badly damaged. Now it was my turn. I was full of excitement as we searched for another target in the silence of the woods. It was truly going to be a great day....

A few minutes later we came across the most beautiful bird I had ever seen. Its beauty was so magnificent, as the verdant foliage surrounded it, that words can only begin to describe the picture it portrayed. The bird was splashed with colors around its neck and on the tips of its wings. The colors seemed to jump off the black feathers which encased the bird. Blue, red, and yellow;

what a picture this bird was. There it was, aloof from the rest of the world, perched peacefully on a branch—doing harm to no one. The bird then turned and faced its fate. The rifle was lifted, aimed and fired. I waited for what seemed an eternity to see the results. The bird seemed to float off the branch like an angel from heaven and descended to the ground.

Full of excitement we sprinted to see where the slain bird had fallen. It lay motionless as if time stood still, surrounded by an aura of death. Derrick examined the bird, since he was the "expert," and surmised that the bird had died instantly, with no pain. I felt so proud to have earned such a beautiful trophy. Man, how cool it was to kill that bird. After gloating over my prize, we took the bird back to my house and buried it in my backyard near the field. The hunt was over.

Later that day I thought about what I had done to that poor defenseless bird—who did nothing to deserve death. I turned off my radio and thought about how good life really is. Tears began to swell in my eyes. I cried. Thoughts of my dead grandparents entered my mind and tears flowed down my face for the bird I killed. From that moment, my outlook on life has been very different. I realized how important it is just to be alive, because one day God might snatch the breath from us like my pellet did to the unexpecting bird.

Looking back on that day many thoughts enter my mind. How can one tiny bird have such an impact on my life? Why does there have to be violence before people understand what is wrong and right? Today I see that the bird was there to teach me about life and its value. Like a small child who touches something that is hot and learns that it burns, I learned by killing a bird that life is worth more than anything else in the entire world.

((13))

Wellness = Balance = Thriving

"You need the right balance between data and gut feeling."

– TOTO WOLFF

Todd R. Otten, M.D.:

((OCCUPATIONAL WELLNESS))

"For 744 hours, I felt like a normal person again. No crazy work hours, no administrative headaches, no educational responsibilities. For the first time in my life, it felt refreshing to 'disconnect' from being a doctor."[88]

– EMERGENCY CARE SPECIALISTS (ECS) PHYSICIAN

ECS is a large independent emergency medicine practice in Michigan who is "...culture driven, with a focus on data-driven quality, business innovation, and physician engagement." The group is a progressive, forward-thinking physician-led group that is far ahead on the curve of Our Quadruple Aim. In November of

2022 they published an article in *NEJM Catalyst*, "A successful sabbatical program to reduce burnout in emergency medicine physicians." As healthcare organizations look for ways to mitigate burnout, their program has resulted in sustained career satisfaction, low attrition, and reduced feelings of burnout in their physician group. Given that their sabbatical program was started in 2008, this is most impressive.[89]

Thinking outside of the box is not without cause for concern, and initially the sabbatical program was met with some resistance. The article discusses the initial obstacles and how they were overcome. But as with many successful healthcare initiatives: "...passionate physician champions provide high value in realizing desired outcomes." Their sabbatical program allowed the physician to do whatever they wanted during their month off, except work for ECS. The program was instituted as a calendar month—a block of protected time. Fully compensated, these sabbaticals have proven to be more than cost-effective.[90]

"You can do anything you want; you just can't work for ECS."[91]

The ECS sabbatical program led to additional benefits, beyond provider wellness. During its implementation, assistant leader positions were created to support existing leaders (while on sabbatical). These mentoring opportunities allowed for improved succession planning, with assistant leaders gaining valuable experience, confidence, and building relationships over time. Subsequently, intervals between sabbaticals were shortened based on tenure, allowing older physicians to extend their careers. Turnover for ECS is less than the industry standard for emergency physicians. Not surprising, the sabbatical program is attractive to new candidates who appreciate the work-life balance.[92]

Lest we forget the impact on quality, cost, and patient experience, the impact of burnout on the other three components of OQA is well-documented. It is detrimental to say the least.

ECS has proven that a sabbatical program can be implemented in a cost-effective manner. Their long-term vision in lieu of short-term financial gains—priceless. The *NEJM Catalyst* article offers a calculator to determine staffing, financial, and full-time equivalent (FTE) counts for those interested. "Modeling variable intervals from a financial standpoint may make entry into a program more palatable, as could a phased, tiered, or partial compensation solution.[93]

The work ECS is doing embodies Our Quadruple Aim. When providers are at their best (i.e., well), patients are the primary beneficiaries—but ultimately everyone wins. I would encourage other emergency medicine groups to explore this sabbatical program. But could this strategy be entertained at a macro level? Improved physician retention provides innumerable benefits to an organization. A daring executive may consider such a program for nursing and beyond. I would encourage others to ask if a sabbatical program is right for them.

((PHYSICAL WELLNESS))

"I need to stop exercising with my fork."

– PATIENT

I have played fútbol (soccer to many) since I was 8-years old. Despite three ACL (anterior cruciate ligament) reconstructions, I continue to play. Often limping around the office the day after a game, many friends question why I still play. More than once, I arrived at work using crutches. But the physical activity is cathartic and provides a welcomed stress reliever. My mind is free during a match, and stress seems to melt away as the adrenaline flows. Recently, I have been blessed to play in an over-18 league with my eldest son, Josh, and my brother, Jonathan. What an incredible opportunity. Josh floats around the field effortlessly as I limp up and down the pitch. Regardless, I am thankful to still play.

Physical activity is just as important for the mind as for our muscles and bones. Copious studies have proven the benefits of regular exercise—both physically and emotionally. Whether it is improved pain control for the arthritic sufferer or an improved mood for those with a psychological affliction, exercise is extremely beneficial. My disposition improves and my knees don't hurt when I exercise regularly. Maintaining a healthy weight is integral to physical wellness. This may be easier for some, but I have yet to meet a patient who doesn't feel better after intentionally losing weight. It is one of my favorite things to do for a patient: stop medications as blood pressure or blood sugars improve as a result of weight loss.

For those who have sat in an ice bath or simply used ice packs, the first five minutes can be a challenge. Throbbing is how I would describe the initial discomfort, then numbness. Taking your mind to another place is a must. However, the benefit outweighs the initial pain—less inflammation and a faster recovery. As I iced my aching knees after an over-40 soccer match, inspiration came to me. Who better to interview regarding physical wellness than a professional athlete? To properly introduce Cooper Rush, we will need to rewind the clock a handful of years.

"Cooper, would you mind autographing this paper for my son, Josh," I asked the mild-mannered starting quarterback for Central Michigan University.

"Sure," as he signed the office letterhead.

I first met Cooper when he was 17 years old, playing football for Lansing Catholic High School. A tremendous talent. Unassuming, with a smile that would light up a room. I had the privilege to be his primary care provider for a handful of years. As he progressed from high school to Central Michigan University, I would follow his football career from afar, occasionally checking the box score to see how he performed. I remember watching a bowl game in which he threw seven touchdown passes—he was even nominated for an ESPY award. My gut told me he was going to make it into the National Football League (NFL), although, I don't think many of my friends believed me.

Currently, Cooper Rush is entering his fifth season in the NFL with the Dallas Cowboys as their backup quarterback. It has been a thrill to watch him prove himself as a player and earn his roster position. His initial success occurred last season when he started against the Minnesota Vikings during a Sunday night game. Watching him drive the Cowboys down the field for a game winning touchdown pass was incredible. As he prepares for the upcoming NFL preseason he was gracious enough to do a short interview regarding physical wellness.

After some brief introductory comments regarding the crux of the project and congratulations, our conversation focused on the physical requirements as a professional athlete. We discussed the transformation from being a collegiate athlete to the professional ranks. Going from an environment where the coaches dictate your every move to a livelihood that demands you are in peak condition on a daily basis—self motivation is required. Improved nutrition, mental well-being, and physical condition are a must to excel. We talked about how caring for his body helps him as a father and husband. As Cooper and I discussed the nuances of his physical transformation and current well-being, he made a comment that resonated with me.

"People don't realize how good they can feel."

A poignant yet incredibly powerful statement by a young man whose career demands he maintains his physical well-being. In a world where people are too busy to exercise regularly and high caloric foods are too easily consumed, Cooper's statement is brilliant in its simplicity. Obstacles and excuses are everywhere. But I know I made some individual changes after we spoke. I find myself eating more fruit and exercising more consistently. And yes, I feel better. I would encourage you to start small, make some changes and see how good you can feel.

Mini-epilogue: Cooper started five games for the Dallas Cowboys in 2022. He finished 4-1 filling in as the starting quarterback. I was blessed to attend a game in Dallas and watch him throw two touchdowns in a victory over the Washington Commanders. Not bad for an undrafted free agent. Something to be said for taking care of yourself.

((SOCIAL WELLNESS))

"I was disappointed in the dietician.
They told me bacon was not meat; that it was fat."

– PATIENT

"It was like being a doctor in a fraternity," I joke about my time as a flight surgeon. During my tenure as the flight surgeon for VP-10, the challenges were tremendous. I was responsible for the health and well-being of every person in the squadron—pilots, navigators, air crew, maintenance team. Immunizations, routine health care, flight physicals, malaria prophylaxis, and more. I served in Brunswick, Maine for three and a half years. These were wonderful years and I have very fond memories. Despite the hard work and a six-month deployment which took me away from my family, there was a healthy work-life balance. I was happy and fulfilled.

The biggest challenge was preparing and implementing a tri-site deployment for over 500 service members. Our main contingent was in Sicily, Italy. But part of the squadron was in El Salvador, and another group in Qatar. Logistics and medical decision-making took on a new meaning. I remember talking with an orthopedic surgeon in the U.S. about a patient with a torn quadriceps tendon in El Salvador while I was on a diplomatic mission in Cannes, France. Thank goodness for my satellite phone.

VP-10 included approximately 60 officers and we were all friends. This resulted in a unique dynamic for sure, balancing roles as friend and primary care physician. But the comradery was amazing. It is rare for a flight surgeon to earn a call sign other than "Doc." Eventually I became "Dr. Evil" for the Red

Lancers of VP-10. A term of endearment certainly, and a story better told in person.

Imagine a regular Sunday pizza night off the coast of Maine. The smell of the marine air with waves crashing into algae covered rocks. The gentle breeze felt cool on the skin. The warmth of Angie's hand in mine as we watched the sun set. Laughter and smiles were abundant as creative pizzas were made by one of the pilots. Spicy pepperoni and seafood to name a few. The aromas filled the seaside home and the homemade dough was mouthwatering. The pizza routine was near Portland, Maine, a 45 minute drive from our home near the base, but well worth it.

Not all of the settings were so serene. About a month into my tenure, Angie (who was nine months pregnant) and I attended a squadron function. The mood was festive and spirits high. The beer and wine flowed, along with dishes to share. People were laughing, dancing, and playing games on the cool May evening. Some of the more adventurous officers were playing games of chance. We enjoyed the moment, but made an early exit as I was on call and Angie was understandably tired.

"Doc, we need you to come back to the party," an urgency in the voice as I awoke.

"What's the matter?"

"Jim needs stitches."

"How bad is the cut," I asked, getting my flight suit back on. A short trip to the clinic to grab some supplies. Sutures, needle driver, scissors, antiseptic solution, gauze, dressings, and more.

I arrived back at the scene, the mood now somber. Many had gone home; only a handful of officers remained, including the Commanding Officer (CO) and Executive Officer (XO). The event was described as Jim sat on the toilet, while another pilot held a bandage to his forehead. Apparently a drunken wrestling match turned ugly between two hulking officers. Jim was on the losing end of a coffee table during the match.

I pulled the bandage back to inspect the wound. The wound was approximately two inches long. More concerning: I could see his facial muscles. This was a deep wound. I suggested we take him to the emergency room, despite being experienced enough to repair the defect. My fellow officers knew I had done a year of general surgery and was quite proficient at suturing. Despite my concerns, I agreed to suture the wound. Perhaps currying favor with my squadron, or avoiding potential disciplinary action for Jim. The reality—I was certainly qualified for the task at hand.

Jim was rather intoxicated. His self-induced anesthesia mitigated the need for any local anesthesia. After irrigating and cleaning the wound, I placed 20 interrupted sutures (both deep and superficial), while Jim was propped up on a toilet. A clean dressing was applied and he was given water to drink. I must admit, the wound healed quite nicely, and was barely noticeable some two years later.

Are there logistical and perhaps even ethical concerns suturing an inebriated colleague? Potentially. Was I qualified and competent to complete the job? Absolutely. Did that event solidify the trust of my fellow officers? Without a doubt. Even better, Our Quadruple Aim was achieved at that moment. Low cost, quality care was delivered at the correct time. And yes, the patient was satisfied and the provider was as well. Certainly a different version of pajama time (stay tuned).

((EMOTIONAL WELLNESS))

"American physicians are now increasingly suffering from a similar condition, except our demoralization is not a reaction to a medical condition, but rather to the diseased systems for which we work."

– ERIC REINHART, M.D.[94]

"Make today awesome," suggests the sticker affixed to the bottom right hand corner of my laptop. A gentle reminder. The pastel colors are soothing and the lettering written to jump out at you as if in 3-D. I cannot help but smile as I reflect on the past six months. A whirlwind of emotions, memories, experiences. And I would not trade any of them. My emotional state is the best it has been in years. One month into my retirement and I feel blessed (don't worry, I'll explain). Peace and happiness fill my days. I have been afforded more time to spend with my wife and children. Time to write and encourage a *Ripple of Change*.

A table of three lovely women with silver hair politely listened to my spiel regarding the book. I even offered them a chance to read this section. But the topic of dysfunction in healthcare immediately sparked an interest. My brain constantly returns to this passion. A quaint coffee shop tends to be an area where ideas flow freely, much like the creamy brown flow of a well-drawn espresso.

The irony is I just completed some paperwork for my prior employer. As I pulled into the parking structure, strange emotions started to sour my bubbly disposition. I felt nervous, jittery, angry, guilty, and somewhat nauseated. All I was doing was pulling into a parking structure of a hospital. A place I have been countless times before for meetings and strategic planning. Why does driving into an open concrete structure evoke such a strong response? I attribute it to moral injury.

Moral injury is not the intentional killing of another human being as in military service, but rather the failure to prevent or witness events that are in direct opposition to moral beliefs and expectations. There is certainly some overlap with PTSD, but in healthcare, this equates to observing preventable adverse patient events and the inability to deliver high-quality care. Guilt, shame, disgust, and anger are feelings that can occur when physicians consistently fail to meet patients' needs. The altruism that called most providers into healthcare led to many personal sacrifices. And now, the obstacles to deliver Our Quadruple Aim have grown to be insurmountable for many. One in five physicians plan to stop practicing in the coming years, only worsening the current physician shortage. And what about Dr. Linus Silver? Worse yet, many feel a lack of support or even betrayal from leadership.

Moral injury results from this complex interplay in attempting to deliver care and results in adverse psychosocial repercussions for the affected individual.[95, 96, 97]

Back to the coffee shop. I took a chance and asked the trio of ladies if they would like to read the first three paragraphs above. They kindly obliged and responded with some kind words. However, a slight correction was noted. One had chestnut brown hair with a hint of silver.

But the most interesting part was the immediate connection. A short conversation ensued regarding emotional responses to supervisors. One of the women had worked for the Social Security and Disability Department. She recently retired, but her husband had the same boss. During the pandemic, her husband was working from home. She happened to be passing by her husband as he toiled away, and overheard her former boss' voice. She reports just hearing that voice immediately invoked a panic attack. In talking with her, she described the pessimism and negativity of her prior supervisor, which often triggered these emotions. In just reliving this experience I could see her affect and emotions change. Powerful.

Simon G. Talbot, M.D. and Wendy Dean, M.D. provide a wonderful overview of moral injury in their article "Physicians aren't 'burning out.' They're suffering from moral injury." The authors eloquently describe burnout versus moral injury and the factors that contribute. They suggest burnout is a symptom or, rather, a result of our broken healthcare system. The conflicting allegiances and misalignment of incentives have created an ecosystem that degrades resilience. The resulting moral injury negatively impacts care and leads to increased costs and poorer experience. I can attest—this is spot on. "Continually being caught between the Hippocratic oath, a decade of training, and the realities of making a profit from people at their sickest and most vulnerable is an untenable and unreasonable demand."[98] I couldn't agree more. Moral injury is the antithesis of Our Quadruple Aim.

((SPIRITUAL WELLNESS))

"We are impatient, anxious to see the whole picture, but God lets us see things slowly, quietly."

– POPE FRANCIS

Bohemian Coffee House is located in Brunswick, Maine and has been in operation for 29 years. I owned a tattered tee shirt displaying their gecko logo in a verdant shade of green and black that has since been procured by my eldest. I last walked into one of all my all-time favorite coffee places in 2007, just prior to moving back to Michigan. As I reintroduced myself to the previously frequented establishment, memories consumed my brain. A mix of the present and past with a swirl of emotion. Aromas of sweet smelling pastries filled the air and 1920s jazz music softened the mood. Inviting, peaceful. I decided to splurge. I grabbed a double espresso while I wrote and an iced latte for the road. The owner/ barista was wearing the same beard as 15 years gone by, with perhaps a few more gray hairs sprinkled in.

My family and I had arrived in Brunswick the night before. As we exited Highway 1 onto Main Street, nostalgia consumed me. Hard to believe how much changed in 15 years. Yet, much the same—a fitting analogy to life. We drove by our old home and stopped at the local hospital where my two eldest children were born. Brandon and Josh reluctantly posed for a few photos in front of the Parkview Hospital sign. Full circle. I have been longing to show my children the quaint New England town where their lives began. Another bucket list item checked. What a blessing.

My foundation in spiritual wellness is in my religious beliefs. Born and raised Catholic, I still attend Mass weekly. My faith is very important and has helped me through some dark moments, including surviving burnout, and dealing with moral injury. Historically, I am soft spoken regarding my faith. However, as the years have mellowed me, I find myself more open. Frequently saying "amen" or "have a blessed day" to patients, or even to a complete stranger. Not trying to impose on them, rather spreading peace. Usually a reciprocal smile or a positive reply is offered in return. These short interactions have a symbiotic effect, and selfishly they help my well-being.

At times my faith did not hold the priority it should. But, dealing with life and death on a regular basis can take your mind to dark places and contribute to burnout. Traditional medical training sets physicians up to struggle: just work harder, be more resilient, do more. And this superhero mantra has been exploited over the years. Pajama time has resulted and is all too frequent for my colleagues, which takes time away from faith, family, friends, life. Pajama time is the term used to describe charting/documentation that occurs at home, typically one to two hours per night for the average family physician. I occasionally joke, "I am not a stenographer."

Earlier, I alluded to a homily I heard years ago at St. Gerard. At the time, I was struggling with burnout. My emotional capacity was low and my empathy was limited. I was going through the motions at work; patients came and went. The days were a blur as my anger and frustration built. Joshua experienced this first hand. The priest suggested that when we had a difficult interaction—pretend as though you were talking with Jesus Christ. Imagine he was sitting in front of you. How would that change your demeanor? How would that change your words? Simple, powerful. This soon became another tool in my burnout toolbox. I used this technique regularly during my struggles. This tool helps me stay in the moment. A deep breath, time slows down—peace, balance.

Prior to heading to Bohemian Coffee, I was reading Joshua's *Losing the Blueprint*. As I got further into the story I couldn't help but ponder fate. Fate that Angie and I were celebrating our 21st wedding anniversary as we drove into Brunswick? Fate that Joshua and I were connected as physician and patient? But is it really fate, or rather a higher power that has interwoven our lives? The latter for me. Comforting. It allows me to use my God-given talents to help others, practice medicine without fear, and free my mind to focus on the patient in front of me. It allows me to block out the distractions of life, assimilate the information presented, and do the best I can for my patients. All the while knowing that Jesus Christ is with me in this journey.

As I looked up from the computer screen to watch my children enjoying their breakfast on the porch of The Brunswick Hotel, I looked left and a rainbow flag had the quote "God is still speaking" written in the middle. A reminder that life has many beginnings and endings, changes are constant, but our spirituality is ever present. I know nostalgia often creates a spiritual awareness or awakening for me. It's like it shows the passage of time and is a reminder that we're not here for forever. I pray people will have an introspective look into their spirituality. Regardless of one's religious beliefs, my take home point is the same—spiritual wellness is a tie to something bigger, and vital for a well, balanced life.

((INTELLECTUAL WELLNESS))

"Not sure why I need an ECG (Electrocardiogram). My three ex-wives said I do not have a heart."

– PATIENT

An interesting corollary to this endeavor is I am once again a voracious reader. Usually I am actively reading three or four books, fiction and nonfiction alike. Books on medicine, politics, cryptocurrency, espionage, inspirational, leadership, and even a few on writing. For many years I did not consistently read for pleasure. Always reading and writing at work was my excuse. But now, I increasingly find myself wanting to improve, not only as a writer, but as a physician, father, husband, and brother. A fellow soccer parent recently commented that I was always carrying a book around, like I was studying for my boards. I laughed and explained why. Maybe he was just being cordial, but he genuinely seemed interested as I gave a brief synopsis of Our Quadruple Aim.

Physicians tend to be lifelong learners. Continuing Medical Education (CME) has been a staple in my life for the past 20 years. I am required to finish 50 CME credits annually and recently completed a longitudinal board recertification process in family medicine. There are various educational opportunities—journals, lectures, online activities—and I have always enjoyed live CME events as well. Keeping abreast of current topics and advances in medicine is vitally important to providing quality, cost-effective care.

Reading seems to have become my CME for writing. I have read dozens of books and hundreds of articles during this adventure. Often finding new ideas or inspirational quotes, then typing away (usually before my children, and the sun, have risen). A peaceful and fulfilling part of my day—an hour will have elapsed in what seems like minutes. Currently, one of the books I am reading is *Perfectly Yourself: Discovering God's Dream for You*, by Matthew Kelly. I picked this up at Mass while on vacation in Gaylord, Michigan. An inspiring work written to help find the best version of yourself, Kelly writes: "Our capacity for improvement is unfathomable."[99]

Another section of the book discussed opportunity that avails itself when we fail, as failure presents a learning opportunity. As a lifelong learner I took particular note. Wise leaders should heed the words of Benjamin Barber as suggested by Kelly:

"I divide the world into learners and non-learners.
There are people who learn, who are open to what happens
around them, who listen, who hear the lessons.
When they do something stupid, they don't do it again.
And when they do something that works a little bit,
they do it even better and harder the next time.
The question to ask is not whether you are a success or a
failure, but whether you are a learner or a non-learner."

– BENJAMIN BARBER

Intellectual wellness is multifaceted. Good mental health, reading, writing, and learning all contribute to continued intellectual growth. The pace is up to you. But recognizing your talents, and then expanding your knowledge and abilities, is critical. I often joke at work, "learned something new today." But that is reality. Rarely a day goes by without learning something new or different in the vast world of medicine. Self-fulfillment and improved performance are potentially right around the corner. As you continue your journey toward thriving, consider what role intellectual wellness plays. Regardless of vocation, everyone should incorporate intellectual wellness into their daily routine.

((ENVIRONMENTAL WELLNESS))

"Professionally fulfilled physicians (defined as those who experience happiness or meaningfulness, self-worth, self-efficacy, and satisfaction at work) are better equipped not only to practice the art and science of clinical care, but also to lead the effort to identify and implement much-needed improvements to our systems of care."

– BRYAN BOHMAN, M.D. et al.[100]

A weekend away with family or friends is often a welcome respite for Angie and myself. And occasionally we have the opportunity to spend time independent of one another. Home is always best, but time with friends can be invaluable to recharging your emotional tank.

For the better part of 20 years my friends and I would travel to Northern Michigan to a small town—Rogers City. A serene area built near a large quarry, a very good friend of mine lived and taught school there. A bachelor, his home was the perfect getaway for a group of friends. Secluded in the woods, the silence could be deafening mid-winter. Piles and piles of glistening white snow surrounded the modest ranch style home. Tall pine trees stood like stoic soldiers shielding us from cold winds coming in from Lake Huron, as we unloaded our vehicles of the necessary supplies.

The first several years of this adventure included myself, and my good friends, Rob and Kelly. The inside of the home was consistent with a bachelor's taste. Perhaps best left to the imagination, the water pressure left a bit to be desired. But despite its shortcomings (for those looking for a five-star retreat)—there is something magical about that house. It was often the only three consecutive days throughout the year where I never thought about work.

Over the years the group grew in size. Some were regular attendees and others an isolated appearance. But to a man—everyone enjoyed the environment. Was it the company, the time away from stress and worries, the food (the slowed cooked venison was amazing), the fun, or maybe the games of chance? The adventures and stories accumulated over time. The duration of the event lengthened and eventually the group outgrew the accommodations. Affectionately called "The Summit," this event holds a special place in many of my friends' hearts. Reflecting back on "The Summit"—the environment was perfect.

Today's turbulent workplace is an opportunity for environmental wellness, and as I describe above—it doesn't need to be fancy or complex to be effective. In pondering this section, my mind drifted back to an article I read in *NEJM Catalyst* a few years ago: "Physician Well-Being: The Reciprocity of Practice Efficiency, Culture of Wellness, and Personal Resilience." The article describes a three-pronged approach to physician well-being.[101] However, the principles laid out can be extrapolated to just about any situation, profession, or workplace environment.

Imagine these three principles as the legs of a stool, each leg reciprocally influencing the other. If one leg is disproportionate, the balance of the stool is off. So too, a workplace environment with regards to efficiency, wellness, and personal resilience. Just as high-functioning physicians are vital to the success of healthcare, high-functioning employees are essential to the success of any business.[102]

Personal resilience are the skills, behaviors, and attitudes that contribute to one's overall well-being, and allow a person to withstand or recover from adversity. The onus of personal resilience largely falls onto individuals, and hopefully the reader has gleaned some coping skills from these chapters. But organizational strategies to promote resilience are equally as important.[103] Those little items that enhance a person's day can have a massive impact. A personal example from my office setting is my occasional power nap at lunch time. I check in with my staff and nurse practitioners to see if they need anything, then proceed to rest for 20 minutes or so. A yoga mat and a Spider-man pillow provide my respite. Protected time, respected by my staff, and I wake refreshed, clear mind, good mood, ready for the remaining challenges of the day.

Efficiency of practice and a culture of wellness are largely organization responsibilities that can have a major impact on personal resilience. We have covered or will cover several components instrumental for healthcare efficiency—EMRs, appropriate staffing, and documentation requirements, to name a few. And a culture of wellness is essential to any high-functioning, successful organization. But balance between the three is required to prevent falling off the stool. In a physician's world, the systems, processes, and practices in place can help us provide compassionate, quality, cost-effective, evidence-based care.[104] This type of care typically leaves a patient satisfied and in turn creates job satisfaction for the provider (another component of wellness). Organizations that recognize the importance of these three components are ahead of the curve and well-positioned to achieve Our Quadruple Aim.

((FINANCIAL WELLNESS))

"Financial stress is a widely recognized element in physician burnout, although to those outside of medicine this may seem paradoxical."

– HILARY MCCLAFFERTY, M.D.[105]

Brandon Francis, M.D.:

When people say physicians make too much money, I recommend pausing and considering the following: if your pipe bursts at home, most people call a plumber. If the plumber does everything right, you pay them market rate and all is well in the world. If they do something wrong or they cannot fix the problem, they come back for another opportunity to fix it. It is much more difficult to put a financial and time-value on physician outcomes, good or bad. So it can be argued, some physicians do not make enough as profits are siphoned to insurance and pharmaceutical companies.

Not all physicians make over $1M annually. Some specialties in particular locations barely make $100K. That may be an unimaginably large amount of money to some people. But consider that salary in the context of $450K in loans at an 8% interest rate. Many physicians feel they are locked into a "debt trap." A financial tether that restricts them from operating at their full potential, and limits them from advocating for patients or providers, particularly if they work in a "culture of fear."

This fear can take many forms. One example can be with respect to litigation. There are situations where a physician is truly negligent and those situations require careful review and potentially assignment of liability. However, it should be noted: most physicians have malpractice insurance by their employer and in exchange for full coverage (including associated legal fees), the physician forgoes the right to fight or settle a case. This sets up a scenario where cases are brought against the physician that may not have real merit but are less costly for the malpractice insurance company to settle.

My point is that a physician's salary should be viewed in context. The reality is that some physicians will pick their specialty to ensure they can pay back their loans and have a comfortable life (save for their kid's college, save for retirement, care for their parents, etc.) while they're doing it. Depending on the healthcare system, this phenomenon may be contributing to why we need more primary care physicians but seem to have a surplus of specialists. The legal risk and consequences for physicians are different than it is for plumbing. And nothing against plumbers, just needed a real world comparison.

Some people would argue that physicians should have nothing to worry about because they have access to loan forgiveness programs for working in under-served areas. Should we consider these areas to be underserved because physicians apparently do not want to live there? What about increasing the pay and decreasing the amount of time to qualify for loan forgiveness (typically requires 10 years)? More physicians might experiment with these locations and potentially stay, especially if the pay is better than more 'desirable' markets.

Some people may argue "you knew the loan situation before you started medical school, so you deserve the loan burden, stop looking for handouts." The other side of that argument is to consider why medical school costs so much. If we value the field of medicine, and have a demonstrated need for physicians, why not incentivize the field so the best and brightest want to go into that field. There are many bright physicians, but there are also many bright people who would make excellent physicians but do not go to medical school because of the prohibitive cost. Where is the balance?

Physicians make extraordinary sacrifices to serve others as altruism drives the vast majority of us. Financial wellness needs to be considered as the shortage of physicians seems to grow and grow.

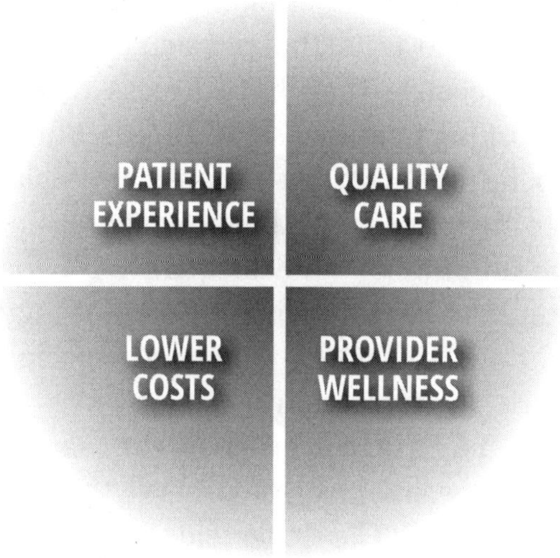
PATIENT
EXPERIENCE
QUALITY
CARE
LOWER
COSTS
PROVIDER
WELLNESS

((14))

Role Reversal

Joshua J. Judy – Patient:

In a memorable visit, I recollected Dr. Otten highlighting the singularity of my situation.

DR. OTTEN: You're my n=1.

Well, at least he hadn't called me his huckleberry. I suppose that's good. Regardless, I was commissioned for the job. What Dr. Otten meant by calling me his n=1 was that I was his sole case study, and I had to find a way forward. My role would reverse with my general practitioner and I would figuratively don a white coat. I poured hundreds and hundreds, if not thousands of hours into research, reading article after article, and journal after journal at the National Institute of Health and other resources, such as the NEJM. Sometimes, I paid for a write-up in a scientific publication if it looked particularly useful.

Along the way, I also stumbled across something called the Post-SSRI/SNRI Sexual Dysfunction (PSSD) forum (pssdforum.org). It was here, in this somewhat underground community, that I first came to recognize there were other damaged and misplaced souls. They were victims describing the chemical disintegration bestowed upon them by multitudes of SSRIs and SNRIs. Women and men.

They all once had been mostly healthy people, living healthy lives with healthy libidos. Motivated. Driven. By and large, they fit my original baseline. I remember people saying their genitalia felt rubberized, assuming they had any feeling left. One woman went as far as using sandpaper to try and feel something, anything. Story after similar story. Emotionally, and spiritually, things weren't any better for these individuals. They were already in their graves. It's a disturbing membership that nobody wanted to belong to. If one's psyche wasn't already damaged enough, these places could do it. Not because the victims weren't telling the truth or what they understood as the truth. Rather, it's because they were. Unfortunately, the general attitude from some of my encounters left me tentative and apprehensive. Emotional and sexual health issues are taboo, stigmatized.

Regardless of one's gender, there are stigmas, challenges, and common grounds. Unfortunately, there are no quick fixes. Sorry folks, when it comes to sexual function with males, a little blue pill isn't always the answer. Coupled with one's own embarrassment, there's rarely more to say... Because of our family planning, Megan and I had asked one of her neurologists if they knew anything about the sexual side effects of levetiracetam. She replied, "Unfortunately, not very much because people won't really talk about it. So, we don't know how to help it."

Stigmas are very real. In the Army, my dad had contracted Hepatitis C sometime in the 1970s. Or, as it was known then, "Non-A and Non-B." Many years later, he had encountered a CDC doctor who was doing a write-up for the *NEJM*. The doctor asked how he thought it was transmitted and my dad replied, "I always felt a strong possibility it came from the air guns they used to give us shots. They weren't sterilized in between uses and we were lined up like cattle." Replying with genuine interest, the doctor said, "That's a good thought. We hadn't considered that. May I use your name in the write-up?"

My dad hesitated and ultimately declined. Why? It was owing to a former encounter at the hospital when he had gone in for testing (many years ago). A receptionist, recognizing what he was there for, in a raised voice asked: "What are you doing in here? Shouldn't you be wearing a mask?" Discretion be damned. All he could do in that moment of gratuitous discomfiture, surrounded by numerous strangers, is counter, "You know, it's not spread in the air." My dad now wishes he had allowed his name to be credited with the CDC doctor to raise awareness.

Grace, or dismissiveness—you pick.

((FOREVER IS A LONG TIME))

At this point I felt alone, dismissed at times. My perception, reinforced by experience, was that candidly discussing side effects of medicine seems nearly as taboo as sexual and emotional health (rare disease or not). So, I said screw it. I started reaching out across the country, eventually across the world. If I found an attentive doctor or scientist, a similar answer came back—

> *"I've heard of this happening in some cases. We know it happens. We just don't know why. Nobody knows, they would say—we just know something is screwed up."*

I then would react with a similarly unhelpful response—*I'm thoroughly screwed*. I wondered with great irony if someone, somewhere wanted to put me back on an antidepressant.

Not all responses were hurried. I remember one distinctly from a gentleman dated March 20, 2020. He had impressive credentials: M.D., Ph.D, FECSM, ECPS and was with the European Society for Sexual Medicine:

> *"There is [the] need for time and motivation and going from deep under and climbing step by step. Luckily you*

didn't lose your motivation to look at all the details of 5-HT receptors. So, you have it.

Start routine daily life with healthy food, regular exercise, going to bed at the same time and have a regular number of sleeping hours etc.—each day the same, like preparing for the Olympics."

I found his response kind. 5-HT, or 5-hydroxytryptamine, is the formal name for serotonin—the intended final target of many antidepressants. When the European doctor said at least I was still motivated enough to look at "5-HT receptors" he was referring to my studying of serotonin receptors in the brain. But here I was in the Challenger Deep, the lowest point in the Mariana Trench in the Western Pacific. It's a chasm approximately seven miles deep and I was being crushed by the pressure, too weak to think or act. I wasn't ready to even slightly entertain a career as a podium-capturing Olympian. Not even metaphorically. Still, despite feeling pathetically sick and lost, I dove deeper.

On March 30, 2020, I located another unexpected but thoughtful voice in the dark—a psychiatrist from California:

"I don't do phone consultations outside of California. In general, I don't do PSSD [Post-SSRI/SNRI Sexual Dysfunction] consultations because I have no solutions to the problem.

Other practitioners have tried various hormonal and dopaminergic agents. While I did identify the problem early on, I have never tried to treat it. It can improve slowly over a year or two or it may persist unchanged. Your problem sounds like it is embedded in global numbing. Generally, this improves with time.

Good luck to you."

A reasonable response if not utilitarian. Global numbing and a bit of good luck sent from sunny California to wintery Michigan. However, there was something far more perceptive here, a genuine acknowledgement that some of what I was experiencing existed. A licensed professional had admitted to it. He had seen it. There was that, and the suggestion of time—I needed more time.

Or, according to him, maybe—forever.

((THE STRAW THAT BROKE THE CAMEL'S BACK))

Fine. If that's your timeframe, why not beat my head against the wall a little longer? I came across another doctor and researcher in this arena, Dr. Hope. I noticed he was oft-quoted in the online communities. Here is what I wrote him on December, 7, 2019, as I felt then in the raw, and without the benefit of hindsight:

> *I'm off duloxetine completely as of Monday, November 18 [2019]. After a couple days, I was randomly emotional and had some memories returned that I hadn't felt/recalled from many years ago. There was a day or two where I could actually feel music, feel the notes. Then came the flu symptoms but of course without a fever. I was always worse at night. Fatigued, achy and anhedonia, and dark thoughts.* ***This really robs you of your empathy and feels like you could witness violence–even someone close to you, and not blink. It's truly sad. Makes me realize a few small microscopic chemicals and metabolites are what determines being human or not and being a lost soul or not.***

People who are afflicted by these conditions have discussed similar reactions. Dr. Hope responded to my note and affirmed:

> *"At the moment, no-one has a clue what is causing this problem or even how to investigate it properly. Tons of people have built interesting models but until someone can reliably make a difference, these just remain speculative."*

What could I take from this? It felt like a non-answer at first glance, but it told a story. Very smart people knew it was a problem and they were making attempts to solve it. It was powerful; because, like the psychiatrist from California, another professional recognized this dilemma. I felt some vindication.

Further down the road, I found an Italian scientist and researcher named Professor Roberto Cosimo Melcangi of the Department of Pharmacological and Biomolecular Sciences "DiSFeB"—University of Milano, Italy. His work included spinal taps, exactly like Megan had to undergo in the hospital for her epilepsy. But Melcangi wasn't searching for meningitis[106].

Instead, the professor was looking at hormones in the brain–specifically specialized brain hormones called neurosteroids.[107] Most of us have heard of hormones. Perhaps in the context of a moody male teenager going through puberty with surging testosterone levels or a female reaching menopause and diminishing hormone production. It can be a complicated topic–even squeamish. I never gave much thought to the matter and had no compelling reasons to. Maybe you've had little to no reasons either. Until some firsthand event affects an individual, it's convenient to keep knowledge on complex topics at a cursory level.

What Melcangi wanted to know is if the brain hormones in people exposed to medications like antidepressants or finasteride (the latter commonly prescribed for preventing hair loss) were different from those not exposed (control subjects). He found levels of key neurosteroids disturbingly off between the two groups.[108] I could write an entire book on hormonal cascades but I'll stop short (if you have questions, please feel free to reach out at ourquadrupleaim.com). Just appreciate that our bodies take its version of 'crude oil', which is cholesterol, and using chemical processes with enzymes 'refines' it into a lot of different byproducts such as steroid hormones for use. The brain will also create important local byproducts, neurosteroids, for its own use.

What can Meclangi's study results tell us? Tons, actually–that specific actions create ripples of change, some helpful, others harmful. It matters little whether it's a hospital administrator dismissive of an overburdened doctor's concerns, a doctor dismissive of their patient's side effects, or a patient dismissive of their doctor's warnings to change lifestyles. The downstream effects can be toxic.

My issues existed even if the proper tools to measure them did not (or were out of reach). Think of forensic science and all the advancements over the years. If you were an investigator 40 to 50 years ago, would you possess the foresight to collect a biological specimen that could be later tested with future technology? For astute detectives who did, it may have meant justice for crime victims when testing technology eventually caught up. It's not that the crime didn't occur, rather the testing didn't exist or was unsophisticated. Many examples exist where DNA tests were inconclusive because the sample size was too small and the equipment too insensitive. Years later, when the sample was retested using newer, more sensitive equipment, a different result unfolded–a eureka moment. Were the results of the original DNA sample dishonest? Far from it.

Another example–the widely known movie Avatar took James Cameron 50 years to create from the time the idea first percolated. Why? The technology required to create the film's stunning visuals didn't exist (except in his imagination). In fact, the famed director waited another decade after completing the screenplay for computer-generated graphics to advance.

As a provider, the next time you sit across from your patient, please consider these scenarios if they tell you about their problem–even if the test to prove their case beyond a reasonable doubt is undiscovered. As a hospital administrator responsible for the success of your staff, think of how to healthily engage staff concerns (unless you prefer workforce strikes and early retirements). As a patient, think about how your doctor might be telling you something you don't want to hear, but need to. As Dr. Otten has said, it's okay to say, "I don't know (but am willing to try)." It's not okay to say, "I don't hear you, or I don't believe you."

"Once you eliminate the impossible, whatever remains, no matter how improbable, must be the truth."

– ARTHUR CONAN DOYLE

Rare, adverse side effects from medication brings up an interesting concept: risk profiles. When you think about your own medical risk profile, I want you to think about the following story. A BBC write-up from 2015 called *"The extraordinary case of the Guevedoces,"* tells the tale of the discovery of a small community in the Dominican Republic many years ago. It was a fascinating intrigue—some males were born appearing female only to later grow penises in puberty. In the 1970s, an endocrinologist from Cornell Medical College in New York wanted to know—could it be true? She headed to the Caribbean Island of Hispaniola, shared with Haiti.[109] According to the article:

> *She discovered the reason they don't have male genitalia when they are born is because they are deficient in an enzyme called 5-alpha-reductase (5-AR), which normally converts testosterone into dihydro-testosterone (DHT). This deficiency seems to be a genetic condition, quite common in this part of the Dominican Republic, but vanishingly rare elsewhere. So, the boys, despite having an XY chromosome, appear female when they are born. At puberty, like other boys, they get a second surge of testosterone. This time the body does respond and they sprout muscles, testes and a penis ... Another thing... Guevedoces tend to have small prostates.*[110]

By 1974, this discovery caught the attention of a large, well-known pharmaceutical firm. Their research set in motion the creation of a drug to artificially duplicate the condition of being deficient in 5-AR. By blocking the conversion of testosterone to its more potent form, DHT, the drug created conditions like the genetic abnormalities observed in the Dominican Republic (DHT ramps up in puberty, kicking off the process in males, and gives them that 'alpha' feeling, body hair, teenage oily skin, a deepening voice; in the womb, it determines if a baby is born with male or female genitalia).[111]

Finasteride was born–what some of those harmed by it call an 'anti-puberty' drug.

Unavoidably, you see how peculiar some mass marketed, profitable products that end up in the mouths of patients are. And many people have no clue, not because they aren't inquisitive or intelligent. To the contrary–it's because they're never told and have no reason to ask unless they're one of the ill-fated ones. So next time you swallow a pill, ponder what inspired its creators. **If after reading about the Guevedoces, you've decided to research potential-side effects of medicines, and have an open discussion with your provider before taking them—I've met my goal.**

Some men take finasteride for years with no problem or only lose themselves upon a dosage increase or withdrawal (similar to SSRIs/SNRIs).[112] The drug is routinely used to treat prostate enlargement, benign prostatic hyperplasia (BPH). Practically all men will get to know their prostate gland at one point or another in their lives. It characteristically comes with age. Therefore, let me be clear: ***I'm not anti-medicine.*** What I can offer is that everyone's got a built-in threshold; a problem is that modern medicine rarely knows how to measure that breaking point *ahead* of prescribing. That's where the focus needs to be—how to accurately baseline or predetermine risk/reward profiles while promoting education, for patients and doctors alike.

'So, what's your risk profile?'

– JOSHUA J. JUDY, PATIENT

You can borrow the model of risk assessment from the finance industry—financial advisors ask people all the time about what they're willing to accept in their investment portfolios. There's no more important 'portfolio' than our bodies. In my experience, deep conversations between doctors and patients that assess risk are scarce.

My hormone doctor, Justin Saya, M.D., says, "We commonly see men with low DHT levels if they've been previously exposed to finasteride. We don't know why. It doesn't matter whether they discontinued the medication. At this point, it becomes more a question of management than a cure. I'm treating an affected 19-year-old patient right now. I once discussed this with my late friend and doctor colleague of mine...for some guys, their Hypothalamus-Pituitary Gonadal axis are simply ultra-sensitive and certain medications are the straw that breaks the camel's back."

Shit, I thought! That's pretty young to be chemically neutered. And regrettably, probably long before they've found their partner in life. With my risk profile suddenly in mind, I recalled my exposures to both finasteride and duloxetine. I quietly counted my blessings that I had already found my life partner.

TL;DR—lessons for OQA:

Everyone, it's okay to be bald. Some pull it off handsomely well, and it beats the potential alternatives.

Patients, stay curious about risks. Research and share information. Think twice and set reasonable expectations. Be in front and upfront about everything, not behind.

Healthcare Providers, that goes for you too. Ask your patients what they're willing to accept, good and bad. And if you haven't read the side-effect profiles for what you're prescribing, I'm giving you a homework assignment.

Bottom line, work together to strive and do it right the first time as Our Quadruple Aim illustrates.

((HOMESICK))

As late as August 31, 2021, there was an update on Professor Melcangi's research funding page:

> *Recent observations obtained by the research unit coordinated by Prof. R.C. Melcangi of the University of Milan, has shown that treatment with paroxetine (a SSRI) in an animal model is able to modify the synthesis of steroids in the brain (i.e. the neurosteroidogenesis).* ***In particular, and this is particularly important for PSSD, drug suspension is able to further modify the steroidogenic process, inducing a persistent decrease in neurosteroid levels.***
>
> *This is interesting as neurosteroids, being important regulators of brain function, could therefore be responsible for many side effects found in Post SSRI/SNRI Sexual Dysfunction. Furthermore, as we have demonstrated in an animal model, an alteration of neurosteroidogenesis is also found in the post-finasteride syndrome (PFS).*
>
> *These observations support our hypothesis, namely that the pathological mechanisms that induce PSSD and PFS may be similar.*[113, 114, 115]

I read this as permanent alteration in brain function—maybe I was right all along? You may have heard of neuroplasticity, where the brain can bounce back or adapt by forming new neural connections throughout life. But in the above circumstances, it sounds like the rubber band had been stretched too far. I remembered what a sleep technician had once told me about children's brainwaves and their vibrancy (see Chapter 17, "The Unseen Hand"). But I was far beyond childhood and had to play the hand dealt.

While these online communities and studies are invaluable to sufferers, many people talked of stepping away. One victim didn't need another's story of misery when they could stare in their mirror. Self-inflicted death was often mentioned–ironically, most were too voided to go through with it. This lack of progress honed a collective depression, and people felt they would never find their own escape velocities. It was somewhere between hell and nowhere.

I knew it all too well. In the back of my mind, I fought to ignore the prior words of the doctor from California—*persist unchanged.* Intensely rooted were these two words, like daggers wedged in my brain. I just kept hoping against hope that somehow down the line, I'd make it back home.

((15))

Office Utopia

"...we must be in service to others, but when we don't have the energy, enthusiasm, and excitement within us, it is darn near impossible to have it for others."

– GREG HIEBERT, *YOU CAN'T GIVE WHAT YOU DON'T HAVE*[116]

Todd R. Otten, M.D.:

The simple day-to-day efforts towards wellness in our family medicine office might go unnoticed. Yet, these efforts are invaluable to our well-being, and potentially emulated in most work environments. Staff and patients flourish in this atmosphere. A simple "good morning" can start the day on a positive note, or asking how someone is feeling, perhaps offering your unexpected assistance, or showing your colleagues you care. Not only will your staff notice, but patients appreciate it as well. As physicians and leaders, we set the tone—good or bad. Learn to lead by example, the ROI is priceless.

This chapter will highlight some simple routines to facilitate working in an environment that embodies Our Quadruple Aim. Remember, wellness is a lynch pin. If you and your staff are well, quality, patient experience, and provider well-being will begin to align, leading to decreased overall costs for our system. When you care for yourself and others—it is incredible how doing the right thing seems to work out in the end. Our office was a utopia and thrived on OQA.

But, these ideas don't need to be limited to a physician's office. Wellness and its benefits can be extrapolated to just about any setting. Whether you work in a law office, school, or restaurant—people want to be happy at work. And when they are, productivity goes up and mistakes go down. Maybe just give it a try and see what happens, and let naysayers be naysayers. Smiling and being kind cost nothing. Before we get into the nitty gritty of our office utopia, I would like to offer a simple example of how wellness can transform a relationship.

((PAY IT FORWARD))

"Stir some shit up with your book, it's needed."

– PATIENT

A simple tap on the shoulder and the receipt was set on the table. I was finishing breakfast with my family at a local restaurant. Brandon was already off with Angie to a driver's training class. Probably not the healthiest of meals, but everyone was in good spirits after Mass and looking forward to the day. The receipt had some writing on it: "Thanks for being my favorite doctor. Your favorite Polish patient." I looked down and scribbled on the paper: "You're welcome."

I was caught off guard and turned to see Michael, who indeed is one of my favorite patients. A broad, inviting smile on his face and hand extended in gratitude. I grabbed his hand and we shared a warm exchange. That pleasant feeling of peace washed over me. I introduced my family and thanked him for paying for our breakfast. We then went our separate ways: I, fulfilled both physically and emotionally. Gratitude and kindness.

Let's rewind the clock several years to when I first met Michael after a severe battle with pneumonia which nearly ended his life. After an extended hospitalization and intensive care unit stay, we were meeting to establish his care. Michael tends to be somewhat skeptical of healthcare and my role as his doctor was no exception. Tough questions were asked of me, both personally and professionally. Michael wanted to know me—not only as a physician, but as a person.

Fortunately, I tend to be honest with patients, even blunt at times. I appreciate that people generally want to know the truth, as did Michael. We discussed his hospital stay and current well-being, and I got to know him as a person. Over the years we developed a good working relationship. Michael coached football and would ask how my children were progressing in high school, wanting to hear about their accolades in athletics. Additionally, I had the honor of caring for his parents before they passed away.

After my battle with burnout, our office developed a wellness committee (see Chapter 18). At one of Michael's appointments, he mentioned his love of singing and playing guitar. I asked if he would be interested in performing for our office staff. Without hesitation, he agreed. We made some arrangements and finished his appointment.

A few months went by, but I had not forgotten my request. I reached out and a date was set for: a lunchtime waiting room concert. I had no idea what to expect, but was excited for the show. Michael arrived with guitar in hand. The staff of about 15 ate lunch while Michael began to perform. As he strummed his guitar, Michael began to sing. A deep, somewhat gruff, but pleasing voice filled the waiting room. Everyone's affect changed, smiles appeared, and people sang along. The country and rock and roll songs were belted out for nearly an hour. To say I was impressed is a massive understatement. Michael has a lot of musical talent and it was a blessing to share with the staff. Life is about sharing, caring, and calculated risk.

Circle back to breakfast, just a few days before a hip replacement for Michael. The surgery went well and Michael has no pain and is back to work—he described himself as a miraculous recovery. Our doctor-patient relationship grew even closer that day over a simple gesture of kindness and thanks. I have a feeling there will be more stories to tell in the years to come.

((ACHIEVING OUR QUADRUPLE AIM))

"It's kinda like putting a screen on a window to prevent the rain from coming in."

– PATIENT (DISCUSSING MASKS AND COVID-19)

Imagine an office setting where laughter and smiles are abundant, and people enjoy being at work. Patients feel as though they are family and well cared for, with video or telephone visits if appropriate, and evening hours four days per week. Providers covering for one another during vacations and off hours. The hours fly by and when you are finished seeing patients, your charting is done, messages completed—no pajama time. (Well, maybe some for the nurse practitioners, but less as they become more proficient). An open door policy for the nurse practitioners and staff to ask questions. Just a snapshot. This was our office utopia for a little over two years.

There is no magic button or switch to flip to achieve this type of environment. Rather, it is necessary to have a commitment to a process—a culture. Before we discuss examples from our office utopia, I would like to review a recent article from the *American Academy of Family Physicians* (AAFP) entitled "Leadership development, well-being, and performance improvement: Achieving the quadruple aim in your practice," from August 2022. AAFP offers a Leading Physician Well-being Program with three goals: leadership development, performance improvement, and well-being advocacy.[117]

The article reviews the importance of physicians as leaders. Without a doubt, my disposition can set the tone for the day in the office, and I strive to set a positive example for the staff (and patients). Perfect—no. A reminder: as human beings, we all have good days and bad. While personal resilience is important to maintaining well-being, the systems we work in can strain this in a multitude of ways. To offset this, the author Jason E. Marker, M.D. suggests that: "Successful leaders learn that the best traits for success include motivating staff, partnering with other leaders, listening to feedback, and supporting teams through their successes and failures."[118]

In regard to continued process improvement, Dr. Marker suggests a four step approach: assess, strategize, accomplish, and celebrate. Start with determining your work environment baseline. Strategize with all team members, openly communicate, and leverage assistance and existing talents. Create a game plan for success. As Dr. Marker writes: *"Do something!"* The tiniest of interventions can yield amazing results. Finally, celebrate wins and learn from defeats.[119] When the office is functioning efficiently and staff are well, the other three components of Our Quadruple Aim follow naturally, and seemingly effortlessly.

((HUMOR))

"The New England Journal of Medicine reports that 9 out of 10 doctors agree that 1 out of 10 doctors is an idiot."

JAY LENO

"What do you mean your name isn't Carl?," I replied in shock.

Let's rewind the clock six months.... Chad was a new receptionist at Family Care Specialists. A fantastic employee with a natural warmth in his demeanor. Combined with a witty sense of humor, he was a welcome addition to our office family. Patients enjoyed interacting with him, as did I. For six months,

I thought his name was Carl and referred to him as such. Little did I realize, his name was actually Chad. He thought it was hysterical, and carried on the charade for six months. I still laugh and share that story regularly. Chad went on to become a respiratory therapist, but his legend lives on at the office. Humor—an undervalued resource.

Recently I was listening to *The Hidden Brain* podcast entitled "Humor Us" with Angie. The podcast reviewed the decline of humor in the workplace and resulting adverse effects, including decreased productivity and lower morale.[120] I agree. To offset this, I have made a concerted effort to incorporate humor into the office routine. It is rare that laughter cannot be heard numerous times during the course of a busy day. I would go so far to say the majority of my patient visits involve laughter. How? Why?

Angie often does not think I am funny. I suppose "Dad jokes" are aptly named, as my morning jokes are intended for a different audience. However, the podcast pointed out one form of humor that resonated with me. Taking everyday observations and redirecting them into a humorous statement. At the office, this is my style of humor. I think Jerry Seinfeld would approve, as his style resonated with millions. The humor in *Seinfeld* made a lot of sense to me. Physicians are inherently observant. We assimilate data and transform it into a diagnosis and treatment plan routinely. If sculpted correctly, these ideas can quickly be turned into something funny, ease tension, and build rapport.

As I try to incorporate humor into the daily routine, my office staff is in lockstep and laughter is commonplace. Ironic that a place where life and death decisions occur regularly should include levity? Why not? Laughter is good medicine. It is sad when laughter is absent from the workplace. If gloom describes your work environment, I implore you to make this change.

Of course there are risks with change. People can take humor too far, and there is no room for humor at others' expense. Boundaries and respect are of the utmost importance. Occasionally a mistake may occur, but a quick apology and forgiveness usually solve the problem. The upside far outweighs the occasion blip in my humble opinion. I offer the following examples during ONE day of seeing patients.

I was seeing a patient with some disabilities who works at a very accommodating facility. Apparently, his co-workers have been teasing him about his height, as he is five feet tall. As I was encouraging him to ignore the barbs, his sister chimed in, "I just tell him to say—dynamite comes in small packages." We all shared a hearty laugh.

Typically during a routine complete physical I will examine the patient from head to toe. As a creature of habit I follow a routine. Often I will look into a patient's ear early on. Seemingly this is a natural entry point for humor—typically from the patient. *Can you see anything in there? Is the light coming out on the other side? How many fingers am I holding up?* These may have lost their potency after several hundred times. Some of my colleagues may be rolling their eyes at some of these quips.

Another example of humor that day occurred while I was evaluating (you guessed it) another ear. Fairly routine, minimal wax, no lesions or tumors. The middle ear drum was intact. The cone of light reflex was immediately apparent. Normal. As I continued examining the ear, a voice queried, "how many fingers am I holding up?" I answered, "two." A brief pause, and then we both started laughing.

The very next day, I heard my MA laughing with our first patient. A quick joke was made between staff members. The patient chuckled and said, "office humor is a good thing." Amazing how this can permeate the workplace if allowed. Balance.

Humor is considered a mature defense mechanism, and I can attest. It helps me deal with death and disease on a regular basis. Self-deprecating humor is occasionally my tool of choice. What better way to level the playing field during a visit. I speak candidly with patients. I wear my heart on my sleeve, and often I poke fun at myself. This tool helps me, and it helps my patients. They let down their guard and reveal those invaluable pieces of information that help me, help them.

As a litmus test regarding how pervasive humor is in our office, I asked the office manager to poll the staff. "How many times a day do you laugh?" Now, keep in mind there is no p-value or statistical analysis associated with this. (Remember, dry sense of humor.) Yet, the answers were telling. My staff did not give specific numbers, but rather a general impression. Telling. Most answered either 1) at least once per hour or 2) all day long. Laughter is good medicine. Humor can exist in medicine, and I encourage you to try.

((SPIDER DAYS))

Joshua J. Judy – Patient:

Dr. Otten isn't joking about laughter. It works. I invited Megan to recount a time from her veterinary technician days:

> *I was using the bathroom. As I sat there, I casually noticed something dark just inside the corner view of my eye. Eerily close. Hairy. It couldn't have been my own legs, for I had recently shaved. Oh Lord, no. There he was, a basketball-sized if he was an inch wide, spider. I stared at him and he at me, as I went about my business. No sudden moves and there could be peace.*
>
> *I heard distinctive footsteps approaching. My trance briefly paused. When you work side-by-side with your co-workers in a relatively confined space, you begin to recognize certain characteristics about them. Even their shuffling and pace become signature moves. It says a lot about how we often spend more hours with teammates than our own families. It also helps when your co-workers wear Dansko shoes, popular in the medical*

industry for all day comfort. A bonus—their clodhopper nature lets them double as a smashing device.

Which is why I instantly knew who it was before they knocked, "Is anybody in there?" It didn't matter that the door was shut. I recognized their presence before any words escaped. It was my unsuspecting co-worker and one of my favorite veterinarians. While I may have disliked spiders, she had a particularly nasty disposition towards them—a primal fear that wouldn't be reasoned with.

I knew what I had to do. As "Ride of the Valkyries" by Richard Wanger began to triumphantly play in my mind, I quietly finished up. Washed my hands, dried them and stepped into the hall. I paced my stride very carefully in gleeful retreat. Trap set, I didn't want to risk missing any of the action that would soon unleash.

"Aaarrggh." Boom—a heavy bricked boot had left my co-worker's foot and gone flying. Still bushy but a bit flatter, the spider resembled a freshly pressed penny.

The door burst open and my lovable veterinarian came hopping out on one-foot, weaponized shoe in her other hand.

"I can't believe you didn't tell me! I can't believe you didn't tell me!"

As I burst into a fit of giggles, the grief-stricken doctor waltzed herself clumsily out of the building to the grass to wipe her shoe. She preferred this, if it meant not cleaning the spider carcass off by hand. Highly ironic knowing the doctor's fine surgical skills and ability to handle the qualms that accompany. "Ride of the Valkyries" had been replaced with Beethoven's "Ode to Joy."

As the story spread, the rest of the staff, including the doctor, joined in the laughter. Don't worry–I soon got what was coming to me. Knowing how much sugar gliders (devilish little creatures, a bit like flying squirrels) gave me the heebie jeebies, the doctor teamed up with another technician and set their phones' tones to the gliders' distinctive chatter. Whenever I was in ear shot, they made sure to blast off a text and watch me jump.

In this profession, we always say laughing beats tears since there's so many chances to cry.

((BIRTHDAY FUN))

"I was reviewing my labs and noticed my chloride was a little low. Does that mean I am not drinking enough pool water?"

– PATIENT

Todd R. Otten, M.D.:

I have a birthday tradition in my office. Some see it as quirky, and maybe so. But try and remember to celebrate numerous birthdays among all of the other stressors of practicing medicine. Alright, probably an ineffective excuse. But ask my staff if they like receiving a birthday present every year.

The process goes as follows. Every year I bring a catalog to work which sells fair trade items from around the globe, supporting various charities. All of my staff members get to choose their present from the catalog. I then take the catalog home and order the requisite items. Of course, I often forget the catalog is in my briefcase for several weeks, and a new catalog comes out, requiring us to revisit the subject. But that is besides the point.

Eventually, items are actually ordered; once the package arrives, I choose a day to celebrate everyone's birthday. Regardless of the month, we celebrate the entire staff's birthday together, on some random day. Who wouldn't like to choose their own present? This has become a tradition in our office. The seasoned staff know the routine. And yes, smiles are abundant.

Another recent encounter may turn tradition. Don has been my patient for many years. Don jokes he is going to live to 105 and recently celebrated his 90th birthday. My staff had a birthday card and gift waiting for him. After his appointment, the entire staff gathered in his exam room and sang him happy birthday. Just thirty seconds and Don was moved to tears. Medicine is about caring and compassion for people. Birthday fun.

((CULTURE))

"Culture is what motivates and retains talented employees."

– BETTY THOMPSON

Culture in healthcare is a complex topic with many interpretations. How culture is defined can vary tremendously—whether on an individual, office, hospital, or even at a system level. What drives culture? How is it fostered and cultivated? A colleague of mine equates cultural development and maintenance to weeding a garden. Without proper weeding, a garden will soon be overrun with weeds—with little yield. So too with culture...without proper care and attention, it can become negative, perhaps even toxic. Much like a neglected garden, a neglected culture can create an atmosphere with many untoward consequences.

"Culture of wellness is defined as a set of normative values, attitudes, and behaviors that promote self-care, personal and professional growth, and compassion for colleagues, patients, and self."

– BRYAN BOHMAN, M.D. et al.[121]

I equate culture in healthcare to the lubrication that allows a machine to run smoothly. When a positive, nurturing culture exists in healthcare it's incredible. Unfortunately, the current cultural climate in healthcare often gums up the gears. Thinking about culture given all of the dysfunction can be daunting—but there is hope. My mantra over the years has been "do the right thing." Simple, powerful, and effective. For me, the basis for a positive and productive culture can be gleaned from Our Quadruple Aim. I have lived OQA for many years, just ask my patients and staff. When you do your best to practice quality medicine, be a good fiduciary of healthcare dollars, treat patients like human beings (or better yet, family) and live a balanced, well life—culture becomes intuitive. Work becomes easier and the joy of medicine returns.

Establishing and maintaining a positive, forward-thinking culture is integral to achieving OQA. Easier said than done... It is not plug and play and cannot be lip service. Culture needs support at the highest levels of an organization and leaders need to set the cultural tone. A positive workplace culture can improve teamwork, raise morale, increase productivity and efficiency, and enhance retention. Job satisfaction, collaboration, and work performance can be enhanced with a positive workplace environment and stress reduced for employees.[122] In a time when burnout is pervasive and employees are leaving in droves, I would suggest leaders take a moment to reflect and ask if the culture in their workplace is aligned and supports their mission statement.

We will discuss a just culture in a subsequent chapter. But what is your mission statement? How does that impact your culture, or does it? Is it possible to be happy at work and be productive? Ultimately, the question that needs to be answered is:

"What are you trying to achieve with your culture?"

In 20 years of practicing medicine I have seen the full spectrum of culture, both good and bad, and at a micro and macro level. High performing entities in healthcare typically harbor a culture that incorporates most (if not all) of Our Quadruple Aim. Cultures that focus on patients and providers (in lieu of profits and data) have been more efficient, had less staff turnover, less patient complaints, and ultimately more profit. Yes, this is my anecdotal opinion. Yes, I have seen a positive culture yield these results. Perhaps, it's time cultures within healthcare revert to including commonsense. Keep the metrics simple. I would argue staff recruitment and retention rates are excellent barometers of culture. Any employer with poor retention rates probably needs a cultural assessment. If nothing else, this should be a red flag for leadership.

I would like to share the cultural example from the office utopia. Considered a pilot program, I was the sole physician supervising three NPs. The office was seen as very successful and the system wanted to emulate our success. We scheduled a meeting and discussed ideas. I emphasized that culture was paramount. The office culture paralleled OQA, despite a lack of support and resources (at times). For example, six exam rooms for four providers (~50% less than ideal) creates a bottleneck—impacting flow, and increasing wait times. Despite the obstacles, our office flourished. The culture was empowering to the staff, allowing them to excel in our healthcare microcosm. Most days our office had been full of color, despite our surrounding world of gray.

Creating a positive culture in the workplace must start with leadership. In my office that role resided with myself and the office manager. At the hospital or system level, a top-down approach is required. The power of positivity cannot be underestimated and actions must be taken consistently to foster the desired culture. Transparency, collaboration, honest communication, and regular feedback are mandatory. Teamwork, clear goals, aligned incentives, and inclusivity are required. When leaders value culture and the requisite components, the workplace culture can galvanize the staff.[123]

But let's digress. Perhaps a brief discussion on how data and evidence influence culture. Maybe leaders should consider the role of commonsense and anecdotal evidence. Lest we forget that **medicine is a world of gray**...

Practicing medicine is very fluid and data is constantly changing. Many situations arise that do not fit an algorithm, nor have supporting data prior to a decision being required. This happens regularly as a family physician and throughout healthcare. Data is important, but often only part of the story. Take for example the diabetic whose hemoglobin A1C (a measure of glycemic control) is elevated because they could no longer afford their medication. That skewed data point clearly has been impacted by a financial component.

Data should be a tool for further questioning, process improvement, quality improvement, and cost savings. Data should not be a shield to hide behind the status quo. Nor should data be manipulated or twisted to serve the myopic view of profits. Data should be used to align incentives. Data should be used to facilitate a culture that embraces Our Quadruple Aim.

What about evidence? I would like to review an article that appeared in *The British Medical Journal* (BMJ), "Parachute use to prevent death and major trauma when jumping from an aircraft: Randomized controlled trial."[124] This is an important pivot when discussing culture. Why? There will be many cultural issues that do not have a black and white solution. A randomized controlled trial is unlikely to exist for the exact cultural crisis a particular organization is experiencing. And maybe the available evidence doesn't add up—so don't jump to conclusions. Evidence should support cultural transformation, but anecdotal evidence and commonsense should also be considered when discussing solutions.

The parachute trial in *BMJ* was a clever randomized trial intended to be humorous and thought-provoking (regarding evidence-based medicine). The authors note, "Our groundbreaking study found no statistically significant difference in the primary outcome between the treatment and control arms. Our findings should give momentary pause to experts who advocate for routine use of parachutes for jumps from aircraft in recreational or military settings." And they acknowledge the study's limitations, "First and most importantly, our findings might not be generalizable to the use of parachutes in aircraft traveling at a higher altitude or velocity."[125]

I am a huge proponent of evidence-based medicine. But I am also a huge proponent of commonsense. This trial is well-designed, but if you only extrapolated the title there is potential for disaster. Hopefully logic and commonsense prevail while using parachutes. The article is fantastic; I laugh every time I read it. I would encourage those with further interest to read the complete article before taking a leap of faith. The authors conclude:

> *"Parachute use compared with a backpack control did not reduce death or major traumatic injury when used by participants jumping from aircraft in this first randomized evaluation of the intervention. This largely resulted from our ability to only recruit participants jumping from stationary aircraft on the ground." The article continues, "Therefore, although we can confidently recommend that individuals jumping from small stationary aircraft on the ground do not require parachutes, individual judgment should be exercised when applying these findings at higher altitudes."*[126]

Brilliant. As a staunch believer in OQA, I believe if your culture emulates these four principles, you can thrive in healthcare. But don't just blindly jump from the airplane. Do your due diligence. Survey your caregivers and patients, ask their opinion. Maybe hire a consultant or visit a successful organization. Have the courage to suggest or even lead cultural transformation. But if your status quo isn't working, what do you have to lose with aligning your culture to Our Quadruple Aim?

((EMR – ELECTRONIC MEDICAL RECORD))

"...a physician sitting at a computer performing the clerical task of data entry and note-taking is a low-value use of a high-dollar resource."

– JILL JIN, M.D. et al.[127]

Imagine a pilot having a completely different instrument panel every few years. Or perhaps a CEO having to learn a new language to present to the board? How would an executive chef feel about documenting the intricacies of every entree they prepare, as they cook? What about a Formula One driver documenting the engine performance while driving the car? Yet physicians and other providers are expected to document every nuance of every interaction while they are seeing patients. I have heard countless stories of patients recounting, "The doctor never even looked at me." It is a myth that a physician has to be the provider that documents every aspect of an office note.

Certainly there are components of the EMR that improve patient care, and data capture is tremendous. The ability to review information on a patient is amazing (if you can find it). Radiographs are at the tips of your fingers and viewed almost anywhere. Long gone are the days of medical students tracking down a hard copy of an X-ray. But EMRs have brought along many challenges, leading to many inefficiencies and waste. The toll on physicians has been prodigious as evidenced by burnout, early retirement, moral injury, and suicide. In order for EMRs to help achieve Our Quadruple Aim, they must improve. The pendulum must shift towards those whom EMRs are intended to serve: patients and providers.

EMRs must become a user-friendly, streamlined device that improves patient care.

In my career I have endured learning five different EMRs. I had such disdain for the EMR in residency that I chose to work at the clinic utilizing paper charts. Each system has its pros and cons. I suppose they are a necessary evil, and they certainly are here to stay. But change is inevitable and desperately needed. Documentation and data gathering needs to be patient-centric and provider-friendly. It needs to be streamlined to capture the essence of the interaction, rather than a bullet-proof document.

Chart bloat has become a major issue, and documentation requirements continue to grow. Chart bloat results from overly verbose notes for a myriad of reasons, including: copying, pasting, and over-documentation, and copying, pasting, and over-documentation. Routinely I have seen notes five to 10 pages long for a common cold. Regurgitating data embedded in a patient's chart occurs for many reasons—billing and insurance to name a few. Current estimates are 6,000 characters for notes in the U.S. By comparison, specialists outside the U.S. average 1,200 characters. [128]

Fortunately, recent billing and coding guidelines have acquiesced to advocacy groups working toward reducing regulatory requirements for less meaningful work. Changes in 2019 allow for documentation by other clinical team members (MAs or nurses) and non-clinical team members (i.e., scribes, students, patients); and 2021 changes allow for coding to be based on medical decision-making or time. Both of these changes have allowed proactive providers to be more efficient with their documentation and workflow. The AMA nicely highlights these changes in their toolkit: *Simplified Outpatient Documentation and Coding*.[129] I would highly encourage providers to review this article to reduce their amount of documentation and incorporate a team-based approach.

There is no magic to improve one's efficiency with EMRs. The inherent tedious nature of EMR utilization has taken its toll not only on provider wellness, but also detracts from the real work of providing care for patients. Many of my colleagues have joked that we are treating the computer, not the patient.

Early in my practice I committed to finish charting immediately after seeing a patient. This requires commitment, particularly when running behind. However, when combined with team-based documentation, diligence toward this endeavor can eliminate pajama time. Areas of opportunity are bountiful, and a deep dive could encapsulate an entire novel. Rather, I will impart some tips, ideas, and a few key skills I have honed over the years to improve my efficiency and well-being.

"I did a calculation, and we are still writing the equivalent of War and Peace *every 9 months."*

– SAM BUTLER, EPIC CHIEF MEDICAL OFFICER (CMO)[130]

1. Allow patients to document prior to the visit.

Many EMRs will allow for patients to complete certain components of the visit prior to being seen. The Review of Systems and History of Present Illness are staples of an office note that many patients can complete. This creates a fantastic starting point for the provider that can be tweaked or edited as required. Initially, I had some trepidation for this change, but it facilitates the visit and improves efficiency. What about aligning incentives even further? Perhaps a discount on the patient's bill if they complete questions prior to their appointment?

2. Allow staff to document.

Within the scope of their practice, MAs, nurses, and other medical staff should be documenting. Providers can easily review and make appropriate edits. A few examples: nurses calling to prepare charts for a Medicare Annual Wellness visit or MAs documenting medications, refills needed, chief complaints, and a basic History of Present Illness. By allowing team documentation, the note can organically grow as the visit evolves—allowing the provider to think, make decisions, edit, and document their thought process.

3. Don't write essays.

Recently I reviewed a 17-page note, a follow-up visit from back surgery. The amount of superfluous information was overwhelming. I had to scroll to find one key sentence, "The patient was healing well from surgery without complications." Why did it take 17 pages? Clerical burdens can be overwhelming and physicians' ingrained work ethic has perpetuated the problem. Instead of verbose dissertations, clinicians should try the less is more approach. Focus on capturing salient points, and reference key studies that were ordered or reviewed. Use abbreviations, key phrases, templates, short sentences, and don't sweat the punctuation. I am not suggesting cutting corners—I am imploring my colleagues to spend their valuable time correctly. Below are a few examples.

Verbose Dissertations	Salient Points
Copying and pasting an entire normal MRI report into a note.	MRI normal
The patient has been to the urgent care three times in the past year for ear infections. Each infection has been treated with antibiotics. One time was keflex, another amoxicillin, and the third was azithromycin. Grandmother took the child in for two of the visits and the mother a third, Mom is wondering about an Ears, Nose, and Throat doctor referral.	Repeat otitis x 3, resolved on abx via UC, ? ENT per mom

4. Start the note before you walk into the room.

While reviewing a patient's chart prior to a visit I will add an appropriate template. This creates a starting point with normative values, reducing time-consuming free texting. For example, prior to a diabetic visit I will add my diabetic template—and make adjustments as needed. The time spent creating templates is invaluable. Talk with your colleagues, borrow the best templates, and use them. Learn your EMR by collaborating with super users or local champions. As recommendations or practice style changes, spend the time to adjust your templates and charting behavior. If you know you will be discussing certain diagnoses during the visit, add them to the assessment prior to entering the exam room. This small amount of work (pre-visit) allows for increased eye contact and a better rapport. Staring at a screen is far from what medicine was intended to be.

5. Chart during the visit.

This is perhaps the most arduous task for many of my colleagues. I am a vestige of the era where a typing class was not mandatory in high school. "Old and cold," so say my children. Typing proficiency is a must for effective EMR utilization. For those who are not strong typers, I would encourage you to work on this. Take a class, practice. Perhaps there is a CME course that includes typing, if not, there should be.

Assuming you have done some component of pre-charting, this will allow you to spend precious time talking and listening to the patient. After all, this is what we went to medical school for. Look up, be engaged! But spend a few moments to document during the interaction as well. Your History of Present Illness and Review of Systems should certainly be complete prior to walking out of the room, perhaps some diagnosis as well. And, tell patients what you are doing when documenting or looking for a diagnostic study—transparency is rarely not appreciated.

#6 and #7 are intended to be a humorous

6. Don't regurgitate.

See number three above (example of chart bloat).

7. Salient points.

See number three above.

Improved EMR efficiency goes beyond an individual's skill set, and workflow solutions should incorporate other key stakeholders as well. Clinical leaders, physician champions, IT, billing and coding, nursing, and the compliance officer all play their part in successful, efficient utilization of an EMR. Time should be set aside and staff compensated for EMR and billing and coding education that includes live support. Mass emails and mandated after-hours training are less than ideal.[131]

During my career, I have invited many administrative leaders to shadow me for a day in the office, and only one CEO accepted. I think all administrators should shadow their providers to see how the day-to-day operations within an EMR work, or better yet, have them document for part of a day. Many will be shocked, perhaps even appalled. We must remember two key components of Our Quadruple Aim regarding EMR use—Patient Experience and Provider Wellness. If those components are forgotten when implementing, utilizing, or updating an EMR—no one wins.

((THE DAY THE MUSIC DIED))

"Control your own destiny or someone else will."

– JACK WELCH

Tuesday, August 2nd, 2022

Listening is arguably one of my greatest strengths as a physician. Encouraging patients to open up about their hopes and dreams, fears and concerns. A probing question can often lead to the correct diagnosis. In the harried chaos that exists in healthcare, this valuable tool is often forgotten. Today, I needed to restrain my emotions and just listen.

My clinic is a dream scenario; busy providers, enthusiastic staff, and satisfied patients. Three brand new NPs have honed their trade and their confidence grows with each passing day, with solid decision-making and practicing good medicine. I am extremely proud of them. And the staff genuinely cares for one another. The collegiality shows, and patients are energized by it. It's no wonder we have outgrown our space and currently do not have enough exam rooms. But six exam rooms for four providers sufficed for two years.

I walked into a meeting regarding facilities, coffee cup in hand. *Careful or you will end up in my novel*—written on the side of the cup. After being asked if those words were a warning, pleasantries were exchanged, and I sat down. I listened as two upper-level executives explained why they were moving the clinic—back to the town where I experienced burnout. (I still struggle with those emotions.) Of course the explanation was sugar-coated, but the reality is, finances were the primary driver. I was even quoted a number of theoretical savings. Even worse, this transition is supposed to occur in three months. I was seething during the meeting, but maintained my cool and said very little. Perhaps it is a blessing, and maybe a new beginning. I was speechless. Numb. I suppose my coffee cup was a warning.

I poured my heart and soul into making our clinic a success—and it is. But of course finances trump people, patients, and caregivers. A seemingly brilliant financial decision from on high will have many repercussions. The boulder thrown into the pond will affect many. But when I saw the pain in my wife's eyes—I struggled to even consider returning to a toxic environment. For nearly 13 years I gave everything I had to my profession—still it was never enough. My wife and I both shed tears today—the day the music died.

((LEAD BY EXAMPLE))

On Wednesday, August 3rd, 2022 I emailed my formal resignation. The morning after the day the music died. After 13 years of treating patients with my current employer, I decided to step away. Some may consider this a rash decision, but I beg to differ. For over a year I had been transparent on my plans to work part-time. I had been discussing this regularly with patients to help them transition, and my staff was well aware. I had informed my employer and pleaded with them to work on a succession plan. I wonder if I was ever taken seriously. Ultimately, the proverbial piece of straw that broke the camel's back was placed. I was done.

In the months that followed, I did my very best to ensure a smooth transition for patients. I went out of my way to contact my colleagues and facilitate the process. I wish I could say the transition was well supported, but instead our office routinely had fewer MAs than providers. Some even made the case I was vilified—becoming the target of frustration and anger because I took a stand. I took a stand for what I felt was right. I took a stand for my colleagues. I took a stand for my family. I took a stand for Our Quadruple Aim. I am not a chess piece to be moved around at will. I am a person who dedicated 11 years of my life in school to help others.

It was during those last few months I realized I was being called to something else in healthcare. Writing this book? Perhaps. Ultimately, I feel there will be many challenges and opportunities ahead to help others. Who knows what doors may open? Every ending is another beginning.

I debated writing this section for several reasons. Predominantly, would my words be used against me? Would I be portrayed as burning bridges or selfish? Blacklisted? Ignored? Would legal action be taken? I suppose that speaks to a culture of fear, rather than embracing Our Quadruple Aim. I even asked Joshua what he thought. He responded with very thought provoking comments and some questions that follow. I will give some brief retorts, but much of what Joshua wrote is rhetorical. My responses are preceded by TRO. Frankly, the transparency is refreshing.

((THINKING PARTNER))

Joshua J. Judy – Patient:

1. Your resignation to me seems like the ultimate culmination of everything wrong with the system—how everything is viewed via $$ rather than doing the right thing. Where is the humanity, in a system that is supposed to care about humans? Once again, who ends up being last in the 'pecking order'? It needs to be flipped.

2. It's part of your journey and kind of reflective of another step of your burnout—there's another part of your story earlier that asks what makes a 45-year-old doctor consider retirement—direct tie here. Seems like a major 'ripple in the pond.'

3. You're going to be free soon—do you feel it burns any bridges? Less risk of offending now that you'll be outside the system? Or are you concerned with future ramifications? i.e., if getting back into medicine later?

   TRO: I am sure I burned a few bridges with my honesty. It is unfortunate that others feel the need to have a certain narrative. For me, it is all about caring and advocating for patients and providers.

4. If you don't write it, will you regret holding back? You can always draft it now to get things off your chest, delete later if it ends up feeling wrong prior to publication.

   TRO: Ah, the catharsis of writing. I believe my integrity stands for itself. Hopefully others can learn from this process.

5. By sharing, will you help other doctors facing similar feelings or how to weigh their own situations? Do you see yourself becoming a voice or spokesperson for others? I know with *Losing the Blueprint (LTB)*, I have a feeling I'm going to end up there myself eventually.... Will it help drive the changes you want to see?

   TRO: Not sure yet, lots of opportunities to help others and our current state of healthcare.

6. You implemented Our Quadruple Aim in practice, of which the book itself was originally titled—a real life success story—despite that, decision makers still drove you away. Seems like a way to counteract their obliviousness (obtuse—is it deliberate?) or narrow viewpoints, and why the system continues to decay.

Shortly after the music died, I proposed these questions to Dr. Otten. And answers came rather swiftly. It was telling. I know his decision to resign wasn't taken lightly given its impact on many people. That felt like an obvious answer to a question I never bothered asking him: Did you decide too hastily? I didn't have to bother. The years of thoughtful care I received as a patient, one of his many, told me of course not. How he chooses to share this part of his story is ultimately his. Still, I appreciated being asked to help. To serve as a thinking partner is endearing.

((KEEPING IT REAL))

Sometimes, simply having someone outside of yourself ask the questions you've already considered, even subconsciously, helps cement positions. It doesn't mean it necessarily changes the outcome, but maybe makes coming to peace with them easier. A vote of confidence if you discover you're asking similar questions, or reaching the same conclusions independent of one another. It helps settle the dust. Puts things in their proper place. Once in place, you walk forward carrying less. And there's tremendous relief and value in that.

Should we do the right things only when expecting favors in return, or facing reprisal? Or do we strive to do things because they're the right thing to do? My mind drifts back to something one of my old bosses used to often say, "Just because you're paranoid doesn't mean they're not after you." He used to say it half-jokingly, but then again, half-seriously. And they say there's a grain of truth behind every joke. It speaks volumes if you find yourself in a culture of fear.

Dr. Otten had led by example. He made a point all along to do the right things for his patients. Good news or bad, he was transparent with them. He called me when he decided to resign. He shared he wanted to make sure I heard it from him, not someone else. That openness translates to this book. If he hadn't, maybe offering my views would have been harder. It wasn't. Instead, the questions largely answer themselves.

So, it should be no surprise—Our Quadruple Aim is built on transparency. Against that backdrop, our dream is that this project creates a thriving, open-minded community. One that offers things like partnership and mentorship, among other benefits. If you're an American healthcare consumer, we're speaking to you.

((16))

Role Reversal Cont.

Joshua J. Judy – Patient:

((THERE ARE NO ABSOLUTES))

Every night after work, the first thing I would do is slump onto the couch in the living room and fall asleep. If dinner was missed, it was missed. If I barely had the energy left to brush my teeth, I would hear about it from my dentist. I can only imagine the important family moments I missed, time unrecoverable. Would I own this problem or would it own me?

Still empowered by my figurative white coat, nothing was off the table. If you know where to look, it's amazing what you can get without a doctor's orders (and outside the choking grip of the "unseen hand" of insurance). I found a lab to measure neurotransmitters based on a urine sample (containing byproducts of the neurotransmitters after the body processes them). This lab came in a kit via mail with specific pre-test instructions. Cheese and bananas had to go, as they could affect the results (you are what you eat). It was April 19, 2020 and I was 38 years old.

Neurotransmitter Test Results
Joshua J. Judy, Patient (at age 38)

Analyte	Result	Unit per Creatinine	L	WRI	H	Reference Interval
Serotonin	53.2	µg/g				50–98
Dopamine	107	µg/g				110–200
Norepinephrine	15.0	µg/g				18–42
Epinephrine	0.6	µg/g				1.3–7.3
Norepinephrine / Epinephrine ratio	25.0					<13
Glutamate	12	µmol/g				9.0–40.0
Gamma-aminobutyrate (GABA)	4.4	µmol/g				1.6–3.5
Glycine	1194	µmol/g				350–1500
Histamine	9.9	µg/g				12–30
Phenethylamine (PEA)	25	nmol/g				26–70
Creatinine	178	mg/dL				35–240

What do you see when you look at the chart above—nothing, or everything? How odd for so many of my major neurotransmitter metabolites (serotonin, dopamine, norepinephrine and phenethylamine) to be so low–and GABA high. I wondered to myself if I was looking into a window of my future self, where Parkinson's and dementia were possible, or arriving early. Somewhere in that porridge of unbalanced molecules was supposed to be love for my family, laughs, sadness, elation–lost to a robotic existence.

I didn't know if the test results were precise. Plausible–absolutely, but there's no simple way of measuring neurotransmitters in the brain. Unlike Megan's case or Melcangi's study, a doctor wouldn't be seeking a spinal tap for a more direct look. In my hand was a proxy (at best). Hormones are similar–with blood serum tests stand-ins for measuring activity at the cellular level. In a later conversation with Dr. Saya, he offered, "**When it comes to hormones, there are no absolutes.** Everybody is different where they feel best. I hope to be in medicine long enough to see that next step, which is to see what is happening at the cellular or receptor level." The pioneering doctor meant that blood serum levels only tell part of the story. Dr. Otten's poem says it all: **Medicine is a world of gray.**

((IT HAS A NAME))

While I literally had hundreds of hours of research under my belt, I fortuitously came across the following recent write-up available at the National Institute of Health, "What I have learnt from helping thousands of people taper off antidepressants and other psychotropic medications" by Adele Framer, published online March 16, 2021.[132] When my journey started, no single writing I knew of existed that so precisely conveyed much of my travails. After all these years, there it was in words. Finally, a fitting name: **Protracted Antidepressant Withdrawal Syndrome (PWS).**

Here was a woman who had endured 11 years—*yes, 11 years*—of PWS herself after coming off paroxetine and started a community called SurvivingAntidepressants.org. Astounding! Not only was it the same antidepressant in Melcangi's study, but I wasn't alone in my toils, not in the least. There were many others—with nearly the same outcomes. Some cases were approaching 20 years, and counting.

Despite documented cases, data is lacking. Highlighting this point is an article Dr. Otten shared with me, "Protracted withdrawal syndrome after stopping antidepressants: A descriptive quantitative analysis of consumer narratives from a large internet forum."[133] Three points:

1. A detailed quantitative analysis of specific symptom manifestations in antidepressant PWS is still lacking.
2. Can be severe and long-lasting, and its manifestations clinically heterogeneous (meaning differences in patient characteristics such as age, dose, dosing frequency, etc.).
3. Long-term antidepressant exposure may cause multiple body system impairments.[134]

According to an article in *Medical News Today* titled, "Understanding anhedonia: What happens in the brain?" anhedonia is the inability to feel pleasure during pleasure activities.[135] Mayo Clinic offers, "depersonalization occurs when you persistently or repeatedly have the feeling that you're observing yourself from outside your body or you have a sense that things around you aren't real, or both."[136] Once Megan and I discovered the right words to describe our internal states, we realized both depersonalization and anhedonia captured the spell she feels under on levetiracetam—especially during her first year on it. Anhedonia appropriately described mine under duloxetine. Simply, both states deliver the sense of being buried alive.

The PWS name was encompassing and I felt some justice. Not only did the moniker represent protracted sexual dysfunction known among sufferers as Post-SSRI/SNRI Sexual Dysfunction (PSSD)—despite dosage reduction or upon drug discontinuation—it described many other ruinous effects. Utter dread, numbness, anhedonia and depersonalization. I read Ms. Framer's publication in outright amazement, my reflection staring back. Ms. Framer writes:

> *"Off paroxetine, I initially experienced hypomania, sweating, and electrical-feeling 'brain zaps', the last continuing for 7months. After several weeks, my acute withdrawal symptom pattern changed to other odd symptoms, among them disorientation, depersonalization, insomnia, light and heat intolerance, indigestion, palpitations, and unease, punctuated by spontaneous weeping spells, attacks of sheer terror, or sudden plunges into unprecedented contentless black holes of pure dread. I felt a vacuum of positive emotion as well as genital anesthesia (post-SSRI sexual dysfunction or PSSD), which took several years to resolve. I had never felt anything like this before. It did not feel like [a] 'relapse'. I spent hours hunting for journal articles about antidepressant withdrawal syndrome."*[137]

For the first six months off duloxetine, I experienced troubling brain zaps. I would be walking in a store or down the hall at work and feel these random electrical shocks in my head. I experienced the "countless black holes of pure dread" and "a vacuum of positive emotion and genital anesthesia." Also, erectile dysfunction, the latter of which persists to this day. I understood too well the lamentable pastime of hunting for journal articles.

Later, I experienced cold intolerance, terror attacks, and palpitations among other troubles due to acquired thyroid dysfunction (and being prescribed the wrong thyroid replacement dosages) as my endocrine system further weakened and prematurely aged. More on that ahead.

Poking into one's neurotransmission system should never be taken lightly. These drugs may aptly push on buttons never designed to be pushed on blindly or inhospitably. Yet, we regularly do it with impunity and without the ability to baseline. No reliable prediction of the influence on far-reaching systems. To a large degree, I believe the neurotransmission system is designed by a higher power. I believe it governs the most fundamental levels of our humanity, and thus should carry a commensurate level of reverence. It's essential to the human experience. Hence, I refer to neurotransmitters as the 'God molecules.'

This shouldn't go unmentioned—paroxetine is the same SSRI that harmed Ms. Framer and that Professor Melcangi used in his animal to show persistent alterations in brain neurosteroid levels. Stands judgment that because of their similar mechanisms, various SSRIs or SNRIs can and do produce similar outcomes.

And what can make PWS or Megan's levetiracetam experience so incredibly vicious, so detrimental, is that for once a baseline *does* exist—**your original self.** It's that old blueprint, before the medication's effects. You know what you should feel like; despite your innermost wishes, that place dwells—just out of reach. Each day you get further away from that person, the memories and schematics fade by and by.

((LIAR LIAR PANTS ON FIRE))

Exactly five years after taking my first pill of duloxetine, on March 27, 2019, I started testosterone replacement therapy (commonly called TRT). Thyroid hormone supplementation would shortly follow.

Understand, your body is the world's most advanced flight control system—directing biochemical signals day and night to the right places. One subset of that system is the Hypothalamus Pituitary Gonadal Axis (HPG). It's responsible for controlling many of the body's hormones like testosterone–mine was clearly jacked.

I had settled on a men's clinic that specializes in hormone care and wellness. It was out of state so treatment would be via telemedicine. They were ahead of the COVID-19 pandemic in this sense, practicing what would become commonplace. Before the clinic would start me on testosterone replacement, I was required to take a baseline test–part of their standard approach to care. Below is my baseline before starting TRT for the first time, taken February 22, 2019.

Test Name	Result	Reference Range
Estradiol, Sensitive *(Sensitive is version for males)*	16.8	8.0 – 35.0 pg/mL
Progesterone	0.1	0.0 - 0.5 ng/mL
Sex Hormone Binding Globulin (SHBG)	22.6	16.5 – 55.9 nmol/L
Luteinizing Hormone (LH)	4.5	1.7 – 8.6 mIU/mL

Follicle Stimulating Hormone (FSH)	4.4	1.5 – 12.4 mIU/mL
Testosterone, Total	363.3	264.0 – 916.0 ng/dL

The above results provided a look into my body's weakening HPG; actually, quite pitiful. Notice the wide range for total testosterone of 264.0–916.0 ng/dL. The closer you approach the bottom of the range, expect men to complain and begin to present hypogonadal symptoms. 363.3 ng/dL at my age was nothing to write home about. Mind you, I was still on duloxetine at 60 mg.

By December 2020, I woefully 'tipped the scales' with a total testosterone value of 250 ng/dL and a free testosterone level in the bottom quartile of 7.75 ng/dL, but I'm getting ahead of myself. For context, it's helpful to know average total testosterone ranges by age (note, these are just averages with variances among men abound):

Age	Total Testosterone (ng/dL)
25 – 34	616
35 – 44	667
45 – 54	606
55 – 64	562
65 – 74	523
75 – 84	470
85 – 100	376

138, 139

At my initial baseline of 363.3 ng/dL, I was giving 80-year-old men everywhere a strong run for their money. Later at 250 ng/dL, I was hanging out with the centenarians. No wonder something as pedestrian as tying my shoes felt insurmountable. For my foray into hormones, I was given a starting protocol of 100 mg a week of testosterone cypionate, injected (this is a common starting dose and subsequently adjusted). Some men need a little more and some need less, like me.

In about two weeks, I noticed my body responding. For the first time in a long time, I had increased energy levels. My motivation lifted. This early and robust response, that many men try to continue chasing, is called the 'honeymoon' period of TRT. But that doesn't last forever and tapers off as your body hits the brakes (downregulates).

I've been on several modified protocols since, due to the dosages being too high or too low, thickened blood, not feeling well with mood swings, fatigue, brain fog, consistently low DHT levels, or a host of other symptoms. TRT is not a panacea. The late marketing personality Ron Popeil became known for the phrase "Set it, and forget it!"—TRT is not this. It takes a considerable amount of dedication, and is often a life-long treatment because many men's own hormonal production, once weakened, doesn't come back online (see Chapter 19, The Sack). Many trials later, I've found a multipart, workable protocol (beyond injections alone). There's a lot behind it–If you want to discuss details, please feel free to contact me (ourquadrupleaim.com).

Every time you make a protocol adjustment, you typically need to give your body six-eight weeks to readjust, if not longer. It's a long slog before you even have a clue that the protocol moved you in a better direction or write it off as failure and retry. People will struggle having that kind of patience. Roadblocks and unhelpful characters abound.

Before finding my current TRT doctor, Dr. Saya, I remember a particular encounter with a pair of endocrinologists. One, responsible for solely treating my thyroid, barked, "You can't inject testosterone more than once a week!" because I would get an infection. I let them go on. But when it was my turn, "So how do diabetes patients inject insulin multiple times a day using the same needles I am when I only inject three times a week?" Sidestepping my question, I was told I would have other adverse reactions like blood clots. I was also told there's no way my testosterone levels could be at the higher levels they were at the dosage I was on. That it had to be a lab error (then, my dosage was 70 mg a week total by injection only).

Initially, this seemed a passable statement but wouldn't hold water long. At this early stage on TRT, I admit my levels were running on the elevated end. But, not for the reasons hinted at. They continued, "You have to be careful about seeing a naturopath." Instead of asking, they led with that assumption. This looked disparaging since Dr. Saya is a medical doctor, which I assured them. I too was fully aware that more is not always better when it comes to hormones.

The second endocrinologist leaned in, "If your testosterone values come in high again, I can't work with you." His partner rather capriciously added in a subsequent visit, "You really should try to get to the low end of normal." In no part of the conversation was I asked, "How do you feel, or how are your symptoms?" I shot back, "Why? I feel like shit there. Am I supposed to?" I was met with silence.

Annoyed. I guess to him, the most important aspect was treating a number and not the patient. His apparent concern was that my hematocrit values, while in range, were borderline high. I reassured them, Dr. Saya was monitoring that. Nonetheless, I modestly lowered my dosage. I retested and came in with a total testosterone in the mid-400s. I'm unsure what was accomplished except more bullshit, and box-checking.

That in mind, Dr. Otten educated me that in medical school, a resident had a term—euboxic, defined as having certain tests within normal ranges. They would teach, "Make sure you get the patient in normal range." It makes perfect sense. The best residents would correlate the test with the clinical picture.

But nowhere in there is a directive to optimize the patient for their body's needs. Testosterone reference ranges are broad, and encompass the entire population at various ages—young, old, sick, and healthy. Why else would a lab's reference range go from the 200s to 1000 ng/dL, and if you fall anywhere on that continuum, you're allowed to skate. A level of 400 ng/dL, while in range, might suffice for a 50 or 60-year-old man. Why suggest that target for one in his 30s who's still symptomatic?

The same can be said for treatment plans in general. I believe optimization separates good to great care from just adequate or less. Are you still feeling symptoms? What about your quality of life? In my opinion, these are must-ask questions—I repeat, treat not only the numbers but the patient.

If nobody is asking these questions, everyone needs to go home and start over. Then, not only ask the questions, but listen to the answers.

Given the insinuation about my earlier relatively higher testosterone values, I investigated how replacement dosages stacked up against those who are labeled 'juicers' in the bodybuilding community. I wanted to know what most providers would consider abuse. At least it would satisfy my curiosity.[140]

While available information is vague and anecdotal, a bodybuilder might inject roughly 500 mg weekly during competition season and 200 mg to 250 mg weekly in the off-season. The 500 mg per week may effortlessly put their total testosterone over 3000 ng/dL (supraphysiological)—a level no human can achieve without cheating, lab error, or a hormone secreting tumor. This on/off cycling—high doses followed by backing off—is called 'blasting and cruising.' There are tall-tale signs. Ungodly vascularity (where the veins themselves look like they lift weights), water weight or bloat, muscles on top of muscles bulging where you didn't know they could even exist. My curiosity fulfilled, I had read enough: I wasn't anywhere near these levels.

By contrast, 1000 to 1200 ng/dL approaches the body's natural biological limit. Based on the endocrinologists' viewpoints, I wondered to myself if they had run into trouble with other patients who had abused hormones by taking mega doses. Testosterone is a controlled substance. Had they been burned before?

I had no way of knowing definitively. All I could do was educate and advocate.

I later relayed my endocrinologist encounters with Dr. Saya. Rather than imply something unbecoming, he constructively offered his thoughts about possible causes of thicker blood (high hematocrit):

1. You don't smoke, which can cause thicker blood.
2. You don't live at high elevation, which can cause thicker blood.
3. After you lowered your dosage, your testosterone levels at your last test were in the mid-400s. That's not concerningly high but your hematocrit, while in range, remained elevated.
4. You mentioned you snore.
5. How about seeing if your primary care doctor could order a sleep study? (Which later showed sleep apnea. See Chapter 17, "The Unseen Hand".)

In contrast, during those early days of my toils, information often wasn't presented so convincingly. Some bordered on absurd or laughable. There are men out there who have been on TRT for at least two or three decades, in their 50s, 60s, and 70s with highly improved quality of life. That means a lot of needles, creams, gels, and adjustments along the way. I hope it is under the thorough and competent monitoring of a skilled and experienced provider.

Because of hormone replacement, I enjoy occasional 'windows.' Levothyroxine (thyroid hormone) and two modes of testosterone application (injections and cream) are able to fiddle with neurotransmission, possibly neurosteroids, enough to momentarily 'flick the circuits just right.' In these moments, I find partial equipoise in my body. It's known that hormones have a direct impact on neurotransmitter production, and it's something Dr. Saya and I have discussed. For example, independent of its anabolic muscle building effects, testosterone has the ability to act on the serotonin system.[141]

Today, without supporting hormones, and five years of ongoing healing, this partial thaw would be a pipe dream. My body simply can't or won't do some things on its own anymore. My body never fully re-sensitized after duloxetine. Do I respond to hormones as effectively as before duloxetine? In short–no. Is there some inner cellular resistance to the hormones? Perhaps. I have no way of knowing other than to say, I'm changed—going from over-firing to under-firing.

Of course, some part of the equation is age progression, which nobody escapes. How much exactly remains unmeasurable, but it's far from explaining everything away. I have my moments, some moderately good ones even. But answers remained elusive. At one consultation with Dr. Saya, I asked, "May I have my androgen sensitivity genetically tested?"

"I may not be able to interpret the results, but if you can find me a lab, I'll help with the paperwork. I'd be curious to see the process myself."

Refreshing, it was Dr. Saya's way of saying *I don't know (but am willing to try)*. His curiosity met with mine, and in early July 2021, I tested two genes for androgen insensitivity: my androgen receptors (AR) and 5-AR, responsible for converting testosterone to DHT. No genetic abnormalities were found:

RESULT: NEGATIVE

About this test

This diagnostic test evaluates 2 gene(s) for variants (genetic changes) that are associated with genetic disorders. Diagnostic genetic testing, when combined with family history and other medical results, may provide information to clarify individual risk, support a clinical diagnosis, and assist with the development of a personalized treatment and management strategy.

Next steps

- This test did not identify any pathogenic variants known to cause disease. This result should be discussed with a healthcare provider, such as a genetic counselor, to learn about the appropriate next steps for further evaluation. Clinical follow up may still be warranted. This result should be interpreted within the context of additional laboratory results, family history and clinical findings.

Seemingly, another dead end but not a loss. I had taken a brave step to all but eliminate the impossible, leaving behind a truth.

TL;DR—lessons for OQA:

To Patients: Dead ends, at times you'll have them. But it's another data point. Take the knowledge you gain from what something is not as a step closer to knowing what something is (or could be).

((CELEBRATE THE SMALL WINS))

In my spreadsheet journal, I recently rediscovered a note captured from an office visit prior to fully coming off duloxetine later that year. It's dated May 30, 2019:

> DR. OTTEN: *Did not agree with Wellbutrin right away due to mixing too many things. Later said maybe it's not a bad idea, but wants to see how I do simply by cutting from 60 mg of duloxetine to 30 mg for a month and then decide.*
>
> ME: *Brought articles. He took them to read so we can get on the same page by next visit. Before leaving, he asked, "no libido with testosterone, really?" Confirmed, no. Said I think it is brain/dopamine related (pointed to my head and said I think it's in here).*

We had been considering dopaminergic enhancing medications like bupropion hydrochloride as a possible option. Later, we would trial a low dose immediate release amphetamine/ dextroamphetamine salts. In people with Attention Deficit Hyperactive Disorder (ADHD), stimulants like amphetamine/ dextroamphetamine salts calm them—or in some cases, overly downregulate them. Some people even call it legalized speed (why it's a Schedule II controlled drug). In people who do not have ADHD, it provisionally amps them up, causing neurons to release some of the dopamine the cells have stored away.

The trial lasted about three to four weeks. Yes, I would perk up after taking a pill. I guess I could finally appreciate why some college students tried it when cramming. This was a notch above my own coffee or Mountain Dew study habits. But it felt unnatural, followed by an unpleasant lull four hours later. I couldn't stick with the yo-yoing effect. Longer-term, I don't think it would have been healthy—all that central nervous system tinkering and here mine was, already pissed off. The system's 'overclocking' effect would find a way to catch up, and my cardiovascular system probably silently thanked me. Still worthwhile because it was eliminated from the 'what-if' list.

On the last point in my May 30, 2019 note, what I had relayed unfortunately held. Not even the almighty androgen, testosterone, the hormone that many rudimentarily equate to all things masculine, could fully conquer the grasp of these stubbornly altered conditions. Far more complicated than a single variable. There's incredible interplay and all components require a delicate equilibrium. Balance. Simple restoration of one item doesn't always restore the system. During this time, I had two doctors who were open-mindedly listening and working with me. More restorative than any chemical, partnerships like these heal.

((N=1))

One day in November 2022, I opened my inbox. Awaiting me was an email forwarded from Dr. Otten with the subject line "Fwd: Antidepressant Discontinuation Syndrome- Updated treatment guide." He had never sent me anything from his work email. Sensing importance, I scrolled until I saw a link.

Had I not been down enough rabbit holes? Clicking, I found myself staring at a database for clinicians. I skimmed over some parts with familiarity while other sections reinforced my understanding–until the words leapt off the screen:

> *"Long-term use of reuptake inhibitors ---> down-regulation of postsynaptic receptors. [Downregulation: A decrease in the number of receptors on the surface of target cells, making the cells less sensitive to a hormone or another agent.]"*[142]

I read it again, my mind hanging on the phrase: *Making cells less sensitive to a hormone*. The one word, if given only one, to describe my body's behavior. **Reluctant.** My body seems to resist inducing proper hormonal signaling. I relinquished my white coat back to Dr. Otten. He was *my* huckleberry now. In the end, the thing that mattered the most—grace—had triumphed over dismissiveness.

TL;DR—lessons for OQA:

Patients, just know, you'll always be battling wildly different opinions. Keep arming yourself with the latest information to educate yourself and others.

If others have no interest in expanding their paradigms or narrowed views, don't let it stop you from growing.

Everyone, let's please aim to start talking to, and not down to each other. When up to the task, we become each others' huckleberries.

((17))

"The Unseen Hand"

Joshua J. Judy – Patient:

It was time for my appointment. I packed a bag, said goodbye to Megan and my kids with hugs and kisses all around, and headed into the local hospital. It was time for my in-lab sleep study. It wasn't a foreign concept to me. I'd had sleep studies in the past, always with mixed or borderline results. In fact, it was an at-home study that paved the way for this in-person one. What *was* different this time was that I went in hoping for a definitive answer. Did I have sleep apnea or not? What else could explain my incessant snoring?

Sleep studies always seemed slightly paradoxical to me because sleeping away from home can be restless. To walk away with a borderline result again–or worse, empty handed–would be highly discouraging. What about all the equipment that would soon adorn my body? That would surely compound things. I remained on high alert knowing I was part of something bigger through the creation of this book.

Upon arriving, I checked in at registration. Everything was routine. I was asked to confirm my name, address, emergency contact, employer, and health insurance. There was one last question, "Do you want your doctor to get a copy of the report?" I had multiple doctors, so which one? I answered in the affirmative, but part of me thought the inquiry slightly odd. I followed-up with, "Doesn't the ordering doctor automatically get a copy anyway?" I was told, yes.

Maybe I wasn't presenting the right follow-up question. In turn, a better question from me would be, "Doesn't my primary care provider automatically get a copy (even if they're not the ordering doctor)?" Lots of what-ifs. If a specialist you were referred to ordered the sleep study, could your primary care doctor be left out of the loop? I imagine the more referrals that happened from specialist to specialist, communication only deteriorated.

Still, in what case would it make sense that your primary care doctor not be copied on results even if they weren't the ordering doctor? Aren't they responsible for your overall care? I ultimately figured saying yes to the receptionist was the best bet against another medical mystery. I could keep going but didn't. That was enough exploration down the rabbit hole—like I said, everything so far was routine. A few actual turns down the hall and I made my way to the sleep study. A woman was waiting for me. She introduced herself and verified my identity. I was told to change into my pajamas and leave the door open to flag her when I was ready.

For those who haven't had a sleep study before, it's an engrossing process. A lot of wires, as if fashioned from Frankenstein's laboratory, decorate your body and are hooked to nearby equipment. If you need to use the restroom during the night, you call the technician's name. They come and temporarily unhook you from the base machine so that you drape this bundle of wires over your neck. That leaves the electrodes fixed atop your head to avoid reapplying.

As my technician busily tended over me, skillfully routing cables, I felt like a construction job site. However, she made it comfortable and through the process, we chatted about our families. I relaxed a bit and shared that I hoped the study provided a conclusive answer. Meanwhile, in my mind echoed my primary care doctor's voice, **"medicine is a world of gray."**

"These electrodes will measure brainwaves and tell us if you're getting enough of the different stages of sleep. It's entrancing to watch the brainwaves of the elderly and children. I once had someone around 90-years-old come in and their brainwaves were very small and shallow." While sharing this, she made very slight up and down motions with her finger and exclaimed, "With children, they're really big and all over!" Her fingers dramatically wagged up and down, giving me pause. The explanation caused me to ruminate about Megan's epileptic condition.

The different waveforms between the young and old made sense, but I found it fascinating. After further introspection, I let my thoughts escape, "Kind of like a measurement of life, huh? I guess getting old is for the birds." Emitting a small chuckle, the technician agreed, "Yup, sure is." I felt melancholy and happy at the same time. The children in those studies radiated brightly. I assumed they had their entire lives ahead of them, while the elderly had faded to a dim glow.

If my oxygen saturation levels dropped to 80%, the technician said she'd come into the room and hook me to a CPAP that night! However, she didn't anticipate I was, "that bad." CPAP stands for continuous positive airway pressure, and a CPAP machine provides a constant level of pressure greater than atmospheric pressure for assisting with breathing.

One of the last pieces of equipment to be hooked up were the electrodes running down my legs to measure for restless leg syndrome. I asked, "Isn't that caused by dopamine issues in some individuals?" In my near endless wonder about all things medical, I recalled reading that several years earlier. She replied with a tinge of inquisitiveness in her voice, "You know, I'm not entirely sure what's behind the cause. Do you ever notice your legs jumping or twitching?" I replied that I didn't and my wife never indicated I did either. No unprovoked nighttime kicking from me–just gentle nudges from Megan to get off my back (I snore less on my sides).

It seemed like it took forever to fall asleep. I lay there in an unfamiliar room, draped in equipment. Before leaving me (the first time) my technician had adjusted the firmness of my bed to my liking. It was a nice option. She asked if I wanted a noise maker on. A small but thoughtful touch, I said yes, thanking her (we used one at home consistently). I was told she had to remove the comforter. It wasn't allowed but I could sleep with an extra blanket. "They just need to stop making the bed with it," she remarked. Her words uncovered another box being superfluously checked.

For at least the first 30 minutes, I tried to ignore the building urge I sensed. I thought I could outrace it by drifting off first. Nope, I had to pee. I had gone while changing into my pajamas but guess I had too much water earlier. I called out to my technician who arrived promptly and assisted in unhooking me. She left a second time so I could finish my business. Returning, she plugged me back in, and left for a third time.

In spite of a few hiccups, it was soon 5 a.m. The technician opened the door and wished me good morning all in one fell swoop. I was already stirring about 15 minutes earlier. Her equipment could 'see' that so she had stopped the recording to begin working on her report. Before leaving me alone to dress and clean up, my technician divulged in passing, "You know, with Medicare, Medicaid, Tri-county, and home studies, we're looking for a 4% oxygen desaturation otherwise we have to mark you negative for apnea. With commercial insurance or in-lab studies, it's 3% oxygen desaturation or if it causes arousal for you." She ever so marginally paused before continuing, "Some nights, it's maddening. Sometimes we're asked to re-score our reports."

Wait, did I hear that correctly? I was tired but coming to. Her disclosure jolted me. Was she saying that the patient's determination was essentially dependent upon the insurance plan, regardless of circumstances? Could I explain it away? Was

I overreading things? I didn't want to conflate what she said about being maddening with something else. Was the answer simply that the in-lab equipment was far more comprehensive and sensitive?

At first brush, maybe. If she instead said that they were looking for 4% oxygen desaturation with home studies and 3% in-lab, I wouldn't question it. That would be clean enough. She hadn't though. She had clearly placed different insurance plans into those two oxygen level groupings, with an additional qualifier of "arousal" for one of them. It was those plans, supposedly to a fair degree, that determined if the patient received a positive or negative result. The situation became muddled. Even so, I hoped my interpretation was wrong.

I asked, "Did you hear my snoring?"

"Yes, I marked you a three out of five," with five being the worst on the snoring scale.

Strangely, I registered satisfaction with that score. It was a shade of gray, but dark enough to stand out. I reflected on what she had said, *"some nights, it's maddening."* I knew listening to snoring all night had to be agitating, but there was more to what she meant. Apparently sensing my trepidation, she offered, "So, I looked up what you said last night. Yup, you were right. Restless legs can be caused by dopamine issues, heredity traits or medications," before adding, "The doctor will interpret the results but don't be surprised if he calls you back in to trial a CPAP machine. Don't worry, I think we got you there."

Through this experience, the "unseen hand" of insurance made repeated uncloaked appearances. Decidedly, I also was getting better at paying attention as a patient—whether a doctor, technician or staff person spoke. And I roused my technician, other than by snoring. She became inquisitive about the cause of restless legs. Mutual listening and learning are a beautiful thing.

Before leaving, my technician gestured to three face masks on a small end table near the exit, "Different setups depending on what you're most comfortable with." I took that as a strong clue of what was to come. One last thing I should disclose is my conversation with the sleep doctor who arranged my prerequisite home study–the same person ultimately interpreting my in-lab results. We had an insightful chat early in the process:

> **DOCTOR:** *We'll have to possibly do two at home studies with negative results (meaning showing no sleep apnea) before we can proceed with an in-lab study.*
>
> **ME:** *Okay, what's the thinking there?*
>
> **DOCTOR:** *Well, it's just kind of the game we have to play. You know, insurance. In fact, I'm not sure how you last managed to get an in-lab study without doing the home study first (to the reader, I had an in-lab study about a year before because of my snoring and hormonal problems). They don't like that. They don't like them too frequently either. Anyway, there's nothing we can do about it so we just work around it... (he can kind of trailed off and sounded a bit tired).*

There it was—a marked tone of resignation. The unseen hand strikes again.

((FREE TO GO))

As I type this in my home office, *The Shawshank Redemption* movie poster hangs on the wall behind me. Adapted from a Stephen King story, *Rita Hayworth and the Shawshank Redemption*, it's easily my favorite movie of all time and nothing I've watched has ever quite replaced it in my heart or mind. Consider me a super fan. I first saw it when I was around 15-years-old; it was the first film that ever moved me to tears.

I've even visited the former real-life prison where many scenes from the movie were filmed in Mansfield, Ohio. The now defunct penitentiary was, unsurprisingly, named the Mansfield Reformatory. Several of the buildings have been razed and a newly built replacement looms close by. What remains standing today of the original monolithic structure lives out its days as a museum. Other scenes were captured in the surrounding area and nearby towns.

One of my visits was on the movie's 20th anniversary. Mansfield had put on a celebration and some of the film's actors came to celebrate. There, somewhat by accident, I saw Bob Gunton who plays "Warden Norton" in the film. My friends and I were at a woodshop that functioned as one of the movie's backdrops. While we stood there looking around, a side door abruptly popped open and my friend whispered, "Hey, look who it is!"

It seems Mr. Gunton was on his own private tour, reliving moments of the film. I figured it was my chance to ask for an autograph. This was right before requests for signatures became fairly passé and selfies rose to popularity. Mr. Gunton was being escorted by local law enforcement and our close proximity allowed me to ask, "Would Bob mind please giving us an autograph?" The lawman leaned over to say something in Mr. Gunton's ear. A quick exchange. Without uttering a syllable, the officer solidly shook his head no.

We were slightly taken aback. It was basically just me, two of my close friends and a couple staff members around. I wondered if Mr. Gunton had chosen to get back into character as Warden Norton. Maybe he never got out of character. Snickering, we quietly debated if we should ask if he was being obtuse and if it was deliberate. My friends and I could be real smart asses. But we decided it was against better judgment. There was a fundraiser later that night at the Reformatory where he would be in character and might have been saving autographs and photo ops for that. Or perhaps he had been pestered one too many times that day.

Despite the disappointment from his rejection, I love his work.

I've had the movie poster since first seeing the film. It's an original two-sided poster, from the movie's 1994 theatrical release. Such posters are rare because only so many are made for each release. Their dual-sided nature makes colors pop more vibrantly from a display box's backlighting. They're the ones you see hanging outside theaters or in their lobbies. My particular poster hung outside a theater in Florida. Reproductions and single-sided posters are far easier to come by.

The movie came on *HBO* late one evening and I remember my father saying to me before heading to bed, "Hey, watch this. You'll like it. It's a great movie." The film might be considered a classic today but it flopped in the theaters. I tell you this because I often see art imitating life and vice-versa. While I admire many of the film's scenes, one distinctly epitomizes how I feel during various affairs.

For those who haven't seen the movie, I'm warning you about a spoiler: A man is up for parole after 40 years of a life sentence. He's appeared before the parole board two times before, each time being asked if he's been rehabilitated and each time, his parole is denied. This was his third time. Played by Morgan Freeman, the inmate's name is Ellis Boyd Redding, or Red for short. The exchange between the parole board and Red's character was one of the best tell-offs ever. If you haven't seen the film, go see for yourself.

After a long pause, Red's parole form is loudly stamped APPROVED in big bold letters. It seems once there was nothing of value left to take anymore, Red was free to go. I see a parallel in Red's release to the health afflictions my grandfather faced in the twilight of his life.

((MORE WALLS, MORE GUARDS (MORE FUNDS)))

My paternal grandfather passed away when I was eight years old. I remember visiting him as a child but was unaware of his health issues until I was an adult. Recently, my father retells an incident to me:

> *Your grandfather had gone into the hospital for hernia surgery. He had his surgery but never really came out of it. He got sick and went into a coma for about two months. He was in the hospital for approximately three months, and his bill was getting really big.*
>
> *A point came where they asked me to consider taking him off life support. They wanted me to pull the plug. Their reasoning, "Well, even if he comes out of it, he'll never be the same. He'll never be right. He's probably got brain damage. Plus his quality of life even if he comes out of it..."*
>
> *They made sure to add, "Oh, he's got this half a million dollar bill too." They started asking who was planning to pay. You have to understand, it was half a million dollars in 1989. A lot now, and a LOT then.*
>
> *I knew I didn't have that kind of money to pay it off. I told them, "No, you don't even know what's wrong. You want me to pull the plug and can't even tell me what's wrong with him. I can't do that. I'm not going to live with that on my conscience. Not going to agree to it. You don't even know why he's in a coma."*

I had been visiting him while he was in the coma. I would talk to him. You're never sure if they can hear you. But you know how they say it can help being there and talking to them, right? So I spent time with him.

Very shortly after this exchange–within 2-3 days, they contacted me again. They called in the middle of the night. "Hey, we ran some tests. He has a blood infection." They gave him some antibiotics. Within one to two days, he came out of the coma and they sent him home. He was the exact same guy I knew before going in.

A flood of questions: What had happened in the limited time between my father telling the hospital a hard no to removing life support, and the decision to give him antibiotics and send him packing? What caused the sudden treatment epiphany, or change of heart? Why the inclination to run tests after three months? Was it sudden inspiration or did incentives align for breakthrough thinking? After my father firmly denied the hospital's haphazard request, their newfound eagerness to cure, peculiar. The timing of their follow-up call, suspect. Of course, a significant bill had accumulated. With each passing day the balance grew. It was taking on a life of its own. Who was going to ultimately be responsible for the bill? Not my dad, and certainly not the hospital.

What's to be gained from this encounter? One undeniable takeaway is that if something doesn't feel right, it probably isn't. Don't be afraid to analyze a situation from a few different angles. Ask yourself if you'll live to regret a decision that seems hasty, or a bit coerced. Was it made under duress? Are there ulterior motives at play? Don't be afraid to step back and assess the situation before acting.

Another thought is that perception is often reality. In the absence of clear answers, people draw their own conclusions.

The hospital in this case didn't do any favors or provide good alternatives. Why had the time come to hurriedly get my grandfather out and clear the way for the next body? My father's hardline stance apparently forced the hospital's hand to dig a little deeper. What if he hadn't pushed back so firmly?

Sadly, my grandfather was gone about a year later, but it had nothing to do with any blood infection. He didn't change his lifestyle. Despite nudging from family, he didn't quit smoking and didn't exercise. Nevertheless, he enjoyed another year of life and his choices were his own.

Doubts about the hospital and its principal players' motivations lingered long after my grandfather's passing and endured decades later... Are the easy cures sitting there all along? I guess that depends on how big the bill becomes. Was there anything left of value to take? After all that time, just like Red, my grandfather was free to go.

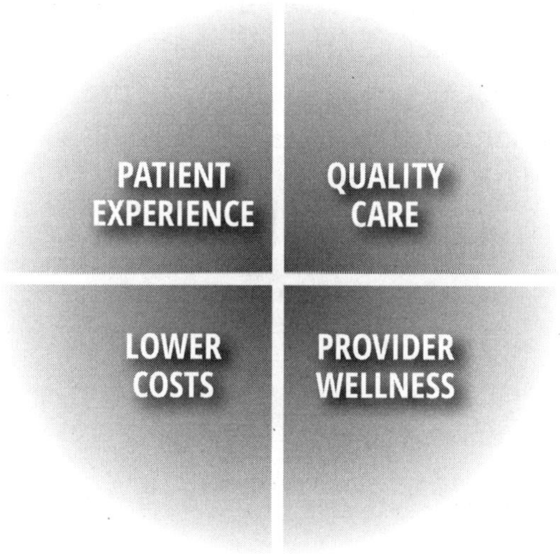
PATIENT EXPERIENCE
QUALITY CARE
LOWER COSTS
PROVIDER WELLNESS

((18))

ROI (Return on Investment) for a Health System

((FLIPPING THE SCRIPT))

"I suspect the percentage of groups that will ultimately install the Quadruple Aim in 'the way we do things around here' will be around 10%. And I have faith that those 10% will deliver care, performance, engagement and quality in a way that establishes the Quadruple Aim as a massive competitive advantage in the years ahead."

– DIKE DRUMMOND, M.D.[143]

Todd R. Otten, M.D.:

Healthcare has transformed more and more into a business model during my career. Undoubtedly, accounting for finances is important when running a large health system. But, it should not be paramount—too often the primary drivers in healthcare are financial. In my efforts to "save the world," I have participated in countless meetings and offered nearly as many suggestions/

ideas for improvement. Only to hear: "What is the ROI?" I have seen where quality is used synonymously with the almighty dollar. There are fundamental flaws in this line of thinking, and unfortunately this has contributed to many of the struggles in healthcare. Physical assets tend to depreciate over time, while investment in human capital tends to appreciate.

A short digression. As Joshua and I have grown closer, our commonalities are uncanny. *The Shawshank Redemption* is also my favorite movie—the plot and character development are incredible. The scene where Red incredulously responds to the parole board echoes what many in healthcare feel: we have nothing left to give. After 20 years, that's exactly how I felt as I penned my resignation.

There are a multitude of factors that have led to the current disconnect with healthcare spending and quality outcomes. Fraud, waste, and abuse are pervasive. But there are many other contributing factors, and they go far beyond healthcare. STOP. Set the book down if you are tired, maybe grab a cup of coffee, or a power nap before continuing. This is important.

I am proposing that hospitals and health systems flip the script. I am imploring the investment be made in people. It is human beings who provide care and who create the data for quality metrics. Ultimately, it is their efforts that hold the potential to lower costs. It is also our belief that healthcare is largely made of good people who are trying to make a difference.

Yes there are exceptions to every rule, but the rates of burnout should be a warning. An alarm of epic proportions. Burnout leads to decreased empathy, negative attitudes, substandard professionalism, poor retention, increased medical errors, and lower quality. And we all depend on healthcare. Do you want care from a burned-out provider? The status quo must change. A tsunami (of problems) is on the horizon and has been accelerated by COVID-19. Changes need to be made at an institutional level to address burnout, moral injury, and their ripple of negative effects.[144]

ROI (Return on Investment) for a Health System

"The high level of burnout should be considered an early warning sign of dysfunction in our healthcare system."

– AMA CEO MEETING 2016[145]

Leaders need to retrain themselves regarding healthcare spending. Short-term investments rarely yield high numbers, unless of course, you own cryptocurrency. We need to think about dollar cost averaging, long-term yield, and diversification—not just ROI. I find it fascinating that hospitals are run like a business, but rarely, if ever, do you hear about investing in our most important asset. People are our most valuable commodity, yet they are often seen as replaceable, or plug and play. This is an inherently flawed mindset. The cost of losing personnel reaches far beyond physicians—no matter the role of the individual replaced. Here are some (theoretical) examples to ponder.

((WHAT IS THE COST?))

- Of a new sanitation worker, whose novice cleaning practices (or lack of training) unwittingly transmits a case of Clostridium Difficile from one patient to the next? Clostridium Difficile is a transmissible disease associated with hospital-acquired infections and poor hygiene.
- Of a new MA who sends in an incorrect refill for a patient (with a significant drug interaction or allergy)?
- Of an administrator who is burned-out and quits, with a sentinel event report buried on their desk in paperwork? A sentinel event is a safety event that leads to an unprecedented poor outcome for a patient, including permanent harm or death.
- Of a brand new nurse who is trying to care for too many patients and administers an incorrect medication?
- What is the cost of leadership and physicians not working together?

- What is the cost of a burned-out physician?
- What is the cost of a physician who dies by suicide?
- What is the cost?

How would these theoretical events impact Our Quadruple Aim? A rhetorical question, but worth pondering. Certainly there are real world examples of how when provider wellness suffers, the other three components of OQA suffer as well. Burnout and moral injury are pervasive and go far beyond healthcare. Profit-driven, corporate mentality is creating problems far and wide, and workers are frustrated. Thankfully, the ideas we present can be tailored to most work environments. I have included a reminder of OQA here, before we flip the script!

OUR QUADRUPLE AIM

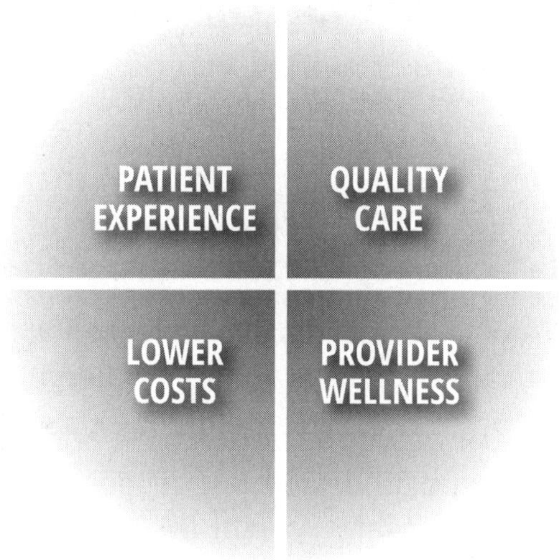

1. **Patient Experience**
2. **Quality Care**
3. **Lower Costs**
4. **Provider Wellness**

((THE CHALLENGE))

"Do unto others as you would have them do unto you."

– JESUS CHRIST, MATTHEW 7:12

At this point, you may not agree with everything presented. I would be surprised if you did. Yet, here we are and something has urged you to press forward. A gut instinct? A lost wager or perhaps I guilted you into it. Or is your mind churning with ideas? Hopefully the latter. Thoughts such as: "yes, we could do better here, or perhaps try this!" If so, the rest of this book should be very intriguing. The topics will be plentiful. The more of us who recognize an opportunity and have the courage to advocate for positive change, the more our ripples will turn into waves.

I would like to present 10 challenges for every leader in healthcare to contemplate. Better yet, every leader in every industry should consider these challenges. Ponder the risk/reward, present the idea, and see what traction you gather. Even if you implement just one, I think you would be hard pressed not to see improvement.

1. Be kind, smile, and thank your co-workers
2. Conduct wellness rounds
3. Allow front-line providers to give feedback to leadership
4. Hire a wellness officer
5. Create a wellness committee
6. Finance (y)Our Quadruple Aim (or wellness) journey
7. Incorporate (y)Our Quadruple Aim into your strategic planning
8. Stop allowing finances to be your primary driver

9. Consider every decision through the lens of Our Quadruple Aim
10. Incorporate wellness into your culture (aligned incentives)

Evidence-based medicine is critical in delivering high quality healthcare (and I am a big proponent). However, we live in a world of gray, and anecdotal evidence does matter as much as data in certain scenarios. Think parachute. I have witnessed OQA work—in the office, at a hospital, and at the ACO level. The metrics a hospital or healthcare system uses need to be tailored to its problems and to the subsequent solutions it hopes to attain. I would suggest picking one (or if bold—many) of the challenges; create a roadmap, set realistic metrics, and see what fruit is yielded in 12 months. Don't just throw stuff at the wall to see what sticks. Constant, poorly contrived change has the potential to kill morale. Be purposeful and well-intentioned. Below, I will present these challenges in an escalating degree of difficulty.

((#1 KINDNESS AND KUDOS))

"If there's one essential element in leadership and life, it's gratitude. Do what you can to show appreciation, be grateful, and say thank you."

– LOLLY DASKAL

Simple gestures can have a major impact on another person. A small effort can fill another's day with joy. But this is not simply a dial to be adjusted, but the transformation can start with one act. However, there needs to be many people who commit to a spirit of generosity. Kindness and gratitude need to permeate your landscape, and preferably from a top-down approach. Think of kindness and kudos as two small snowballs you toss into the snow at the top of a mountain. This small effort has the potential to create an avalanche at the base.

This challenge has very little cost. But the return—priceless. The majority of individuals want to be recognized and appreciated. So tell them. People (whether providers, patients, or any employee) want to be treated with respect. The following excerpt is from a patient of mine. A thank you card—to me, despite her suffering. It speaks to the power of kindness.

> *"I can say without hesitation, for one minute, that I would not have made it through these past few years without your kindness and understanding. I am so sorry for any trouble I have caused you. I wish you could have known the happier, better version of myself. She is in there somewhere, but the depression and pain is excruciating at times that it gets in the way. But every time I think I can't go another step, you are right there giving me the strength to keep trying. You are a blessing to so many. 'Thank you' is not enough. But that is all I have."*

This reminds me of one of my favorite patients. Randy had a long history of chronic pain due to his cerebral palsy and contractures. Essentially his legs were contorted, stiff limbs, rendering him unable to walk without great effort and pain. He was a very intelligent man with a sharp tongue and biting sense of humor. I always cherished seeing Randy, and had the honor of being his physician for 10 years. Despite his tough exterior, he had a warm heart and our visits were filled with laughter. Still, this relationship nearly didn't happen.

For Randy, listening and hearing were two distinct things, and I agree. Randy was strong-willed, even obstinate. Prior to our meeting, he had a solid relationship with his former physician. Unfortunately, a move necessitated a change of providers, and there we were. Little did I know that "listening" to him was his top priority.

During our first encounter Randy knew what he needed from me, but I knew very little of him. It had taken years for him to develop a rapport with his prior physician. Years to get his chronic pain under control. I started to ask pretty standard questions, hoping to learn more about Randy. He was persistent on continuing his existing pain regimen. I wasn't opposed, but pressed on with more questions, as his plan included opiates. (The opiate crisis can make for a difficult encounter to say the least).

At one point during the interaction Randy smacked his fist into his palm and proclaimed, "we're done here."

At that point, I had a decision to make. I could let him walk out the door or try to de-escalate the situation. I chose the latter. Randy calmed down and we made a deal. I would reach out to confirm his pain regimen, and we would follow up in a week to discuss options. A week later the regimen was confirmed and our relationship began.

The years went by and our bond grew closer. I knew Randy struggled with life at times due to his limitations and chronic pain. Knowing this, I tried to make our visits special. I wrote a note telling him he was one of my favorite patients, which was true. Another time, I wrote a simple note saying "happy birthday."

Apparently Randy would remind his caretaker that he was my favorite patient and that she could not make that claim. That encapsulates Randy's sense of humor. Sharp, just like his mind. Randy appreciated that I not only heard him, but listened. Those efforts made Randy feel important.

Unfortunately, while on my sabbatical, Randy ended up in the hospital and passed away. When I returned to work, his friends brought in a framed picture of him holding the notes, proudly displaying them. That photo sits next to my desk to this day. I tell the story of Randy to illustrate how simple acts of kindness can go much further than one realizes.

Patients want to be cared for in a loving, empathic manner—not in the harried pandemonium that often exists in health care. Word of mouth is a powerful tool. It is no wonder a physician with a good bedside manner never has a want for more patients. Is it a surprise that a caring nurse, who had time to tend to a sick patient, noticed a problem before it turned into a disaster (i.e. more cost, lower quality)? These are simple examples. A straightforward concept, easily initiated, can improve your institution's reputation. A better reputation leads to more patients, which leads to increased revenue. It all comes full circle, every stakeholder can thrive with Our Quadruple Aim.

((#2 WELLNESS ROUNDS))

"Gratitude provides inoculation and protection against life's storms and adversities."

– GREG HIEBERT

Sir William Osler is a pioneer in the practice of internal medicine, credited with its introduction to the U.S. He studied in England, including his training at Oxford, as well as other prestigious institutions in Europe. He is credited with the development of the first housestaff system for residency training as well as bedside rounding. He engaged patients as active participants in the diagnostic process. My favorite quote from Sir William Osler is: "The good physician treats the disease; the great physician treats the patient who has the disease."[146, 147]

In researching his career, certainly Sir William Osler was ahead of his time. Treating the person is integral. But too often in modern medicine a person is identified by their disease process—and not their name. I tell my patients I view their health care as a team game, with the key players being them and me. I am very forthright with my suggestions. Most appreciate this approach. I certainly don't treat the disease only. The biopsychosocial aspect is paramount.

Rounding reminds me of a story while I rotated through trauma surgery as a surgical intern. Our trauma teams were rounding in the ICU with a prominent trauma surgeon. A legend at the institution. Full of knowledge, confidence, even a swagger. Interns and medical students were often stumped, even shamed for their lack of knowledge. The learning was tremendous and the curve steep. I enjoyed the rounds. I felt like a saturated sponge just trying to soak up a few more drops of information.

On a particularly busy day, we gathered for rounds. Everyone was exhausted from a lack of sleep, being on call every other day, overloaded with patients, and trying not to drown in the tasks of the day. The first patient was knocking at death's door. An elderly patient with numerous comorbidities had barely survived a motor vehicle accident, whose blood pressure was being maintained with vasopressors. The outlook was grim. One of my colleagues was presenting the case. Ultimately the lead trauma surgeon (in his neatly pressed white coat), asked my friend, "What should we do?"

A pause. Then my fellow intern physician answered, "I would let the patient expire."

Mouths dropped. An uncomfortable silence ensued. The lead surgeon stared out of the window for what seemed an eternity. No one said a word, nor moved. The tension—palpable.

The conversation that ensued was something of legend. A discussion of life and death. Right and wrong. Modern medicine versus the natural course. It was the bravest statement I have ever seen anyone make in my career. It took courage and it was correct. After a discussion with the family, suffering was needlessly avoided, and the patient did indeed expire in peace.

What are wellness rounds? Healing for the healers. A chance to refill your tank. An opportunity to ensure your colleague is ok. They represent a unique environment to engage staff with ideas and tools for wellbeing. In an era where more and more is asked of frontline providers, wellness rounds are a chance for a pause. A respite. A chance for healing.

The superhero era of compartmentalization and resilience in medicine is changing. And rightly so. The suicide rates among physicians are alarming. The rate of burnout—unacceptable. And the dissatisfaction goes far beyond just physicians. Caregivers must learn to care for one another. I will offer a few examples, but your wellness rounds are only limited by your imagination.

The opportunities for these potential endeavors are endless. Humor, mindfulness, relaxation, emotional, and psychological replenishment. Caring for caregivers. Entities that embrace this concept will flourish. Should you need a metric—retention would top my list.

Orlando Health offers compassion rounds as part of their physician health and wellness program. Facilitated by a physician coach, these rounds focus on the human dimension of medicine. The sessions are an opportunity to discuss the social and emotional issues that are encountered while caring for others. These rounds offer a respite for providers, while replenishing their emotional bank account. Physician coaching is offered—an opportunity for growth (both personally and professionally). Compassion rounds are just part of a multifaceted approach offered to providers to enhance wellness. I would encourage those interested to explore their website for additional information and ideas.[148]

Rush University System for Health in Chicago, Illinois (RUSH) was a leader in the Illinois COVID-19 response. As part of their robust and innovative strategy for the pandemic they commissioned a special Wellness Task Force. The task force established Wellness Rounds, a Wellness Consult Service, Wellness Plus, and a central Wellness Resource Hub in an effort to maintain the well-being of their frontline workers during the crisis. The online toolkit is an excellent resource, rich with ideas.[149]

RUSH identified one best practice of: utilizing an executive sponsor. This is critical to developing a wellness program that goes beyond lip service. A high-level executive can accelerate funding and serve as an intermediary between executive leadership and the wellness response team. This direct line of communication allowed RUSH to remain agile and empowered their wellness response team to quickly address emerging issues during a time of crisis.[150]

Many institutions have rounds performed by executives or hospital leadership. However, the wellness rounds created by RUSH are unique in many ways. Each team consisted of a physician leader, a psychologist, a nurse, a chaplain, and a social worker. The focus was wellness with an emphasis on self-care, encouragement, and reflection. The formal structure, consistency, interdisciplinary composition, and empowerment allowed the teams to address immediate issues through a real time feedback loop at the highest levels of the organization.[151]

Wellness rounding offers many opportunities. Frontline workers have unique insight into what is working well and more importantly where issues lie. Whether with an individual or a larger systemic problem, these endeavors can mitigate or even solve issues before they escalate. Frequently, healthcare has become reactive, rather than proactive. Wellness rounds are a chance to swing the pendulum, and perhaps even create a culture of wellness.

((#3 FEEDBACK))

"Successful leaders hold career development conversations with their physicians, inspire, and empower their physicians to do their job well, and recognize the physician for a job well done."

– AMA CEO MEETING 2016[152]

I am blessed to have worked with Cari (my MA) for nine years. I remember during her interview, I asked, "who would she be if she could be a superhero?" Over time our relationship strengthened, we evolved, and we are now good friends. When Cari started, I recognized her ability, but some molding was required. Now a stalwart of the office, Cari has honed her skills to the point she can anticipate many of my questions, which allows me to do my job—think and treat patients. She is an invaluable team member and allows us to operate at the highest level. Our relationship is of mutual respect, honesty, and immense joy. Constructive criticism is welcomed, in both directions.

This type of relationship is of utmost importance not only in primary care, but medicine in general. The more in sync a provider is with their team, the better the care. Teams that allow for bidirectional communication work in harmony. Far better than a top-down or worse yet, a siloed, or micromanaged approach. Having worked in many environments, my happiest and most productive years occurred when providers and leadership were on the same page of music.

Some of the most successful organizations utilize a feedback system from providers to leaders. CEO performance scorecards at the Mayo Clinic not only include financial and quality metrics, but staff engagement, satisfaction, and burnout measures. This information is subsequently shared with the board. Transparency. Physician well-being is measured annually and physicians are asked to evaluate the leadership skills of their immediate supervisors as well. Over time the data between how empathic, engaged, and involved leaders were with their staff was compared to burnout rates. No surprises here: there was a inverse linear relationship between positive leadership attributes and rates of burnout.[153]

While writing *Ripple of Change* with Joshua, we requested feedback from a multitude of people—friends, family, colleagues, patients. As you might imagine the spectrum of responses encompassed a bell shaped curve. Good, bad, and everything in between. Some critiques were as simple as "that's good" or "I like it." I appreciate not wanting to hurt feelings, but to truly facilitate change—some cages are going to need to be rattled. So, I would preface any feedback requests with a footnote: "Don't pull any punches, we can take it." Joshua and I want Our Quadruple Aim to shake things up in healthcare. As such we wanted to put our very best into *Ripple of Change.*

Ask and ye shall receive, so the saying goes. The same could be said of the feedback we received. The most constructive, thought-provoking, and probing comments and questions were by far the best criticism we received. This input often led to rewrites of sentences, paragraphs, even complete sections. We engaged in fantastic conversations, some of which were cathartic and invigorating. The conversations and revisions led us to conduct more research and exploration. Without open and honest feedback, *Ripple of Change* wouldn't be nearly as in depth. Thanks to all those who shared their true feelings. I encourage you to do the same.

((#4 HIRE A WELLNESS OFFICER))

"The time is always right to do what is right."

– REV. DR. MARTIN LUTHER KING

Many high-performing companies already emphasize employee wellness. Disappointingly, many healthcare systems are just trying to catch up. Baffling. The epidemic of burnout and moral injury, and growing primary care and staffing shortages, have been building for years. This is telling. If the COVID-19 pandemic taught us nothing else, people are our most valuable commodity. People listen to the cries of a newborn. Administer life-saving CPR. Remove the infected appendix. Change the soiled sheets for those dying. People run clinics and lead healthcare systems. People make the difference in healthcare—it's time we invest in them.

Family and friends know that I like to play poker. The psychology, the math, the comradery, the emotions. Poker is far from a game of pure chance. Yet those who don't understand it often call it so.

I still remember the first time I played. I was 9-years-old and intrigued by my Uncle Bill's game with his friends. I pleaded with my father to let me play. He gave me $5 and said I would have to pay him back. Three hours later, I returned his $5, having won another $9. I was hooked. Whether or not my Uncle Bill and his friends let me win is unknown. I like to think I was a natural.

But I suppose most 9-year-olds would like to believe this. Over time, some of my most cherished moments with my friends have occurred around a poker table.

What in the world does poker have to do with hiring a wellness officer? Everything. A game of poker is more than who wins or loses money. You don't even need to play for money. A poker game is about friendship and quality time. It promotes well-being among friends and family. Stories are told, conversations are had, life is enjoyed. Sure, it is fun to win. But honestly it is more fun to just play.

Hiring a position that doesn't generate an immediate ROI can constitute a perceived risk at your institution. Perhaps a real risk depending on your financial situation. I would make the case that hiring a wellness officer is a calculated risk. A risk that, if taken, has potential for infinite yield. A risk that if not taken has many untoward consequences. Hiring a wellness officer is far from a gamble; with staffing shortages, can you afford not to?

How to start? What are your metrics? Is this a full- or part-time position? What is the goal? There are no canned answers. The real question is do you believe in Our Quadruple Aim? If so, like in poker—I suggest you go "all in."

Perhaps the ultimate challenge is "buy in." Just like in a poker game, there is an ante. An ante is a set amount of money that each player puts in the pot before starting a hand. Your entity, whether an office, hospital, or system needs to decide what the ante is. Perhaps a volunteer at the start? But in the end, this must be a compensated position to perpetuate a culture of wellness. Good intentions are a start, but time is valuable. And hospital staff are already stretched to their breaking points. Dollars must be allocated.

If your wellness officer's efforts can retain one physician in a five-year period— the position will have paid for itself.

This concept of a wellness officer is simple, yet often meets staunch resistance. Fortunately, there are numerous consultants, programs, webinars, and coaches that can help you along this journey. Below are just a few resources to facilitate your wellness journey.

Dike Drummond M.D. from thehappymd.com
- offers The Quadruple Aim Blueprint
- build a system-wide program, matched to your needs[154]

Stanford Chief Wellness Officer Course[155]

American Academy of Family Physicians (AAFP) Health and Wellbeing Conference[156]

So, find the leader in your institution that embraces wellness and OQA. Trust me, they are there. Preferably a physician, nurse, or other provider fits this mold. Is there a burned-out provider who needs a fresh start? Have a crucial conversation and encourage them to facilitate. Or maybe it's you. Present to your board. Talk with your CEO. Discuss your problems in the institution and how many are affected by wellness. How does this affect quality and cost? How does it affect your bottom line? Develop metrics. Then create the position that fits your institution's needs.

Start simple and grow. Allow for creative freedom and growing pains. Once you find this key individual, create the position and hire them. Throw your stone into the pond. See what ripples are created. Just like a poker game, there is an element of risk to hiring a wellness officer. But, can you afford not to sit at the table and play?

((#5 CREATE A WELLNESS COMMITTEE))

"Do not wait for leaders; do it alone, person to person."

– SAINT TERESA OF CALCUTTA

1. Find your champion
2. Define your issues
3. Get buy-in from executive team
4. Fund the wellness committee
5. Create your wellness committee
6. Develop strategy
7. Implement
8. Measure

((#6 FINANCE YOUR QUADRUPLE AIM))

"It is not enough for leadership to give lip service to caring about their people."

– DIKE DRUMMOND, M.D.[157]

One of the most fascinating aspects of writing has been writer's block. Those moments where the words are difficult to translate from thought to paper. And what is perplexing is that the topics that seem so intuitive have been the most challenging. For example, I have yet to hear good reasons why not to invest in Patient Experience, Quality Care, Lower Costs, and Provider Wellness. So why does ensuring wellness for your employees require an immediate ROI? I thought healthcare was supposed to be about "caring" for others. This is where Our Quadruple Aim elevates its predecessor: The Quadruple Aim. In the end aren't we all responsible for health and well-being?

"What happens if we invest in developing our people and then they leave us?" – CFO
"What happens if we don't, and they stay?" – CEO

– PETER BAEKLUND

There is so much to unpack in these two questions that an entire chapter could be devoted to it; in the midst of writer's block, a simple example seems sufficient. Current estimates to replace one physician are between $500,000 and $1 million dollars. Estimates vary depending on the source and factors considered, but it is an expensive proposition. Let's review the expense associated with my three-month sabbatical (as a result of burnout)—$700,000. With the current and anticipated physician shortages, these costs will skyrocket. Lest we forget the costs of traveling nurses and other financial factors related to retention issues. Ergo, why not invest in your current staff? Keep them happy and engaged. I suspect the cost of investing in a medical staff member's well-being would be a fraction of what it is to hire new physicians. We are a valuable asset—not a commodity.

((#7 INCORPORATE OUR QUADRUPLE AIM INTO YOUR STRATEGIC PLAN))

"A mission-engaged culture lives and breathes strategy."

– MATT RUSH

To say the practice of medicine is complex is an understatement. Those who master the art of medicine are special and often followed by patients regardless of distance. The complexities of delivering cost-effective, quality care, and aligning patient experience and provider wellness can be a daunting task. Many feel as though it is impossible. But sometimes the most complex problems require the simplest of solutions. And sometimes, the simplest solutions are the best. Perhaps we need to declutter and find the elegance in simplicity.

My suggestion is rather simple: incorporate OQA into your strategic plan. In principle, this is a simple notion; in reality, the implementation may be extremely complex. Regardless of the situation, there is room for improvement. Start simple and see what evolves. Remember, cultures won't shift overnight. But I believe those who embrace Our Quadruple Aim will outperform those who don't, whether in healthcare or beyond.

As a senior in high school, one of my favorite memories occurred while taking honors physics. We had an outstanding teacher—firm, yet fair. She didn't tolerate shenanigans. But her passion for imparting knowledge was evident and I soaked it up. The second semester of the year-long class involved a series of projects. Whose cooler could retain cold temperatures the best? Whose mousetrap racing car was the fastest, or could travel the farthest? Whose matchstick bridge could support the most weight? Whose paper airplane could travel the farthest?

Keep in mind, I was in high school before the Internet was commonplace. No Google searches, with potential answers at your fingertips, and the grade was dependent on your performance. The better your project performed, the better your grade. Seemingly complex problems—often with simple solutions.

It was 1994 when I was a senior in high school. A full 10 years prior to taking aerodynamics as a lieutenant in the Navy. The particular assignment was to create a paper airplane that could stay airborne the longest. The instructions were very simple. Use one sheet of paper, folded in any manner you choose, to create a craft that will stay aloft the longest. Paired with two classmates, we worked on the project in the classroom and at home. My colleagues tried numerous designs with varying success. I mainly just watched.

"Todd, aren't you going to practice your design?" asked my classmate.

"Don't worry, I got this."

I never did tell my teammates my plan. Perhaps overconfident or even cocky. Or maybe the overexuberance of youth. But I was certain my design would prevail the day of the test. Moreover, I didn't want the other teams to catch on (high schoolers tend to gossip). Definitely not a stellar example of transparency.

Time went by, and the day of reckoning arrived. There were numerous designs and unlimited trials. Paper airplanes were flying all over the room. Stopwatches clicked everywhere. The atmosphere was frenetic at times, but smiles were abundant. Fortunately for me, our teacher didn't allow for copying a design once it had been unveiled. My teammates were testing their designs with decent results. Then it was my turn to reveal the masterpiece. My teammates, still in the dark regarding my plan, watched in anticipation.

As I took center stage, a quiet calm seemed to spread over the room. Attention was drifting toward me. Perhaps knowledge of a secret plan had spread. So I grabbed a piece of blank, crisp white copy paper. Fresh out of the package. Pure, clean, no folds or wrinkles. I held it in my hands for a brief moment as if holding a baby bird, letting the anticipation build. Looking around, paper airplanes stopped flying and 20 pairs of eyes focused on me. My teammates looked on with expressions of cautious optimism. I grabbed a school chair and stood on my tippy-toes reaching for the ceiling, the unfolded piece of paper prominently displayed. I held the piece of paper as flat and as close to the ceiling as possible.

Time slowed down. The memory remains vivid in my mind, nearly 30 years later. I let go. Like a leaf falling from a tree—the piece of paper moved back and forth as it floated to the pale ceramic tile. Left, then right; back and forth. Peaceful, rhythmic. The first flight beat the nearest competitor by two seconds. Some were angered by the simplicity, others laughed, and congratulated me. I think our teacher felt a little of both. Needless to say, our team triumphed in the paper airplane trial. The 100% grade was secured. This particular model of airplane was subsequently banned in honors physics. A complex problem, with a simple solution. Makes me smile to this day.

After writing this story, I asked for feedback from my office staff, including the NPs. One critique noted the growth of a cocky, intelligent high schooler to the current physician and leader I strive to be. Elizabeth, an NP, noted: "Keeping a solution to yourself makes for successful individuals, not necessarily healthy teams or the best outcomes. Healthcare has to be a team effort for the best patient care."

As a medical student I learned about Occam's razor: we allow the simplest answer to guide us. I feel Our Quadruple Aim follows this mantra, being a simple concept in and of itself. However, implementation can be another story entirely. Limited resources and financial pressures can be tremendous impediments. Many do not even know where to start. Simply incorporating OQA into strategic planning would be an incredible start. Just talking about and sharing OQA is even simpler. Possibly, your mission statement needs to be addressed or refreshed. Perhaps a leadership course with a new twist—emphasizing the four components of OQA. Maybe the concept needs introduction at the board level or a medical staff meeting. Our Quadruple Aim is simple in concept, but far from easy to master. But doing nothing is exactly that—nothing.

((#8 STOP USING FINANCES AS THE PRIMARY DRIVER))

"Money is only a tool.
It will take you wherever you wish,
but it will not replace you as the driver."

– AYN RAND

Does your mission statement talk of treating patients or making money? I can't imagine many hospitals' mission statements focus on finances; rather, they emphasize quality care, patient centricity, or even evidence-based medicine. A quandary then—why is profit so often at the forefront of healthcare? What is the bottom line? How many days cash on hand? What is the next big investment? How much revenue can a specialist generate? A shiny new building?

When finance is the primary driver, OQA suffers. In fact, the current modus operandi is paradoxical to lowering costs. Moreover, when the focus is on creating more widgets, the quality of widgets generated declines. The pendulum becomes unbalanced—and both providers and patients suffer.

Widgets in health care? What? Is healthcare a business or a service? The pressures to see more patients, do more procedures, order more tests, and refer to specialists are real. Time pressures exist, physician salaries are largely driven by productivity. The goals of Our Quadruple Aim have all too often become secondary to revenue generation.

Having finance as the primary driver in healthcare has contributed to the inefficient, bloated system that exists today. Unfortunately, healthcare has turned into big business and trillions of dollars are on the line.

This problem won't be solved for many years to come. But things must change as the current fiscal trajectory is not sustainable. Increasing costs with worsening outcomes undermine OQA. As healthcare attempts to transform from fee-for-service to value-based reimbursement, many leaders struggle to shift their mindset. Our Quadruple Aim can help this transition and align the incentives for all stakeholders, but we will need a multitude to reverse course.

((1ST-TIME QUALITY: COPIES OF COPIES))

Joshua J. Judy – Patient:

Dr. Otten tells me, "Unfortunately, many patients just want a quick fix. I try to offer options and have patients consider them. But many just want me to decide. It can be daunting." There are tradeoffs. How would the tenants of Our Quadruple Aim guide this balancing act? The four tenants are: Patient Experience, Quality Care, Lower Costs, and Provider Wellness. Quality Care doesn't always have to mean most expensive (especially when all the downstream costs of a decision are considered). And if you allow for Provider Wellness that results in a great Patient

Experience, now all cylinders are firing. Is that even possible? Absolutely!

Have you seen organizations that only consider initial ROI for decision-making? If you answered yes, you recognized this common trap. It's where only the face value of a decision dictates whether to go forward rather than the total cost of that decision. What about doing things right the first time to avoid a ton of rework and waste on the backend (which often exceeds many multiples beyond the initial outlay)? In my profession, that's called the Total Cost of Ownership.

Over my career, I can think of many times where decisions were made to buy the cheapest goods or services without considering the accumulating harm of poor (or absent) quality standards. What about if you pay or invest a little more now by not just defaulting to the quick fix and save far more in total costs later? Think of it as dollar-cost averaging.

Dr. Otten and I discussed the 2022 quality initiatives that were disseminated to the primary care physician group he was a part of, which included grading medication reconciliation performance. If you recall, medication reconciliation is used to confirm what medication a patient is taking, and that it matches their chart (see Chapter 5, Our Quadruple Aim). After-the-fact surveys were sent out to patients asking them to confirm their prescriptions. The theory is a reviewer could then verify if doctors and staff had typed them in correctly on patients' charts. One big problem: occasionally, these are the same patients who couldn't explain what medications they took while in the doctor's office. How would their answers be any different while filling out the survey later?

In sympathy, the patient might take a lot of medications. One where even a photographic memory would struggle. At home, at least they'd have their medicine cabinet in front of them. But who feels like repeating themselves by filling out a survey? Garbage in, garbage out.

Alternatively, it bears repeating what Dr. Otten asked: What if hospital administrators allowed hiring of additional staff to help educate patients on how to best track their medications, embracing first-time quality? Save the postage, save the time, and save the all-around frustration. This aligns perfectly with the tenants of Provider Wellness leading to a satisfactory patient experience, while maximizing quality, and minimizing total costs.

I'm reminded of an early job from long ago. At the end of each quarter, I prepared a report. A second party was required to validate my output. Off the report went. Without fail, this person proceeded to make an exact copy of it, exclaiming, "They match, so it must be right!" They're replicas of the same information–of course they would match (even if mine contained mistakes)! No matter how many times my then-boss and I tried to point out the absurdity of this exercise, the reviewer didn't want to rock the boat. There was little motivation to change.

Unfortunately, the point was lost and this poorly conceived process lived on. A real quality control step would have been investing time to check my math upstream. Considering a process's Total Cost of Ownership requires an open mind. My then-boss, who sadly passed away in 2022, would roll his eyes and drolly remark, "The behavior exhibited is the behavior incentivized." Wise words.

((#9 LENS OF OUR QUADRUPLE AIM))

"If you want to see a better world,
change the lens through which you see it
and do the work to make it better."

— JEFFREY G. DUARTE

Todd R. Otten, M.D.:

Flight conditions were ideal—a warm late August day, somewhere over north Africa. No turbulence, cruising at about 25,000 feet in a P-3 Orion. We were returning from a diplomatic mission in Uganda, to refuel in Spain. It was 2005 and about halfway through our deployment at Sigonella Air Base in Sicily, Italy. I was the squadron's flight surgeon and at that particular moment was actually flying the aircraft.

"Keep it straight and level doc, you're doing great," said my co-pilot (an actual P-3 pilot).

As part of our training to become a flight surgeon (for the U.S. Navy) we attended eight months of training in Pensacola, Florida. We learned about weather, aeronautics, navigation, and numerous maladies that could occur and/or impact one's ability to safely pilot an aircraft. The training was full of didactics, including how to conduct a mishap investigation. As part of our indoctrination, we also learned how to pilot an aircraft, including eight familiarization flights in a T-34, accompanied by a naval pilot. A T-34 is a small dual seat turboprop aircraft. If you are thinking Maverick from *Top Gun*, that's about right.

"Thanks, Mike!" I replied.

As we continued our journey toward refueling, my mind was focused on the task at hand. What was our altitude, speed, attitude? Was I following the flight plan? All seemed to be in order. The clear, endless blue sky seemed to reach out forever. My thoughts drifted home—to Angie and our 1-year-old son. Then suddenly, a radio call on my headset rudely interrupted my thoughts.

"American aircraft, American aircraft! You have entered protected airspace, you must land now." The voice was stern, and the accent was hard to place.

I turned toward our XO, "Sir, would you like me to get out of the seat?"

"Doc, just keep it straight and level," he replied.

"American aircraft, you must land now!"

My mind was racing—nothing made sense. I kept the aircraft in control and again questioned if I should allow another pilot to take the yoke. The radio calls continued. At one point, I was instructed to take my American flag off of my flight suit and hold it up to the window. I was completely perplexed—there is a large "U.S. Navy" written on the fuselage.

"Doc, there are two H-57's on the wing," someone exclaimed.

I looked. "I don't see shit!"

Then, one of the senior navigators entered the cockpit and revealed who was making the radio calls. "American aircraft," he said and laughed hysterically. H-57 was the name of the two engines on the wing. I joined the laughter, and I often recall that story.

Why did I tell the hazing of a flight surgeon by his fellow officers? That day over north Africa, there were several perspectives in the cockpit of the P-3 Orion. My perspective (as the flight surgeon), the pilot's, the navigator's, the XO's; each of us had a job to do, and apparently mine was to provide entertainment for my colleagues. Sure, the story is humorous and clearly no one was injured, except my pride. However, the story helps to solidify my point regarding viewing healthcare delivery through the lens of Our Quadruple Aim.

Whether you are a patient, provider, nurse, administrator, cook, or housekeeper, we all need to be working toward common goals. Goals in healthcare need to be simplified to their core values. What better way to encapsulate OQA than to examine each and every decision under this purview.

An important distinction: I am not saying every decision needs to be microdissected. Rather, Our Quadruple Aim should be considered (in some capacity) when decisions are made. This is particularly true for decisions that impact both patient care and providers. For example, our current EMR requires the provider to hit the refresh button prior to signing their note. Simple enough, but multiply that by 4-5,000 visits per provider per year, times thousands of providers. The refresh button needs to be hit millions of times. Logical to think this step might get forgotten on occasion. The real problem becomes when subsequent readers are not able to see the completed note. Rest assured, the information is there, but only the author can see it. Lunacy. This obviously can lead to errors due to lack of transparent information.

I am not sure how this decision was made, or even why it persists (despite several inquiries). Unfortunately, this mandate remained in the EMR as I wrote this chapter. I would make a case that this decision has the potential to negatively impact each component of OQA. Patient experience is negatively impacted when an ER physician cannot read the note the family physician wrote. This can lead to unneeded testing, higher cost, and potentially lower quality. Worse yet, an error when a documented allergy cannot be reviewed. And provider wellness—my sarcasm speaks for itself. In many ways, it was easier to write this book.

It boggles my mind that decisions like these are made. Yet, this happens regularly in our healthcare landscape. Silos and fragmented care are everywhere and create unneeded complexity and frustrations. Decisions need to consider how they will impact not only the patient, but also the end users. If done correctly, and balanced decisions are made—high quality and lower costs will follow.

I am imploring healthcare leaders at every level to take a step back and consider all four components of Our Quadruple Aim when making decisions. Patient Experience, Quality Care, Lower Costs, and Provider Wellness. Every choice has the potential to impact others—legal, finance, IT, housekeeping, administration, patients, and providers. Good people making seemingly sound decisions can have devastating consequences to the end user. Certainly one component of OQA may be the primary driver in a particular situation, but all facets need to be considered.

((#10 INCORPORATE WELLNESS INTO YOUR CULTURE, USING OUR QUADRUPLE AIM TO ALIGN INCENTIVES))

"If you want your people to be courageous (and you do), then you as a leader need to rethink your organization's culture and ask yourself if it supports and encourages acts of courage, both great and small."

– LOLLY DASKAL

The Soup Spoon Cafe in Lansing, Michigan is a quaint restaurant that serves delectable offerings. It sits on the corner of Michigan Avenue, a block away from a local hospital. The type of place that invites conversation. If you have eaten there—you understand. A logical choice for two physicians to meet. This is where I first met Brandon Francis, M.D., a fellow physician about to embark on a new chapter in his career.

Dr. Francis is board-certified in internal medicine, psychiatry, neurocritical care, and critical care medicine. He completed a combined internal medicine and psychiatry residency program, followed by three years of active duty in the U.S. Army, and then a neurocritical care fellowship. He currently serves as the CMO for an acute care hospital. Impressive. Despite his superlative training, and some loan forgiveness, Dr. Francis has a significant loan burden and has been working in "underserved" areas his entire career. As we heard from Dr. Francis previously on financial wellness in Chapter 13, and will again, it is important to understand his perspective.

After some small talk, we dove into a rich conversation about Our Quadruple Aim. Considering this was our first interaction, it was remarkable how quickly we let our guard down. Things that worked well in healthcare, and a much bigger discussion on those did not. The conversation was full of hope and enthusiasm. Ultimately, when our lunch was finished, my spirits were renewed and motivation restored. We spoke for two hours. Trenchant.

There were several items that I hastily jotted down in my notepad during the conversation. Brandon was full of wisdom and probing questions. We spoke of aligned incentives and areas that desperately needed improvement. The conversation flowed naturally, covering a variety of issues. I was taken aback when he asked how I became a writer. Up until that point, I hadn't considered myself a writer. Me—a writer?

"So why do we continue to accept the current state of healthcare," I queried.

"It's the evil I know."

"The evil I know." A respected neurointensivist says this. My goodness—I was speechless. I knew this statement would make it into the book. At the time, I was uncertain of where, but inspiration hit me on my drive home.

The evil I know; this speaks volumes when it comes to describing an existing culture. Whether that culture is at your office, hospital, or the highest level—evil does not have a positive connotation. No doubt this is felt outside healthcare. No wonder why we are in the midst of the great resignation, the quiet quitting. Imagine trying to transform this type of culture into one of wellness. Difficult, yes. Impossible—no. So I will pose the challenge nonetheless.

"Must genuinely LIVE your culture from the heart, mind and soul (the concepts of Our Quadruple Aim). Such that, they become part of a 'belief system' that everyone believes in and holds themselves and others accountable into perpetuity. Aspire to create a culture where every interaction and every decision encapsulates Our Quadruple Aim. Undeterred by failure or disappointment—after all, every organization or system in healthcare is composed of human beings, beautiful and fallible at the same time. To lead is to understand this, and rise above!"

– MATT RUSH

Without a doubt, transformation of a culture is a massive undertaking. No blueprint, specific instructions, not one set answer. Numerous layers have to be peeled back and often years of dysfunction unwound. Politics and bureaucracy stand as immovable objects. So where do you start? I humbly offer suggestions.

Leadership is key, and belief in wellness is essential. Without effective and committed leadership, your efforts will be doomed from the start. Cultural transformation will never succeed without a strong leader. Whether a key physician leader or a top executive—this person must practice what they preach. The Provider Wellness component of Our Quadruple Aim cannot be lip service—it cannot be another BOX CHECKED.

Believe it or not, a champion exists in every institution. Trust me, they are there. No one wants to work in a dysfunctional culture. People are often locked into the evil they know. If there is not an obvious candidate—find them. Send a probing email, have conversations, ask questions. I would imagine several candidates emerge when you are transparent about cultural transformation (particularly one that includes wellness). People want to enjoy their work. People don't want to work in fear. Patients want their providers to be at their best. If the culture is transformed into one that includes wellness, the other three components of OQA should naturally follow.

The COVID-19 pandemic has accelerated many issues that predated the devastation, and the frustrations extend well beyond healthcare. The number of conversations I've had with good people who express similar concerns in their line of work is ever growing. The issues in healthcare are mirrored everywhere, and workers are fed up. The emphasis on wellness can and should be expanded to every industry.

Tracy Bower from Forbes.com discusses how the pandemic has changed the future of work in her article, "6 ways to reinvent your wellness strategy—according to the experts." Senior level executives were gathered and I found their titles intriguing: Chief

People Officer and Chief Human Capital Officer (to name a few). She speaks of transparency, changing expectations, and caring and compassion for employees. She highlights six strategic shifts to reinvent your wellness strategy.

((WELLNESS IS...))

1. Central
2. Strategic
3. Holistic
4. Systemic and Integrated
5. Data-Driven
6. Demands Action[158]

Some of the simplest examples of cultural transformation occurred when I served as Chief of Staff. I utilized components of the aforementioned challenges regularly. Simple gestures often transformed meetings. Levity often precipitated engagement. Routinely I would begin a meeting with an anonymous quip from a patient. Watching a stale, agenda-laced meeting transform into a high-energy, efficient meeting (full of wellness and collegiality) was magical.

"I don't know why doctors ask if it burns when I pee,
I have never tried to light it on fire."

– PATIENT

Of vital importance to cultural modification are aligned incentives. Individuals in an organization need to row in the same direction—working towards common goals. Imagine the port side of a boat rowing forward and the starboard reverse—you will only go in circles. So too with organizational infrastructure. Framing incentive structures towards common goals is only logical. As our incentive structure became more and more aligned, the hospital thrived well beyond its finances. This should be a top-to-bottom approach, and I would offer utilizing Our Quadruple Aim as the foundation.

((ALIGNED INCENTIVES))

1. **Patient Experience** – Happy patients are the best form of advertising. A solid patient experience involves everyone in an organization. Spend less on advertising and more on positive experiences. Incentivize or reward your employees to deliver (think outside of the box; it doesn't always have to be money).

2. **Quality Care** – A patient's outcome can be impacted by every single employee (positive or negative). Does your incentive structure reward EVERY employee as patient quality metrics improve? It should.

3. **Lower Costs** – Appropriate testing and fair and transparent pricing will retain patients and yield loyal, potentially lifelong customers. What a radical idea—to align incentive structure with your customer base. Doing more is just that. Inflated bills lead to lower retention.

4. **Provider Wellness** – Happy, content employees make recruitment and retention easier. Employee turnover is expensive. Play nice in the sandbox and imbed employee wellness into the culture—the ROI is infinite.

((19))

The Sack

Joshua J. Judy – Patient:

During our health deluge, Megan and I still had dreams of having a second child. We heard the clock ticking grow into ever louder thuds. Through most of 2020 and before, we had been actively trying to conceive. It had been a full year. I use the word 'active' loosely because there was one major, unrelenting problem. Our brains were hardly signaling like they used to and as a result, little to no desire or physicality existed. With the after effects of the duloxetine, I had significant dysregulation and dysfunction of my hormonal system and who knows what else. And under levetiracetam's spell, Megan was in the same boat, floating adrift.

We had to force ourselves to try once or twice a month, often with many fits and false starts—mostly subdued and joyless. Indeed, it was an 'empty home,' upstairs and downstairs, if you get my drift. Literally, our home wasn't going to be as full as dreamed with family planning on hold. My God, how was this supposed to work?

I wondered what damage had been done to our systems. With our son, everything was straightforward and worked out. Megan became pregnant, had a natural birth, and there were no complications. We wondered if fertility was ruined in me, her or both. We wondered even if we could conceive, would there be any lurking birth defects? But life often has no regard for your plans. Overnight, when your most sensitive body part becomes relegated to a vestigial structure, family planning is out of the question. I'm speaking of the brain, which controls the other parts—and yes, that *other* part was now dead too.

Whatever fertility I had, I knew on TRT, it would be next to nothing. When you use exogenous (external) testosterone, endogenous (internal) production becomes suppressed. A negative feedback loop prevents 'cheating the system.' If you could hear your body talking, it would say, *"I can kick my feet up. You're getting your fix elsewhere."* Production signals like Luteinizing hormone (LH) and Follicle Stimulating Hormone (FSH) are practically guaranteed to go to zero.

To get around this, some hormone doctors will prescribe a supporting compound like Human Chorionic Gonadotropin (HCG) to directly stimulate the testicles while bypassing the hypothalamus and pituitary gland (which controls the feedback loop). For some males on TRT, HCG is often a complementary part of their protocol. When LH and FSH disappear, many men struggle with atrophy of the 'boys.' Like most things, when no longer stimulated, they shrink. Begets new meaning to use it or lose it, right? This can be painful for some men, literally through physical change, and mentally too. To compensate, men may be prescribed HCG at a lower dosage when fertility is not the main goal. If fertility is the main goal, HCG may be prescribed at a higher dosage.

Beyond that, HCG can directly stimulate your body to make some amount of endogenous testosterone, called intratesticular testosterone (ITT). Essentially, you're bypassing your own system and directly sending an auxiliary signal to the 'boys.'

I remember one visit with yet another endocrinologist, not Dr. Saya. She and her female assistant walked into the room with a rope. On that rope were different sized elongated spheres. I'm sure you can imagine what they were supposed to represent. I was asked to point to the one that best embodied the size of my two fellas. Not your everyday visit, is it? Oh boy(s).

An analogue to LH, HCG resembles LH to the body enough to activate the target cells. As Dr. Saya says, "Past that, we don't know if it functions exactly the same at the transcription level." He prescribed me HCG to inject into my belly fat, or adipose tissue. 500 International Units (IUs) on the same days I injected my testosterone for a total of 1500 IUs weekly. It's not a perfect science. Given that estrogen is aromatized in the Leydig cells, some men have estrogen problems on HCG due to the ITT while others feel great.[159]

For those where HCG contributes to estrogen problems, it occurs because it's somewhat unnatural compared to a healthy body's pulsatile LH delivery. HCG has a longer half-life and is said to be several times stronger than the body's own LH on a per-IU basis. These factors may lead to excessive intratesticular aromatization, almost certainly circumventing any attempts by the body to adjust estradiol (E2, a form of estrogen) levels naturally on its own. Recall the feedback loop that is deactivated on TRT–the body's own tools to balance now bypassed.

As a fertility standalone, HCG failed me. For atrophy, it assisted restoring to about 60% of pre-TRT. FSH was then added, at a cost of $600 a vial out-of-pocket. To save on cost, I would inject 50 to 75 IUs twice a week.

Again, not enough. I would have to come off TRT for a chance to regain fertility. Whether my body had anything left in it was anybody's guess. It had weakened, hence why I went on TRT in the first place, so why would it launch a comeback story now? As before, I'm sure feeling miserably low energy would be part of the experience, which of course is self-defeating in family planning. We would have to roll the dice. Megan and I paid a visit with Dr. Otten.

ME: Are you able to order a fertility test?

DR. OTTEN: Sure. I'll put the order in. Just a heads-up, typically if you've successfully had one child, and experience problems conceiving the next, the problem often lies on the woman's side.

This was news to us and good to know. We would attack this problem in two parts: (1) Megan would do an at home fertility test. (2) I would be taking a trip to the hospital lab, once I could provide them what they were looking for—a fertility specimen.

Between production and delivery of said specimen, I had about an hour to safely deliver the goods, or else they would start spoiling (at least for testing purposes). Well, there was no avoiding it. I strode down the hall of the hospital carrying a plain brown paper sack. It wasn't lunch. The cargo inside the bag was whatever fertility I had left. Oh shit. There's a check-in station. Of course, it's April 2020 and COVID-19 pandemic is just ramping up. Isn't there a lane directly to the labs in the back or something? I saw the receptionist, perkily checking in others. Don't you ask what's in the sack. Don't you dare. It was my turn–

"What are you here for?"

"I have a specimen for the lab."

"Do you know where the lab is?"

"Sure do." Wasn't it good enough that I knew how to read signs?

She then picked up the phone, "There's a patient coming back. He'll be there soon with a specimen."

I liked the ambiguity of it all. Ever the stickler for details, it's one of the few times I felt generalized terms availed. Zagging my way back through the bright and polished halls of the hospital, I found the window to the lab. Here, another bouncy staff member was in wait. I extended the brown paper sack across the threshold of the counter, "Here you go. Fertility sample."

"Perfect, I'll get this under the 'scope' right away and take a real good look!" Because of the intensifying global pandemic, masking was in place. Twinkling, her eyes readily betrayed the face cover. I knew there was a big smile under there. I guess some things are easier to keep under wraps than others.

"How was it produced?" She needed to validate the method.

"Carefully," I said, tapping the intake form where I had checked the proper box. A perfectly honest answer. Under the conditions, I didn't feel I could afford anything less than judicious handling.

With a giggle, she volunteered, "Don't worry, you'll know something this afternoon!" Everyone sure is cheerful around here. I realized some people take a lot of pride in their jobs and I appreciated it. The lab tech was true to her word and I didn't wait long. Less than two hours later, the results came back. Unfortunately, I couldn't hide behind ambiguity this time—a low flag. I was at the bottom of the range. Whether I liked it or not, I felt like that mostly empty paper sack was a metaphor for many things.

((BIRTHDAY WISHES))

Meanwhile, Megan ordered a fertility kit with hormonal testing specific to females. Her report came back. One value flagged a little high but no immediate showstoppers. The arrow turned back towards me. Where to next? That's when Dr. Saya and I discussed another option: enclomiphene.

A medication called clomiphene may be more popularly known. It's a medication that contains two isomers (two or more compounds with the same formula but a different arrangement of atoms in the molecule doing different things), zuclomiphene and enclomiphene. The former is a weak estrogen agonist and the latter is a strong estrogen antagonist. Agonism means activation of a target receptor and antagonism means blocking action at the receptor.

Recall the Hypothalamus Pituitary Gonadal Axis (HPG) (Chapter 16, Role Reversal Cont.)? In a healthy male, the way that your body knows to make testosterone is for the axis to 'scan' for low estrogen. Once it realizes that estrogen has dipped too low, it in turn knows that any testosterone must also be low. Enclomiphene blocks, or antagonizes estrogen at the pituitary and hypothalamus and in essence tricks the HPG into thinking there is none in the body.

Estrogen in males is made from testosterone via a conversion process called aromatization so you can't have one without the other. Thinking that there is no estrogen in the body, the brain starts screaming at the pituitary to produce more LH to signal to the testes to make more testosterone, which will in turn result in more estrogen being produced until it feels 'topped off.' It's quite the parlor trick.

When it comes to clomiphene, there's just one problem: Potentially permanent eye damage with floaters. Scientists suspect zuclomiphene, not enclomiphene. Given my eye condition, that was an immediate no go for me. I had been doing my own research and so when I had my next consultation with Dr. Saya, I brought my concerns up. Because of this, I was able to assist my doctor with recognizing potential risks.

"All fair concerns. I can prescribe enclomiphene alone. It's offered at 12 mg and 25 mg. We'll do the higher dosage for you and you will take one pill daily," he offered.

Compounded by only one pharmacy in the U.S., off my script went. I started treatment on a Friday at the end of August 2020. The day I stopped TRT is the same day I took my first enclomiphene pill. Several weeks later, I got my test results. LH was at 6.3 IU/L and FSH at 6.4 IU/L. My natural total testosterone rose to 640 ng/dL and free testosterone to 16.0 ng/dL. When hoodwinked, my hormonal system had some fuel, but not without the support of the medication.

It wasn't going to last. By seven weeks in, I had to come off enclomiphene. I felt sick. I was slipping on much of the progress made towards thawing from the 'global numbness' caused by the duloxetine.

Dr. Saya shared, "Men on things like enclomiphene can feel poorly because of blocking estrogen. Everything in balance."

It's a lesson all men should know—contrary to popular belief, estrogen in the right amount in their bodies is just as critical as testosterone, with some of testosterone's own effects facilitated through its conversion in the brain to estrogen. Put another way, testosterone will fail some key duties in the brain without assistance from estrogen.

Low estrogen, beyond the obvious effects like bone loss and fat accumulation, leads to poor mood, depression and a host of other problems in men. Like many things in the body, it's there in the proper amounts for a reason. Balance. Counterintuitive but amusing to realize that a man needs certain levels of estrogen to be more manly.

Subsequently, I was offered phosphodiesterase type 5 (PDE-5) inhibitors. These help control the mechanical aspect of the 'plumbing' by increasing vasodilation–but not libido. It would have to suffice, hopefully, and get the job done so to say. And it did, barely, but our daughter was conceived later that year, and three years after our initial plan. We're blessed to have just celebrated her first birthday! Miracles can happen—sometimes you just have to be willing to take the extra steps and time to make them come true.

Dr. Saya: If you're reading this, thank you.

TL;DR—lessons for OQA:

Everyone, this wasn't an easy section to write but hardly any of this experience is.

My wife and I have always been private people. However, we feel the greater good comes from transparency, in hopes others can learn from our experiences. If you can take something from our stories, please do. And if you can't, perhaps you know someone who can. Sharing is caring.

((ONE VARIABLE AT A TIME))

Not too long after starting TRT, my thyroid values started behaving strangely. Was my body not keeping up with the increased metabolic demand placed by the restored androgens? Maybe, or my pituitary is just weak and destabilized in general, or both.

Thyroid hormone is epochal to the body; its importance cannot be trivialized. There are thyroid receptors in every cell in the body, including the thyroid gland itself. The hormone is responsible for metabolism, governing the rate at which the body uses energy. This affects everything from temperature, to digestion and brain function. Thus, thyroid hormone must be done correctly—too little or too much leads to deleterious effects.

As it does with many of the body's important hormones when low, my brain was asking my pituitary to nudge my thyroid gland for more production. It does this by releasing Thyroid Stimulating Hormone (TSH), just as the pituitary would release more LH in a healthy male to signal the production of more testosterone.

Baseline TSH = 2 u[IU]/mL	(ref range = 0.35 - 4.01 u[IU]/mL)
New TSH = 5.43 u[IU]/mL	(ref range = 0.35 - 4.01 u[IU]/mL)
Free T4 = 0.6 ng/dL	(ref range: 0.82-1.77)

Diagnosis: hypothyroid.

Initially, I was given Armour Thyroid. One grain, or 60 mcg a day. Armour is desiccated thyroid, meaning extracted from dried up pig thyroid glands. Because it's derived from actual animal gland, Armour contains a mix of thyroid hormones in a ratio specific to the animal it's taken from. Understand that thyroid glands make different thyroid hormones, and pigs are no exception.

Armour contains a mix of T3 (called triiodothyronine), T4 (called thyroxine) and unmeasured amounts of T2, T1 and calcitonin. Armour comes in a 4:1 ratio of thyroxine (T4) to triiodothyronine (T3). A human thyroid gland produces T4:T3 in a ratio of 11:1 (some literature offers 14:1) while pigs produce in a ratio of 4:1. Interestingly, desiccated thyroid has been available since the late 1800s and was the very first therapy available for low thyroid hormone, a pioneer in hormonal treatment. By the 1960s, it started losing favor as the pharmaceutical companies developed ways of making synthetic levothyroxine, or T4, that can be dosed more precisely. By the 1970s, blood testing improved.[160, 161, 162, 163]

Not all providers like or agree with Armour. A cardiologist at a hospital once told me, "It's dirty, it has impurities. Go with a T4 only solution, like levothyroxine." The thyroid gland primarily produces T4, which is converted to bioactive T3 in tissue throughout the body by a process called deiodination—where enzymes called deiodinase cleave off iodine molecules on the T4, resulting in T3 that the cells use. Predominantly, until the T4 is metabolized by deiodinase, it is considered a reservoir or prohormone for T3. While T4 does have some biological effects, T3 is far more active, ranging from 3x-4x more. Much activity within the cell occurs once T4 is converted to T3.[164, 165, 166]

A few of T3's responsibilities are increasing cardiac output and heart rate, basal metabolic rate, and raising the effects of neurotransmitters like dopamine and norepinephrine through higher sympathetic activity. You might think of thyroid hormone as a controller of your cells' internal clock speed. Because of the higher T3 to T4 ratio in Armour, it can lead to hyperthyroidism if not dosed correctly. However, too much T3 in the body presumes the patient converts T4 to T3 well.[167, 168, 169] Balance: A theme that regularly applies with hormones just as it does with Our Quadruple Aim.

The thyroid gland does make a small amount of T3 directly and releases it into the bloodstream. Some patients do not convert T4 to T3 well due to genetic deficiencies with their deiodinase enzymes (three known enzymes exist called D1, D2, and D3). Hence, why some patients fail to feel better on T4-only therapies. Those patients may end up requiring a hybrid approach, supplemented with T3. Thyroid hormone typically has a narrow therapeutic range, which means dosing must be precise to prevent harm.[170, 171, 172]

Along the way, I was paired up with an endocrinologist who switched me from Armour to T4. She started me at 100 mcg. Her reasoning, "I want to make sure we get enough hormone to peripheries."

By two weeks in, I was ablaze. My skin burned uncontrollably. It appears we had reached the peripheries, just as the doctor had wished. I placed call after call to her office. I'm overmedicated, I pleaded. *Sorry. She's not here. Sorry, she's at the hospital doing biopsies.* My blood pressure began spiking. Headaches. Chest pains. Shooting down my left arm. Racing heart. I wanted to crawl out of my skin. But I was afraid to just stop taking the medication. If she couldn't be there for me, maybe the emergency room could. On December 18, 2021, I checked myself in. They ran bloodwork. The attending doctor and I deliberated:

"Don't you have an endocrinologist you're working with?"

"Yeah, I do. I'm not getting a response. I'm sick."

"Well, we have to make a call. What do you want to do?"

"Cut it in half. Write me for 50 mcg. Start there."

"I'm okay with that. It's not like you have no thyroid function."

Again, I briefly donned my figurative white coat. Looking at my test results later from the hospital (before the dosage drop) confirmed my suspicions. Free hormone right on the upper end of the range, TSH terribly suppressed at 0.03 and well out of range; hard data to confirm my feelings all along. Weeks later, I saw a cardiologist and worked with his assistant. She was merciful and compassionate. Her words:

"You had a stress test, multiple EKGs, wore a Holter monitor and had an echocardiogram. All fine. I agree. 100 mcg was just too much. It's not like you need a full replacement dose. It's not your heart that's the problem, it's the things that are acting on it like the thyroid hormones. I want to see you feeling better."

I didn't have a T4 to T3 conversion problem. Too much hormone in means too much hormone out.

The endocrinologist, evidently listless from her other obligations, directed her nurse to write back. "It appears too much hormone made him go from hypothyroid to hyper." Old news by now. Also, she wanted me to stay off TRT while dialing in my thyroid values. Since I had stopped taking enclomiphene a couple months before and back on my own HPG, I was given another test. A new record—a new low.

LH = 1.2 [IU]/L	(Ref range: Male Age 20-70 years 1.5 - 8.1 mIU/mL)	Flag = Low
Total Testosterone = 250 ng/dL	(Ref range: 240 - 950 ng/dL)	

This goose was cooked. Fried. My body's hormonal system had left the building. This travesty became unsustainable. I have a family, a career, and a house to support. Whether on anybody else's radar, I still had to function. And a wait-and-see-while-receiving-minimal-communication was not a reconcilable strategy. What should I do? Afterward, I asked Dr. Saya:

"What she probably believed, though falsely in my opinion, is that by attempting to restore your thyroid values to normal levels, your testosterone values would come back too. I just don't see it in your numbers or your

body's response. Your testosterone values are low and I don't see them returning. It's a glaring issue so you can at least start addressing that now. My recommendation is to restart TRT and stick with the lower thyroid medication for a while."

I was sent to another endocrinologist's office. We would customarily spar as doctor and patient, bobbing and weaving on my treatment plan. At first, one provider alternated levothyroxine at 50mcg one day and 25 mcg the next. Absolutely unsustainable—a dizzying array of semi-hyper/hypo/hyper/hypo. Another then told me why not stick with 50 mcg? I liked your numbers better there. I told him I don't like how I feel there. I was depleted and finished. I said I want to try 38 mcg. By now, it didn't matter who wore the white coat.

He relented. 38 mcg of brand name levothyroxine, Tirosint. Not more. Not less. The right dosage not just for anyone, but for me. I made the point that given Tirosint is essentially pure T4, without fillers found in generics, how much is absorbed varies (i.e. 50 mcg of generic could be close to 38 mcg of branded medication). The "unseen hand" wanted me to try five other generic brands first while disregarding my doctor's pre-authorization requests (these inefficiencies are a blaring siren as to why the U.S. spends nearly one-fifth of its GDP on medical costs). Because the "unseen hand" refuses to pay, I choose to work with a specialty compounding pharmacy and pay out-of pocket.

There are approximately 37 trillion cells in the adult human body.[173] Each one must re-adjust to taking exogenous thyroid, at the nucleus level for months and months. There was no way in hell I was going to slog through five other formulations after grudgingly re-regulating on my current formulation over the past year and a half. One day, to prove how sensitive my body is, I ran a thyroid panel as soon as the lab opened and before taking my daily thyroid medication. I baselined with a FT4 of 0.6, just below range (my trough value). The next time, I took my medication and waited 3 hours before running the same labs (my peak value). FT4 had more than doubled. I sought Dr. Saya's weigh in:

> *"You're obviously very sensitive to hormones. T4 has a very long half-life. Yet, 24 hours later, you'll be right back at the bottom of the range. Then you take 38 mcg of T4 and a few hours later practically double your values at peak. The bloodwork explains some of the effects you've described.*
>
> *That kind of jump is uncommon. I wouldn't expect it. Same goes for testosterone with you. Many guys I work with wouldn't even feel a difference by increasing their dosage 10 mg, yet your values swing greatly and you feel it.*
>
> *You could split your thyroid dosage to twice a day to lower the peak, but that might not work for lifestyle reasons."*

On the last point, thyroid hormone must be taken on an empty stomach for proper absorption, which is why it's commonly taken first thing in the morning before eating. I personally set my phone alarm to remind me. I then wait one hour to eat. It must be taken at the same time each day to keep blood values in the proper zone. Splitting doses is difficult for most patients—once the busy day starts, people are eating or snacking throughout.

Further complicating matters is if you are modifying your thyroid treatment while adjusting testosterone dosing because of indirect influence on binding proteins. Binding proteins help move hormones throughout the body and dictate how much freely circulates at any given time. TRT can expose an underlying thyroid weakness. See excerpt below from *"Sex steroids and the thyroid"* by Rundsarah Tahboub, M.D. and Baha M Arafah, M.D.:

"Gonadal steroids exert their influence on thyroid function primarily by altering the clearance of thyroxine-binding globulin (TBG). Despite the gonadal steroids-induced changes in serum TBG concentrations, subjects with normal thyroid glands maintain clinical and biochemical euthyroidism without changes in their serum free thyroxine (T4) or thyroid-stimulating hormone (TSH) levels.

In contrast, the administration of gonadal steroids to patients with thyroid diseases causes significant biochemical and clinical alterations requiring changes in the doses of thyroid medications. Similarly, gonadal steroid therapy might unmask thyroid illness in previously undiagnosed subjects. It would be prudent to assess thyroid function in subjects with thyroid disease 6-8 weeks after gonadal steroid administration or withdrawal."[174]

The above translated: a body, when healthy, may find and maintain harmony easier than a treated one. With so many variables at play, Dr. Saya frequently reminds me, "When it comes to hormone treatment, you'll never know how you'll feel until you try." He and I often discuss changing one variable at a time. Absent that, patients will have a hard time sorting out what change did what.

I would undergo further HPG-related testing. Because of headaches during this period, two MRIs of my pituitary were performed. The headaches were always in the same place—about two or so inches from the front of my forehead, between my eyes. I would say a respectable approximation for where my pituitary gland sits. The MRI confirmed a partially empty sella, unforeseen for my age, called Empty Sella Syndrome (ESS) and what could be considered a small pituitary tumor or incidentaloma.

The pituitary gland sits in a small bony pocket outside the brain called the sella turcica (or Turkish saddle) and is surrounded by brain fluid for protection. Excessive brain fluid in the sella can put pressure on the pituitary gland, squishing and flattening it. From there, perchance a resulting biochemical weakness or interference—hypopituitarism.

I was informed, "You went through puberty fine. You fathered two children fine. But, for whatever reason, your pituitary just kind of gave up eventually. A small defect or pinhole perhaps from birth allowed extra brain fluid to leak in back then. Hard to know. Either way, something triggered things now."

Yes, a straw heavy enough finally landed on the camel's back. In the end, my current treatment protocol is not a perfect savior, and while TRT combined with thyroid hormone has provided me some relief and restored some parts of the spectrum, not all and unevenly.

((THEY GOT THE GOLDEN ARCHES, MINE IS THE GOLDEN ARCS))

I recalled earlier in childhood experiencing bad headaches for a stretch of time. Undoubtedly, a parallel to my experiences as an adult. Relative to classmates, I was short for my age. A specialist ordered an MRI then too. Rummaging through storage, Dr. Otten's staff gallantly located a copy of the report from roughly 30 years ago. It read in part, "Start of what appears to be a partially empty sella."

In my memory remains one scrap of my childhood conversation with that specialist, "You probably won't have any problems from this later in life. If you want to grow, just eat more cheeseburgers, okay?" As a kid, who could disagree with more cheeseburgers? These days, and several cheeseburgers later, I'm down to two doctors—Dr. Otten and Dr. Saya. I had learned a valuable lesson I would never forget: Quality over quantity, if you're lucky enough to find it.

TL;DR—lessons for OQA:

Your body is smarter than any test. It will find ways to communicate with you, even if you've never experienced them before. It doesn't automatically mean it's gaslighting you. Listen to it.

It's a good idea to keep your medical records around. You might need them later, much later. The second half of my dad's hepatitis C story is a perfect example (see Chapter 23, Horrible v. Helpful: Making a List, Checking It Twice)

((SHARE THE 'WHYS'))

At first, it might seem like a good thing I can write all that I have about the patient experience. But is it? Rather, isn't it a little wretched that I didn't have to reach far to find these words? It means the experience can be completely demanding and taxing. It means it is frustrating and baggage inducing. It means our healthcare system needs dire fixing. I offer the next evolution of **"I don't know"** is:

> *"I don't know. But, here is what I've commonly seen in clinical experience with other similar patients or heard from my colleagues. I can give you a range or a reasonable expectation. I believe I can get you to 70-80% based on my prior observations and experiences. We'll keep testing and adjusting until we get you there."*
>
> *"It might take up to one year or more for you to feel better. I've seen it vary from person to person. Hang in there. I'm here for you."*

Also, I believe offering the 'whys' behind a treatment decision are paramount to the patient's confidence level in their provider.

If a provider is uncomfortable with what a patient is asking for, then they should say so while making absolutely sure to take time and explain why to the patient.

During my thyroid troubles, not once did anybody ever mention the possible time frame involved. Nobody said it might take at least a year to adjust. Instead, a friend told me. One who had gone through many fits and starts herself—that is, until she landed under the care of a thorough provider who was there for her.

Earlier in my journey, I'm reminded of when we were trying different solutions, Dr. Otten wrote to me in the patient portal, **"I'll help you anyway that I can."** Ever a servant leader, the good doctor offered the perfect example of saying: **"I'm here for you."**

TL;DR—lessons for OQA:

Everyone, when something terrible happens, all you have left is your attitude: Either start trying or finish dying.

I think it's fair to say that whatever ails you, your ultimate liberator or enslaver will be your attitude. Whether your attitude is your best advocate or strongest antagonist lies in your willpower to reframe your circumstances.

I accepted Dr. Otten's words. With a young son, daughter, and wife who depended on me, and others I cared about who I didn't want to let down, I had to choose life and hoped it in due time chose me back.

Perhaps my favorite part written by Ms. Framer's AWS account is this: *"We encourage members to 'pay it forward' and support other members."*[175] 'Paying it forward' is the primary reason my wife and I are open to sharing our experiences. I wish for our stories to help contribute to a groundswell of awareness regarding potential side effects caused by medicine in certain patients.

TL;DR—lessons for OQA:

Providers, medication risks aren't negligible and caretakers need to do a better job of saying, "Here's what the available literature says" BEFORE prescribing, regardless of whether they've ever clinically encountered it.

Patients, there's always the chance you will be your doctor's n=1. Then, after the damage is done, you find you are actually n=10,000 and counting among the population.

If the literature says nothing, the action doesn't stop there. In fact, it has just started. You as a patient must research possible effects before swallowing that first pill and weigh them–cautiously.

YOU MUST. Again, details matter.

((20))

Higher Quality

"The aim of medicine is to prevent disease and prolong life; the ideal of medicine is to eliminate the need of a physician."

– WILLIAM J. MAYO

Todd R. Otten, M.D.:

How do you measure quality in healthcare where the inevitable outcome of every patient, every single human being is death? Every case has the same endpoint, but a different timeline. Morbid? Perhaps, but reality nonetheless. So who determines the standard against which excellence is measured?

As an experienced physician, difficult questions become easier to ask. Quite frequently (with sicker/older patients) I will ask a question that is essential to determining their course of care. I will even inquire at a visit to establish care (if appropriate). I preface the question with my thoughts on quality of life versus life expectancy. Describing these as balancing on a pendulum, I will ask where their priorities lie: "Quality of life, or quantity of life." Potentially surprising to some, a good percentage choose quality of life. And others want heroic measures enacted until their dying breath. There are a few simple keys to this exercise—asking the question, and listening to the response.

Rhetorical questions dominate the gray world of medicine. How do we capture a quality endpoint for the 40-year-old breast cancer survivor, whose disease has returned with such vigor, that her goal is to live to see her youngest graduate from high school?

There are so many factors that contribute to quality care in healthcare, both subjective and objective. Add in endless surveys, data on everything imaginable, and quality being equated with costs. Lest we forget our sicker and aging population. What about fraud, waste, and abuse? In a society where anything less than five out of five stars is deemed subpar, healthcare is in a precarious position with regards to quality measures. The quality strings pull at both patients and providers and blur the picture tremendously.

Before we continue to open Pandora's box, we must remember that Our Quadruple Aim is about balance. If all of our energy is spent on quality, other components of our tetrad may suffer. Healthcare dollars are not infinite and we have proven that spending more doesn't always yield better outcomes. If we don't listen to our patients and providers, I doubt their experience will be ideal. Unfortunately, in our quest for perfection we have left both patients and providers behind.

Is there a simple solution? Many would argue no. As part of this chapter I will offer a contrarian view—**a rainbow of gray**. We will review some clinical examples of success using OQA as the reference encyclopedia, and discuss population health and aligned incentives.

Certainly data and finances are important, but we mustn't forget these are an amalgamation of many individual data points—patients. Spending more time entering data, satisfying alarms, and checking boxes has led to less time with patients. Less time to comfort the sick child, less time to comfort the hospice patient. It's time to take a step back and reassess what we are trying to accomplish in healthcare. If we remember that medicine is a world full of different shades of gray, the picture (of quality) starts to become clearer and clearer.

((CT (COMPUTERIZED TOMOGRAPHY) SCANS))

"My goal for my health care is not to use my cemetery plot."

– PATIENT

Christopher Port, M.D. is one of my best friends. We attended medical school together at Wayne State University and he is the CMO for a forward-thinking, independent emergency medicine physician group in Grand Rapids, MI – Emergency Care Specialists (ECS). We still debate who sat next to whom on the first day of medical school. Chris, I am putting it in writing: I sat down and introduced myself to you. Not sure that will end the debate, but at least it's in print.

During medical school, we spent countless hours together. In class, dissecting cadavers in gross anatomy, rounding on patients, studying for step one of the USMLE (United States Medical Licensing Exam). Quite often we would play some golf and then study for hours upon no end. Lattes and coffee were a staple. Needless to say, we became lifelong friends.

Recently we had the opportunity to spend a few days together in Northern Michigan during a fall golf outing. If you haven't seen Michigan in the fall, you're missing out. My favorite season for sure. The crisp, clean, refreshing air. The bright red, orange, and yellow on the trees as winter approaches. Stunning. One round of golf involved rain, snow, sleet, sun, and wind—all during just a few holes. Thank goodness for cart covers and heaters. Some consider this sort of adventure too much, but the smiles and laughter dominated the day, even with the inclement weather.

I thought this section was about CT scans? As Chris and I drove north for our golf endurance test, we chatted about life. Family, hobbies, golf, cryptocurrency. But, soon our conversation turned to our work and I was excited to update Chris on my progress with the book. We discussed both good and bad in our work environments, and the overwhelming issues that exist in healthcare. I was fascinated with the discussion, particularly the evolution of Chris' career. He has transitioned from a full-time clinician to his current state of 50/50 (ER physician/CMO). I recalled explaining OQA (while I was an ACO medical director) a few years prior (ironically on our way to another golf outing). And now, as I listened to some of the quality improvement projects his group was working on, it was clear his efforts embodied Our Quadruple Aim.

The project is titled, *The Impact of Standardized Use of Head CT Decision Rules on Computerized Tomography Imaging Utilization in Adult Minor Head Trauma*. The purpose of the quality improvement project was as follows: to determine if using clinical decision aids during the evaluation of minor head trauma (in adults) would decrease head CT utilization. Without getting into the minutia, it was a well-designed study that yielded some impressive results. Using the Canadian Head CT rule as their guide, they monitored CT utilization in minor head trauma over an 18-month period.[176]

Part of the process included developing an internal expert Quality Improvement team, workshop meetings, adoption of standardized pathways, a robust education plan, individualized performance feedback, and data transparency to track metrics. Over the 18-month intervention, the group achieved a 57.5% increase in appropriate CT utilization. Even more impressive, they were able to have a 17% reduction in CT utilization rates which resulted in a potential avoidance of 255 CT scans. An anticipated cost savings of $237,915. Translating education into savings for both payers and patients alike.[177]

As Chris continued to explain, I couldn't help but interject and tell him how proud I was of the work he was doing. Whether they knew it or not, ECS was exemplifying Our Quadruple Aim. His group's efforts are incredible and go far beyond this one example. The two hours of driving to our golf destination flew by. Brainstorming about healthcare improvement, who knew this could be so stimulating. Practicing quality medicine, working on lowering costs—wins for both patients and providers. This conversation surely helped us endure the pending gray Michigan weather.

1. **Patient Experience** – Less CT scans leads to decreased radiation exposure, lower costs, and shorter visit times.
2. **Quality Care** – Quality outcomes were sustained despite less testing. More is not always better.
3. **Lower Costs** – Avoiding unnecessary testing translated to less expenditures for insurers and patients.
4. **Provider Wellness** – Dollars saved translate to value-based reimbursement for providers. Quality work that is compensated, as it should be.[178]

((LISTENING))

"Change happens by listening and then starting a dialogue with the people who are doing something you don't believe is right."

– JANE GOODALL

"How are you today?," I queried.

"Yes I am," replied Terry.

I can't help but smile writing this. I have known Terry for over a decade and saw him as a patient for the last time today. Terry quickly reminded me that I pulled his "chestnuts" out of the fire a few times. He went on to clarify, "You saved me from being paralyzed; and, another time you saved my life." Prior to Terry's appointment, I had been debating how to begin this section. What better way to explore effective listening than real-life examples?

Before I impart Terry's stories, I feel compelled to convey

how listening has eroded from the art of medicine during my 20-year career. This is unfortunate as the patient will often tell you the diagnosis before you even start your examination. They will open their hearts and minds to you. They will tell you their darkest secrets and loftiest of goals. They share their feelings, emotions, and experiences—on every level. But, you must be paying attention to hear it. The skill of listening is often sacrificed in favor of data collection, box clicking, clerical burdens. As with any skill, there is a continuum. Many providers are great listeners, others not so much. As healthcare becomes more complex, the detractors to listening continue to grow.

Beyond clues to what their disease process might be, patients will tell you where the issues are in your office, the hospital, the healthcare system, the insurance company, and more. Some of the concerns are unfounded or perhaps unrealistic; often, many are truths. Patients with similar experiences that are not captured on a survey. Patterns of dysfunction will display themselves like a vibrant rainbow after a fresh spring rain. But you must see the rain and hear the thunder first, before looking for the rainbow.

The following stories highlight two ends of the spectrum of listening, and how it can make all of the difference in the world. Just ask Terry.

The first time I pulled Terry's "chestnuts" out of the fire occurred 10 years ago. Terry had been seeing my predecessor on a regular basis, but had an appointment with me regarding neck pain. The visit began with his customary greeting (see above) and quickly we developed a rapport. After a few laughs, we dove into his concerns. Terry recently had surgery on his lumbar spine (lower back) and had been routinely seeing several specialists. But his lower back wasn't the issue. Terry complained of neck pain, worsening numbness, and weakness in his upper extremities. These symptoms had gotten progressively worse in the preceding months, and were severely limiting his daily functioning. After a neurological exam, I was certain a major issue affected his cervical spine. I was shocked he had seen three specialists prior to me, with the exact same complaints. Terry conveyed they weren't listening and kept focusing on his lower back. This created several layers of delay.

My staff will confirm I rarely order any imaging STAT, but I was so concerned about Terry's presentation—I ordered a STAT cervical spine MRI. The result: severe spinal stenosis with edema (swelling) of his spinal cord. Essentially his spinal cord was being squished, causing the swelling and progressive neurological dysfunction. I was happy to have an actionable diagnosis for Terry, but disgusted with my colleagues who failed to hear his complaints. Terry had emergent surgery less than 48 hours later. For those of you not in healthcare, an emergent neurosurgical case diagnosed by a family physician is rare. Fortunately, most of Terry's neurological deficits resolved over time. Had three of my colleagues listened to Terry, the delay could have been prevented.

I pulled Terry's "chestnuts" out of the fire again after he had been seen in the emergency room for back pain. Terry had recently been treated for lumbar osteomyelitis (an infection in the bone of his lower spine). He was following with a few specialists and previously had improved. The antibiotics were stopped, but within a few weeks his pain returned and progressively worsened. Over a weekend, the pain got so severe that he presented to the emergency room. I had to rely on Terry's account at the follow-up visit, as no ER record was available (the dictation was not finished).

Terry reportedly expressed concerns (in the ER) that his spinal infection had returned. Despite his pleadings, only a basic work up was performed, some pain medication given and Terry was discharged home. No antibiotics. More labs and another urgent MRI was performed: recurrent lumbar spine osteomyelitis. Fortunately after another lengthy antibiotic course, Terry made a full recovery. I question how much the opiate crisis detracted from Terry's ER visit, as chronic pain patients were often stigmatized and viewed under a different lens. But, better listening certainly would have expedited appropriate care for Terry.

Effective listening takes practice, patience, and time. Unfortunately, this tool is not effectively utilized enough in our tumultuous healthcare landscape. Listening is invaluable to Our Quadruple Aim. Take a deep breath, slow down, free your mind, and listen. You might be surprised what solutions arise.

((POPULATION HEALTH))

"Risk isn't a word in my vocabulary. It's my very existence."

– SLASH

Population health deals with the health outcomes of a certain group of individuals, often a specific cohort or within a geographical location. This overarching approach looks at the entire group rather than individuals. The goal is to maximize health outcomes of a community or a particular group. It is strongly rooted in primary care and preventative medicine. Population health addresses individuals' health needs throughout the continuum of care through participation, engagement, and interventions with the overall goal of improved health outcomes of the collective.[179, 180] Unfortunately, healthcare is fighting an uphill battle to achieve Our Quadruple Aim, as productivity and profits are often prioritized before outcomes.

Thinking back, I have been working with forms of population health since 2004, when I assumed my role as the flight surgeon for VP-10 in the U.S. Navy. Our goal was keeping the squadron healthy to assist in protecting America's freedom. With the assistance of two Navy corpsmen, we were responsible for every aspect of the squadron's medical care. Granted, this is a relatively healthy group of individuals, having been medically screened prior to entry into the Navy. But we certainly had our share of pathology: achalasia, thyroid cancer, lymphoma, normal pressure hydrocephalus, arterial thrombus, and body dysmorphic disorder (just to name a few). My colleagues affectionately called me "the zookeeper," as we diagnosed a handful of uncommon or rare disorders.

I formally learned the term population health in 2014, concordant with my introduction to ACOs. The concept immediately struck a chord, particularly the preventative care component. I was Vice Chief of Staff, and considered how to incorporate the concept at Hayes Green Beach Hospital. I saw the value of team-based care to improve the health of our patients, and I started to campaign for a population health position. The initial response: "What is the ROI?" Dumbfounded. What is the return for a position to help order appropriate preventative tests for tens of thousands of patients? This task routinely, logically falls on PCPs. Family physicians typically handle several complaints at any given visit, and depending on time constraints, ordering preventative tests fails to be the priority.

Despite the initial resistance—I persisted. I don't have a MBA (Master of Business Administration) but I am a strategic thinker and numbers are intuitive. As such, a population health position seemed a no-brainer, including from a financial perspective. But it also encapsulated every component of OQA. Improved Patient Experience through team-based care, getting appropriate preventative tests, catching major problems early, and avoiding hospitalizations. Ergo, Higher Quality and Lower Costs. And a team-based approach certainly reduces clerical burdens, leading to improved Provider Wellness. Essentially a win for everyone involved, yet I struggled to gain traction and subsequent approval. Frustrating.

Undeterred, I decided to make a bold move. When it comes to doing the right thing for patients and providers I tend to be fearless (for better or worse). At the time, I routinely attended the hospital board meetings as a medical staff representative. I typically updated the board regarding the medical staff and often shared rewarding stories. As I was not getting any traction for population health, I made a pitch to the board. And it worked—less than a month later we had a pilot program for population health. Starting with colorectal cancer screening, a medical assistant was the first member of our population health team. The year was 2015—success immediately. The number of colonoscopies increased dramatically (as did revenue). Fast forward eight years, and our population health team was emulated and now an integral part of the health system. And now the larger system looks to our efforts as a template for success. Darn those pesky physicians who advocate for patient care.

There are many key components to a successful population health team (or whichever title you prefer). But engaged PCPs, teamwork, care coordination, and aligned incentives are critical to a successful program. And population health teams align quite nicely with Our Quadruple Aim:

1. **Patient Experience** – Helping patients be proactive while navigating the complex healthcare landscape.
2. **Quality Care** – Helping with data capture, ordering preventive tests, and care coordination.
3. **Lower Costs** – Avoiding hospitalization, readmission, unnecessary procedures, and redundant testing, while capturing revenue for appropriate testing and value-based reimbursement.
4. **Provider Wellness** – Reducing clerical burdens and box clicking, teamwork, and improved patient outcomes. Returning the joy to medicine.

((E(QUALITY)))

"Even before the pandemic,
our system was failing the people it was designed to serve."

– FARZON A. NAHVI, M.D., *CODE GRAY*[181]

Brandon Francis, M.D.:

We have an equity problem in healthcare. To complicate matters, some people believe that delivering equal care is the answer. It is not. The answer is to engage all necessary resources to achieve equitable outcomes. This means care may not be equal. For some, to achieve a desired outcome, no specific interventions may be required. For others to achieve that same desired outcome, they may need multiple providers, transportation, food, and childcare services. We need to stop running from the reality that we have disparities in healthcare that are strongly rooted in race and ethnicity.

We should move past arguing about the quality of the data and start collaborating on solutions. Some people are content dissecting the data to the point that they miss the forest for the trees. The data is not perfect. But the trends are clear.

Healthcare outcomes are not isolated to what happens within the healthcare facility. There are many factors that influence an individual's health status. The spectrum of things that influence health range from genetic factors to what zip code they live in. Consider this: does your zip code have access to healthy food options? Let that marinate for a moment. Your zip code may communicate more about your health than you realize. And yes, your health insurance company knows this.

((ALIGNED INCENTIVES))

"Show me the incentive and I will show you the outcome."

– CHARLIE MUNGER

Todd R. Otten, M.D.:

Having aligned incentives is essential to maximizing quality. The more a team works together, the greater potential for a win, whether on the football pitch or the hospital ward. Cohesive units increase the opportunity for success. My favorite fútbol club (soccer in the U.S.) is Arsenal. Located in North London and boasting a long history of success, the recent years have been a bit more turbulent. After a long stint in the Champions League, Arsenal has been notably absent for several years.

However, the start of the 2022 season has been amazing: 14 wins, two draws, and one loss in the first 17 matches—43 points and sitting top of the league. What changed? Probably more than I will ever truly know. But a new manager, Mikel Arteta, was appointed and difficult decisions were made. A former Arsenal player, Arteta's leadership style is infectious. With a clear vision and depth of knowledge, the culture shifted. This type of transformation is not instantaneous, but incentives certainly seem aligned towards a common goal. The team plays with a decisive, attacking mentality. As Ray Hudson (world renowned fútbol commentator) would describe: "magisterial."

Benjamin Schwartz, M.D. writes: "Incentive alignment involves ensuring that all stakeholders strive for common goals and pull in the same direction. In theory, aligned incentives can eliminate practices that run contra to the greater good while discouraging the waste, fraud, and profiteering that plague American medicine."[182]

Brilliant in its simplicity, I couldn't agree more. But, the obstacles quickly appear, making implementation near impossible at times. Certainly patients want affordable, quality care, and a positive experience; the majority of providers want to deliver these while maintaining their well-being. But, as Dr. Schwartz notes: "...existing stakeholders have often had disparate goals and have been unable or unwilling to work together to address the system's shortcomings. In fact, there remains distrust and lack of consensus with many of these entities as evidenced by resistance to price transparency, surprise billing horror stories, network confusion, physician burnout, and on going battles about patient data and interoperability just to name a few."[183]

As mentioned in the introduction, Our Quadruple Aim is a stripped down, bare bones approach to aligned incentives. The four tenets are easy to understand and extrapolate. No convoluted concepts. Simple, actionable, malleable. I encourage you to take Our Aims, mold and transform them, and make them yours.

Our Quadruple Aim	Coach's Quadruple Aim
1. Patient Experience	Player wellness, development
2. Quality Care	Winning, having fun
3. Lower Costs	Fan experience, fair ticket price
4. Provider Wellness	Coach's wellness

Healthcare in America needs a unifying force that demands an end to excessive profit seeking and selfish behavior. OQA requires compromise, understanding, and alignment. Not siloed, fragmented care that creates more widgets. Yes, I believe OQA can be the driver for equitable, affordable, quality care for all, with a positive experience for patients and providers. I have seen it work. If enough stakeholders adopt Our Quadruple Aim as a transparent tool for facilitating change we have a chance to turn our ripples into a tsunami.

((EMULATE, THEN AN EXODUS))

"I go where Dr. Otten goes.
I want to retire with him, when he does."

– CARI, MA

Quality in healthcare comes in many forms; it is ever an evolution of science, blended with the art of medicine. Metrics and data abound, but sometimes it is the simplest of adventures that yield the highest quality. As noted, my practice achieved an "Office Utopia" as a pilot program. Despite the fact the clinic was only open for two years, we accomplished incredible things—both in infrastructure and patient care. In fact, after being open for less than one year, we were asked by several hospital executives how "the system" could emulate the practice in other offices. But "systemness" didn't seem to appreciate independent thought, and in the end—finances won. Black and white trumped my world of gray.

I would like to impart some of the highlights from our experience. Some anecdotal evidence is involved, but quality care certainly has a subjective component and when performed well exemplifies Our Quadruple Aim.

My office manager (also a nurse) is superlative and underappreciated, as she advocates for both staff and patients assertively and honestly. She has a special place in my heart for her efforts. As we saw patients while short-staffed, she filled in as a MA and receptionist and even assisted me with performing procedures. All the while not shirking her duties as the manager, achieving both PCMH status and a rural health clinic designation. Yet, nary a position has been found for her.

No wonder healthcare employees are leaving in droves. Why do healthcare leaders allow for short-staffing to be so commonplace? I am sure you guessed. Unacceptable staffing-to-patient ratios are becoming the norm (with finances driving the proverbial bus). Just read the current healthcare headlines:

"'Only a Sociopath Could Work for a Large Health System,' Doc Says Sardonically."[184] Patient volumes are high as ever and we do our best with limited resources. Is this a just and safe culture? Would a commercial airliner be allowed to take off, if the pilot was acting as the baggage handler, refueler, and flight attendant as well?

The front office staff in a primary care office often takes the brunt of patients' frustrations with healthcare as a collective; their attitude and effort can make or break an office. My front office staff is instrumental in our ability to provide quality care. A perfect example: facilitating referrals as our office neared its final days—ensuring patients got the care they needed. I would be remiss if I didn't include our nurse navigator, who ensured appropriate care for our complex Medicare patients and would troubleshoot just about any logistical problem I may throw her way.

As I re-read the section entitled "The day the music died," I was reminded that good things often come to an end. Unfortunately, the quality care we delivered wasn't enough to trump the theoretical savings on rent by relocating our office. I equate the decision to relocate our office as the first domino in a long line. That first domino hit the second: my decision to retire.

From there, the dominos quickly diverged into many lines—falling faster and faster. The impact on staffing regarding these decisions has been tremendous. Fortunately, the vast majority of the staff have landed in wonderful positions—some closer to home, closer to family. A few retired or left healthcare, and others transitioned (to positions described as their dream job). A few stories have yet to play out, but that first domino reaffirmed my decision to step away. I feel I am being called to something different through *Ripple of Change*. Time will tell.

Data is important to OQA, so let's review the numbers. The initial numbers are as of the day after the music died (after I set the second domino in motion). I am only documenting known transitions, as at least three of the staff have yet to determine their paths. The numbers represent staff within our office and are public knowledge. The information is telling, just imagine the exodus of patients.

	Our Office Utopia: ***The day the music died***	**The ROI:** ***Four months later***
M.D.	1	0
NPs	3	1
Nurses	2	1
MAs	5	2
Reception	4	2
TOTAL	**15**	**6**

And what about the two MAs who work with me? Fortunately, both are thrilled for their next adventure. Both are transitioning with the office and working with the remaining NP. I anticipate their working relationship will blossom and they will continue to provide superlative care.

So after two years of the pilot program, the office doors will close permanently in 2023. The pilot office, with three brand new NPs, was successful on many levels. Not everything was perfect, but for a large stretch of time the office embodied Our Quadruple Aim. But in the end, a decision to save money on facilities cost the system much more. Starting with known estimates to replace a physician of $500,000 to 1 million dollars, the costs of the second domino that fell were much greater (in my humble estimation, but what do I know).[185, 186]

Ironically, if I had been asked, not told, the office was moving—I may have stayed.

In a recent conversation with a colleague, he discussed the fear of mutual destruction and described how that exists in the corporate workplace. The fear of mutual destruction is the military notion that nuclear war would assure complete destruction of both warring parties. This notion creates a level of deterrence regarding nuclear powers and the potential for war. Seems a little drastic to utilize this tactic with employees? But it does seem to exist, with leaders making decisions hoping employees don't call their bluff and have a "nuclear" response. Surely, some consider my decision one of mutual self-destruction. But that would mean both parties were destroyed—wouldn't it?

However, I am more at peace with my life now than I can remember in a long time. Far from being destroyed. Cari has reminded me regularly how good my mood has been, often humming as I walk to see patients. Laughter and smiles abound. Will I return to direct patient care at some point—maybe. Will I ever be a full-time family physician—doubtful. The days of working in an environment that doesn't respect Our Quadruple Aim are long gone.

((21))

Set Points

Joshua J. Judy – Patient:

The experiences of the last several years caused me to reflect back—before finasteride, tramadol, duloxetine, and the rest. To better understand my baseline, I reached to my childhood. A young boy, closing my eyes at night, I could feel each sway and tumble of the roller coaster earlier that day. I effortlessly replayed each vivid memory–the smell of cotton candy and popcorn perfuming the air, the warmth of the sun glinting overhead, and children giggling in delight only to scream as they crested over the ride's next hill. My senses had been tantalized with each sight, scent, and sound of the amusement park. Every detail lucid, recall sharp, and emotions wide-ranging and intense.

I could be described as shy and contemplative. I was a bit compulsive and a perfectionist but also creative–writing poems, and making music. Later in life, I picked up playing guitar and even composed an instrumental score for my wedding.

As a teenager and into adulthood, I would get anxious easily. Public speaking in front of large crowds was torturous. The mere thought set my mind racing. But the act left me looking for the nearest exit as my heart pounded furiously in my chest. The opposite sex made me nervous and antsy. If a pretty girl looked my way, I'd furtively look down at the floor rather than flirt. Going into a major meeting would cause my hands to get ice cold. *"Several lines of evidence suggest specific neurotransmitter system alterations in social phobia, especially with regard to the serotoninergic, noradrenergic and dopaminergic systems. During anticipation of public speaking, heart rate was elevated in patients with social phobia compared to controls."*[187] These are the same neurological systems duloxetine influences.

Another quirk—growing up, I used to get night or sleep terrors (referred to as parasomnia). They continued into adulthood as well. When I began taking duloxetine at 30 mg, they increased significantly. After upping to 60 mg, they nearly vanished. Events became much more static and dulled–a gray, filtered existence. Many times, they're just that, events. The world felt considerably flatter and recollections subdued. Of course, the big question that remains is why?

Nearly everyone I've spoken with who is afflicted by my condition describes a similar neurological and psychological makeup—going from a highly sensitive individual within themselves and their environment, to a far more robotic-like state. In many cases, those presenting with AWS or PSSD have hormonal profiles that even look normal. So where do the inflicted alterations hide?

((CHANGING PERSPECTIVES))

Partnering with my primary care provider to write this book has opened a lot of channels, breaking open an overdue conversation. During an office visit, Dr. Otten caught me off guard:

DR. OTTEN: "I have a serious question for you, and I want you to think before answering: What will you do with all this knowledge? You should consider going to medical school."

Flattered, I wasn't sure how to answer. For Megan and me, the medications had either destroyed or reshaped something critical. But I think I can answer now: **For the same reason Dr. Otten went into medicine—I want to help others.** Feeling a flutter of motivation, I started asking Megan things like:

1. Do you still get enjoyment from food?
2. Do you laugh just because you know it's what you're supposed to do in a social situation or does it come naturally?
3. Does your skin feel as ticklish? Does it still tingle from touch?
4. Do you still dream much at night?
5. What about daydreams or fantasies?

The answers to questions 1-5 are at the bottom of this section.

She asked me the same questions along with: Was the opposite sex still attractive?

Megan shared with me that once the kids are grown, she fears she won't remember their childhoods. I too shared this fear, along with questioning if a loved one died, would I feel nothing. It was our new reality with our brains entirely restructured and governed by these medications. For her, it's because of the daily intake of the levetiracetam and for me, the ruins of duloxetine.

We found out—just like I got good at faking being able to read a classroom board or screen from far away—I got proficient at knowing when to laugh. Not by choice, Megan learned to excel at faking social cues too. Because it's all on the inside, we can't prove it beyond a reasonable doubt. Society is all about, "show me the data—show me the evidence." Everything is a court case, an overplayed mantra. Anecdotal evidence matters.

Data has its time and place, and I would overload you with it if I could. But until scientists produce tests for precisely diagnosing adverse side-effects, openly sharing experiences is the best available option. For all your visual learners, I present two basic illustrations I rendered:

**Normal Emotional Profile:
A Balanced Spectrum**

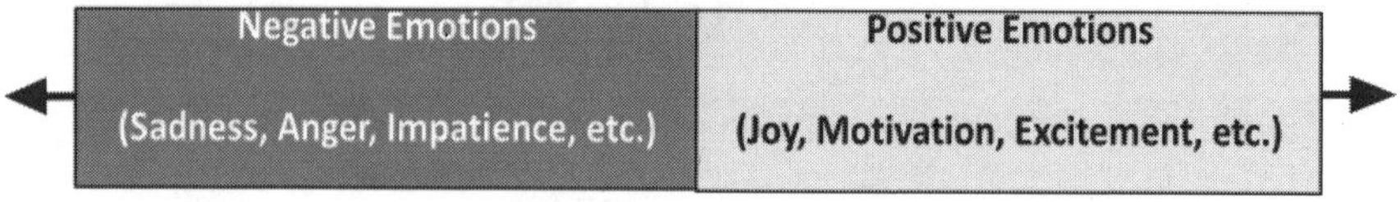

**Levetiracetam Emotional Profile:
Lopsided to the Negative, Capped on the Positive**

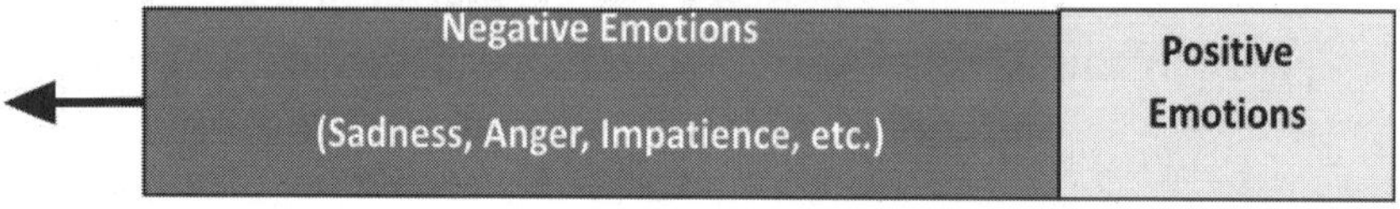

We had new set points...life just takes a much stronger lift. Megan helped me figure out my reality only because her feelings were essentially mine. We had been 'checking the box,' in quiet suffering. During this prolonged and disconsolate time, Megan mostly continued to fight her own war and I mine. I'm cognizant I hadn't been there for her in the way I now wished I could have been. I was so insular and focused on finding a solution to my troubles that I had nearly forgotten anyone and anything else.

Answers to the above questions Megan and I asked of each other. The first five answers weren't dissimilar enough to separate:

1. Do you still get enjoyment from food?

   Some, not as strong.

2. Do you laugh just because you know it's what you're supposed to do in a social situation or does it come naturally?

   Often laughed because I remembered the social cues, not because my body was still responding spontaneously.

3. Does your skin feel as ticklish? Does it still tingle from touch?

   Quite diminished.

4. Do you still dream much at night?

   No, or if I do, they're so weak I don't remember them in the morning.

5. What about daydreams or fantasies? *Rarely.*

As for my question:

6. Was the opposite sex in general still attractive?

   While I could still tell females were aesthetically copasetic, that's where it ended. Predominantly, the opposite sex, once beautiful to me, manifested as office furniture. Replaced in my mind as inanimate objects where strong attraction had once been.

((CHEAPSKATE TREASURES))

I reminisce on when I proposed to Megan. It was late spring 2011 and I had been meticulously planning for weeks. We were going to go on a 33.5-mile bike ride along an old railway, abandoned by a train company some 20 years earlier. The railway sat unattended and overgrown for years until given new life when converted to a riding trail. It ended near the beach at the lakeshore.

I was cheap then—mostly by circumstance as I was early in my career—so I zip-tied milk crates to the back of our bikes on behind-the-seat shelves and loaded all our supplies up. Some 70 pounds of camping supplies, water, and snacks haphazardly stacked in a top-heavy mess. If we survived this hairbrained scheme and I didn't lose the engagement ring along the trek, I would get down on one knee and propose.

We passed through many small towns, whizzed by blueberry patches, deciduous forests, and an occasional stream that spun like an entwined ribbon near our path. It was nearing dusk. We had been riding for at least eight hours. We were exhausted, grossly underestimating the demand of this trip. With little choice, we sluiced through the obscuring landscape around us. We had mostly stopped conversing, rationing what little energy we had left. The hum of our bicycle tires against the compacted gravel path melted seamlessly into the noise barrier created by our labored inhaling and exhaling.

Yet something else registered just above the whirr of the surroundings. It was subtle and nearby. I glanced over. Megan had been chanting quietly to herself for the past 30 minutes. I called out, what are you saying over there? *"Just keep swimming. Just keep swimming."* I had no idea what she was referring to but if it was helping, I'd say it too. I guess I was too fatigued to feel silly. *"Just keep swimming. Just keep swimming,"* I whispered. I was a little slow to catch on, but I would finally understand its magnitude years later.

((OPEN HEARTS, OPEN MINDS))

Does a one-size-fit-all approach crystalize the epitome of lazy thinking? Or does everybody have a native sweet spot? Is everyone affected by diseases and medications differently? This line of thinking is not abstract, hence why one person might drink copious amounts of alcohol without severely ill effects where another becomes inebriated after only two drinks. Alcohol is a substance and so are medications. They have intended-effects, or side-effects.

How do we enlighten and lead others to consider this? Long-haul COVID makes for a strong case study. A May 4, 2022 article by Jamie Ducharme highlights the downsides of broad-brush and closed-minded approaches to healthcare:

[Senator] Kaine won't name names, but he says he's been approached by at least one "person of importance" in Washington who has Long COVID but doesn't feel comfortable talking about it. "The person said, 'You can talk about having nerve tingling. I can't talk about brain fog and confusion, doing what I do.... People would be nice to me, but they might not entrust me with the things they entrust me with now,'" Kaine says.

Others have struggled to convince doctors and loved ones that their symptoms are real and worthy of treatment. Advocates hope public conversation and acceptance could go a long way toward easing the stigma, not only for long-haulers but also for people who suffer from other complex chronic conditions like myalgic encephalomyelitis/chronic fatigue syndrome and chronic Lyme disease."[188]

I remember early in the COVID-19 pandemic a brief exchange with Dr. Otten during an annual physical office visit.

ME: "We're going to learn a lot from this pandemic."

DR. OTTEN: "Yes, I suspect we're going to learn a lot about a lot of things, not just about our bodies."

It's hard to argue that burdensome times in life are only valuable if we walk away learning something useful from them. How do you convince the skeptical? The sometimes maladaptive yet ubiquitous response is with data. So, what happens when you don't even have the tools or tests to measure the data? You keep telling your story until you raise awareness, that's how. You get more and more eyeballs on it until the data can be produced.

In Mr. Kaine's case, it probably doesn't hurt to have the title of Senator behind your name. However, if he was struggling to convince others about a medical condition that (so far) only exists in people's words and stories, I definitely empathize. And pause to reflect: If even a U.S. Senator deals with the taboo of a situation in light of evidence, how many other ill-fated people are suffering from a rare disease in silence?

Because science is ever-evolving, I suggest the answers lie in what breakthroughs come next. In a June 9, 2022 article published in *Nature*, titled, **"COVID and smell loss: answers begin to emerge,"** it states,

> *"Early in the pandemic, a study showed that the virus attacks cells in the nose, called sustentacular cells, that provide nutrients and support to odour-sensing neurons.*
>
> *Since then, clues have emerged about what happens to the olfactory neurons after infection. Researchers including biochemist Stavros Lomvardas at Columbia University in New York City examined people who had died from COVID-19 and found that, although their neurons were intact, they had fewer membrane-embedded receptors for detecting odour molecules than usual.*
>
> *This was because the neurons' nuclei had been scrambled. Normally, the chromosomes in these nuclei are organized into two compartments—a structure that enables the neurons to express specific odour receptors at high levels. But when the team looked at the autopsied neurons, 'the nuclear architecture was unrecognizable,' Lomvardas says."*[189]

I suspect there are many matches to the damage caused by long-COVID and other mysterious ailments like Lyme Disease, Chronic Fatigue Syndrome, and possibly Antidepressant Withdrawal Syndrome (AWS), Post-SSRI/SNRI Sexual Dysfunction (PSSD), or Post-Finasteride Syndrome. Whether it's chronic inflammation, immune system shifts, neurosteroids or systemic hormonal imbalances. Up or downregulation of certain enzymes, changes in receptor sensitivities or counts, gene silencing, premature aging, and indiscriminate scrambling of sorts inside cells.

Our bodies simply might not metabolize key inputs and outputs as they once did, hence previous signaling is suppressed. Time will tell how accurately these hypotheses play out.

TL;DR—lessons for OQA: Ways to be less silent.

Patients, things you should be asking your doctor before devotedly accepting a treatment plan:

1. **Have you ever tried this in other patients before, or am I the first?**

2. **What is your confidence level for what you're proposing? Why?**

3. **What side effects have you seen in practice?**

4. **What side effects have you heard or read about, from colleagues, patients, or otherwise?**

5. **How long of a transition period when switching dosages or meds? Is there a wash-out period (meaning where the old dosage is leaving your body while you wait for the new amount/med to stabilize)?**

6. **What do you expect to see happen from this therapy or change?**

Oh, by the way–I got down on one knee and Megan said yes. 🙂

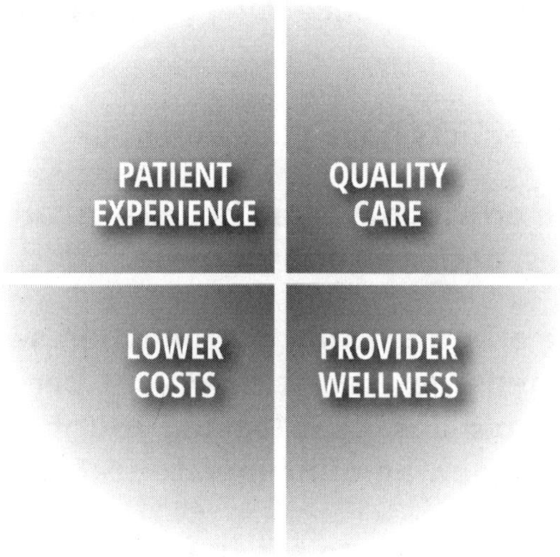
PATIENT EXPERIENCE
QUALITY CARE
LOWER COSTS
PROVIDER WELLNESS

((22))

Patient Experience

"You can please some of the people some of the time,
all of the people some of the time,
some of the people all of the time,
but you can never please all of the people all of the time."

– ABRAHAM LINCOLN

Todd R. Otten, M.D.:

In my spare time I like to go "picking" and "antiquing." I enjoy the treasure hunt and some even say I have an eye for it. More than once I have stopped on the side of the road to "pick" something out of another's trash. The end table, crafted with care and displaying a beautiful patina, now sits next to my sister's bed. The old adage that one man's trash is another man's treasure could never be more true. I say this quite often as I justify my hobby, but interestingly it does parallel patient experience.

"Dr. Otten, what are you doing here," asked Matt, one of my long-time patients. There I was, wearing a Spider-Man tee shirt, vintage shorts (procured at a resale shop), and flip flops. Drinking a bottle of water in the sweltering heat. It was 90 degrees out, thankfully the tent overhead provided a respite from the blistering sun. Sharing the experience with me were Daniel (my son) and two of my best friends. Scattered around us were comic books, collectibles, and antiques. If you wandered onto the scene it was akin to an unkept dorm room.

"Just having fun," I replied.

"Never thought I would see you here."

As we exchanged pleasantries, my mind went back to the day I diagnosed Matt's cancer. A thorough exam on a routine concern saved his life. It was my turn in the conversation. "I enjoy treasure hunting and interacting with others. Did you notice there are no price tags on anything? Make an offer if you see something you like."

What I found most fascinating about this approach is the majority of people offer a fair price. Some would even over pay. Yet others failed to reach a deal. The whole experience was a microcosm of the human experience. It is so enjoyable that my friends and I have set up at no less than five or six flea markets. We are a staple at the local Mega Mall and our investment club is even named after our booth, A10.

Unfortunately, Matt has passed since that hot July day (unrelated to his cancer). We crossed paths several times in the interim, occasionally for an office visit, but more frequently looking for treasures scattered about on an asphalt parking lot. I wish he could see me writing with a grin ear-to-ear. I believe he still can. I wonder what his view of the flea market exchange would be. What would be his criteria for the experience? Trash or treasure?

Patient experience is inherently difficult to accurately capture and extremely subjective. What one person sees as valuable, another sees as insignificant, perhaps even detrimental. Yet, this component of healthcare is often painted as black and white. Perhaps, a shade of gray is required.

Should the focus be on episodic points of care? Or perhaps a longitudinal approach? Maybe even how patients feel about their health in general? For sure, there is not one correct answer to this dilemma. We have evidence, we have data, but eventually there is a person sitting in front of us, in all of their beauty and uniqueness. What are their hopes and dreams? What is their goal for their health care?

As I pondered this topic, my mind went to another patient. Kit is currently an inpatient with COVID-19 pneumonia on high-flow oxygen. He was born with Lennox-Gastaut Syndrome and is currently in his forties. He is severely developmentally disabled with the cognitive ability of an early toddler. At his best, Kit is the star of the show. A bright smile and booming voice. He commands attention with his family and he loves every minute of it. In turn, his family pours on the affection. It is a beautiful sight to see. Love.

Unfortunately, his health has declined with age. Two prolonged admissions for both status epilepticus and a fractured hip (complicated by infection, subsequent surgeries, and eventually total removal of the hip joint). These episodes have taken their toll. Currently Kit is non-ambulatory (not able to walk) and has minimal verbal skills along with his severe cognitive impairment. So how do we measure his satisfaction with the care he is receiving, as visitation is severely limited due to COVID restrictions?

Writing is often a stream of consciousness. This chapter should be considered as such. I don't believe there is one simple answer to the question of how to improve patient experience. But rather improvement requires a multifaceted, balanced approach, that includes quality care and low costs. It requires listening. Not just physicians listening to patients, but listening at the highest levels in healthcare. Listening to where the problems lie and having the courage to implement change. We will explore ideas, foster conversations, and ask questions. The journey is undetermined, but Our Quadruple Aim is an excellent guide. We will build towards suggestions and some brainstorming. Let's get started.

((SUBJECTIVITY))

"Your most unhappy customers
are your greatest source of learning."
– BILL GATES

Subjectivity is defined as the quality of being based on, or influenced by personal feelings, tastes, or opinions. Not whether a correct diagnosis was made, but rather how the patient felt about, or their opinion of, the interaction. Subjectivity definitely plays a role—both for the patient and physician. Yet, satisfaction scores are typically a one-way street in healthcare.

Medicine is an art. It blends science, evidence, psychology, interpersonal skills, data, emotions, finance, and disease. Not to mention how cultural, political or religious beliefs contribute to experience. What about the patient's priorities? They may differ completely from the provider. Without a doubt, the list of components to providing care are extensive. Assimilating all of those pieces is akin to working on a difficult puzzle. Trying to balance an interaction with a patient can be daunting. At times, even impossible.

In our modern society, unrealistic expectations are becoming more and more pervasive, so too in healthcare. Our fast food society surely plays a role. The mantras of "do more with less" and "just one more thing" threaten to worsen the exodus from healthcare (that is already occurring). Now just imagine expectations regarding the mountains of paperwork providers have to complete, far from instantaneous. Or angry family members who don't comprehend their loved one is dying, despite your best efforts. I have heard numerous stories of both physical and verbal abuse of healthcare providers, though the providers did nothing wrong. These components need to be considered in the subjectivity of patient experience.

I appreciate the patient as the consumer of healthcare. A patient's attitude, beliefs, and compliance are vital to not only the success of an interaction, but their vitality as well. These factors play a role in the perception of experience as well. An interaction can go in the wrong direction in the blink of an eye. Sometimes, it has nothing to do with the provider, sometimes it does. A few examples will follow—mostly good, just a tincture of bad.

(("SHE IS NOT MOST PEOPLE"))

"And the King shall answer and say unto them, '
Verily I say unto you, inasmuch as ye have done it unto one of the least of these My brethren, ye have done it unto Me.'"

– MATTHEW 25:40

The following is a heart-wrenching story told by the parents of their late daughter, Miracle. Miracle was born with a severe de novo (random) chromosomal abnormality. This manifested in a multitude of medical conditions, which included but was not limited to: absent forearms, no thumbs, non-communicative, deaf, non-ambulatory, severe cognitive impairment, with an adult weight of 50 pounds. Her loving parents have hearts of gold, caring for her every need for over two scores. Unconditional love epitomized.

I met with Miracle's parents to review her case for *Ripple of Change* in hopes of inspiring many (including families who face similar challenges) to advocate for change. As I listened to their story for just over an hour, I couldn't help but don my proverbial white coat. Empathy for their plight filled my being as time melted away. Without getting into the minutia regarding her final years, I was saddened and frustrated by the travails of the tale her parents unfolded. Her father meticulously recorded her history in tests, letters, emails, complaints, and inquiries. And who would know the patient better than two parents who had cared for Miracle her entire life. Her very existence demanded selfless love.

The narrative that was conveyed was almost too much to believe. Complication after complication, many iatrogenic (induced by medical care). Miscommunication, and a lack of listening and coordination, led to delays in diagnoses and more problems. I would like to share just a few comments and quotes from her father. I have little doubt in how Miracle would describe her patient experience in those final years (if capable).

- "There should be no difference in health care for our disabled patients."
- "That seemed to be lost on them." (referring to Miracle's baseline capabilities)
- "It is another failure to communicate. The ER had an attention deficit problem."
- "...each time we have come here, we have endured notable failures."
- "...your units are many times the last resort between life and death, and must be held to a higher standard."

Honestly, I was embarrassed as I listened to some of the misfortunes Miracle and her parents had to endure in the last years of her life, and some of the comments they heard from healthcare workers were appalling. In an attempt to honor her life and legacy, her parents were involved in the development of a program to address the well-being of patients with disabilities. Over the course of several years progress was made and seemingly Miracle's parents succeeded in advocating for those who cannot speak for themselves. Her obituary even recognized the efforts to honor Miracle's legacy in helping others. But then COVID-19 put a halt to everything. Miracle's parents believe the program never came to fruition.

Just when I thought the story couldn't be anymore frustrating and depressing, Miracle's father shared two separate news stories of parents with severely disabled children that both tragically ended with murder-suicides. Patient and parent. What desperation, anguish, and hopelessness must have existed to reach such a conclusion for those parents.

Hearing stories such as these is frustrating and heartbreaking for anyone who has an altruistic bone in their body. And they are way more common than they should be. Miracle's parents put in an inordinate amount of time and effort to advocate for those patients who are less fortunate. Their hope: to make healthcare a better place for those after Miracle through a task force focused on patients like her. Our Quadruple Aim is about delivering quality, cost-effective care to everyone, regardless of disability, handicap, special needs, socioeconomic standing or any other confounding factor you can imagine.

After our interaction, Miracle's parents each sent a follow-up email expressing their gratitude for Miracle's story being included in A *Ripple of Change* and their excitement in celebrating her life. I would like to share two comments. "Thank you for the time you spent with us today, listening to our long-lived frustrations and entanglements with the medical community. Bringing this all back up has strengthened my resolve to visit again with the Patient Experience Department, and see if, post-Pandemic, the task force still exists and if it does, what form has it taken on."

Perhaps your ripple is advocating for those who are less fortunate, just as Miracle's parents have.

((PERCEPTION IS REALITY))

"When people talk, listen completely.
Most people never listen."

– ERNEST HEMINGWAY

This story goes back a few years...early 2010. I joined Family Care Specialists in January of that year. Busy immediately, I saw 20 patients my first day. With one superstar MA and paper charts,

I dove head first into the daily grind. Thrilling and terrifying at times, residency had prepared me well and I am forever grateful to my mentors. A few months into the routine, I saw Jackson for the first time. Jackson was a pleasant young man, in his early twenties, and was following up for high blood pressure, headaches, and diabetes. His appointment turned out to be anything but routine.

After a brief introduction, we reviewed Jackson's medical history and began a review of his recent blood pressure and blood sugar readings. The data was remarkable, both blood pressure and blood sugars wildly fluctuated, with little rhyme or reason. This was despite two blood pressure medications and an insulin regimen for his blood sugars. Intriguing.

Illogical for a slightly overweight man in his early twenties to have refractory hypertension and diabetes. Like a cold case detective given a new clue, my enthusiasm surged and I volleyed a barrage of questions at Jackson. Chest pain—no. Shortness of breath—no. Blurred vision—no. Diarrhea—no.

No other instant clues, I transitioned to exploring his headache history. Jackson described his headaches as very random, intense, and occasionally he would feel flushed. Minimal relief with medications, and he did not snore. The physicians reading may have already made the diagnosis and, if so, kudos to you. It was then that his girlfriend chimed in; "We checked his blood pressure when he was having a headache, and it was 220/110!" (A normal blood pressure is in the 120/70 range, plus or minus). I felt like I was reading a textbook concerning a particular diagnosis. We made a subtle adjustment to his medications, ordered some lab work and a CT scan of his abdomen, and made a short-term follow up appointment.

After the visit was complete, I ran down the office hall, excited to proclaim my working diagnosis to my partner. "Linus, I think Jackson has a pheochromocytoma!" My exuberance was met with some skepticism, but my confidence undeterred.

A pheochromocytoma is a neurohormonal tumor that secretes epinephrine and norepinephrine, causing elevations in blood pressure, blood sugar, and headaches among other abnormalities. It was as if Jackson was reading the textbook to me.

Finding a rare disease can be intellectually gratifying, despite the angst it causes patients. I saw Jackson back a few weeks later, and two of his tests confirmed the diagnosis of a pheochromocytoma. His 24 urine catecholamines were extremely elevated and his CT scan showed a mass on an adrenal gland. I was ecstatic to confirm a rare diagnosis and a better plan for Jackson. I conferred with Linus and referred Jackson to a local surgeon for evaluation of the adrenal mass. Fast forward a few months, the adrenal mass was resected with pathological confirmation—a benign pheochromocytoma. Jackson's blood pressure and blood sugars normalized and his headaches resolved. An incredible case, rarity presented when I first met Jackson. His parents were so excited they wrote me a letter of thanks, which I have to this day.

My perception of Jackson's care was very different from his preceding care, and his reality dramatically changed after his pheochromocytoma was resected. Perception is reality. This case exemplifies what different viewpoints can mean to patient experience. Depending on one's perception of a particular circumstance, interaction, diagnosis, or hospital visit—their view of reality can vary tremendously. One small variance can take an overall positive interaction to one that is perceived in the darkest of lights. Our Quadruple Aim can help tip the scale in the correct direction.

I would like to highlight two components of OQA in this case, albeit all four components were incorporated into Jackson's care. His experience as a patient dramatically changed after his tumor was removed. No medications, no insulin or blood sugar checks, and fewer doctor's appointments. Shortly after his surgery, Jackson and his girlfriend were married and eventually moved away. Nice to have a happy ending in medicine.

And how did Provider Wellness play a role? A physician who is well-rested, not burned out, and whose life is in balance can think clearer and capture those fine details—which can make all of the difference in the world. The appreciation from patients and family members, as well as the intellectual gratification, can fill your emotional tank and allow you to endure some of the more frustrating components of healthcare.

((ALLOWING PATIENTS TO BECOME PEOPLE AGAIN))

"Sorry for keeping you waiting.
I really like your beard by the way."

– TODD R. OTTEN, M.D.

"Thanks, I didn't have it when I got here."

– GARY, PATIENT

After the initial introductions, and some small talk, Anthony stepped towards the interactive presentation screen. Having previously seen the presentation, I anticipated it would span approximately 20 minutes. I couldn't have been more wrong. He reviewed the information in about two—a "Cliff Notes" version. He then grabbed a dry erase marker and walked towards a series of white boards. Curious as to where this was going, I moved forward in my seat, Joshua to my right, Chad behind us. I opened my notebook, pen at the ready.

The next 45 minutes were a whirlwind of healthcare, economics, and technology, as Anthony Chang, Ph.D., explored how BAMF Health (Bold Advanced Medical Future) embodied Our Quadruple Aim. An impromptu lecture of pure brilliance regarding the state of healthcare and how progressive companies like BAMF Health want to revolutionize care. A review on the interplay of financial drivers, with patients carrying the load.

From start to finish, a smile was on my face. The CEO of the company took the time to share his passion and how well it aligned with OQA. The remainder of the conversation was rich, meaningful, and passionate. Kindred spirits on improving healthcare. Different paths, but the altruism was evident.

Joshua and I were then taken on a tour of the facility. Every detail was well-planned and patient-centric. Anthony's vision and passion had come to fruition in a masterclass of medicine, business, and technology. BAMF Health is a progressive, forward-thinking company that allows patients to become people again. As such, it's worth exploring each component.

The moment you walk up to the building it is evident that Patient Experience is paramount for BAMF Health. A valet parking sign prominently displayed for patients. The driveway extended under the roof to protect patients from harsh Michigan winters. A heated walkway to prevent ice and snow, reducing the risk of falls for frail men with metastatic prostate cancer. This is just the entrance. Every component of the facility keeps patients at the forefront, while respecting the potential dangers of radiation. From the furniture, to the exam rooms—every detail is purposeful, intended. Even the imaging rooms are designed to reduce anxiety for patients as they fight for their lives. The ROI you ask? Priceless.

As BAMF Health is a new company, the Quality Care is just beginning, with unlimited potential. A perfect example was the thank you note on display from a patient with end-stage prostate cancer, previously admitted to hospice care. After treatment through BAMF Health's novel approach, the patient is now in remission. From their website: "Theranostics is an emerging field in medicine with proven results, combining the power of molecular imaging and molecular targeted radiation therapy to accurately diagnose and treat patients. After locating and identifying the disease through molecular imaging, a simple IV injection delivers targeted treatment directly to where it is needed, minimizing damage to healthy tissue."[190]

New technology is not without cost, but Anthony's vision regarding technology as a competitive, disruptive force to ultimately Lower the Cost of care is nothing short of genius. His work with artificial intelligence (AI) and theranostics, once scaled, has incredible potential for cost containment. As we discussed AI in healthcare, the conversation migrated to the current siloing of data and its detrimental effects on patient care and cost. I couldn't agree more. Creating a neural network, combined with a causal model—so promising.

Imagine if my patient (Jackson) with the pheochromocytoma had been evaluated with the assistance of AI? Perhaps a differential diagnosis would have included this as a cause of his refractory hypertension and diabetes. The diagnosis potentially made years sooner. The correct treatment expedited, and expenses truncated: allowing a patient to become a person again.

The trip would not have been complete without Provider Wellbeing. As we toured the facility, I could not help but notice the smiles and positive attitudes on the faces of the staff. The energy: positive and inviting. People happy at work, wanting to help patients. The joy of medicine was clearly present. Well-conceived meditation areas, ergonomic workstations, and a place to take a short nap—all in an effort to maintain provider well-being. Simple, brilliant execution. Dividends in recruitment and retention, netting top notch employees. All in an effort to provide superlative care.

As our tour neared its completion, Chad Bassett (COO), Anthony, Joshua, and I sat down and talked for a few moments. Mission complete: confirmation that BAMF Health is living Our Quadruple Aim. Open and honest conversation. Like-minded individuals who appreciate the current frustrations in healthcare that many patients endure. As we talked, Anthony made a profound statement summarizing the frustrations and obstacles he has heard from patients trying to receive cancer treatment in America. He said: "Many have shared, I would rather die." Enough said.

((GET HIM A BOTTLE))

Joshua J. Judy – Patient:

Megan and I were thrilled—our first-born, a boy, was delivered naturally without complications and in perfect health. Everything was in place. We had researched the best car seat and traveled several cities over to find it on sale. We even asked the store staff to confirm our research, which they did without hesitation. We had gotten a hold of the handmade cradle that my wife's uncle had made decades earlier. Both Megan and her two brothers slept their first nights in it—our son would carry on the tradition.

His room was ready to welcome him, with new curtains and shelves mounted on the wall to hold boundless stuffies and the all-important baby monitor. Adjacent hung a painting Megan had made, complete with a monkey, kangaroo, and a hippo enjoying a drink in a watering hole beneath white puffy clouds. In one corner was a rocking chair with a footrest for mom to comfortably sit and tend to the baby. And in another corner was the changing table, fresh diapers, and several containers of wipes on standby for the stinky messes that would soon arrive.

I recall it started snowing the day we were discharged from the hospital. Before leaving, the birthing center nurses double-checked that the car seat straps were properly secured—no more than two fingers should fit under the center plate, and snuggly. It is apparently a common mistake of first-time parents to leave straps too loose, risking injury to the infant. The nurses gave a nodding approval, and sent me on my way to bring the family car to the hospital's front entrance.

We departed and drove home methodically, taking our time and watching for both deer and slick spots (because of the newly fallen snow). Michigan winters can be taxing and changing weather patterns can and do strike suddenly. So of course, the weather had been perfectly fine leading up to discharge. But we avoided any disasters and pulled into the garage about an hour later. We couldn't wait to show our son his new home and surroundings.

The rest of the day went by quickly and it was time for bed that first night. When you're a new parent, seemingly innocuous sounds like creaks and customary house settling take on potentially ominous significance. You sleep with one ear alert and an eye partially open.

Though Megan was a formula baby, she was determined to breastfeed. I was a breastfed baby, and inclined to agree–especially if it meant keeping Megan happy and our son healthy. Besides money saved, I had heard of the benefits of breastfeeding such as receiving maternal antibodies.

Breast milk is thinner than formula, and because a baby's stomach starts out no larger than a cherry pit, this means frequent feedings–with no more than two hours in between. While chiefly up to the baby to tell us when and where through communicative cries, we were going to watch the clock. It would be hardest on mom, who had to get up routinely. But my wife was young and excited to provide our son all the necessities of his new life, vigorous subsistence being one of them.

We had noticed that our son was sluggish to latch at the hospital, as discerned by the nurses too. But they assured us it's a process, to be patient, and that baby is learning. A lactation consultant could contact us later in the week with advice. So Megan, fiercely resolute to make it work, carried on the best she knew how. There were frustrating starts and stops as Megan continued to work with our son. By all indications, he was eating—getting colostrum as the milk let down process began. Colostrum provides all the nutrients and fluid that a newborn needs in their early days, as well as many substances to protect the baby against infections. Its color and thickness are due to the fact that it is higher in protein, slightly lower in sugar, and largely lower in fat compared to later milk.

Very shortly into our son's first week of life came the post-delivery check-up with Dr. Otten. While we were establishing a baseline as new parents, looking back, our son never overly fussed or cried much since arriving. He has always been a solid sleeper.

Megan had been feeding him every two hours if not sooner. We indicated that while our son had been wetting diapers with expected frequency, he had not had his first stool. Other than the meconium, a tarry stool that comes shortly after delivery, things were dry. We were not quite alarmed but wondered how concerned we should be. This was uncharted territory and we were attentive. Attentive too was our family doctor. Besides his medical training and experience guiding him, he has four children of his own. What better experience is there than when it's first-hand and practical? Looking back, this was a critical juncture—I can say without overstatement, a life-saving one.

Because our son was wetting his diapers, it meant his kidneys were functioning. While he had lost some weight, the recommendation was that if he does not have the initial stool by the end of the week or his urine output decreased, to take him into the hospital and to not hesitate. Our family doctor had enough seriousness to register and move to the forefront of our minds. And there he stayed.

The end of the week arrived swiftly, and without stool. We bundled our son up and as directed, took him to the nearby main hospital. It was not long before one nurse was by our son's side, trying to place a catheter to administer fluids. His veins were small. He was dehydrated. Another nurse was called, apparently more experienced. Soon, a third and final nurse appeared. They brought in a small plank like board to tape to his arm and keep it straight. All three nurses gently took turns poking and searching for a vessel before the eldest and most senior nurse was successful.

Along with my parents, Megan and I watched helplessly. Our son would need a battery of tests. Results would later show his blood was getting thick due to dehydration, with certain markers like hematocrit rising.

During the entire time of placing the catheter, I had offered my right index finger to him. His eyes were closed, but he wrapped his tiny fingers and thumb around it, squeezing. There his hand stayed, never once letting go. I wasn't sure if he was as scared as we were. If so, he was only showing some of his cards.

Not long after our son was hospitalized, I came across a story online. It was the story of Jillian Johnson. Mrs. Johnson's story had eerie similarities. There is a *Washington Post* article written by journalist Lindsey Bever, dated March 8, 2017, and titled, "She listened to her doctors—and her baby died. Now she's warning others about breast-feeding." Bever writes:

> *[,,,] Landon Johnson had been trying to breast-feed almost continuously since his birth days earlier—and screaming each time his mother pulled him from her chest. Just stick with it, the first-time parents were told.*
>
> *[...] But it was not until days after their newborn had stopped breathing [...] that Jillian Johnson said she and her husband learned what might have happened to him. A doctor in a neonatal intensive care unit told them he suspected Landon was so severely dehydrated that his heart had stopped beating, she said.*
>
> *[...] Jillian Johnson said she told the doctor in February 2012. "I couldn't wrap my head around it. I was frustrated with myself because there were these doctors and nurses who kept telling me, 'Just keep feeding him. Just keep him on the breast. You've got a great latch. You're doing fine.' "*
>
> *But she had no breast milk to offer him, she said.*[191]

We stayed at the hospital overnight with our son after being admitted to the pediatric ward. There were tests and more tests.

Lung capacity and function were good. They listened to our son's digestive tract. It sounded like it was moving without obstruction, so that was encouraging. Our son was monitored throughout the night, and we were reassured to keep breastfeeding whenever possible. By this point, our son had lost nearly all of his baby fat stores.

The following morning, the Medical Director of Pediatrics visited the room. After introductions and a short exchange of pleasantries, he donned a medical glove. Next asking for a bit of petroleum jelly, he smeared it on his pinky before momentarily placing it where the sun doesn't shine. Ripping off the glove, the doctor paused. He displayed a somewhat knowing smile before matter-of-factly proclaiming, "Nurse, get this boy some formula please. As far as I can tell, he's hungry." A bottle was produced and our son was on his way to regular eating and the world of gastronomy. The mystery had been solved.

I feel emotional when I think about it all, harkening back to that day in the triage room, and weighing the experience years later. I empathize and feel deep compassion for the parents whose baby did not make it. I feel sorrow for her and her family. What if her doctors had simply looked at the simplest of solutions? What if they had just fed that poor baby some supplemental food? How could our experiences be so similar but with vastly different outcomes?

I have come to appreciate these butterfly effects in life—outwardly innocent decisions that come to carry enormous sway. We don't know which ones will cause us to teeter under a precarious balance, where the slightest variation will send us unpredictably in one direction or the other. We can reach the summit of a mountain while remaining completely oblivious of how dangerously close we came to sliding into the abyss below.

Or we can be fully awake and realize that while not all information matters, often the details desperately do. Being able to pick through the ones that matter over the ones that do not determines our fate.

When Dr. Otten told us to go to the hospital, he cast a stone, creating a ripple. The Director of Pediatrics cultivated the next ripple by deploying a straightforward, effective solution. Their actions leave behind reverberations felt today. Our son recently celebrated his sixth birthday, happy and healthy as ever. He can feed himself just fine and has no problems packing it away. I think he will be a foodie like his father and mother. He is always talking about how he thinks both his parents can cook better than Gordon Ramsay. While flattering, we suspect it's wholly inaccurate. Only once have we tried a Ramsay recipe, and it was delicious! Maybe our son will have his own set of Michelin stars someday.

In the grand scheme, being a breastfed baby was not necessarily superior over being a formula-fed baby, or vice-versa. Our son's still here and the feeding method made little difference. At six, diapers and the abyss he faced early on are long behind him.

What *did* make a difference were two very attentive doctors, parents, nurses, and supporting staff. Having the right amount of food, regardless of source, *was* the critical factor. For the parents who feel guilt or shame of starting out with the best intentions to breastfeed only to end up on formula, we offer our experience. Do not beat yourself up or think you failed. Do not let others make you feel inferior for switching to formula, including overzealous lactation consultants. Rather, feel you succeeded because of your adaptability. You adjusted to changing conditions in the best interests of your child's health and well-being.

Sometime later, my curiosity took over and I had to know what the hospital charged for our stay. $7,000—seven thousand dollars to defecate in a highly supervised and controlled setting. This was indeed a monumental achievement! Smiles aside, I struggle to consider how different our story could have gone? If absent the right support.

So this too came to pass—our son was able to accomplish something many never reach. He managed to take a seven-grand dump even before the end of his first week of life—a story that could be retold at moments requiring opportune teasing or simply celebrating. It was undoubtedly the shit of a lifetime.

((TRANSPARENCY))

"The chain reaction of price transparency begins with patients posing the simple question: 'How much does that cost?'"

– ELISABETH ROSENTHAL, M.D., *AN AMERICAN SICKNESS*[192]

Todd R. Otten, M.D.:

Imagine going to a restaurant, having a sumptuous meal, complete with fine wine, a delectable dessert, without any idea what the final cost will be. No need to pay at the end, the bill will be mailed, and it will amount to several times what you expected. After many months, your credit card bill arrives; with a haphazard list of random items, fees, ancillaries items, facility charges, accompanied by a note with the audacity to expect payment in full. I struggle to think of another industry that operates as healthcare. And yet, patients (the customers) have grown accustomed to this twisted methodology.

The lack of transparency of healthcare in the U.S. is a multifaceted monster wrapped in a shroud of secrecy. Driven by profits, the opacity of the existing culture in healthcare has financially ruined countless lives—all in a quest for higher revenue streams. Unwinding this level of dysfunction will take the effort of many, at both the local and macro level. Fortunately there are examples to look to for inspiration and efforts to improve the existing nightmare in America. Our Quadruple Aim mandates transparency to bend to the cost curve.

Transparency and competition are staples of healthcare delivery in many other developed nations. Singapore is often considered a first-rate example. Using a mixed-financing system, Singapore has achieved universal health coverage with the national government fully responsible. The ministry ensures competition, with prices and bills from various entities on its website, allowing patients to make informed decisions. Medishield Life is the country's public statutory insurance system, while Medisave is a required medical savings account. Medifund provides a limited but effective stop gap for those who have exhausted their savings and government subsidies.[193, 194, 195, 196, 197]

The combination of transparency and financial incentives has led to dramatic disparities when comparing Singapore's healthcare expenditures to the U.S. Singapore spends approximately 5% of its GDP on healthcare compared to that of 18% in the U.S. This equates to $4,270 per capita and only $1,372 out-of-pocket spending in Singapore (as of 2020), compared to $12,914 and $1,315 respectively in the U.S. (in 2021). Furthermore, Singapore's life expectancy exceeds the U.S. by five years. A better outcome at a fraction of the cost. Telling.[198, 199, 200, 201, 202, 203]

The Consolidated Appropriations Act of 2021 is a breath of fresh air for the American healthcare consumer. Enacted on December 27, 2020, this legislature includes the No Surprise Act under Title I and Transparency under Title II.[204] I hope to impart some key components regarding healthcare from this nearly 5,600 page document.

Historically, emergent care would often leave patients (consumers) responsible for high out-of-network costs. As health plans would only cover certain portions of the bill, the remaining portion (often exorbitant, even predatory at times) would be passed on to the patient (known as balance billing). These unexpected costs are known as surprise bills. The new rules are aimed to protect patients and restrict out-of-pocket costs.[205]

The American Hospital Association provides an excellent summary of the health provisions in the Act:

> *"Health care providers (both individual practitioners and facilities) will be required to share 'good faith estimates' of the total expected charges for scheduled*

> *items or services, including any expected ancillary services, with a health plan (if the patient is insured) or individual (if the patient is uninsured). Health plans will be required to send patients an 'Advanced Explanations of Benefits' (EOB) prior to scheduled care or upon request by patients..."*[206]

Protection of continuity of care and up-to-date in-network provider lists are also addressed.[207]

In order for OQA to succeed, transparency is a must. Transparency in pricing should exist at every level of healthcare, not the convoluted shell game we have endured for so many years. We (as patients and providers) should demand fair and honest pricing. But we need continued help, particularly in legislation and at the highest levels of medical leadership.

Elisabeth Rosenthal, M.D. takes a deep dive into the financial landscape of healthcare in her book, *An American Sickness: How Healthcare Became Big Business and How You Can Take it Back*. Appendix A, in her masterclass of writing, involves pricing/shopping tools for the American healthcare consumer.[208] This is a must read for those interested in helping to facilitate change. Capitalism has failed the healthcare consumer. Transparency, when combined with Our Quadruple Aim as a guide, has the potential to right many wrongs.

((QUALITY VERSUS QUANTITY))

"Less is more."

– LUDWIG MIES VAN DER ROHE

Empowering healthcare providers to discuss end of life (i.e. mortality) early on in the course of patients' healthcare journeys has tremendous potential to reduce costs and limit suffering (i.e. morbidity). Previously I described healthcare on a pendulum—quality of life versus quantity. It's amazing how receptive patients are to this discussion. On numerous occasions I have met a 90-some-year-old who has never broached this topic. Open to the discussion, warm, welcoming the idea, like the internal debate was waiting for an invitation. Yet, for many the conversation never occurs. In the hospital, at the end of life, not wanting to extend things, but only wanting comfort. Hundreds of thousands, if not, millions of dollars later...the inevitable occurs—death, peace. And what was accomplished: the antithesis of Our Quadruple Aim?

A major problem in the current healthcare landscape is that providers are incentivized to do things, code things, chart things—often at the expense of preventative measures.

And what about any end-of-life discussions? Modern healthcare would be well-served to value and facilitate these conversations. But insurers routinely don't incentivize end-of-life conversations. When patients turn 65 they routinely transition to Medicare, taking expensive end-of-life care with them. And we all pay for it. Just like taxes, death is inevitable. A complete disconnect with incentive structures.

Without a doubt there are providers who abuse the system as well, doing more than is required. Lest we forget fraud and waste. This is far from what being a physician is all about. Caring for patients, their hopes, dreams, and end-of-life wishes. Isn't that what we went into medicine for? That's why I went into medicine. Maybe it's time many of us reassess what our mission is.

Polypharmacy is the use of multiple drugs to treat one or more disease states. I often equate this as too many medications—especially in my elderly patient population. I find reducing unneeded medications to be very gratifying. The process is intellectually challenging and rewarding on many levels. Removing a medication in a 90-year-old patient who is dizzy and struggles to function, returning their quality of life, is a win (for both of us). Certainly Joshua will attest to the trouble medications can cause, despite the best of intentions. Unfortunately, this is a time-consuming process and doesn't generate another "widget." More than once I have been told by a patient that a provider has dismissed a symptom as being a side-effect of a medication, only to have that symptom resolve after the medication is discontinued. Quality of life.

Time is one of the most valuable commodities in healthcare. Unfortunately, continued pressures and clerical duties have compressed interactions with patients and created many untoward consequences. The simple act of spending time with patients, listening, explaining, and teaching is often sacrificed as a result. This leaves patients confused and frustrated, wandering through the dysfunctional landscape—lost. Often with no place to turn for help. As a result, tests are not completed, leading to delays. Patients are perceived as non-compliant, often through no fault of their own. Yes, I am giving 20 years of anecdotal evidence; I didn't have the time to set up a randomized controlled trial (pun intended).

The negative impact of revenue generation on time cannot be understated. Perhaps, the continued exploration/migration towards value-based reimbursement can improve both quality and quantity of life for patients. Interestingly OQA aligns quite well with value-based care.

((OUR QUADRUPLE AIM IN ARCHITECTURE?))

Jeffrey Johnson, AIA (American Institute of Architects):

In the example of architecture, we'll replace the patient with a building user. As you begin to contemplate the User Experience and what can be designed, Space, Rituals, Policy, Incentives and Roles all come into mind. In a well-designed building, all these design elements work in conjunction with one another to create the overall experience, leaving the guest with a feeling of comfort, care, attention to detail, curation, reward, and inspiration. For many, good design just feels right and not forced.

If the above elements align in a meaningful way, architects are rewarded by meaningful design engagement and the belief they are making a difference in the world.

Our Quadruple Aim	Architecture's Quadruple Aim
1. Patient Experience	User Experience
2. Quality Care	Quality Design
3. Lower Costs	Lower Cost or Increased Value
4. Provider Wellness	Team Health and Satisfaction/Motivation

((PATIENT EXPERIENCE BRAINSTORMING))

Todd R. Otten, M.D.:

Surveys can be helpful, but many (including myself) consider them trite. Many are tired of being perpetually surveyed; particularly if the data is twisted to fit a certain narrative. In a culture where anything less than 5/5 stars or 10/10 is deemed a failure, are these data points truly valuable? Maybe it's time to consider a fresh take or new approach?

Perhaps the correct form of patient experience is where **subjective comments** can be independently interpreted (as positive or negative)? Leadership or a committee offering reasonable thresholds of success. Consider including patients or other key stakeholders.

Mystery or Secret shoppers are individuals who visit stores and restaurants, banks, apartment complexes, and more to assess customer service. These individuals are typically employed by a third-party company to provide first hand insight, which can be used to improve the business.[209] I know a newly appointed healthcare CEO who used a similar approach. Mystery shopping has the potential to be a powerful tool. Perhaps an opportunity for former healthcare workers?

Tying physician compensation to surveys and patient experience, while understandable, can be a dangerous slippery slope. There are instances where the patient's desires are in direct opposition to the best interest of their health. A simple example—a diabetic who loves donuts and you suggest they cut back. Or the patient with COPD (Chronic Obstructive Pulmonary Disease) who doesn't want to quit smoking. Certainly the examples can become exceedingly complex. Surveys should be used to evaluate performance and lead to improvement; tying surveys to compensation has the potential to facilitate bad behaviors.

Longitudinal reporting (or surveys) of patients presents a unique opportunity. Why not a long-term evaluation process? Many patients work with certain providers and even healthcare systems for years, even decades. Why not incorporate their input as things evolve over time?

Blended surveys present an interesting challenge, where both the patient and provider rate the interaction. A two-way street, the Yin and Yang. I wonder if there has been an example of a blended survey result? Let both the providers and patients rank interactions and run a statistical analysis? Random, intermittent. Hmmm.

Dollars will follow **happy patients**, as revenue should be a reflection of satisfied customers.

((23))

Horrible vs. Helpful

Joshua J. Judy – Patient:

When I wrote this chapter, I had several ideas about what proper health care should (or should not) look and sound like. Many of the dialogues I share are firsthand between doctor and patient. Others were shared with me for passing along. I hope the stories lead you, the reader, to reflect on your own encounters in healthcare. Then ask yourself, how do I skip my stone?

When I was in grad school, I had an economics professor. One day in class, he expounded about the benefits of outsourcing and how it resulted in nearly limitless benefits to all consumers through keeping wages low and ever cheaper prices. I raised my hand, asking, "What about when it reaches the point when your own job is outsourced and you're no longer able to be a consumer?" My point was that workers and consumers are rarely mutually exclusive parties—they can and often do wear both hats. Pigs get fat and hogs get slaughtered comes to mind. Balance is key.

He drolly replied, "Job security has nothing to do with outsourcing." The class roared with laughter. Approaching him after class, I asked him if what he said earlier was what he really believed. What he stated next, I filed away in my memory, "Look, I came to this country. My kids live here. I worry about their future too. I just teach this stuff." I wished for him to understand our interdependencies, economic and beyond. Based on his response, perhaps he did, and better than I first gave him credit for.

That exchange years ago between student and professor parallels some of my recent exchanges between doctor and patient. It's always interesting to compare and contrast the "stage performance" with the "after show" conversation, when the lights dim and the hot mic is silenced. When it comes to medicine, or the many other topics of life, you shouldn't be afraid to compare and contrast either.

This leads me to my next point: You must find the right care provider for you. Differentiate the experience early in my wife's epilepsy journey with Megan's current neurologist below.

MEGAN'S NEUROLOGIST: How are you doing?

US: Well, that's a big question, doctor—with what we think has an even bigger answer.

So started our Zoom call visit with Megan's current neurologist.

NEUROLOGIST: Okay, what's going on?

MEGAN: Well, we just want to talk for a bit. Joshua is writing a book with our primary care doctor. And through this writing, we've come to discover how similar our experiences are and how we've come to articulate it. For me, positive emotions are very hard to come by, while negative ones are always on the ready.

NEUROLOGIST: Has this gotten worse after pregnancy? You can feel worse up to a year after having the baby. It's normal findings for postpartum, especially with the hormone changes.

MEGAN: No, it's been pretty much there since levetiracetam.

NEUROLOGIST: Has it been worse since COVID and lockdown?

MEGAN: Yes, naturally some. But it's more than that. There is little emotional attachment to my memories. And as a result, they fade and every day is a blank page.

NEUROLOGIST: While everyone is different, irritability and aggression are well-known and documented side-effects for levetiracetam—the more negative emotional profile.

ME: We fear we'll forget many of the most important memories.

MEGAN: Yes, things that should bring joy because they're joyous moments just come and go. If our daughter takes her first step, I know I should be happy but I can't be—and then I'm upset that I can't be. I'm capped on what I can and should feel.

NEUROLOGIST: And I see you're on 1500 mg, once a day?

MEGAN: Yes.

NEUROLOGIST: It's been four years since your last seizure. Are you thinking about coming off? That's one option, but for some, unacceptable.

US: That's not an option for us given the detrimental outcomes of the first trial. We just wouldn't feel safe.

Megan's previous car crash ran through our minds–we knew what she meant, and she knew what we meant.

NEUROLOGIST: I understand. Let's talk about other options. First, are you done having kids?

MEGAN: Yes.

NEUROLOGIST: Well that opens the door to other medications. I know you've tried lamotrigine before, and that gave you a skin rash. The rash can be very serious. So that's off the table. As you know, lamotrigine is the other one considered safe for pregnancy, like levetiracetam. But there are other options that are more mood-stabilizing that would now be available.

Oh right, lamotrigine. We recalled the hour-long speech from my wife's first neurologist about calling immediately if a rash forms, only to receive no call back.

Speaking of mood-stabilizing, another option would be adding an antidepressant, but I think I know your answer.

My wife and I scooted forwards in our seats and glanced at each other. We remained quiet but slightly tense. The neurologist knew a little about my own experience from a previous conversation. She moved on swiftly.

NEUROLOGIST: You could also split your dose, a.m. and p.m., even on the extended-release pills that you're on. As long as you're getting the required amount daily, this is another option.

One thing I should bring up—and it won't hurt either way—is vitamin B6, 100 mg. I looked back, and it looks like you tried it before without much effect. Potentially worth considering again, as there was a study showing some mood-stabilizing benefit.

At this point, my wife and I were waiting for her to bring up lowering her levetiracetam dose. It was something that had been mentioned in a previous visit. We jumped in—

ME: How about lowering her dosage? One of your colleagues was very adamant against it, noting Megan was already taking the lowest therapeutic dose. However, you were open to this idea before.

The doctor gave a quizzical look, silently questioning her colleague's statement.

NEUROLOGIST: That's definitely an option but further testing would be needed. We would need another extended EEG (5-hour test) and another measure of your levetiracetam blood serum level. If the EEG looks too active, I wouldn't be comfortable lowering the dosage—at least not without adding a second medication.

But I don't understand my colleague's statement. The study of the medicine from the manufacturer says that 1000 mg is the starting dosage, not 1500 mg. And that's right out of their own paperwork.

This brought us some relief. My wife's current neurologist was on the ball. But raised serious questions of the other neurologist's willingness to help and openly accept patient questions—and to know the necessary background on the very medications she prescribed.

Another data point for you. During early pregnancy, when we baselined, you tested at < 0.2 ng/dL of levetiracetam in your bloodstream. Basically, unreadable. And you didn't have any breakthroughs, even with all those hormone changes. It's just one data point, but it's something.

This last point caused the doctor to smile. I asked the next question somewhat already anticipating the answer.

ME: What's the chance that this EEG doesn't show any activity since it's just a snapshot in time?

NEUROLOGIST: That's always a chance because like any tests, they can fail. With medicine, you never know until you try. But we know one thing for certain—**the status quo is unacceptable.**

After some goodbyes and exchanging of appreciation, our Zoom call ended.

A striking encounter! Rather than make us a nonentity, the doctor made us part of the solution. Her last statement was incredibly powerful—her attitude shined, a beacon to guide us forward. A formula of some grit mixed with grace and we loved it. Each interaction is another chance to learn, to course correct, to turn things around—to take a step towards healing a little more.

We learned that there's a wonderful way to practice medicine—patient and doctor, together as one. Interdependent. That means you have to be active in your own care, even if it's when you feel at your lowest. Only you know your body the best. You believe what your body is feeling and telling you, and so too must your doctor.

In June 2022, Megan completed an extended EEG. It was a 5-hour test, with her two previous ones clocked at 30 minutes and 2-hours. It came back abnormal. We quietly read and absorbed the results. It felt crushing, but we reminded ourselves that we needed to hear from Megan's neurologist. We didn't wait long. She always calls personally with news and promptly—in today's busy world of dereliction or delegation, what a standout!

NEUROLOGIST: "Did you already see the report?" she gently asked.

MEGAN: Tentatively answering, "Yes."

NEUROLOGIST: "I want you to get bloodwork done. I'd still be comfortable lowering the dosage if the levetiracctam level isn't already on the low end. Though if it is, we could still lower the amount. But I would want to add something else at a low dosage that isn't mood destabilizing—because, as we said, the status quo isn't an option," she reassuringly stated.

Megan then dropped a question that caused the young neurologist and mother (who had recently given birth to a baby girl) to think hard.

MEGAN: "What if I end up switching completely to another med at some point, but due to it not working, I need to come back on levetiracetam. I've spoken with other epileptics or those who know epileptics, and they said sometimes upon return, the seizures emerge harder to control. The brain has changed too much in the interim."

NEUROLOGIST: After a worthy pause, the doctor replied, "You know, that's a really good question. It's possible and happens in about 6% of cases."

If you're not being heard, keep searching until you find that **equal** partner in medicine. A little moxie goes a long way when used for the greater good. I empathize that the "unseen hand" of insurance may block you or your referring doctor's flexibility to do so. If that doctor is unwilling to assist slapping back coverage denials or pre-authorizations, just keep swimming.

((SECOND OPINIONS ARE NICE, SEVENTH OPINIONS—LIFE CHANGING))

As I wrote this section, my mom recounted an illuminating tale from decades ago. For a half a year, she suffered in pain while urinating. She started with her family doctor, Dr. Silver, who referred her to different urologists. They would take urine samples, but nothing out of the ordinary would show up. Still, logic would lead most to assume it was a urinary tract infection. She would be prescribed a short-course of antibiotics, no more than two weeks, and that was supposed to be that. But the pain remained, unabated, and carried into a family vacation.

My first time in Arizona and quite young, I vividly remember traveling the diverse landscape of the Old West. But as a child enchanted by the pastel sands of the Painted Desert, our next stop was only a fleeting thought. While my sister and I waited outside in the blistering sun, my parents went into a clinic. After introductions, the physician had this to offer, "Maybe she's just got an STD (sexually transmitted disease)."

From the patient perspective, this statement could be interpreted in many ways, most of them negative. Was the provider suggesting adultery? My parents had been faithfully married for many years. Yet, from the provider's perspective, a comprehensive review of symptoms reasonably includes potential STDs. A communication breakdown, proving that context and the order in which things are said are paramount. A moment by the physician to explain the thinking behind their words may have avoided harboring poor feelings years later—the result: a visit in vain.

Shortly, my mom was referred out to gynecologists. A pattern formed, albeit a highly unsought one—the doctors were recommending a complete hysterectomy. Once started, they kept beating the drum. One day, my mom decided to ask: "What if I do this, will the pain go away?" The gynecologist's answer, "Oh, I can't promise."

That moment was a wake-up call. She went back to her family doctor, asking, "Can I go to one of the main universities?" He agreed, "I can do that, but I want to try one last thing. I'm going to send you to someone who comes by locally once a week. He's quite a good doctor in his field." Once there, the last-ditch doctor said, "I want you to take these little white pills for three months. A long course of them. Then we'll see." They were an antibiotic that my mom hadn't taken before, and three months was much longer than two weeks.

She began the treatment and one month later, all pain vanished. It was the seventh and last physician my mom ever saw for this problem. Turns out the infection behind the pain was upstream in the tubes that connect the kidneys to the bladder (and trapped there). But not enough to show up in her urine or flag any tests. Nobody had considered that possibility; a critical mistake averted. A total hysterectomy would have solved nothing—leaving my mom with new problems, as well as the old one.

((MAKING A LIST, CHECKING IT TWICE))

Medical records, in one stroke a necessity, and another, the bane of existence for both doctor and patient. In 1977, my dad needed to complete his Army discharge exam. As a young G.I., he was a world away at Ft. Knox guarding gold while his mom (my grandmother) was back home in the final stages of battling cancer. The Army supported a hardship discharge but that's where magnanimity stopped and ambiguity started, leaving important questions: What is a discharge exam and why does it matter? The military, aka Uncle Sam, a man of few words, let silence do the talking. My dad would have to find out alone–in his words, "I was young, trusting, and inexperienced, not realizing how serious things could have gotten."

"You have Non A/Non-B hepatitis," drawled a disengaged Army clerk.

DAD: *"Is that something to be concerned about?"*

CLERK: *"Not really sure."*

DAD: *"Well, note it anyway, okay?"*

CLERK: *"Yeah, okay."*

Time passed and the memory was buried, until elevated liver enzymes forced the exchange to resurface. Checking with Veterans Affairs (VA) for possible benefits and treatment, they found no mention of hepatitis in my dad's records. With no record came a swift denial.

Twenty years later, after successful interferon treatment, my dad had won his health battle while losing an administrative one. An official letter appeared stating he likely contracted hepatitis in the Army, but benefits remain unnecessary because, "You're now cured and will receive a zero rating (no benefits)." It left an unsettled feeling—what records did they have to suddenly refer to? A check decades earlier by the VA came up empty. An about-face after massive delay–was a missing note found? With impeccable timing, was this a masterclass in payout avoidance while admitting partial fault (and medical record omission)? Or, just an honest mistake?

TL;DR—lessons for OQA:

Patients, it's okay to feel like you can seek multiple opinions. Each one may contain parts of the full answer. And when taken together, put you on the path to wellness. It's prudent to double-check and follow-up on your medical record. Even when made without ill-intent, nobody will suffer more than you while living with someone else's incorrect call, or lack of follow through.

((AS FATE WOULD HAVE IT))

Have you ever heard of the Great Pacific Garbage Patch? The Patch, if you will, is a swirling, human-created mélange of trash released in the North Pacific ocean covering an area twice the size of Texas.[210] With that as a backdrop in my mind, I ruminate on my 20-minute appointments scattered everywhere across a timeline clogged with thousands of other patients and countless forms and checkboxes. Just years and years of buildup.

I loathe to be so blunt but sometimes it can't be helped: There's no room to half-ass our health care expectations, interactions, and end results. But since we have every middleman, middle-process and middle-thing covered, today's system thrives on it. Doctors and patients are left further apart from one another than ever with a mountain of cost, waste, and affliction standing between. Hasn't anybody told you the joke? In today's environment, what's the best way to stay healthy? It's easy. Don't ever get sick.

As I write this near-penultimate section, I'm opening a letter. It's from a collection agency on behalf of the local hospital. Irritated, I figured somewhere was an honest mistake. Perhaps this letter was lost or misplaced, or something else inadvertently overlooked. I pay my bills, and if need be, set up longer-dated payment plans when no fees or interest are charged. If you understand the time-value of money in those cases, why wouldn't you?

When it comes to medical charges, the hospital always seems busy wrestling with the "unseen hand" on final amounts—I've received medical bills two calendar years later. Why is this acceptable? Yet I doubt my experience is unique.

Perfect example: I had just called the hospital's billing department a week ago and asked if there were any outstanding charges that weren't included in the existing payment plan. The answer was no, everything was included. You're good to go.

I next called the collection agency. I didn't want to double pay something already rolled into the existing payment plan. I asked who the charges were for and they confirmed for my daughter. I then called the hospital again and spoke with another agent. The way the online patient portal was arranged, both our son and daughter are linked to my account, as dependents, of course. But I couldn't see any charges under my daughter's name. There wasn't even a billing section on her page. As I explained this, the billing agent said I would have to speak with the IT department. Hold for transfer.

The IT agent came on and as we were talking, I clicked on the billing section of my account. I found a missing clue near the top of the page—"Patients Included: You, Your Son." Bingo. Our son was linked both medically and financially under one guarantor, me. However, our daughter was linked only medically. Any charges for her would keep slipping through the cracks until they went to the collection agency (where I would finally be made aware months later). Those charges, invisible even to the billing agents, never had a chance to be paid upfront. Nor rolled into a payment plan.

A vision popped into my head–a lonesome agent, in a cubicle, entangled by a headset with only the blue, hazy glow of her monitor to beat back stifling, gray walls. Evident were the silos between departments and lack of information sharing. My reverie couldn't be far from the truth. To see all charges, accounts needed to be fully linked. The agent did not have a method to see unlinked open charges. Poor processes left her hands tied. An IT incident ticket was created to work on linking all accounts.

A couple hours later, the hospital's IT group called back. "We've been able to link your daughter but not the same way as your son. The way that he's linked, under one guarantor, is not our standard way. It's the 'mistake way' of doing it. Not sure how that happened. Each person is supposed to have their own guarantor number."

Running through my head were two things—how our son is 6-and-a-half, and his age in terms of how long the 'mistake way' was out there. I replied, "Please don't make me an exception. I don't want to break your processes. It doesn't matter how my son's account got linked. I just want things to be consistent so I can see all charges. Our daughter turns one in two days so it'll be a bit before she's managing her own bills."

"Ha, I get it. But that's upstream if you will. Another group, registration handles that. Not sure how they will allow it—if they will change the way your son's linked, or make an exception for your daughter by setting her up the 'mistake way' too. They'll have to make the call. I'm just the IT guy." His was a genuine answer but I felt drained. I needed a break from writing my patient story. If you're still upright, the health care fight is perpetual!

My first family physician, Dr. Silver, re-enters my mind. I reflect on his gratuitous and tragic fate. I think of my current family practitioner, Dr. Otten, who was able to catch himself and recognize burnout. I think of all the doctors and patients out there, ourselves included, afloat in a large, swirling garbage patch. If the system feels fatal to you, it's because it often is.

As for the final bill: $320. I could afford to pay from my Health Savings Account. Maybe next time I won't be in the same fortunate position. Regrettably, I realize many Americans would be hurt by a $320 surprise bill. Between my time spent on it, the collection agency, and two billing agents, the IT guy, and now possibly a registration department, the invoice was far more billable wages than the original amount. How many more times will bureaucracy triumph over principle before healthy change happens? Dr. Otten and I believe in our hearts a transformation has begun. And we challenge everyone to help us turn the tide for a better system of care. As a reader of *Ripple of Change*, you've cast your first stone.

((FATAL FLAWS))

There's an old adage: Never go around your boss at work. But what if they're failing to listen and help? After you've had a heart-to-heart conversation and gotten nowhere, is it time to escalate matters? Perhaps the same thinking can be applied to the doctor-patient dynamic. If you are in a position to do so, try putting aside funds for a cash-only doctor. They often enjoy greater freedom beyond the dictating confines of insurance. Consider running your own blood work if your physician won't (or can't) place the order, and better arm yourself with information. There are many online services that partner with the major labs like LabCorp or Quest. You simply pay out-of-pocket, get an order e-mailed, and take it to a local blood draw station. I have used places like www.discountedlabs.com with success. Bring the results with you to your next visit and be an informed, engaged patient. Or take the report to another doctor for a second opinion. Be curious about your own ailments and embrace the "whatever it takes" attitude—become your #1 advocate.

If you can't secure the funds through your own means or from family, try services like GoFundMe. It's unlikely to hurt—what hurts is failing to exhaust all available options. As long as you're being upfront and truthful, people can draw their own conclusions as to whether to donate to your cause or not. It doesn't stop others from trying, and neither should it for you. Or sell something you don't use anymore on eBay or Facebook Marketplace. Nothing you do or materially own matters without owning your health.

While it's open for debate, without further change, today's system often makes us sick. In my humble opinion, it keeps us sick too. Asking for help mustn't be stigmatized, otherwise it's dehumanizing. Fortunately, thanks to technology, we have more ways of seeking assistance than ever before. There are like-minded, online communities to lean on, and telemedicine with out-of-state practitioners that removes geographic barriers. And the ripples have just started.

((24))

Prevention, Procedures, and Profits

"Are we doing your physical today?"
– TODD R. OTTEN, M.D.

"I thought we were just padding your paycheck."
– PATIENT

Todd R. Otten, M.D.:

As I dug deeper and deeper into the financial disruptors of healthcare in the U.S.—the number of titles I considered for this chapter was rather extensive. *Fraud, Waste, and Abuse. Stark Laws, PBM's, GFO's...Oh My.* (A nod to *The Wizard of Oz* for the younger readers). *How Capitalism Has Failed the Healthcare Consumer.* I think you get the point: our existing infrastructure has let the American healthcare consumer down. Not only have we failed patients and providers, but we are rubbing salt in their wounds with dollar bills.

The current financial landscape of healthcare in the U.S. feels akin to a shell game. For those unfamiliar, the shell game is one of chance (i.e., gambling). Imagine a small ball lying on a table. Three empty cups stand stationary behind a ball, and a middle-aged man with a bright and charismatic smile draws you in. The object of the game is to ascertain under which cup the ball lies at the finish. One out of three odds to double your money. Once the ball is covered, the curator will move the cups (as much as desired). Quickly the cups will move, faster and faster. Easy to lose track of the ball. Worse yet, with sleight of hand and deceptive practices, the ball may not even lie under a cup when the game concludes. And you must choose the correct cup or your money is gone.

Unfortunately, this is exactly how many patients feel trying to navigate the financial landscape in healthcare. And providers are just as frustrated. Just ask. There are many factors that have led us to this point. Lack of transparency, predatory billing, fraud, waste and abuse, to name a few. Lest we forget big pharma. OQA is not a switch that can be flipped to solve our dilemma. But it can be a starting point, a guide to facilitate change. It can be the underlying theme to provide courage for many of us to speak up. The more people utilize Our Quadruple Aim in their thought process and decision-making, the more we can reign in healthcare spending that is spiraling out of control. When one becomes 10, and hopefully thousands of people promoting healthcare fiscal reform: we will move the needle.

((MONEY DOESN'T GROW ON TREES))

"Today, every piece of good work in medicine, it seems, needs a promising business model."

– ELISABETH ROSENTHAL, M.D., *AN AMERICAN SICKNESS*[211]

Sitting quietly in Panama City Beach. The sun is rising—brilliant oranges and reds. The clouds create a silvery lining. A dilemma:

what golf course to play with my three sons. I am thinking we will play Windswept Dunes. Josh, Daniel, and I will play, as Brandon likes to ride along. A well-deserved respite—spring break with my family. Quiet. Peace.

My phone buzzes. That small pocket computer which can snap us back to reality. An email has arrived—"Happy Doctor's Day," from the Michigan Academy of Family Physicians. Fitting. A reminder of my normal day, both good and bad.

I think back to my adopted grandfather. Both of my biological grandfathers died when I was young, and my family befriended an elderly couple who worked with my father. Over the years we became very close and I affectionately called them Grandma and Grandpa. I distinctly remember sitting with him on his deathbed, trying to offer comfort. I had just been accepted into medical school and his last words to me were: "Don't rest on your laurels."

So how do we unwind the dysfunctional, profit-driven health-care landscape to which we have been acclimated? There is no simple answer. Rather we need to look at the separate components of healthcare that need to change. This chapter emphasizes the financial aspect. Those entities that extract maximum value from our siloed system must be addressed. Unfortunately, dollars are frequently the primary driver of healthcare, and last I checked, money doesn't grow on trees.

((LOWER COSTS PER CAPITA?))

"The health system in the United States is one of the most inequitable when compared to peer developed nations. Despite enormous spending on health care per capita, in fact spending more per capita than all other nations in the Organization for Economic Cooperation and Development combined, the United States has staggering and disappointing outcomes—ranking 28th out of 34 countries in life expectancy, 33rd in infant mortality and 1st in poverty."

– J. NWANDO OLAYIWOLA AND MARK RASTETTER[212]

Not sure if it was irony or serendipity, but as I began this chapter, one of my patients shared an article from the *SaturdayEvening-Post.com*, titled "It's Time We Fixed Our Hospitals."[213] A fascinating commentary regarding the finances in healthcare and concerns with respect to profits as the primary motivating factor. It speaks of maximizing profits at the expense of patients and providers. Although I didn't agree with every aspect of the article, it included many poignant comments. I offer a few examples, but encourage you to dig deeper.

- "It's all about money today, and there is no economic incentive to keep you healthy, to get you well, or for that matter keep you alive."
- "Kindly assistants, competent nurses, and decent physicians try to humanize the widget, but they are constrained by a system driven by the bottom line."
- "Doctors feel crushed by their many masters and miss the authority that they used to enjoy, or that they anticipated that they would enjoy when they decided to go to medical school."
- "Hospitals have an incentive to get you out the door when the revenue stream declines. And insurance companies have an incentive not to pay for your tests and treatment."[214]

Wow, there is a lot to unpack here. This article was blunt, and there is no simple solution to the complex set of questions and comments presented. Yet, I agree with many of the author's sentiments. The article speaks to the broken incentive structure to deliver healthcare in the U.S. Often, the existing compensatory mechanisms are not aligned with what is in the patient's or caregiver's best interests.

The good news is that there are people who are trying to move the needle. Marty Makary, M.D. has written an absolute must-read in regards to the fiscal dysfunction in healthcare in his book, *The Price We Pay: What Broke American Health Care – And How to Fix It*. The book masterfully weaves current examples of waste and abuse with creative, altruistic endeavors to combat them. Dr. Makary traveled the U.S. searching out both good and bad.[215] More importantly, he offers hope. I encourage everyone with the energy and courage to make a difference to read this book—perhaps even twice.

There is a saying about physicians, and it goes something like this. Specialists know more and more about less and less, until they know everything about nothing. Family physicians know less and less about more and more until they know nothing about everything. There are some nuggets of truth in that statement for sure—and levity to boot. Interestingly, the more you know about insurance and the finances in healthcare—the less you are likely to pay. Knowledge is power.

We will highlight several areas of opportunity to reduce waste and expose and remedy fraud and abuse. Bending the financial curve of healthcare in the U.S. will be a herculean effort. But if enough stones are cast into the pond, the ripples might turn into waves. If you aren't the type to cast a stone, share these ideas with someone who is. Just imagine if millions of patients and providers use their collective voice. Transformative. Don't rest on your laurels.

((PREVENTION VERSUS CURE))

"No matter what advances medicine might make,
he'd learned the hard way that doctors occupied
the last line of trenches in a battle
that should have been won at the front line."

– BARRY LAVERTY, *AN IRISH COUNTRY DOCTOR*[216]

My love of flying is a product of being a flight surgeon in the U.S. Navy. A rolodex of fond memories permanently stored from my time in the service. As I peered out of the window on the commercial flight my thoughts drifted between my children at home and my beautiful wife sitting next to me. I prefer the window seat. Angie would prefer to drive. Flying is an opportunity to view the world from a different perspective. Verdant pastures, shades of red and brown, baby blue skies, fluffy white clouds—majestic views.

My sister and brother-in-law sat directly in front of us. We were headed to a long weekend getaway to celebrate a 40th birthday, traveling to Phoenix, Arizona to rendezvous with family. Golf, swimming, and relaxation awaited. Having taken off from Detroit, Michigan, we were about two hours into the flight. Angie's nerves had settled and we had just ordered a beverage when my blissful thoughts were rudely interrupted.

"Is there a doctor on board?" blared the PA system.

This is the last thing you want to hear on a flight—particularly as a physician. I took a deep breath, looked at Angie and stood up, my hand sheepishly raised. My mind snapped back to reality with a work-like determination. Unless there was an emergency physician on board (or EMT), I was likely the most qualified to deal with a medical emergency. The flight attendant made eye contact, feigned a smile, and walked towards me. Time began to slow down. Anticipation and angst were the new emotions...the prior euphoria had melted away.

"Thank you...this way," said the stewardess, as I followed her to the cabin. Trudging forward begrudgingly, my brain reviewed a question I have been asked hundreds of times. When people find out I was a flight surgeon, I am invariably asked if I performed surgeries on a plane. With a smile, I explain the title is a misnomer. So no, I did not perform operations on a plane, and I had no intention of doing so as I advanced in the fuselage.

The walk forward covered about 90 feet, with hundreds of pairs of eyeballs following my trek. I could feel my pulse quickening. The patient was in a semi-recumbent position in the kitchenette, near a restroom. To my surprise, he was wearing a steward outfit. After a brief update from the stewardess, I turned toward the steward and quickly checked his vital signs while asking questions at the same time. The steward now the patient, and I the physician. The ever present white coat.

Pulse – 120 (normal 60 – 80)	Respiratory rate – 25 (normal 8 – 16)	Conversive

The patient started answering questions, but his breathing was labored. He was slightly pale, with small beads of perspiration on his brow. His worst symptom was shortness of breath that had begun approximately 20 minutes prior. We placed the patient on oxygen and I started to ask about his medical history: HIV positive, on testosterone therapy, and had recently been discharged from the ICU after a severe bout of pneumonia. One thought replayed in my mind—who cleared this guy to return to work?

After the initial assessment, I turned back towards the stewardess to see what medical supplies were available. A medical emergency kit was presented, which included some basic first aid supplies and a few medicines including epinephrine (occasionally referred to as adrenaline). This medicine is used in advanced cardiac life support to treat malignant arrhythmias. Angie (a former ICU nurse) arrived at the scene to assist and we administered an aspirin to the patient. I asked the stewardess if any other resources were available and she informed me the airline medical director was available via telephone. I reassessed and reassured the patient.

Pulse – 130	Respiratory rate – 25 – 30	Conversive

I spoke with the patient, and he answered in short sentences, catching his breath in between. He described some slight chest discomfort, but struggled to elaborate. The oxygen remained in place. I listened to his heart and lungs with my newly acquired stethoscope. His heart rate was regular, but tachycardic (too fast). Lungs seemed clear, but clearly the exam was limited due to the background noise. His condition was gradually worsening. Twenty minutes had elapsed, and I asked to speak with the airline medical director.

The phone was at the back of the aircraft. Another walk with all eyes firmly fixated on me. After a brief introduction (including my background), the conversation included: the patient's history and current condition, options and equipment available, and remaining duration of the flight (about two hours). A decision was made to continue supportive care and attempt to land in Phoenix.

I made my way back to the kitchenette to reassess the patient. Again—eyes following. At this point, I had little additional treatment to offer beyond aspirin and oxygen. Several options if he worsened. I prayed that did not occur.

Pulse – 140	Respiratory rate – 30	Lethargic, but responsive

This was not going well. Our attempts to converse with the patient were becoming more difficult. Fragmented. He was slipping in and out of consciousness. No new symptoms, just short of breath and chest discomfort. Another 15 minutes elapsed, but it seemed like an eternity.

Pulse – 150	Respiratory rate – 35 – 40	Somnolent

The patient was conscious only with stimulation, and his cognitive abilities were rapidly diminishing. I asked to speak to the medical director again.

"Hello, this is Dr. Otten."

A barely decipherable response was given.

"I can barely hear you," I exclaimed.

"You know you are on an airplane," said the medical director.

"No shit, I am pretty sure I called you," I said, full of exasperation.

The conversation that ensued was fascinating, with numerous stakeholders impacted by whatever decision made. He asked if we could make it another hour and half to Phoenix. Clearly his primary objective was to complete the flight.

"We'll do our best. If this patient was at my office I would have called EMS already. I suppose I can start chest compressions if he codes (his heart stops)."

"I will talk with the captain," replied the medical director.

A few minutes later the stewardess asked us to take our seats. We would be making an emergency landing in Albuquerque, New Mexico. I get chills thinking about that moment. The walk back to our seats seemed to take forever; it was as if we were traversing through a field of mud. The emergency landing was announced over the PA system. Again, I was the center of attention, for which I had no desire. I worried for my new patient, and was glad we were landing. He needed a higher level of care than I could offer. I sat down and buckled my seat belt.

I closed my eyes and prepared for landing. Another 10 minutes elapsed, but my internal clock was returning to normal. I looked at Angie and I could see the look of concern. As the wheels of the aircraft touched the ground, I felt relieved. An ambulance was parked on the tarmac. My fear of my patient dying started to lessen. As the aircraft came to a stop, I jumped out of my seat to check on my patient.

Pulse – 150	Respiratory rate – 35 – 40	Somnolent

I did a sternal rub to arouse the steward, rubbing my knuckle firmly on his chest. I handed him a slip of paper with my name and cell phone number inscribed. I told him I wanted to hear from him when he was better. The aircraft doors were opened and EMS took over. They asked a few questions, but already had the history. The patient was loaded onto the ambulance and I returned to my seat. The cathartic feeling that I had done my best washed over me, and I was glad the patient was en route to the hospital. I wondered how many of the several hundred passengers were upset with me.

We deboarded the plane to await a new flight attendant, who ironically was flying in from Phoenix. As we walked forward in the fuselage, I was expecting upset stares, perhaps even snide comments. What instead transpired surprised me. No less than 10 people thanked me for doing the right thing. My eyes welled up with tears. As I approached the exit door, the captain stood there with his hand outstretched towards me. I extended my hand, trembling. He grabbed hold of my hand and simply said, "thank you."

"An ounce of prevention is worth a pound of cure."

– BENJAMIN FRANKLIN

This case is a classic example of potential cost savings from better preventative care. Based on the medical history of the steward, he was a high risk to return to work. I never would have let this patient return to active flight status as a flight surgeon. Fortunately, this case ended well from the patient's perspective. But what was the cost to the other passengers and airline? And what about the hospital cost? Surely, the total was in the hundred of thousands. All of that financial outlay could have been prevented with a simple office visit. But our healthcare system favors action rather than prevention. Until the pendulum swings towards Our Quadruple Aim I fear these problems will only intensify.

Epilogue: about a week after our vacation I received a text from the steward: "I had a massive pulmonary embolism (blood clot to the lungs) and spent a week in the hospital. Getting better. Thank you."

((INTERMEDIARIES))

"It's time we banned all kickbacks in medicine."

– MARTY MAKARY, M.D., *THE PRICE WE PAY*[217]

If you truly listen to patients, they will tell you where the problems are. Not only true in diagnosing disease, but what ails healthcare as well. This has never been truer. As Chief of Staff, the insight patients gave often led to quick fixes in our rural critical access hospital. A quick example—throughput for phlebotomy had suffered with long, frustrating wait times for patients. I would hear about this problem regularly from patients. As a solution, a satellite lab station was started as a pilot, then quickly became a permanent fixture, cutting wait times in half while increasing volumes. A win for every stakeholder: a microcosm of OQA.

As I approached retirement, I spent more and more time listening to my patients vent about systemic healthcare concerns. Local issues, complaints about the hospital (and system), financial worries, drug prices, deductibles, insurance, politics; I had to redirect patients on a daily basis—they are fed up.

The financial pressures are at a tipping point. People are choosing to eat over paying for their medication. Second- or third-line medications (often with less efficacy and higher side effect profiles) are being used with increased frequency, as people cannot afford first-line choices. People are avoiding testing and staying home longer than they should when ill; often leading to longer hospitalizations and poorer outcomes. At times, people even prefer death. Talk about moral injury. And who is to blame?

Certainly there are plenty of issues, and everyone who administers and/or utilizes healthcare could and should aspire to participate in a better system. However, there are intermediaries or "middle men" who have mastered extracting dollars from the system (with questionable return for the end user). I am not suggesting that there aren't good people who work in the following examples. Nor am I suggesting that there aren't good companies that are trying to improve problematic areas in healthcare. But I am saying there are far too many bad actors. Far too many leeches that extract maximum value from the average American healthcare consumer. Let's explore some rabbit holes.

While practicing, I could capture macro trends in healthcare just by listening to my patients and compiling anecdotal data. Again—think parachutes. One trend I heard with increasing frequency was prescription drug costs. In recent years, the costs of prescription drugs have spiraled out of control. Patients having to make decisions between medications they could afford and continue to take, or not. Patients are rationing generic insulin so they don't run out. Imagine having to choose between basic staples or their medications.

I have always tried to be a good fiduciary of healthcare dollars. But red flags have been rising for years. A reminder: a red flag in medicine is used when there is concern regarding the gravity of a pending diagnosis (usually not a good sign). Certainly there are many factors that contribute to this price escalation. But many Pharmacy Benefit Managers (PBMs) are contributing to prescription drug price appreciation.

PBMs originated in the late 1960s when insurers were trying to contain costs regarding prescription drugs. Their current role serves as an intermediary (overseeing pharmacy benefits) between pharmaceutical companies, wholesalers, pharmacies, and health insurance providers. Many describe PBMs as the "middlemen" of the pharmaceutical industry, and over the years much consolidation has occurred. Currently the three largest PBMs control nearly 90% of the market, and are also owned by insurance companies. Additional vertical consolidation is occurring as group purchasing organizations (GPOs) are being integrated—blurring the lines even more.[218, 219]

To complicate this process even further, there exists a lack of transparency, complex rebate and fee structures, and a dearth of regulatory oversight—the average consumer has no idea where their hard-earned money is even going when they pay for a prescription medication. Even worse, the PBMs' incentive structure is often completely misaligned with regards to cost savings for patients. What do I mean by this? Well simply put, the higher the price of the medication—the greater the profit for the PBM. Throw in contractually gagged pharmacists and other creative contractual nuances that favor PBMs.[220, 221] This is almost too much to believe—patients are at the mercy of greed. It makes me nauseated to think of my diabetic patients who can't afford their insulin. The opposite of Our Quadruple Aim.

"I had to decide to pay my mortgage or buy my medicine."

– PATIENT

Marty Makary, M.D. eloquently describes "the spread." Essentially this is the difference between what a PBM charges an employer for a medication and what they subsequently pay out to a pharmacy for the same medication. Depending on the difference between the two sums—a tidy profit can be made. In *The Price We Pay*, Makary highlights examples where employers were paying their PBM five to 20 times what the PBM was paying a pharmacy. And we all share in the burden of paying for this. Gross profits for PBMs in 2019 have been reported to 28 billion U.S. dollars—that could pay for a lot of insulin. Fortunately, Dr. Makary and others have spoken up. Dr. Makary suggests exploring consulting firms available to negotiate PBMs contracts.[222]

The PBM Accountability project looks to explore PBMs, their current revenue structure, and how this translates to higher prescription drug prices subsequently passed on to patients and insurance providers. The project discusses misaligned incentives, excess complexity, limited transparency, and lack of regulatory oversight—leading to increased revenue for PBMs. They have a fantastic website that highlights many areas of opportunity for cost savings for patients through policy change and other areas of opportunity within the PBM structure.[223] And we all agree that the American healthcare consumer needs to speak up and voice their displeasure for change to occur.

A sign of progress: The Pharmacy Benefit Manager Transparency Act of 2022 looks to empower the Federal Trade Commission and state attorney general to stop unfair and deceptive PBM practice models. Introduced in May 2022, the Act looks to mandate transparency, incentivize fair and transparent PBM practices, and prohibit unfair and deceptive pricing practices (including spread pricing). As of writing, this legislation was working its way through Congress.[224] Hopefully we take another step towards achieving OQA.

((BIG PHARMA))

"Price is what you pay, value is what you get."

– WARREN BUFFET

Two words, simple, yet daunting. I sat and stared at the title of the section for several minutes. The cursor blinking, almost daring me to set my fingers in motion. How do I succinctly encapsulate the issues within an industry so vital to healthcare, yet, so financially driven? Example after example of profit-driven decisions that are in shareholders' best interests. Are there even examples I can point to that embody Our Quadruple Aim? There must be. Determined to find examples of progress within the pharmaceutical industry towards achieving OQA, I felt obligated to provide an amazing resource that pulls back the curtain.

Elisabeth Rosenthal, M.D. in her book *An American Sickness: How Healthcare Became Big Business and How You Can Take It Back*, eloquently reviews many of the issues in the pharmaceutical industry in her chapter—"The Age of Pharmaceuticals." An intriguing investigative report, giving real-life examples of how the pharmaceutical industry and the quest for profits can have devastating financial effects on patients.[225] I will include a few quotes from the chapter, but her book is an amazing review and offers a clear manifesto for change. For those wanting to further OQA, I highly encourage reading her work.

- "Through that evolution, the price of Ms. Marcus's old drug, long off patent, had increased 500 percent, even as its price decreased for patients in other developed countries."
- "'The only people who win are the lawyers and the patent holders.' David Kliff, editor of Diabetic Investor, regarding patents and insulin therapy."
- "Likewise, cost-saving new treatments have had a maddeningly hard time finding their way into the American medical bazaar, because lower prices for patients often translate into the loss of income for someone with greater clout."[226]

It is unfortunate that the quest for higher profits has contributed to a landscape so contradictory to Our Quadruple Aim. As a family physician it has become increasingly frustrating to prescribe cost-effective medications for patients. Patients routinely have to choose between their medications and other necessities. Why is there such a discrepancy between the U.S. and other developed countries? I am advocating for change at the highest levels in line with OQA. Physician leaders, administrators, politicians need to step back and ask how their decisions affect the macro environment in healthcare. What ripples do your decisions make?

But there is hope as evidenced by the recently passed Inflation Reduction Act (as the measure is known). Passed by both chambers of Congress, this Act was signed into law in August, 2022. The American Association of Retired Persons (AARP) launched a *Stop Rx Greed* campaign in 2018, which, while stalled by the COVID-19 pandemic, was reinvigorated in 2021 with a message of: *Fair Rx Prices Now*. Through a collective effort of petitions, emails, letters, and phone calls to Congress—the campaign was successful. This law is a milestone for patients' and providers' plight against big pharma's greed. I will highlight some of the achievements. Total annual out-of-pocket spending on prescription drugs will be capped at $2,000 starting in 2025. Most vaccines will be free for Medicare patients in 2024. The Health and Human Services secretary is authorized to negotiate a certain number of prescription drug costs, starting in 2023. If a prescription drug price is raised more than the rate of general inflation, penalties will be levied to the pharmaceutical companies.[227]

Considering the average annual price of the top 260 brand-name prescriptions most used by older Americans rose from $100 in 2005 to $303.25 in 2020, this law is a major win. As a comparison, if a gallon of milk had the same rate of inflation, it would have gone from $3.19 to $12.87 (keep in mind inflation affects prices of commodities differently).[228] The importance of the endeavor cannot be overstated. This law embodies everything about Our Quadruple Aim. Patients taking the initiative to encourage Congress to control prescription drug costs screams "Our." This effort begs the question, "what challenge is next?"

((YOUR GUESS AS GOOD AS MINE))

Joshua J. Judy – Patient:

"I don't want cost to be an issue."

Those were the words of the bright, young neurologist engaging her patient. Megan's doctor recognized how well she was doing on her new epilepsy medication, brivaracetam. Although a close cousin to levetiracetam, it's newer (still under patent) with reports of less side effects. It was promising and the doctor wanted Megan to continue the medication.

Megan's neurologist's approach was remarkable. And remarkably simple. If the cost of medication meant choosing failure over success, she wanted us to know that cost-sharing programs existed. Even more important was the doctor's mindset—it's how she chose to lead the conversation. Care in the driver's seat, costs in the rearview.

Earlier in the conversation, Megan had broken down the confusing pricing scheme for her doctor. Megan was originally written for a 30-day supply with four refills. She had three full refills remaining. But the prescription plan provider incentivizes home deliveries. If the patient chooses to utilize a local pharmacy, they're charged more exorbitant prices. And the PBM is a pro at getting their message across. Piles of notifications, e-mails, and letters to switch to home delivery stack up rapidly.

"Looking online, the plan defaulted to a 50-day supply for $350. That's a partial refill–one bottle and two-thirds of another. But I have three full refills remaining. Are you able to write me a fresh script for 90 days and we'll see the cost? It should only come in 30, 60 or 90-day supplies. I don't get it," Megan conveyed.

"What? I don't get it either. I'll call in a new script," replied the doctor.

Certainly, both doctor and patient had seen advanced mathematics during their academic careers. But this was the most complex of equations—prescription quantities and pricing. A black hole. Enough to leave anyone bewildered. Days later, the new script was processed. The price: $198 for a full 90-day supply. Yet, $350 for a 50-day supply. Odd. That raised many questions.

Why did the portal default to 50-day supply? Was it all they had in stock? With three full refills left, it should have defaulted to 90-days for home delivery. Did they get more stock between Megan's appointment and the new script being sent? Ok, how about a message stating such. Why was a 90-day supply so much cheaper than 50? Was the programming behind the provider's portal hardcoded to look for a 90-day supply? And anything less prevented a coupon from being applied? Megan discovered that the manufacturer's coupon alone was $500. Ok, why not account for that? If the portal had originally allowed a 90-day refill, would we have seen $198 instead of $350?

An enigma. Or was it something else? I don't have ready answers to those questions. That's the point—where's the transparency?

((ONCE BITTEN, TWICE SHY))

Could we have called the script plan provider and asked about the above discrepancy? Certainly. However, it's a story of trust. Would it have been a good use of time? Less certain.

I distinctly remember the last time I called the plan provider. I had just opened a letter stating that I needed to switch from name brand thyroid medication to generic. I would be required to cycle through five other generics first. If and only if those failed, I *might* be allowed to come back to the brand name and have it covered. Mind you, I had just taken an entire year to adjust to the current medication (which was covered at the time). I was finally doing better. To a higher power somewhere, I suppose that meant it was a perfect time to tip over the apple cart.

Switching brands went against all of my doctors' recommendations. Once adjusted and doing well, the patient should remain on the brand that got them there. Who could argue with this logic? And what to say about annual formulary changes? When the calendar year rolls, the list of prescription drugs covered by a patient's PBM or insurance plan can and often changes. Brand names dropped for cheaper generics regardless of impact to patients, sudden requirements for preauthorizations, and the list goes on. With this top of mind, prior authorizations were written by both Dr. Otten and my specialist. In an equal but opposite fashion, prior authorizations were denied. A battle staged.

I decided to appeal. I took a half day off of work in case I needed it. Utter insanity. It felt like robbing Peter to pay Paul. These were hours spent away from my actual job so I could be a proxy worker in healthcare. Modern healthcare: a productivity killer across many industries. I phoned the prescription plan provider and was placed on hold. Three hours later, still holding. If I hung up, I'd lose the spot in the queue I had worked hard to climb. Spot 10. Spot 5. Spot 2. Caller, you're next! Oh boy, I felt like I was winning the lotto. Oh no, it was 4:40 pm on a Friday. Surely, as a courtesy, they would check in before closing. 4:59 pm. 5:00 pm. 5:05 pm. They had run the clock out. And there was no way to leave a message—the same annoying music just kept looping. Son of a—

The next day, I reached a supervisor and told them how much I appreciated yesterday's stunt. My words were professional but terse. In return, I was issued an apology–and another denial. Exactly whose pockets were getting heavier as mine got lighter? It's a lesson we often pay for things in life that we receive little value for.

I returned to the specialist's office. I had found a sympathetic front desk staff member. "I recommend you reach out to this compounding pharmacy. I hear they have a deal directly with the manufacturer. Here's a few samples we had laying around to get you through. Good luck." The staff member had a few brand name blister packs tucked away in a front drawer, left behind by who I presume was a drug rep passing through. They'd be expiring soon anyway. She discreetly slid them across the counter, her commiserating half smile punctuating an otherwise soulless transaction. Why did everything, even when doing the right thing, have a back alley feel?

In case you wondered, I'm still on the brand name years later. I pay out-of-pocket and it's cheaper than if I had run it through insurance. Are you surprised? Money might not always buy health, but it sure buys options. Intuitively, we know that concentrated powers generally hate when people have options.

Our Quadruple Aim is about the freedom enjoyed by asking the right questions and having informed choices. And to the front desk staff member out there, thank you.

((PRIOR AUTHORIZATION (PA)))

"Insurers' rationale for prior authorization is simple: it bolsters the bottom line."

– STEVE COHEN[229]

Todd R. Otten, M.D.:

If you read my poem "**Medicine is World of Gray**," you most likely gleaned that I am not a big fan of prior authorizations. In fact, just hearing that term elevates my blood pressure, occasionally gives me a tension headache, and even makes my blood boil at times. Such a visceral reaction to paperwork. Perhaps a vestige from my prior burnout, or maybe pure disdain for the mountain of forms. At the risk of sounding pompous or callous—I didn't go to school for 11 years to check boxes for everyone. I understand the intent—supposed cost savings, avoiding waste, abuse, and perhaps curbing fraud. But what about those of us who are practicing good medicine, advocating for our patients, and trying to be good fiduciaries for the healthcare dollar? Burying us in paperwork perpetuates moral injury.

So what is a prior authorization (PA)? Approval from an insurer (payor) prior to delivering care, i.e., treatment, service, test, medication, and more. Think of a PA as a stop light to the next level of care. The intent is to optimize patient outcomes, ensure safety, and limit fraud, waste, and abuse.[230] Unfortunately the current system is flawed, with manual and cumbersome processes leading to delays in care and potential for adverse outcomes.

"Because precertification has become such a vibrant business in and of itself over the years—and remains a great way for insurers to save money—the requirement for precertification has trickled down to the most trivial medical needs."

– ELISABETH ROSENTHAL, M.D., *AN AMERICAN SICKNESS*[231]

With health care costs spiraling out of control, the essence of PAs seems logical. Rooting out fraud, waste, and abuse is imperative—hence the rationale for PAs. But at what cost? The ripples to Our Quadruple Aim are tremendous. Higher administrative costs—estimates nearing half a trillion dollars. Poor patient outcomes as a result of delays. And I will attest—PAs do not help my well-being. The AMA has been surveying my colleagues for years. In 2019, 83% of physicians report PAs harm continuity of care and 86% report the problem has worsened in the last five years.[232]

Perhaps some examples to highlight the frustrations with PAs is warranted. The unseen cost of doing prior authorizations is difficult to assess—but just ask any provider how they feel about it. The following is an excerpt from a colleague.

"I don't think physicians should be involved in PAs at all, UNLESS the med being prescribed is not FDA-approved for the condition being treated. That's the only case in which I feel a physician should have to justify or do 'paperwork' for prescribing and getting a med approved for a patient. PAs are about cost containment and should be dealt with between patient and insurer. Physicians should be completely left out of that hassle. A physician's job is to make clinical decisions about treatment, not do paperwork to get an insurance company to cover a med for a patient."

– ANONYMOUS

Scathing. Surely it has contributed to my decision to retire. Certainly it adds to the never-ending list of frustrations for many other healthcare workers. Advocating for patients and getting resistance from "the unseen hand" can be mind numbing. Having to tell a patient their insurance no longer pays for a life-saving medicine is disheartening. Their medication is no longer on formulary or didn't follow the algorithm—how do I explain that? Someone who has never seen the patient made a decision in lieu of their PCP. Frustrating for patients and providers.

Approximately seven years ago I met George. George was a patient of my former colleague—Linus. He was following up from a recent admission for a congestive heart failure exacerbation. In short, his heart struggled to keep up pumping blood, and fluid accumulated in his lungs and extremities. He wasn't the most compliant and hadn't been following with cardiology. His medications had been adjusted during the hospitalization and he was following up with me for the first time. He was skeptical and reluctant to adjust his medications.

At the time I was an ACO medical director and had been diligently working on cost savings and reducing hospital admissions. Managing heart failure successfully requires many things—education, dietary changes (particularly salt), exercise, diligence monitoring vital signs and weight, testing, appropriate medications, and more. With the right mixture—patients can do well and live for many years.

That first meeting with George was pretty straightforward. I ensured he was on an appropriate regimen of medications, ordered follow up lab work, offered some education, and made a follow-up appointment. About a month later, George was in my office after another heart failure exacerbation, resulting from chips and salsa at a Mexican restaurant. I altered my approach. I asked George how he felt about being in the hospital—again. We discussed his dislike of medications and having appointments. I was blunt and we made a connection. A rapport was developed. We discussed a newer medication, sacubitril/valsartan. At the time, I had minimal first-hand experience with the medication. However, from a physiological perspective I felt the drug had tremendous potential for heart failure.

George seemed more committed and we made a follow-up for one week. Begrudgingly, George kept his appointment. His labs were better, but his legs were still swollen and he was short of breath. I started him on sacubitril/valsartan.

Fast forward two years. George was doing well. No more admissions for congestive heart failure. We met every three to six months. He still complained about having to see the doctor, but appreciated not being in the hospital. Over time, those complaints melted away. As we had entered into a new calendar year, George needed a PA for his sacubitril/valsartan. I was incensed. Specifically the request asked if a cardiologist had prescribed the medication. If you recall, George had two admissions in less than a month, and now he hadn't been hospitalized in two years. I penned a response.

> *"I have been taking care of George for two years. When I first met him, he was admitted for congestive heart failure twice in a month's time. We maximized his therapy and added sacubitril/valsartan. He has not been admitted since. And yes, I spoke with cardiology regarding this case. Did a cardiologist review his case on your end?" Signature—with a smiley face included.*

Medication approved. Certainly one of my more flippant responses. Imagine having to write hundreds of PAs every time we move into a new calendar year. Hundreds of letters to justify why patients have been on medications that keep them out of the hospital, improve their quality of life, lower costs—achieving three of the four components of OQA. Unfortunately this does not help Provider Wellness and contributes to escalating frustrations for physicians and other providers. This process must change, particularly for those providers who have proven to be good fiduciaries.

The intriguing part of PAs is, if implemented properly, they have the potential to achieve Our Quadruple Aim. Unfortunately, reality often lands far from this ideal. Greed and dysfunctional processes have created the mess that exists today. The burden has been shifted to physicians and healthcare workers. Fortunately many have offered solutions. Let's explore a handful.

Medicare advantage plans routinely look at overall cost of care. Capitated models exist that reward good fiduciaries of the healthcare dollar. The concept of evidence-based medicine should be extrapolated to PAs. Providers who have proven to be good stewards should have reduced clerical burdens. Yet, the current system is designed to flesh out fraud, waste, and abuse—burying everyone in paperwork.

Why not look at overall cost of care (using artificial intelligence) and adjust prior authorization requirements for successful providers?

Steve Cohen eloquently outlines several ideas for reform in the article *"Instead of Prior Authorization, Insures Should go Back to the old 'Pay-and-Chase' Model."* He suggests shifting the clerical burden back to insurers with additional ramifications for fraudulent activities. Moving back to a "pay-and-chase" model, insurers would pay claims up front and use their investigators to recover erroneous or fraudulent payments. In addition, he suggests Congress extend the False Claims Act to all of health care fraud, not just federally funded procedures.[233] Perhaps this would incentivize insurers to focus on OQA—not the bottom line.

An eHealth Initiative Collaborative Project in 2019 established a series of prior authorization workshops with numerous stakeholders, including the AAFP. Their goals included improving the current prior authorization landscape and to address the widespread challenges and dissatisfaction among healthcare professionals. They suggest the focus be on improving, reforming, and streamlining the PA process—to reduce physician burnout, improve outcomes, and increase patient satisfaction.[234] Yet another example that echoes Our Quadruple Aim. They offer four concepts to facilitate transformation. I would encourage those interested to read the full article. I will paraphrase for brevity's sake:

1. Transparency of payer policy and evidence-based clinical guidelines at the point of care may reduce need for PAs and minimize care delays.
2. Reducing overall volume of services and drugs requiring PAs could decrease administrative burdens and costs for all stakeholders.
3. Stakeholders should incorporate existing, industry-endorsed standards and explore new electronic standards that improve the PA process.
4. Stakeholders should explore alternative payment models that promote bundled authorizations for a particular episode of care.[235]

Ultimately for the PA process to align with OQA, legislative changes are likely required. The passage of Senate Bill 247 in Michigan is a brilliant step forward for patients, communities, and physicians. This bill states, "After three years of legislative consideration this bill was signed into law...bringing new transparency, fairness, and clinical validity requirements for the prior authorization process. These positive changes will help ensure patients can get the care and medications they need, when they need them, as determined by their family physicians." Senate Bill 247 provisions include standardizing an electronic prior authorization submission process, ensuring these authorizations are based on peer-reviewed clinical criteria, and instilling timelines for insurers to complete their prior authorization reviews. This legislative change is a breath of fresh air on many levels. Reducing the administrative burdens is a major win for both patients and providers. Postponing care due to clerical burdens can lead to delays in diagnosis, higher costs, and worse outcomes.[236] These legislative changes are a step in the right direction to achieve Our Quadruple Aim on a larger scale. In a state where physician shortage is a major issue, this is a win for reducing burnout and helping physicians care for their patients.

((VENTURE CAPITAL))

"It is health that is real wealth and not pieces of gold and silver."

– GANDHI

Why would private equity firms be buying up physician groups? Simple—there is money to be made. Instead of profit margins going to improve preventative care, they are now going to venture capital groups. Another dangerous, slippery slope. I sent texts to some respected friends and colleagues, including many physicians and business leaders, asking, "Any thoughts on venture capital buying physician groups?" The responses are telling.

- "Seems like a no brainer to make money. But would also put pressure on performance metrics. What may become more important as we enter that world is a focus on ethics and morality to ensure care remains a top priority."
- "It's bad. A dangerous slippery slope."
- "I'm not a fan of venture-capitalism involved in healthcare at all. One more example of middlemen bleeding profits and inflating costs."

Typically a physician does between 11 to 17 years of school to become board-certified in their chosen specialty. Even more with additional training such as a fellowship. Physicians have sacrificed portions of their lives to help others and historically this connotes a level of autonomy in practice. However, in my 20 years of practice the autonomy we earned has eroded. Just another reason physicians are quitting medicine.

The ability of a physician to make a decision for a patient is tethered to many parties in today's modern version of health care—Parties such as third-party payors, PBMs, health systems, and hospitals, to name a few. And now venture capital groups. Healthcare has been largely driven by profit for many years. We are already on that slippery slope. Adding venture capital may turn that slide into a bobsled run. Without autonomy, physicians cannot perform at the highest level.

The biggest concern I have with venture capitalism in acquiring physician groups is: who are the incentives aligned for? Is Our Quadruple Aim at the forefront of decision making? Doubtful. I recently read an article about Ray Brovont, M.D., an ER physician who advocated for additional staffing to appropriately care for patients. An unfortunate theme throughout healthcare. He was fired. Ultimately, a wrongful termination suit was settled to the tune of 26 million U.S. dollars.[237]

I don't know Dr. Brovont personally. I am sure both sides have their story. But who really won in a situation like this? The physician? The patients? The venture capital group? Maximizing profits at the expense of quality patient care, appropriate support, and staffing is a disaster waiting to happen. If this unfortunate trend continues—I fear there will be many similar, lamentable stories in the future.

((CONFLICT OF INTEREST))

"The solution to the current problem
is to fix the broken incentive structure."

– VINAYAK K. PRASAD, M.D., *MALIGNANT*[238]

Who doesn't like a free meal? Imagine your lunch hour, catered by some of the nicest restaurants in town. Perhaps you are a fan of Thai food. I certainly am. Angie and my children will attest that it is one of the few cuisines I will routinely eat at the cost of straining the confines of my stomach. I cannot resist the unique flavors of a well-prepared curry dish. The coconut milk, lemon grass, and spices create a magical allure, and my mouth is watering just thinking about it. In the episode that follows, this catered meal was brought to the office specifically for me.

My office staff often preferred more traditional fare. But the pharmaceutical representatives knew to keep my attention, Thai food was the weapon of choice. Historically, I would let the pharmaceutical representatives talk until I was done eating. Somehow, I seemed to eat just a bit longer when Thai food was on the menu. Typically they would convey some reasonable information, along with the most recent studies of the medicine as well as prescription coverage. The banter was jovial and I would accept their meal along with the information they provided. Many of the drugs presented were me-too medications or prohibitively expensive. And I usually preferred generic medications, the cost-effective choice.

But, occasionally, there were a few gems introduced over the years. Sacubitril/valsartan was one such medication as the pharmacology is brilliant (just ask George). I was an early adopter of this medication, and was able to keep many patients out of the hospital. My anecdotal evidence grew rapidly.

The outcomes with my patients were impressive. Imagine a patient whose legs are so swollen that bullae (fluid filled blisters) cover their lower extremities. Numerous bullae were part of the initial presentation of a patient that I was able to keep alive for several years after starting this medication. A potential hospice patient prior to taking sacubitril/valsartan, his improvement allowed me to foster a strong enough relationship that when hospice was required, he was able to die peacefully at home.

Another example of a medication class I was an early adopter of was the Glucagon Like Peptide-1 (GLP-1) Receptor Agonist class. The first GLP-1 agonist was approved in 2005. Again the mechanism of action made sense. These are diabetic medications that combat the negative physiology of abdominal adipose tissue on several fronts. Mimicking our normal physiology is extremely enticing for those of us who treat diabetes on a regular basis. I continued to use this class of medications on a regular basis, with tremendous victories in blood sugar control and weight loss. In addition, this class of medication allowed me to reduce adverse events from other medication classes, such as hypoglycemia, or low blood sugar.

Recently, I have been reading *Malignant: How Bad Policy and Bad Evidence Harm People with Cancer*, authored by Vinayak K. Prasad, M.D. This is a wonderful journey through the world of oncology, clinical trials, chemotherapy, and associated costs. He discusses the inherent conflict of interest over physicians being paid by both the patient and manufacturers of products. Dr. Prasad makes a compelling case that physicians should not receive compensation from for-profit companies that sell health care products. No drug rep meals, honoraria, or consulting fees. The discussion of bad policy and bad evidence, and subsequent harm to cancer victims was disturbing to read. Numerous solutions were offered—including transparency and policy change. Policy change which puts patients, not companies, at the forefront.[239]

Honestly for a long time I felt as though the cost of a (pharmaceutical) lunch benefited my patients and the healthcare collective at large. Now I question that. The more I read about pharmaceutical companies maximizing profits, PBMs taking hefty margins, conflicts of interest, and healthcare spending spiraling out of control. I wonder if we have other outliers, whose altruism exceeds human nature for greed. I am a lifelong learner for sure, and am always interested in advances in medicine. A simple lunch to learn more about a medication? Maybe—but at what cost?

((FRAUD, WASTE AND ABUSE))

"For the love of money is the root of all evil...."

– TIMOTHY 6:10

Unfortunately, this section can almost write itself. The amount of fraud, waste, and abuse that occurs daily in healthcare in the U.S. is appalling. The examples are endless—just look at recent headlines, or Google it. Disheartening to those of us trying to be good stewards. The few examples I chose to include are purposeful and intended to inspire change, such as improved oversight and subsequent repercussions. As such, I will take a simple, hopefully thought-provoking approach. A simple written illustration will be followed by some comments.

Fraud

A Michigan physician is convicted of defrauding Medicare and faces significant fines and up to 10 years in prison. The crime consisted of billing for bogus visits—even while on vacation. Additionally, controlled substances were prescribed without a documented medical need.[240] There are many issues with a case like this, and at the core is a blatant disregard for the Hippocratic Oath—"do no harm."

Waste

Hemoglobin A1C is the gold standard for monitoring and managing diabetic patients. I explain to patients this test measures how many sugars are attached to their red blood cells. A red blood cell's life span is typically 90 days. Ergo, an A1C level is a good indicator of glycemic control over a three-month period. An interval of time is needed to see appreciable change, typically months. During a hospital follow-up visit for a patient, I noted they had an A1C level drawn on back-to-back days during their admission. Wasteful.

Abuse

Martin Shkreli, a former hedge fund manager, bought the rights to an inexpensive generic medication to treat a parasitic infection in 2015. This medication had been on the market for years, suddenly a pill went from $13.50 to $750.[241] Greed personified.

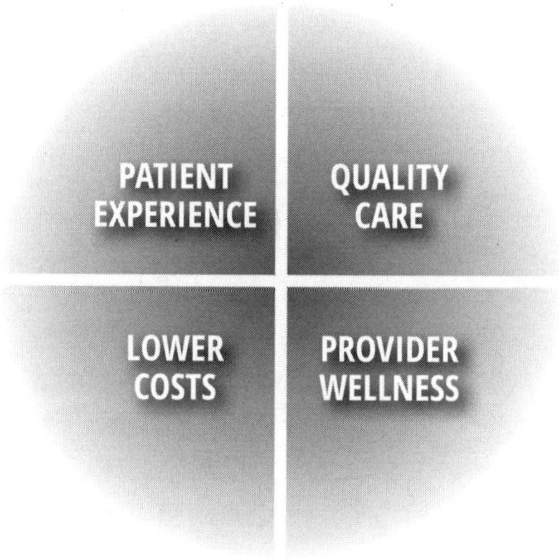
PATIENT EXPERIENCE
QUALITY CARE
LOWER COSTS
PROVIDER WELLNESS

((25))

As We Are Today

Joshua J. Judy – Patient:

In a flawed world, you reach for the things that once brought you joy or comfort—anchors back to happier times. Coping skills. And the promise of what's to come. The night of my wife's first seizure, while we watched TV, she was crocheting. For Megan, crafting has always been that anchor. One of the first gifts she ever gave me was a blanket she crocheted in college. I still use it on cold nights, or when feeling under the weather.

My mother-in-law retired in the summer of 2022. Referring to themselves as "The Crafty Ladies," mother and daughter will craft together and film their escapades for YouTube (thecraftyladies.com): new blankets, jewelry, pet clothing, a wedding dress repurposed into throw pillows (by a friend's special request), and wherever else their hearts and imaginations take them. Regarding the wedding dress project, it was the dress worn by Megan's friend's daughter, who passed away unexpectedly some years back. Life always finds a way.

Today, Megan wears a medical bracelet. Engraved on it are the words, "epilepsy" and "penicillin," the latter signifying she's allergic to it. As for the former, if you weren't told, you'd never know she had epilepsy. We're reminded, most illnesses aren't worn on our sleeves. We always have to look beyond the surface.

With her neurologist's support, Megan parted ways with levetiracetam in late 2022, and switched to brivaracetam. A casual observer probably wouldn't notice any differences. But they don't have the benefit of watching the small, delicate changes unfold—each becoming more pronounced by the day. As weeks turned into months, long lost memories and motivation have stepped out of the shadows. Improved mood, more restful sleep, and the ability to reconnect with herself are firmly in grasp, unthawed after a toilsome winter of separation. She's able to find joy in activities again, laugh, care—as she says, feel human again.

One of the most fascinating observations is how her memories of life events, blocked while taking levetiracetam, now percolate to the forefront. We discovered they were still there, being "recorded" but under lock and key. Levetiracetam and brivaracetam are chemical cousins and if you look at their graphs, they look uncannily similar. It's awe-inspiring to think how the slightest shift of molecules—far below the surface—can outwardly change lives. For Megan, the transformation has been nothing short of miraculous. She's in the closest state possible to her old self while remaining on epilepsy medication.

Thinking of Megan's journey, I'm reminded of the profound differences between Dr. Otten's and my duloxetine experience. What is a savior for someone may be damnation for another—the fundamentally gray nature and yin-yang of medicine.

I recently started treatment with a CPAP for my obstructive sleep apnea. Will it help? It's too early to know yet, but I believe it will. I'm tweaking my TRT protocols, reading the latest medical studies, and working with my doctors in search of remnants of my old self. I read about others' health journeys and find myself thankful. I'm grateful for each new day to keep fighting the fight–and that I've risen to the point where caring matters once again. Because for the longest time, I hardly did. With newfound motivation, I'm co-authoring this book with my doctor as we ask what ventures lay in wait. An inconceivable enterprise not that long ago. I am not entirely my former self. But, like Megan, my will to take risks in life has largely healed.

During the writing of this book, Megan shares that she often held back her own struggles—chiefly because she feared my fragile state and what adding to my plate would do. She confesses, "I would go to bed and the next day, I hated to find out that I would still wake up."

> *To my wife, I'm sorry I didn't recognize we were so equally lost. That we were encased in the same concrete tomb—together. Despite it all, I love you and always will.*
>
> *To my son and daughter, your daddy loves you the universe over. Then infinity on top of that.*

Do you know that tightness in your eyes you feel as you're about to tear up? If you've never lost that, you might not even think much about it. I'm thrilled to say, it's a sensation that I can feel right now. Hell, it only took about five years to find some semblance of regularity. **Welcome back.**

The years of accumulating frustration revealed a truth–we exist perfectly in an imperfect world. Like that day many years ago on our honeymoon hiking the sand dunes to Lake Michigan, the medical journey can be a long arduous trek never knowing if the "water" is truly getting closer or merely a mirage. Still as difficult as it sometimes seems, we just keep taking another step forward.

TL;DR—lessons for OQA:

Everyone: "Just keep swimming," as a popular little blue hippo tang says.

((26))

Who Are the Incentives Aligned For?

"The real opportunity to disrupt American healthcare lies in true, open, and honest alignment of incentives."

– BENJAMIN SCHWARTZ, M.D.[242]

Todd R. Otten, M.D.:

((TAKE A RISK))

Life is full of opportunities. Some are pretty straightforward—others not so much. Risk—reward, pros—cons, good—bad. The shades of gray can be overwhelming. As the years have gone by, my fear in making decisions has largely melted away. But for others it can be paralyzing. Fear of failure, fear of rejection, fear of losing their job. The culture of fear is all too pervasive in healthcare. Money, greed, fraud, waste, abuse, lawsuits: all have warped the profession into a state of dysfunction. I am not suggesting illogical choices. But rather, imploring those who can make positive change to take a chance, speak up, and do what is right. Not only what is right for patients but also right for those providing care.

This chapter was initially titled Macro Wellness. However, wellness is only a portion of Our Quadruple Aim. Lest we forget the quality and financial aspects. Ignoring one or more components of OQA (while focusing on others), has contributed to the current state. So how to lead into such a nebulous topic? A topic of taking risks, challenging the status quo, accepting opportunities, and aligning incentives? Whether patients, providers, insurers or even hospital systems—the incentives must be aligned. What better way to start than to relish in the recent triumph of my son, Josh.

The date was June 4, 2022. My family and I sat in the bleachers at Kent City High School for the Michigan Division 3 State Finals Track Meet. It was a beautiful day, temperature in the 60s, clouds providing a break from the sun. A perfect day to run. The stage was set for Josh and his teammates.

Josh had qualified to run four events his senior year at Lansing Catholic High School. The final event was about to begin, and the boys had a legitimate shot to win the race. Josh had already placed 2nd in the 3,200-meter relay, 3rd in the 1,600 (aka the mile), and 2nd in the 400-meter dash (running 50.19, only 45 minutes after running a 4:20 mile). My family and I could barely stand the excitement. But let's rewind the clock just a bit and review some of the key moments that preceded. Several individuals made courageous decisions—presenting Josh with a golden opportunity.

Key moment number one occurred the prior fall—my son was allowed to compete in two sports during the same season. A privilege. Risks taken by the athletic director, school, coaches, and my son to come to this decision. But Josh was allowed to play varsity soccer and run varsity cross country in the fall of 2021. A grueling combination at times, but Josh has the heart of a warrior and hates to lose. Sure, some minor stumbles occurred along the way (lest we forget he was only 17-years-old). But he gave his all in both sports, leading the soccer team in scoring and finishing fourth place at the state finals cross country meet—earning all-state honors in both.

Key moment number two occurred just prior to spring break. Josh decided he would attend college at the University of Detroit Mercy, having been recruited to run cross country and track and field. Angie and I were ecstatic, as that is our alma mater. Twenty-one years of marriage later, our son would be returning to the place we met. Even more exciting, the current coach also coached Angie and myself. Josh is the first child (of two former athletes) to compete under Guy Murray.

Key moment number three occurred on April 25, 2022. Optimistic and overzealous, I texted Josh's high school track coach (Tim). I asked if he had thought about having Josh run the 400-meter dash at the regional meet. A potentially daunting task, the 400-meter dash is less than one hour after the 1,600. Considering Josh was running the mile in about four and a half minutes—not a lot of recovery time. What seemed possible on paper could be too much for a teenager.

Prior to that text, Tim had been contemplating the same races for Josh. He retrospectively shared some of his concerns in that decision-making process; specifically, that there is a balance in aspiring to win and potential risk of injury. Unknowingly that text affirmed what Tim had been considering—that Josh could handle running both events (physically and mentally). The regional meet was outstanding. Josh won the 400 and also qualified for the state meet in the mile, 3,200-meter relay, and 1,600-meter relay.

Key moment number four occurred at the state finals. Unfortunately, a very talented sprinter on another team injured his hamstring running the 200-meter dash. That same sprinter had already won three events, and surely would have scored points, if not won, the 200-meter dash. But, he earned zero points and courageously limped over the finish line to a rousing applause. The stage was set: if the Lansing Catholic boys won the 1,600-meter relay, they would win the state championship (by a single point).

Serendipitously, we were sitting behind the family of the aforementioned sprinter. The anticipation was building. The slower heats of the 1,600-meter relay were completed, three heats in all. The picture became clearer with every passing moment. Bang! The gun sounded just as I had heard thousands of times before. My heart was pounding. The lead runner started off in fourth place. Leg two maintained the position. The third runner had an inspired run and got the baton to Josh in second place. Just ten meters behind, one lap to go. "It's over," Tim said. Josh ran an inspired anchor leg, with a split of 48.8 seconds. He took the lead on the back straightaway and extended it down the final stretch to win by almost 30 meters. It was surreal. Jubilation.

After the trophy and medals were awarded, the celebration lingered on the infield for nearly an hour. The boys wanted to soak in every moment. Hundreds of pictures taken and a celebratory lap around the track, including Josh's younger siblings. Interviews occurred with the coach and some of the athletes. You couldn't wipe the smile off of the boys' faces. So many decisions had led to this point. So much effort that yielded an extra point here or there. Had Josh not ran the 400-meter dash at regionals, I wouldn't be writing this section. Courage, risk, opportunity.

((PHYSICIANS IN LEADERSHIP))

"Hospitals and health systems
whose leadership and providers are aligned—flourish.
Those that aren't—flail."

– TODD R. OTTEN, M.D.

After 13 years of service to my prior employer, I retired in January of 2023 (at age 46). I had been contemplating retiring for a few years. In preparation I had planned to cut back on my hours and see patients part time in 2023. Open and honest, I notified leadership 15 months in advance. Then, the day came when the music died, which imploded our office utopia. So much for transparency. That moment accelerated my decision and I resigned the following morning. Rash—no. Abrupt—yes.

Out of respect for my employer and patients I gave 150 days notice, when only 90 is required. But as I have found in healthcare, it is never enough. Always wanting more. The reactions to my decision were polar opposite. Patients and my staff were frustrated initially, but accepting in the end. During my final five months, patients were: gracious, kind, understanding, appreciative, and congratulatory. In my opinion, leadership exhibited: anger, frustration, disbelief, fear, blame, and denial. The only thank you—a brief congratulations at one meeting, where my M.D. was annotated as D.O. on the agenda. Prior to retiring, I felt as though I was vilified for speaking up, trying to foster change, advocating for patients and providers, and for doing what is right for myself and my family. A fascinating evolution.

Why such divergent responses? Shouldn't everyone in healthcare be working toward the same goal? In a utopian world, yes—but unfortunately that is far from reality today in the U.S. I subscribed to Our Quadruple Aim when I practiced medicine, and patients appreciated that approach. Striving to deliver quality care, contain costs, and deliver a positive experience for both patient and physician. My incentives were and are aligned. Unfortunately, this is not the case for many administrators I worked with. Lack of engagement and misaligned incentives led to tenuous interactions. This lack of alignment toppled a series of dominos as I approached retirement. Fortunately, the vast majority of my staff and patients navigated the situation rather adroitly—before the last domino fell.

Why do I write about the dissolution of our practice? I firmly believe if a strong physician leader was involved at a higher level in the decision-making process—things would have gone differently. If OQA was the driver, I might still be seeing patients. But rather, finances steered the ship. Administration and the medical staff were not aligned, with a chasm separating us. Decisions in healthcare should be driven by those who understand medicine and how patients are affected—not just the bottom line.

I have worked in many situations where physicians and leadership are aligned. Whether my time as a flight surgeon in the Navy discussing the status of a pilot with our commanding officer, or as an ACO medical director advocating for patients and providers to the board. Or as Chief of Staff at Hayes Green Beach Hospital, leading a medical executive meeting. Our Quadruple Aim was my guide in each of those scenarios, and we flourished. Not only were we solvent financially, but retention was high, and patients were satisfied and well cared for. Some anecdotal evidence, sure. But do you really need a study to prove wearing a parachute when jumping out of an airplane in flight is a good idea?

((STAFFING CRISIS))

"Do I really like healthcare?
Or have I just learned to tolerate it?"

– MA

We are currently in the midst of the "Great Resignation"—an economic trend where employees across different sectors and industries are leaving their jobs because of the COVID-19 pandemic.[243] I believe the pandemic was the accelerant for a fire that started in healthcare staffing long before. Doing more with less. Stagnant pay. Inappropriate staffing levels, particularly with nursing. Burnout. Moral injury. People are tired of being treated in a bureaucratic, corporate fashion in an effort to maximize profits. And patients are noticing—big time. Some days I heard more complaints about the dysfunction in healthcare than patients' health concerns.

A recent nursing strike in New York City highlights the disconnect between employees, leadership, and financial drivers. Over 7,000 nurses failed to reach a contractual agreement; leading to canceled surgeries, diversion of patients, and hiring traveling nurses to care for patients. The current business model in healthcare emphasizes productivity in a fee-for-service driven model. Nursing typically does not generate revenue, so many hospitals keep this component of their workforce as lean as possible. The domino effect often results in an overworked and burned out nursing staff. Nurses with too many clerical burdens, taking care of too many patients. Nursing-to-patient ratios are disproportionate and unacceptable. This is far from a supportive environment and frankly unsafe at times.[244]

The inadequate staffing ratios extend far beyond nursing. As I approached retirement, many of our staff transitioned to new opportunities, and none of them were replaced. For over a month we operated with two MAs for three providers (myself and two NPs). Our office manager routinely filled in where needed. The penultimate moment before I retired occurred when one MA called in sick. That left one MA for three providers—no resource staff were available, and yet no appointments were canceled. Patients were understanding, and we made it work. I helped bring patients back from the waiting room and took their vital signs. Frustrating. An email expressing my concerns to numerous administrators apparently did not warrant a response, as I never got one. Nor was my request for an exit interview with the Board of Directors granted. Denied.

There are a multitude of reasons staffing ratios have created such consternation. Financial pressures, time constraints, clerical burdens, and safety concerns—to name a few. The never ending list of "just one more thing" has reached a breaking point and health care workers are burning out. As Dylan Scott writes in "What the NYC nurses strike reveals about US health care," "Eight of the 25 major work stoppages involving 1,000 workers or more that the U.S. Labor Department tracked in 2022 were initiated by health care workers, the highest share of any single profession."[245]

The four tenants of Our Quadruple Aim have the potential to right many wrongs. If your institution is struggling with staffing issues, retention, recruitment; I suggest you present these ideas to your administration, clinical leaders, and even your board members. Stop trying to expand your footprint, and focus on the core of your business. Is the brand new building really needed? Are executive salaries just, in comparison with staffing pay? Without doctors, nurses, and clinical staff—revenue goes to zero.

I would argue the business case for addressing burnout for physicians should be applied universally.[246] So treat your staff like gold, the dividends are priceless. Little things matter, wellness matters. A healthy work environment yields better recruitment and higher retention. Fair wages decrease reliance on traveling nursing. Competitive wages attract talent. The example below illustrates how OQA can improve your nursing infrastructure (or other clinical staff), leading to a positive, thriving culture.

Our Quadruple Aim	Nursing Quadruple Aim
1. Patient Experience	Improves via appropriate staffing ratios
2. Quality Care	Through adequate support structure
3. Lower Costs	Fair pay reduces utilization of travel nursing
4. Provider Wellness	Nursing wellness, improving recruitment/retention

((JUST CULTURE))

"The just culture is a learning culture that is constantly improving and oriented toward patient safety."

– PHILIP G. BOYSEN, II, M.D.[247]

In healthcare we often hear about a culture of safety and a just culture. Both environments require transparency and a supportive leadership who lead by example. Unfortunately, this is far from reality at times. Having spoken with thousands of people regarding Our Quadruple Aim, I have heard comments like, "I work in a culture of fear" and "It's the evil I know." Listening to the culture subsequently described, I doubt a just culture existed. A culture of fear doesn't exactly encourage open and honest conversation. The following story from Anne highlights an approach that is all too pervasive.

Anne, R.N.:

"Nursing is a calling," my mom always told me. Inspiration comes in many forms. My journey into nursing started with a warm, familiar voice. Growing up, I was unsure what I wanted to do, enjoying childhood too much. My mom, ever confident in my potential, suggested I look into nursing programs. That suggestion changed my life. I transferred into a nursing program my freshman year of college, and have been caring for patients for over a decade.

Every profession has rules and regulations, policies and procedures, disciplinary actions and commendations. But the stakes are even higher in medicine—lives are on the line. I try not to think about the myriad of potential mistakes. But I am human, and on occasion, being a nurse can be frightening. Fortunately, I've worked with amazing nurses and doctors who have always taught and supported me along the way.

I used to have horrible anxiety the night before a shift. I would arrive early to prepare as much as possible. I questioned every decision, always asking the opinion of my charge nurse. I wanted the best for patients, and certainly to avoid harming anyone. Ultimately, patient care had nothing to do with my firing. A simple, honest clerical error would be one of the hardest lessons of my life. Looking back, I was about to enter a perfect storm.

The summer of 2011 was much anticipated by my family. My brother and sister-in-law were expecting twins. Everyone was excited with the prospect of cuddling not one, but two babies. My sister-in-law went into labor early and delivered via c-section on July 2nd. Having recently broken up with my boyfriend, I decided to switch my shift to help a colleague who wanted the holiday weekend off. I decided to visit the new arrivals after my shift. My new niece was having some breathing issues and was in the neonatal intensive care unit. Not wanting to bother my brother (during such a stressful and joyous time)—I looked up my sister-in-law's room number at work.

What I failed to remember was that there were two ways to search a patient's room number. One method was HIPAA compliant, the other not. An honest mistake. And my nightmare began.

I look back and wonder about so many things. What if I didn't switch my shift that weekend? What if I wasn't getting over a breakup? Would I have questioned my decision more? Would I have stopped short? I had been trained on HIPAA compliance, more than once; but a few weeks later I was shocked when I was fired, and stunned by the reason why.

I was called to have a meeting with my manager and a representative from human resources. I walked into the room not knowing why I was there. I was grilled about the prior event, and essentially told that I was a horrible nurse (for what I had done). Yes, I should have known better, but this wasn't a pattern. Rather an isolated, honest mistake. This wasn't even about my performance as a nurse. I had never even been written up for anything in my preceding three years. But because I was an at-will employee, and the hospital had a zero-tolerance policy for HIPAA violations, I was out. Fired.

Even today—it hurts to remember. No one likes to feel like a failure, and I felt like I failed not only myself, but my family, and the whole nursing profession. I am still bothered by the lack of acknowledgement: I made a human error and no harm came of it. My co-workers were flabbergasted and failed to understand the logic behind this decision. The hardest pill for me to swallow was when I learned that if I had simply gone to my manager and informed her of my mistake, I would not have been fired. Salt in an open wound.

For the next few weeks I tried my best to keep on living life. My calendar was wide open. I tried not to panic about how I would pay my mortgage and bills. Then things got worse—the nurse licensing board contacted me.

You might think attending nursing school teaches everything you need to know. In reality, you learn most of what you need to know on the job. In retrospect, my first few years as a nurse I was terribly naïve. I had never considered what happens when you're fired. I soon learned. The employer notifies the board of nursing and there's an inquiry. Not only did I lose my job, but I now have to have a meeting with a licensing board member with my nursing license and career hanging in the balance.

As scared and nervous as I was, the board member showed empathy. She was very straightforward, professional, and didn't berate me. Unlike the HR department at the hospital, this board member treated me like a human being. I was exonerated and kept my nursing license. I was ecstatic I could continue working as a licensed nurse, but the next hurdle would be finding a job.

I struggled with how to explain the gap in work on my resume without blacklisting myself. In a phone interview I was told this was a red flag, and I most likely would not get a second interview. But I was not comfortable lying. I applied for many positions and even started the process to become a travel nurse. Luckily I applied for a position with a manager who was an angel. In my interview she asked all the questions I feared, but also felt that I deserved a second chance. Redemption. Ironically, I have applied for other positions and never been asked about the gap again.

I'll never forget how self-assured the Human Resources representative was telling me how terrible of a nurse I was. Someone who has presumably never done direct patient care, telling me I'm terrible at my job for making a clerical mistake. Is this what a just culture is?

I was, and am, a great nurse. I have had to convince myself of this over the years as self doubt was burned into me. Fortunately, I have a wonderful support structure. My parents are my biggest cheerleaders. They are my reminder: that I am a dedicated and caring nurse. I do it for them.

Todd R. Otten, M.D.:

I would argue Anne's institution followed a flawed line of thinking regarding a just culture, as described by Dr. Boysen in his article in *The Ochsner Journal*. "One organizational approach has been to seek out errors and identify the responsible individual. Individual punishment follows. This punitive approach does not solve the problem. People function within systems designed by an organization. An individual may be at fault, but frequently the system is also at fault. Punishing people without changing the system only perpetuates the problem rather than solving it."[248]

A just culture cannot be lip service. It requires time, transparency, teaching, learning, patience, and even forgiveness. Human beings make mistakes. Mistakes can lead to poor outcomes. Certainly I am not encouraging errors, but mistakes are opportunities for learning and corrective actions. A just culture balances these needs to reduce future errors. But time pressures and institutional infrastructure often line up the swiss cheese holes for an error. Just as in military aviation, a mistake typically occurs after a series of flaws (holes) line up just right. Organizational issues or flaws are no different, and should be addressed when an error occurs. A just culture allows for this. Does yours?

((DISRUPTIVE INNOVATIONS))

"A leader is someone who knows the way, goes the way, and shows the way."

– JOHN MAXWELL

Healthcare continues to have amazing technological advances. A heart valve can be repaired through a small incision, with camera and equipment being guided to the area of need through a small tube. The patient is left with a small incision, rather than a thoracotomy (large incision in the chest with ribs then spread apart) and severe postoperative pain.

Yet an antiquated form of communication is commonplace in healthcare. I simply asked my four children if they knew what a fax machine was? Natalie, age 8—"No." Daniel, age 11—"No." Brandon, age 15—"I don't know, something with paper?" Joshua, age 17—"Are you still using those? Aren't they used to scan and transmit images?"

So much for a paperless system with EMRs. My office went through a ream of paper every day. Inefficient, wasteful. The office staff had to print off incoming faxes, scan them into the EMR, and then route them to me for review. Outgoing paperwork went through an additional step of me having to sign endless forms, orders, and more. Again, the red folder of death reminds me how many silos exist in healthcare. The sharing of patient data electronically is essential for the continuity of care, but is expensive and negatively affects the bottom line—so manual processes continue.

The responses are telling. At times, a medical office's technology feels like it's 1985, fax machines and sticky notes everywhere. Can't we do better? These cumbersome processes still exist in medicine and further complicate the existing chaos.

The amount of time and effort spent on paperwork is inordinate. HIPAA laws, secure communications, and lack of interoperability have created many issues with information flow. Can you imagine seeing your provider after a complicated hospitalization and they have no idea you were even admitted? No records to review. I cannot even begin to estimate the number of times I have seen a patient who was recently discharged from a hospital with no records to review. Nothing. It's 2023 and I know I am not alone in these frustrations. Isn't it time we move forward?

Vinayak K. Prasad, M.D., eloquently dissects issues in oncology in *Malignant: How Bad Policy and Bad Evidence Harm People with Cancer*. Dr. Prasad's book is a thorough investigation into historical and existing pharmaceuticals, drug and research trial developments, conflict of interest, policy and more. He asks many potent questions of our existing healthcare infrastructure. In discussing solutions for the development of cancer trials he suggests: "Ideally, some sort of computerized system should be in place nationally, so that patients can be enrolled on trials at any site in the country, whether or not they live close to an anointed cancer center."[249] A tremendous idea that would certainly propel Our Quadruple Aim to another level. Is this possible with today's technology—yes. Is it possible with existing healthcare infrastructure—no.

While researching AI, I was reminded of *Fantastic Voyage*, a medical science fiction film from 1966. The crux of the movie involves shrinking a medical team and their submarine, The Proteus, to enter a patient having a stroke and break up the blood clot. The movie chronicles their microscopic journey through the patient's body, prior to returning to their original size. In many ways, the themes in the movie parallel medical advances on the horizon capable with AI.

"Artificial intelligence simplifies the lives of patients, doctors, and hospital administrators by performing tasks typically done by humans, but in less time and at a fraction of the cost." A fascinating and rapidly growing sector, AI collects, perceives, synthesizes, and interprets data points via machines rather than human beings. The technology has the ability to handle large volumes of data and rapidly interpret the information, identifying patterns and insight beyond human capabilities.[250, 251] As a physician who interprets data on a regular basis, I see infinite potential with this emerging field in healthcare. AI is a tool that can improve healthcare's existing modus operandi on many levels. If utilized responsibly, AI can undoubtedly augment OQA.

As we reviewed previously, BAMF Health in Grand Rapids, Michigan is treating patients with metastatic prostate cancer with AI and radiopharmaceuticals, directly targeting a ligand on cancer cells with short-acting radioisotopes. Having visited their treatment facility, the patient experience is just as important as the quality of care delivered. BAMF Health diagnoses and treats patients on the same day, utilizing AI to guide the medication dosing. Incredible. This company embodies Our Quadruple Aim.

The metaverse is another emerging technology with potential to revolutionize healthcare. A single, shared immersive blend of reality, unreality, and data—the metaverse is where people experience life in unique ways they couldn't in the physical world. One key component is Web3, the internet of the future, where individuals control their data rather than third parties. This user owned approach (to data) would allow patients to switch from one application to another, without having to register every time.[252] This has potential for a major impact on an industry in which privacy and consent are paramount. Web3 has the potential to reduce many silos that currently exist within healthcare's data infrastructure.

Virtual reality has been used by the Virtual Reality Medical Center in La Jolla, California for decades to treat phobias, PTSD, anxiety, and other conditions. What's next with the metaverse? How about a novel, immersive way to obtain informed consent, where a patient could experience what a procedure entails prior to ever having a scalpel touch their skin? The metaverse and Web3 have limitless potential.[253]

What about blockchain technology? Blockchain is a digitally distributed, decentralized, public ledger that exists across a vast network of computers. Information is recorded permanently in sequential blocks. As Adam Hayes, writes in "Blockchain facts: What is it, how it works, and how it can be used," "The innovation with a blockchain is that it guarantees the fidelity and security of a record of data and generates trust without the need for a trusted third party."[254] Most people associate blockchain with cryptocurrencies such as Bitcoin, Ether (native token of the Ethereum network), or TEL (the native token of Telcoin, a mobile money/remittance platform). But blockchain technology will revolutionize many industries, including healthcare.

Blockchain has an amazing amount of potential in healthcare, particularly with secure transfer of medical records, managing the medicine supply chains, and helping researchers unlock genetic code. Numerous innovative companies are exploring these opportunities.[255, 256] I am particularly excited about the management of medical records. The cumbersome processes that exist (including the routine use of faxes) create silos, which negatively impact a provider's ability to provide care.

Imagine a world where a complete medical record is available using the blockchain, information assimilated using AI, and a patient encounter occurs in the metaverse. These tools have tremendous potential to streamline processes, tailor a physician-patient interaction, and deliver high quality care. Redundancies and waste are reduced or eliminated. Decreased clerical burdens on physicians. Certainly there are risks associated with new technology, and those must be accounted for. But, Our Quadruple Aim craves these innovations, I urge everyone to entertain these disruptive technologies and consider their adoption.

((BURIED IN PAPERWORK))

"The practice of medicine is an art, not a trade;
a calling, not a business;
a calling in which your heart will be exercised equally
with your head."

– WILLIAM OSLER

This section, though very straightforward, was one of the last I wrote. I detest paperwork, as my former staff and patients can attest. The clerical work for providers, particularly those in primary care, has rapidly spiraled out of control. I appreciate that documentation is intended to root out fraud, waste, and abuse. I respect risk stratification for value-based reimbursement. I understand the documentation to justify reasons for medical supplies and equipment. But burying providers in paperwork does not achieve OQA. The lack of transparency makes oversight both difficult and incumbent on providers, and the dominos continue to fall....

The amount of documentation in medicine has been conveyed as "just one more thing," which never ends. Clerical burdens are routinely listed as a top cause of burn out.[257, 258] As previously mentioned, I jokingly nicknamed the folder of paperwork (needing my signature) as the "red folder of death" and more recently I had introduced the "Hulk hate paperwork" folder (with numerous images of the large, green, angry superhero). Fitting, as Hulk's rage is a reflection of how I often felt having to sign hundreds of documents each week. And many of these documents exceeded 10 pages—wasteful. Superfluous and disheartening.

Some examples are warranted. I'll start with a list of expected documentation for a family physician (not all inclusive, and can vary depending on appointment type). Then, we'll move into some humorous real-life examples, and finally ideas for improvement.

"Each new administrative initiative brings us more tasks to complete and less time with which to complete them."

– FARZON A. NAHVI, M.D., *CODE GRAY*[259]

((REQUIRED DOCUMENTATION FOR A PRIMARY CARE PROVIDER (PCP)))

- Pain Scale (1/10)
- PHQ-2 or PHQ-9 (depression screening)
- Medication Reconciliation
- Past Surgical History
- Past Medical History
- Family Medical History
- Allergies
- Alerts (medication interaction, insurance alerts, etc.)
- Preventative Health
- Immunizations
- Vital Signs
- Order Labs, Radiographs, Other Testing
- Associating Diagnostic Codes with Testing
- Reviewing Controlled Substance Registry
- Evaluation and Management Codes
- Procedure Codes
- New and/or Refilling Medications
- COVID-19 Screening
- Diagnostic Code Gap Closure
- Hierarchical Condition Category Codes (HCC)
- Patient Centered Medical Home (PCMH) Questions
- Travel History and/or Screening
- Insurance Documentation
- Consent Forms
- HIV Screening
- Cancer Screenings (breast, colon, lung, cervical)

- Patient Understands Button
- Chaperone Present, Absent, or Declined
- Physical Exam Findings
- Assessment and Plan
- Sexual History
- Follow up Interval
- Procedure Notes
- Review of Systems (ROS)
- History of Present Illness (HPI)
- Alcohol and Substance Use History

By the way, for many providers it is expected that all of this documentation is accomplished in 15 to 30 minutes. Many providers struggle to accomplish these exorbitant requirements, which leads to pajama time. As described, pajama time is the term used to describe charting/documentation that occurs at home, typically one to two hours per night for the average family physician. A recent *Forbes* article reports physicians spend twice as much time doing non-clinic duties as caring for patients.[260] This isn't what I signed up for—just another contributor to burnout.

((ANECDOTAL IDIOCRACY))

"Why do I have 15 patients on my schedule?"

– TODD R. OTTEN, M.D. (WORKING A HALF DAY)

"Because they couldn't fit 19."

– CARI, MY BEST MA

If I do not hit the refresh button before I sign my note (in the EMR), half of the note is blank. I tried to rectify this several times. The response from IT typically was, "you just have to hit refresh."

Interruptions are non-stop while attempting to deliver patient care. Having to sign an emergent form for hearing aids.

Having to sign an emergent death certificate. I appreciate time is valuable, but if everything is urgent/emergent, is anything truly?

Diagnosis of carotid stenosis (plaque build up in the carotid artery) would not qualify to order a carotid doppler (diagnostic test using ultrasound); additional documentation and a different diagnostic code was required from the insurer.

((THINK OUTSIDE OF THE BOX: OUR QUADRUPLE AIM BRAINSTORMING))

1. **Patient Experience**
   a. Reduce clerical burdens, allowing providers to increase time with patients.
   b. Delegate paperwork completion to the appropriate provider (i.e., clinical staff).

2. **Quality Care**

   c. Enact regulatory/policy changes to reduce burdensome paperwork.

   d. Increase transparency to improve oversight, allowing providers to focus on patients instead of paperwork.

   e. Stiffen penalties for "bad actors," targeting fraud and abuse.

   f. Move towards rolling averages for formulary changes, quality metrics, and more (start with two or three years).

3. **Lower Costs**

   g. Utilize AI to target fraudulent activity. Less oversight/regulation for good fiduciaries of the healthcare dollar. More scrutiny on the opposite end of the spectrum.

   h. Establish a national provider license to expand opportunities for providers who are doing good things.

4. **Provider Wellness**

   i. Improve documentation efficiency—see EMRs in chapter 15, which includes streamlined and team based documentation.

   j. Initiate or augment your wellness efforts, you cannot afford not to.

((COMPETITION OR COLLABORATION?))

"Currently, there exists a somewhat adversarial relationship among payers, providers, and patients, and a lack of transparency is intrinsic to the way money gets made."

– JOHN HAMMERGREN, *SKIN IN THE GAME*[261]

As my acumen in the world of cryptocurrency grows, the phrase "down the rabbit hole" reminds me of my introduction into this fascinating asset class which includes blockchain technology, cryptography, and decentralized networks. I was hooked, intellectually and financially. It's an intriguing world with limitless potential. Certainly not all cryptocurrencies are Ponzi schemes. Due diligence will separate trash from treasure.

In researching healthcare, there are rabbit holes everywhere, waiting to be explored. This is particularly true with regards to opportunity for improvement. Aligned incentives and transparency are two topics worth a substantial investment of time. Both are essential to achieve Our Quadruple Aim.

Before we move forward, some rhetorical questions. Regardless whether you are a patient, physician, frontline caregiver, provider or other stakeholder:

Are your...
insurer's...
hospital's...
provider's...
incentives aligned with yours?

Not just lip service, but truly aligned? Take a moment to ponder. Do some research, ask difficult questions. Then come back to these questions. You might be surprised how often the answer is: NO.

If incentives were truly aligned, would there be a long history of contractual gag clauses that precludes price transparency in healthcare? Doubtful. Imagine shopping for groceries and having no idea what anything costs. Or filling up your tank with gasoline, only to receive a multitude of bills in the coming months. A functioning marketplace would not tolerate this opaqueness. Yet, many of these bad behaviors have been perpetuated in healthcare for decades.

John Hammergren, CEO of McKesson Corporation from 1999 to 2018, first published *Skin in the Game: How Putting Yourself First Today Will Revolutionize Health Care Tomorrow* in March of 2008. In re-reading his work 15 years after its first edition, I see that, unfortunately, many of the issues he discussed still exist today.

Mr. Hammergren eloquently conveyed his thoughts on the existing relationships between payers, providers, and patients. He discusses adversarial roles among these stakeholders and a lack of transparency. He suggests: "...the current system is a nightmare of paperwork and confusion." And patients: "... feel as though they are lost in some absurd bureaucratic nightmare." Perhaps my favorite: "... the average American home or office... is far more sophisticated than the average clinic where the fax machine is still the administrator's best friend."[262] Ouch, so much for progress.

While researching transparency, Joshua shared the following article from *The New York Times*: "Hospitals and insurers didn't want you to see these prices. Here's why." Wildly disparate prices are reported within a given institution. The cost of a simple pregnancy test ranged from $10 to $93 at one institution (depending on which insurance carrier versus a cash price). The $10 was if you had no insurance. A nine-fold difference.[263]

A simple analogy: the price of a gallon of gas would depend on which credit card you use or whether you pay with cash. The final price varies by several factors. Who wouldn't adjust their payment preference with this type of methodology. And yet, somehow the American healthcare consumer has grown accustomed to this muddied playing field. Try playing the shell game with your eyes closed—good luck.

The *New York Times* article reviews numerous hospitals' responses to a federal law enacted in 2021 which mandated an increased transparency of prices hospitals negotiated with insurers. Despite the mandate, compliance has varied and data difficult to interpret for consumers, if available.[264] The historical lack of transparency regarding pricing and subsequent response by institutions is appalling at times. But increasing transparency is a step in the right direction.

A particular section of the *Times* article caught my attention regarding gag orders from Richard Stephenson, a former employee of the Blue Cross Blue Shield Association.[265] In a subsequent conversation between Richard and myself, he noted these clauses were commonplace and often precluded development of pricing tools for patients. Surprised? You shouldn't be.

Richard founded a medical data transparency start-up: REDU Health. Their company's motto: to insert market forces into the healthcare system. What better way to increase competition and reduce costs than transparent pricing data? Does your insurer and hospital offer pricing information if you ask? Is it on their website?

As our conversation continued, we agreed; we are both disruptors in the healthcare space. As I explained *Ripple of Change*, I suggested we need an army of disruptors to facilitate change. The American healthcare consumer is tired, frustrated, and often broke.

For capitalism to succeed for all stakeholders in healthcare, a revolution may be in order. A revolution that inspires thousands and thousands to voice their opinions, write letters, ask questions, and fight for cost-effective, quality care. Care that is accessible and equitable for everyone. Care that respects the experience of both patient and provider. What better way than Our Quadruple

Aim? Starting is easy, take the OQA lens to your next healthcare challenge and see what evolves.

As our conversation morphed, kindred spirits aligned. The topics came quickly, with different perspectives but similar goals. Transparency, aligned incentives, and improvement of the healthcare marketplace topped the list. Richard asked where the problems are in healthcare. My retort: "It may be easier to list where they are not."

As the conversation flowed back and forth, I explained my recent resignation and why. This prompted Richard to ask about my non-compete clause. The question caught me off guard, but I knew the answer. One year and 25 miles. Essentially, for the next 12 months I could not see patients within a very large circle in mid-Michigan. Non-compete clauses limit competition. In an era where physicians are growing in ever short supply, this seems quite counter-productive to delivering care. But, it does limit competition for hospitals. So who does a non-compete clause benefit? Not patients—I assure you.

Fortunately, The Federal Trade Commission (FTC) proposed a new rule on January 9th, 2023 regarding non-compete clauses: *Non Compete Clause Rule (NPRM)*. The following is an excerpt from the summary:

> *"The Federal Trade Commission ("Commission") is proposing the Non-Compete Clause Rule. The proposed rule would, among other things, provide that it is an unfair method of competition for an employer to enter into or attempt to enter into a non-compete clause with a worker; to maintain with a worker a non-compete clause; or, under certain circumstances, to represent to a worker that the worker is subject to a non-compete clause."*[266]

I applaud the FTC's effort towards non-compete clauses. Increased competition is paramount to improved marketplace conditions and subsequently lower costs. Last I checked physicians and other providers are integral to caring for patients. Creating geographical restrictions to provide care in an effort to limit competition is not patient-centric. As Richard reminded me: "Health insurance is not equivalent to health care."

((POLICY CHANGE OR FREE MARKET?))

"The United States has the best healthcare;
if you know where to get it and can afford it."

– GEORGE CLAASSEN

Historically, I rarely watch the news as I often find it polarizing, biased, and sensationalized. It typically frustrates me as I would prefer to hear the facts, do some due diligence, and make an informed decision. Furthermore, I admit politics have never been my forte. However, seemingly we need these entities to facilitate change. Or do we?

As I reminisce on my son Josh's athletic achievements, I wonder if he would have gotten an athletic scholarship had we waited for bureaucracy to unravel. The precedent at Josh's high school precluded students from playing two sports simultaneously. Sound historical logic behind this decision, but it also restricted high-caliber athletes. Under the guise of transparency and aligned incentives, a pilot program was introduced. All stakeholders were involved in a discussion to set expectations, guidelines, and more. The current "market" if you will, suggested a change from the existing policy. The result: two seniors were allowed to dual sport. Josh earned all-state honors in both, and another soccer player kicked for the state championship football team.

Recently, I was answering a series of continuing medical education (CME) questions. One of the questions caused me to pause: "What is the only group of patients in the U.S. that is constitutionally guaranteed health care?" I knew the answer and yet was disappointed in the affirmation. People who are incarcerated are constitutionally guaranteed health care. No one else is. It seems to me that *everyone* should be constitutionally guaranteed care for their health and well-being.

Is our current government nimble enough to create meaningful policy change—so desperately needed to improve our current healthcare infrastructure? A loaded question. Oversight and regulations are needed, but who should be leading the charge?

I spoke with George Claassen, the President and Founder of Class Insurance Consulting (CIC), who focuses on high-performance health plans. George is affiliated with Mitigate Partners and works to reduce costs for employers through improved access, direct primary care (DPC), reference-based pricing (RBP), data, transparency, and aligned incentives (to name a few). In bringing healthcare straight to employees, this fresh approach requires an open-minded employer looking for a transformative value-based model. It requires the will of an organization to be aligned with the change George offers.

Some highlights from a Mitigate Partners case study are warranted, as these efforts highlight aligned incentives and embody Our Quadruple Aim. Tasked with reducing insurance costs, employees' outlay, and minimizing member disruption, Mitigate Partners worked with Gasparilla Inn and Club in Florida to create a self-funded insurance plan. An inclusive approach produced an actively managed, valued-based, self-funded plan for 185 members, which reduced overall costs dramatically. With an emphasis on DPC and affordable preventative measures, the results are impressive: a 1.8 million U.S. dollar reduction in healthcare spending over three years, no premium increases in the first four years of the plan inception, and deductibles were eliminated.[267] Incredible.

As our conversation evolved, many healthcare topics were covered in a rapid fire approach (during our 55-minute discussion). Educational and thought-provoking. A few comments stood out and are worth sharing. George conveyed that if a patient has an exceedingly complex or rare case in their models, they "look for the highest quality care and travel if required, which often results in a lower overall cost. A healthy side effect." Brilliant. George is also a strong believer that, "A transparent, free market is required to solve the dysfunction in the American healthcare landscape."

For a free market to succeed in delivering OQA, transparency is essential. The obscurity that prevails in healthcare is akin to a curtain restricting a warm morning sunshine, illuminating a bedroom as pleasant dreams fade away.

But our current system is a nightmare for many, and I am imploring my colleagues to take a stand on innumerable levels—including proactive policy changes that assimilate Our Quadruple Aim. Certainly there are many already doing phenomenal work, but more are required. The exodus of providers is alarming. And medical bills are destroying families. We need more clinicians at the highest levels involved in the decision making—embracing and advocating for Our Quadruple Aim. Recent legislation increasing transparency is a start, but far from complete, as the future state of U.S. healthcare is in jeopardy. As more and more clinicians burn out...who will be left to care for patients?

((27))

Tomorrow's Blueprint

Joshua J. Judy – Patient:

I had been drifting in a vast fog for a long time that had been unwilling to dissipate. One day, out of that fog came a figure—a faint silhouette also drifting. At first, it was hard to make out but I could see the outline of a coat. The coat was white and approaching. You do remember, I had been here before but this time it was different. Suddenly, the figure beneath the coat materialized—and there he was, my doctor. Just like me, he was another human being overtaken with feelings of frustration and burnout.

As a patient, I had been the one always asking for help. It's just what patients do. This time, though, I knew my doctor was subtly asking me for help, and that was rewarding. I felt like I was finally wearing my own white coat.

I learned that one of the healthiest things you can do for yourself is to try stepping in somebody else's shoes for a while. When I was able to do that, it opened the door to better understanding myself and others. The outcome is *Ripple of Change*, and the deepening of a wonderful and lasting friendship.

It also resulted in a strong marriage made even stronger. I didn't realize it at the time, but my doctor's request to *"just write"* was a subtle yet incredibly cathartic treatment plan. Recall the paper airplane project from Dr. Otten's honors physics class. Often, the simplest solutions are best.

I implore you: never lose your desire to get better. Never lose the drive to help yourself. And keep trying and learning so you can help others you care about. You will be fearful along the way. You will be in doubt. Your pain will try to make you fall down the mountain or stay down in the abyss. As you know, these pitfalls have claimed others. We remember those who have gone before.

You will find yourself at times believing in your setbacks—more than your steps forward. Some of the time, you'll wish for black and white. Other times, you'll hate that everything seems so black and white. Many times, you'll find the world is gray—and you'll wish for color.

My story of patient burnout was of relearning to care for others after losing the ability to care about oneself. Dr. Otten's story of doctor burnout was of relearning to care about oneself while still caring for others. When you accept that it's okay to keep going, even if you don't know what awaits you atop the summit, you've achieved everything you need to start healing. So when you find yourself again caring about conquering the next summit before even ascending the first, you've won.

I have many people to thank for the resolve to keep going: my wife, children, parents, extended family, friends, supporting doctors, and my health hero and friend, Dr. Otten. To give each other faith is to give each other life's blueprint—I think it's the best treatment possible.

((CROSSROADS))

"Two roads diverged in a wood and I—
I took the one less traveled by,
and that has made all the difference."
– ROBERT FROST

Todd R. Otten, M.D.:

Two months prior to my retirement, the office was struggling. The majority of the staff had left for new positions or had committed to others, and no one was replaced. Two of three NPs accepted new positions outside of the health system, and patient visits were as high as ever. I became frustrated with the lack of staffing at the office. Despite being transparent about my retirement, the narrative was seemingly quite negative, and the weight of my decision was starting to take its toll. Saying goodbye to patient after patient. Many tears, and occasionally anger or frustrations towards me. Worse yet, I was receiving little support from administration. I penned a frustrated email and sat on it for a day, debating whether to send it.

I tend to be a morning person—just ask Joshua, my wife, and kids. Five a.m.—and I am wide awake. Off to the computer. I tend to do my best writing very early. No distractions. As I sat on the love seat, feet propped up, steam emanating from a freshly made latte, I pondered the preceding week and the email pending in my draft folder. Would sending the email change anything? Do I have the emotional energy to help a system that doesn't want to change? What about my staff and patients? What would be the ripples?

I decided to take the road less traveled and deleted the email. I asked my office manager if we could have an impromptu "huddle." I wanted to reverse course and make the last eight weeks of my tenure a positive experience. At the huddle I quoted

Robert Frost as above. I thanked everyone for all of their efforts, particularly regarding patient care. I explained that the decision to move the office was the first domino to fall, but my decision to retire was the second, and a major one at that. I knew my decision had affected the trajectory of many lives, including everyone in the room.

But I also knew that most of the staff had found excellent jobs, shifted careers, or planned to reunite with loved ones. And patients were finding their way, often with the help from the office and myself. Frankly, the process has gone pretty well at the office despite our isolation. I encouraged the staff to continue their best and that the last eight weeks remaining were going to be the best ever. At that meeting I instituted a weekly wellness champion. A weekly prize was my small token of appreciation to a devoted staff member who gave their all for two amazing years.

The following day, it was as if a switch had been flipped. The laughter and smiles had returned. In less than two hours—work became fun again. The email was never sent and never will be. Our Quadruple Aim shaped that decision and the office was better off for it.

((28))

The... End?

"Dr. Otten is retiring? Well, I guess I am gonna die."

– RICHARD, PATIENT

Joshua J. Judy – Patient:

The end was fast approaching. Completion of this book was in sight. And the good doctor's closure to two decades of seeing his many patients was practically in lockstep. As I grappled with that thought, my phone vibrated. It was early November 2022. I had just walked out of an all-day work meeting and a brief text message awaited:

TODD: Any interest in being my last patient?

It was my friend. Saved in my contacts was not Dr. Otten. In its place, Todd. As our relationship had grown over the weeks and months, he had hinted it was okay to stop greeting him with "doctor." Laughing one day, he had made clear that it made him feel too old. I made it clear that he could still expect to hear the title while at the office. Deal.

He was at it again, throwing another stone and watching the resulting cascade. I felt that quick rise, a flutter of emotion. The ones that travel up your chest and make a beeline for your eyes.

ME: Hold up. As in last, last? Let's chat if you have a min tonight.

Soon on the phone, we discussed the topic at hand. I shared that there was only one answer, and the answer was of course, yes. That it would be a tremendous honor. I already had a scheduled check-up coming. To coincide, we would simply slide it out by a couple weeks. My friend felt it could make for an interesting ending. Importantly, I think we both knew it was a new beginning—of another positive ripple. The date was set: Friday, *December 23, 2022.*

((NEVER AGAIN))

During the holidays, Megan loves to bake. She does it for the love of gifting to family and friends, as much as the act itself. Cookies, pies, fudge, popcorn balls, Rice Krispy treats, puppy chow—this time of year, there's as much powdered sugar dusting our kitchen as snow blanketing the yard.

By our door Megan left a treat-filled box ready. The recipient—Dr. Otten and his loyal staff. Tomorrow, the office would be closing its doors forever. But not before my physician saw his final patient and I saw him at 11:40 a.m. Who knew what the final day could bring? We thought twice of it. I would take the goodies a day earlier so there was enough time to enjoy them. For the delivery, I asked my son James if he wanted to ride along. In the car, I heard from the back seat, "Daddy, why does it smell like peanut butter in here?"

"That would be the puppy chow your mommy made."

Pulling into the office's parking lot we found it empty. I wondered if they had already closed.

"Daddy, their light is on so I think we're okay."

We grabbed the gift box and headed in. I saw two smiling receptionists at the window. One was busy on the phone so her colleague slid the window open. "Merry Christmas!" as I handed her the homemade goods. Several thanks later, we were back in the car. Turning away to buckle my seat belt while simultaneously turning the key, I didn't see him standing there in the winter wind. Quickly rolling down my window, "Hey Dr. Otten!"

He was without a jacket in short-sleeved scrubs. Like a worried parent, my first thought was, "my friend's going to get a cold." Laughing inside, I half brushed it away. Years of diagnosing everything from diabetes to cancer, while surviving burnout. I figured he could fend for himself. The other half of me—still worried. At 46, he was too young to be driven away.

I let my mind drift back to our first appointment long ago. The young, clean-shaven physician entered the room. He appeared as poised to solve world hunger as he was to take my blood pressure. Reaching to check my lymph nodes, he didn't notice my dress shirt buttoned at the top, and pulled a little too tightly. Slightly embarrassed, he smiled warmly and apologized. I liked him immediately.

Dr. Otten's voice snapped me back to the present, "Hey guys, come back inside! No sooner than thinking of you, appears this gift box." A subtle reminder that mindset is a powerful thing.

He walked us back to his office. Gone were the heart-shaped glitter, balloons, rainbow unicorn decorations, and Lego figures. All that remained was a desk, a few chairs, a monitor and his laptop he carried into appointments. James sat in one seat and I the other—we were about to get a crash course in what happens beyond the appointment room.

I noticed the monitor flickering and Dr. Otten readjusting the docking wire. "That's the laptop you bring when you see patients? Does it need to be unplugged and plugged back in each appointment?"

"Yeah, I.T. tells me I just need to plug it in to make it work." I quickly realized the silliness of that statement—knowing from my own office experiences that the hundreds of times it had to be detached wore the cable out.

"This is the charting software and this is your chart," he said. My chart, zero HIPAA concerns.

I sat and observed. Squinting, I could hardly make out all the text. There were dozens of panes, tabs, folders, inboxes for countless notifications, drop-down menus, radio buttons, free form text boxes, and a bunch of other buried prompts. I didn't know what the hell I was looking at. Impressive and intimidating in the same glance.

Dr. Otten started walking me through, "Here's your last appointment, a check of your body systems, your cardiovascular risk factors, scripts, and more." He explained, "If you're on a controlled substance and need a refill, I need to work through these prompts. Then do two-factor authentication on my phone for the script. It texts me and I answer back. I once counted. 27 clicks per medication."

"That's 27 clicks for one patient and one med?" I saw a graph in my mind, one with an exponential curve shooting towards the stratosphere. All for one task.

My physician and teacher continued, pointing to a box that read, "Does the patient understand their care?"

"This is one of my favorites. If I answer no, there's a hard stop. For example, if a patient has dementia, how do you think they would answer? I then have to fill in why they don't understand."

But I understood. The provider would have no choice but to answer yes to move on. I asked, "Does that data if the patient answers 'no' go anywhere or change anything? What happens?"

"Nothing, it just collects it. I tested it. After putting in flippant comments for a year, it finally worked its way through to someone's desk and they improved the form—a little. By the way, we haven't gotten to coding and billing yet..."

As Dr. Otten continued, I realized one thing more than anything—I would fail as a doctor. Not like you might think. I think I would have made it through medical school. I would come to deeply care for my patients and staff. I would find passion and interest in the science, clinical data, and improving lives. No, my failure would boil down to everything that would prevent those things. A system that proactively fights for no more than

20-minute appointments and large dollar signs, with care for provider and patient long forgotten.

I turned to James who had sat quietly during this lesson. "Son, are you ready to go to medical school?" I saw a twinkle in Dr. Otten's eye, the mask poorly concealing his chuckle, "We better talk first, buddy."

"My appointments have been winding down. I'm not being tugged at as much today, so we could spend more than five minutes walking through it. Given the weather tomorrow, the office will be closed."

My last appointment wasn't anything like I expected. Sometimes things turn out differently. In this case, things turned out for the better. I felt sadness, but also a release. This book has unshackled me from patient ignorance; and my retiring provider from a form of systemic sickness. Never again would I sit blissfully unaware in an appointment room wondering why it was taking so long to see me. Once you see something, you can't unlearn it. I appreciated everything I saw—the gift of walking in someone else's shoes. The gift of caring and being cared for. I appreciated the dire need for Our Quadruple Aim more than ever.

((WHITE COAT NO MORE))

"What we call the beginning is often the end
And to make an end is to make a beginning.
The end is where we start from."

– T.S. ELIOT

Todd R. Otten, M.D.:

"White coat enters the room." Only five words. Five words that caused me to instantly stop reading Joshua's work the first time I encountered them. My eyes were unable to move past them. Locked on. Memories, thoughts, and emotions began racing through my mind as if my career was being replayed in that instant. A lifetime of effort and achievement distilled into five words.

The symbol of everything I aspired to be as a young man transformed into something else. Something cold, callous, without empathy. The magical aura that centuries of trust had created, evaporated in five words. I was taken aback with the simplicity and magnitude of that sentence.

Ironically, I stopped wearing my white coat many years ago. Superficial reasons, sure. The office I worked at had a terrible HVAC system and was unyielding in the summer heat. My white coat exacerbated the already uncomfortable temperatures. The coat felt stuffy and sweat routinely dripped down my face. Administration suggested I remove a layer—off went the white coat.

Besides, I knew the majority of my patients very well, having cared for them over many years. Who wants to be so formal when such intimate details are required? Who wants to let their guard down with a wall of white cotton fiber blend standing in the way? The erosion of trust is symbolized in the sentence "white coat enters the room." I suppose subconsciously taking off the white coat was freeing. I don't regret that transition for an instant, and with time, patients grew to cherish the causal familiarity.

Joshua's sentence speaks to me on so many levels. The white coat is seemingly a metaphor for my career. Wanting so desperately to be accepted into medical school. I recall wearing that white coat for the first time, beaming with pride. Years of schooling and training. The endless hours of studying, countless sleepless nights on call—I sacrificed many things, missed many important life events. All to achieve one of the most important goals in my life: wearing the white coat, with M.D. after my name.

So much to unpack: "White coat enters the room." Perhaps the title of another book. Surely another touch point in what has become more than a doctor-patient relationship. Joshua and I have become good friends, and closer day by day. Our paths were destined to cross: to share in healing, mutual empowerment, our spheres of influence ever growing on one another. Fate. Our stories symbolize so much of what is wrong in healthcare.

And a coat is just a coat. Not wearing a white coat doesn't diminish my abilities as a physician. Losing the white coat doesn't change the thousands of lives I have touched. Would I do medicine again? Absolutely. I wouldn't alter a thing. I am proud of my career to this point, and I will always advocate for patients and providers. I am humbled by what life has given me. But the day the music died was a turning point, and I chose the road less traveled. And here I write, at peace, life balanced. No longer practicing medicine, and burnout but a distant memory.

My faith has been augmented in many ways through this discourse. A simple request to "just write" has taken Joshua and me on an unbelievable journey that seems almost predetermined. A unifying bond as physician and patient, a commonality with duloxetine—with radically different responses. Our stories overlap in so many ways, and ultimately helping one another through some of the most difficult times in our lives. It's as if a higher power has been guiding our hearts, minds, and hands in trying to inspire positive change. I feel as though we are being called in another direction with a future unknown. But it seems like we may just be getting started with Our Quadruple Aim.

My white coat was last donned many years ago, and now that white coat has left medicine entirely. Permanently? Doubtful. I love caring for people too much, but I don't have a crystal ball. Perhaps the last vestige of my white coat is the pen that adorned my breast pocket, adjacent to the letters—M.D. My ripple started when I dipped my pen into the metaphorical murky pool of dysfunction in healthcare, attempting to create lasting change. Despair is pervasive, but hope springs eternal. As the book closes, we hope you learned and felt inspired and empowered. Everyone has their part to play—what will be your ripple of change?

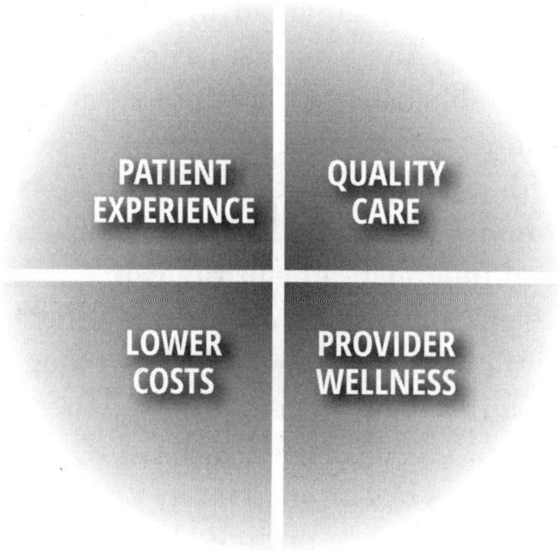
PATIENT EXPERIENCE
QUALITY CARE
LOWER COSTS
PROVIDER WELLNESS

ACKNOWLEDGEMENTS

"As we express our gratitude,
we must never forget that the highest appreciation
is not to utter words, but to live by them."

– JOHN F. KENNEDY

As it seems that healthcare has aspirations to become a Rube Goldberg machine, we decided to take a streamlined approach to our acknowledgements. No matter how many words we type here, "thank you" is not enough to express our gratitude. The collection of people who contributed and supported this effort goes far beyond the list of names below.

Each and every person in our sphere was instrumental to translating our memories, thoughts, research, and ideas into the preceding score of chapters. Those countless, seemingly insignificant moments in life have lined up in perfect harmony to yield *Ripple of Change*. We are humbled and blessed to have you in our lives and to share in this opportunity. As we thank you, all we ask in return is: find your stone.

We extend our thanks to:

Angie Otten, Megan Judy, Fred Merry, Mary Neville, Andre Carter, Ben Neville, Matt Rush, John Adams, Emily Milanowski, Brandon Francis, Mike Ranville, Ruth Otten, Jay Otten, Anna Criddle, Gary Fraylick, Chris Port, Jeff Johnson, Mike McNearney, Gary and Yong Judy, The Kemerling Family, The Biergeder Family, all of Dr. Otten's patients, Diana Debnar, Cari Reynolds, Elise Wildern, Devon Kruger, Elizabeth McDowell, Jessica McKillop, Donna Davidson, Kimberly Friar, Tony Marl, Kerry Lefere, Dike Drummond, Jonathan Otten, Juliet Kavanaugh, Kevin Kavanaugh, Derek Crombie, Ellen Crombie, Dana Kirk, Rex Nelson, Rob Leuken, Vickie Swisher, Justin Saya, Paul Sieving, Kermit and Debbe Douse, Cooper Rush, Richard Stephenson, Amy Wallace, George Classaan, Anthony

Chang, Chad Bassett, Catherine Dobrowitsky, Sarah Otten, Jerid Minnich, Jeremy Dull, Mike Tobin, Mark Cantazzaro, Susan Sanford, Lowell Fernander, Lori Pray, Chad Rogers, John Findley, Lynn Barr, E.W. Tibbs, Travis Criddle, Tim Simpson, Ara Pridjin, Dave Kruger, Father Mark Martin, Sandy Gould, Tammy Merrit, Julie Coenen, Linda Chermak, Patrick Sustrich, Kelly Murray, Jeff Whitson, Jessica Larkin, Russ Hicks, John Vandermolen, and all of the family, friends and colleagues whom we may have inadvertently excluded.

Thank you.
– Todd R. Otten, M.D., and Joshua J. Judy, Patient

ACRONYMS

(5-AR) 5-alpha-reductase
(5-HT) 5-hydroxytryptamine
(AAFP) American Academy of Family Physicians
(AARP) The American Association of Retired Persons
(ACL) Anterior Cruciate Ligament
(ACLS) Advanced Cardiac Life Support
(ACO) Accountable Care Organization
(ADHD) Attention Deficit Hyperactive Disorder
(AI) Artificial Intelligence
(AIA) American Institute of Architects
(AMA) American Medical Association
(APP) Advanced Practice Practitioner
(AR) Androgen Receptors
(BPH) Benign Prostatic Hyperplasia
(BAMF) Bold Advanced Medical Future
(BMJ) The British Medical Journal
(CEO) Chief Executive Officer
(CFO) Chief Financial Officer
(CIC) Class Insurance Consulting
(CIN) Clinically Integrated network
(CME) Continuing Medical Education
(CMO) Chief Medical Officer
(CMS) Centers for Medicare and Medicaid Services
(CO) Commanding Officer
(COO) Chief Operating Officer
(COPD) Chronic Obstructive Pulmonary Disease
(CPAP) Continuous Positive Airway Pressure
(CT) Computerized Tomography
(DHT) Dihydro-Testosterone
(DMC) Detroit Medical Center
(DPC) Direct Primary Care
(ECG) Electrocardiogram

(ECS) Emergency Care Specialists
(EEG) Electroencephalogram
(EMG) Electromyography
(EMR) Electronic Medical Record
(ER) Emergency Room
(ERG) Electroretinogram
(ESS) Empty Sella Syndrome
(FSH) Follicle Stimulating Hormone
(FT4) Free T4
(FTC) Federal Trade Commission
(FTE) Full-Time Equivalent
(GABA) Gamma-aminobutyric Acid
(GDP) Gross Domestic Product
(GPO) Group Purchasing Organization
(GSW) Gunshot Wound
(HCAHPS) Hospital Consumer Assessment of Healthcare Providers and Systems
(HCC) Hierarchical Condition Category
(HCG) Human Chorionic Gonadotropin
(HGB) Hayes Green Beach Hospital
(HIPAA) Health Insurance Portability and Accountability Act of 1996
(HPG) Hypothalamus Pituitary Gonadal Axis
(ICU) Intensive Care Unit
(IHI) Institute for Healthcare Improvement
(IT) Information Technology
(ITT) Intratesticular Testosterone
(IU) International Unit
(LARA) Licensing and Regulatory Affairs
(LH) Luteinizing hormone
(LTB) Losing the Blueprint
(L.V.T.) Licensed Veterinary Technician
(M and M) Morbidity and Mortality Conferences
(MA) Medical Assistant
(MBA) Master's of Business Administration

(MBI) Maslach Burnout Inventory
(MRI) Magnetic Resonance Imaging
(NFL) National Football League
(NP) Nurse practitioner
(NPRM) Non Compete Clause Rule
(NSAIDs) Non-steroidal Anti-inflammatory Drugs
(OQA) Our Quadruple Aim
(PA) Prior Authorization
(PBM) Pharmacy Benefit Manager
(PCMH) Patient Centered Medical Home
(PCP) Primary Care Physician
(PDE-5) Phosphodiesterase-5 Inhibitor
(PFS) Post-finasteride Syndrome
(PSSD) Post-SSRI/SNRI Sexual Dysfunction
(PTSD) Post-traumatic Stress Disorder
(PWS) Protracted Antidepressant Withdrawal Syndrome
(RBP) Reference Based Pricing
(ROI) Return on Investment
(RUSH) Rush University System for Health in Chicago, Illinois
(RVU) Relative Value Units
(SJS) Stevens-Johnson syndrome
(SNRI) Serotonin Norepinephrine Reuptake Inhibitor
(SSRI) Selective Serotonin Reuptake Inhibitor
(STD) Sexually Transmitted Disease
(SUDEP) Sudden Unexpected Epilepsy Death
(TBG) Thyroxine-binding Globulin
(TL;DR) Too long; didn't read
(TRT) Testosterone Replacement Therapy
(TSH) Thyroid Stimulating Hormone
(U.S.) United States
(USMLE) United States Medical Licensing Exam
(VP-10) Patrol Squadron Ten
(WHO) World Health Organization
(W-I-F-M) What's in it for me?
(XO) Executive Officer

ENDNOTES

Chapter 2—History of Present Illness

1 John Hammergren and Phil Harkins, *Skin in the Game: How Putting Yourself First Today Will Revolutionize Health Care Tomorrow* (John Wiley & Sons, 2008), 41.

2 Benjamin Schwartz, "Aligned Incentives," *Www.Linkedin.Com*, accessed January 2023, https://www.linkedin.com/pulse/aligned-incentives-benjamin-schwartz-md?trk=portfolio_article-card_title.

3 American Medical Association and American Medical Association, "How the Last Year Has Forced Rethinking on Physician Burnout," *American Medical Association*, March 10, 2021, accessed 1/2023, https://www.ama-assn.org/practice-management/physician-health/how-last-year-has-forced-rethinking-physician-burnout.

4 American Medical Association and American Medical Association, "How the Last Year Has Forced Rethinking on Physician Burnout," *American Medical Association*, March 10, 2021, accessed 1/2023, https://www.ama-assn.org/practice-management/physician-health/how-last-year-has-forced-rethinking-physician-burnout.

5 "AHA House Statement: America's Mental Health Crisis February 2, 2022 | AHA," American Hospital Association, February 3, 2022, accessed February 17, 2023, https://www.aha.org/2022-02-03-aha-house-statement-americas-mental-health-crisis-february-2-2022#:~:text=behavioral%20health%20services.-,Workforce,meet%20Americans'%20behavioral%20health%20needs.

Chapter 3—Journey Beyond the Triple Aim

6 Institute Of Medicine and Committee on Quality of Health Care In America, *Crossing the Quality Chasm: A New Health System for the 21st Century* (National Academies Press, 2001), 5-6.

7 Institute Of Medicine and Committee on Quality of Health Care In America, *Crossing the Quality Chasm: A New Health System for the 21st Century* (National Academies Press, 2001), 1.

8 Institute Of Medicine and Committee on Quality of Health Care In America, *Crossing the Quality Chasm: A New Health System for the 21st Century* (National Academies Press, 2001), 1

9 Donald Berwick, "The Triple Aim: Why We Still Have a Long Way to Go," accessed November 17, 2021, http://www.ihi.org/communities/blogs/the-triple-aim-why-we-still-have-a-long-way-to-go.

10 Institute for Healthcare Improvement (IHI), "An Overview of the IHI Triple Aim", accessed 11/2022, http://www.ihi.org/Engage/Initiatives/TripleAim/Pages/default.aspx.

11 Niñon Lewis, "A Primer on Defining the Triple Aim", accessed 11/2021, https://www.ihi.org/communities/blogs/a-primer-on-defining-the-triple-aim.

12 Institute Of Medicine and Committee on Quality of Health Care In America, *Crossing the Quality Chasm: A New Health System for the 21st Century* (National Academies Press, 2001), 6.

13 "Accountable Care Organizations (ACOs): General Information | CMS Innovation Center," accessed 3/2023, https://innovation.cms.gov/innovation-models/aco.

14 Thomas Bodenheimer and Christine A. Sinsky, "From Triple to Quadruple Aim: Care of the Patient Requires Care of the Provider," *Annals of Family Medicine* 12, no. 6 (November 1, 2014): 573–76, https://doi.org/10.1370/afm.1713.

15 Thomas Bodenheimer and Christine A. Sinsky, "From Triple to Quadruple Aim: Care of the Patient Requires Care of the Provider," *Annals of Family Medicine* 12, no. 6 (November 1, 2014): 573–76, https://doi.org/10.1370/afm.1713.

16 Dike Drummond, "The Battle for the Quadruple Aim—Its 3 on 1 and the Outcome is UnClear", accessed 11/2021, https://www.thehappymd.com/blog/the-quadruple-aim-vs-physician-burnout.

17 C suite solutions, "Why the Quadruple AIm Plays an Important Role in Health Care", accessed 11/2021, https://csuitesolutions.com/press-releases/why-the-quadruple-aim-plays-an-important-role-in-health-care/.

18 Privis Health, "What is the Quadruple Aim and What Role Does it Play in Healthcare", accessed 12/2021, https://www.privishealth.com/what-is-the-quadruple-aim-and-what-role-does-it-play-in-healthcare/.

19 Eric Reinhart, "Opinion | Doctors Aren't Burned Out From Overwork. We're Demoralized by Our Health System.," *The New York Times*, February 7, 2023, https://www.nytimes.com/2023/02/05/opinion/doctors-universal-health-care.html.

20 Wendy Dean, Simon G. Talbot, and Austin Dean, "Reframing Clinician Distress: Moral Injury Not Burnout.," *Federal Practitioner : For the Health Care Professionals of the VA, DoD, and PHS* 36, no. 9 (September 1, 2019): 400–402.

21 Joe Cantlupe, "Number of Healthcare Administrators Explodes since 1970 | Athenahealth," *Www.Athenahealth.Com*, accessed December 15, 2021, https://www.athenahealth.com/knowledge-hub/practice-management/expert-forum-rise-and-rise-healthcare-administrator.

22 Alicia Phaneuf, "What is an EMR System? Definitions, benefits, problems and trends for electronic health records," accessed 12/2021, https://www.businessinsider.com/electronic-health-records-benefits-challenges.

23 Focus for Health Foundation, "A Growing Crisis: Physician Shortage," Focus for Health, November 4, 2020, accessed 12/2021, https://www.focusforhealth.org/a-growing-crisis-physician-shortage/.

24 Elisabeth Rosenthal, *An American Sickness: How Healthcare Became Big Business and How You Can Take It Back* (Penguin, 2018), 86.

25 Leigh Page, "'I've had it with medicine!': 16 options for second careers," accessed 12/2021, https://www.medscape.com/viewarticle/827680.

26 Leigh Page, "'I've had it with medicine!': 16 options for second careers," accessed 12/2021, https://www.medscape.com/viewarticle/827680.

Chapter 4—Losing the Blueprint

27 Jun Shan, "The Meaning of Yin and Yang," accessed 9/2022, https://www.thoughtco.com/yin-and-yang-629214.

28 Julia Neuberger and Raymond Tallis, "Do We Need a New Word for Patients? Let's Do Away with 'Patients' Commentary: Leave Well Alone," BMJ 318, no. 7200 (June 26, 1999): 1756–58, https://doi.org/10.1136/bmj.318.7200.1756.

29 John Gilbert et al., "Open Stand-Up MRI," *Journal of Spinal Disorders & Techniques* 19, no. 2 (April 1, 2006): 151–54, https://doi.org/10.1097/01.bsd.0000188665.54014.8d.

Chapter 5—Our Quadruple Aim

30 Andrew Yang, *Forward: Notes on the Future of Our Democracy* (Crown, 2021).

31 Tom Janisse, "Relationship of a Physician's Well-Being to Interactions with Patients: Practices of the Highest Performing Physicians on the *Art of Medicine* Patient Survey," *The Permanente Journal* 12, no. 4 (January 1, 2008): 70–76, https://doi.org/10.7812/tpp/08-041.

32 C suite solutions, "Why the Quadruple AIm Plays an Important Role in Health Care," accessed 11/2021, https://csuitesolutions.com/press-releases/why-the-quadruple-aim-plays-an-important-role-in-health-care/.

33 World Health Organization: WHO, "Quality Health Services," *Www.Who.Int*, July 20, 2020, accessed 3/2023, https://www.who.int/news-room/fact-sheets/detail/quality-health-services.

34 David A. Kindig and Greg L. Stoddart, "What Is Population Health?," *American Journal of Public Health* 93, no. 3 (March 1, 2003): 380–83, https://doi.org/10.2105/ajph.93.3.380.

35 Vinayak K. Prasad, *Malignant: How Bad Policy and Bad Evidence Harm People with Cancer* (Johns Hopkins University Press, 2020), 56-57.

36 www.CMS.gov, "National Health Expenditures 2021 Highlights," accessed 1/2023, https://www.cms.gov/research-statistics-data-and-systems/statistics-trends-and-reports/nationalhealthexpenddata/nationalhealthaccountshistorical#:~:text=The%20data%20are%20presented%20by,spending%20accounted%20for%2018.3%20percent.

37 Joshua Cohen, "Dismal U.S. Life Expectancy Trend Reflects Disconnect Between Dollars Spent On Healthcare And Value Produced," Forbes, November 1, 2020, accessed 12/2021, https://www.forbes.com/sites/joshuacohen/2020/11/01/dismal-us-life-expectancy-trend-reflects-disconnect-between-dollars-spent-on-healthcare-and-value-produced/?sh=53290ec53847.

38 Marty Makary, *The Price We Pay: What Broke American Health Care—and How to Fix It* (Bloomsbury Publishing USA, 2019).

39 BioSpace, "Caravan Health ACOs Save Medicare $58 Million and Achieve Outstanding Quality Scores in 2018," *BioSpace*, October 2, 2019, accessed 1/2023,

https://www.biospace.com/article/releases/caravan-health-acos-save-medicare-58-million-and-achieve-outstanding-quality-scores-in-2018/.

40 C suite solutions, "Why the Quadruple AIm Plays an Important Role in Health Care," accessed 11/2021, https://csuitesolutions.com/press-releases/why-the-quadruple-aim-plays-an-important-role-in-health-care/.

41 Jina L. Sinskey, Rebecca Margolis, and Amy E. Vinson, "The Wicked Problem of Physician Well-Being," *Anesthesiology Clinics* 40, no. 2 (May 1, 2022): 213–23, https://doi.org/10.1016/j.anclin.2022.01.001.

42 Tait D. Shanafelt, Joel Goh, and Christine A. Sinsky, "The Business Case for Investing in Physician Well-Being," *JAMA Internal Medicine* 177, no. 12 (December 1, 2017): 1826, https://doi.org/10.1001/jamainternmed.2017.4340.

43 Tait D. Shanafelt, Joel Goh, and Christine A. Sinsky, "The Business Case for Investing in Physician Well-Being," *JAMA Internal Medicine* 177, no. 12 (December 1, 2017): 1826, https://doi.org/10.1001/jamainternmed.2017.4340.

44 National Academies of Sciences Engineering Medicine And, National Academy Of Medicine, and Committee on Systems Approaches to Improve Patient Care by Supporting Clinician Well-Being, *Taking Action Against Clinician Burnout: A Systems Approach to Professional Well-Being* (National Academies Press, 2020).

Chapter 6—Anatomy of Burnout

45 Psychology Today, "Burnout," *Psychology Today*, December 1, 2021, accessed 1/2022, https://www.psychologytoday.com/us/basics/burnout.

46 Mackenzie Bean, "7 Stats on Physician Burnout amid COVID-19," *Www.Beckershospitalreview.Com*, accessed on 1/2022, https://www.beckershospitalreview.com/hospital-physician-relationships/7-stats-on-physician-burnout-2.html#:~:text=Sixty%2Done%20percent%20of%20physicians,the%20Physicians%20Foundation%20released%20Aug.&text=The%20survey%20is%20based%20on,May%2026%20and%20June%209.

47 Maria Clark, "50+ Shocking Physician Burnout Statistics You'll Never Believe—Etactics," *Etactics | Revenue Cycle Software*, December 3, 2021, accessed 1/2022, https://etactics.com/blog/physician-burnout-statistics.

48 DNYUZ, "Physician Burnout Has Reached Distressing Levels, New Research Finds," *DNyuz*, September 29, 2022, accessed Sept/2022, https://dnyuz.com/2022/09/29/physician-burnout-has-reached-distressing-levels-new-research-finds/.

49 Mackenzie Bean, "7 Stats on Physician Burnout amid COVID-19," *Www.Beckershospitalreview.Com*, accessed on 1/2022, https://www.beckershospitalreview.com/hospital-physician-relationships/7-stats-on-physician-burnout-2.html#:~:text=Sixty%2Done%20percent%20of%20physicians,the%20Physicians%20Foundation%20released%20Aug.&text=The%20survey%20is%20based%20on,May%2026%20and%20June%209.

50 Maria Clark, "50+ Shocking Physician Burnout Statistics You'll Never Believe—Etactics," *Etactics | Revenue Cycle Software*, December 3, 2021, accessed 1/2022, https://etactics.com/blog/physician-burnout-statistics.

51 DNYUZ, "Physician Burnout Has Reached Distressing Levels, New Research Finds," *DNyuz*, September 29, 2022, accessed Sept/2022, https://dnyuz.com/2022/09/29/physician-burnout-has-reached-distressing-levels-new-research-finds/.

52 Simon G. Talbot and Wendy Dean, "Physicians Aren't 'Burning out.' They'Re Suffering from Moral Injury," STAT, June 23, 2021, accessed 1/2023, https://www.statnews.com/2018/07/26/physicians-not-burning-out-they-are-suffering-moral-injury/.

53 Maria Clark, "50+ Shocking Physician Burnout Statistics You'll Never Believe—Etactics," *Etactics | Revenue Cycle Software*, December 3, 2021, accessed 1/2022, https://etactics.com/blog/physician-burnout-statistics.

54 "Addressing Primary Care Workforce Challenges: Practical Solutions and a Way Forward," *Resources.Aledade.Com*, accessed 2/2022, https://resources.aledade.com/policy-regulation/addressing-primary-care-workforce-challenges-practical-solutions-and-a-way-forward.

55 Dike Drummond, *Stop Physician Burnout: What to Do When Working Harder Isn't Working* (Heritage Press Publications, LLC, 2014), page 22.

56 Simon G. Talbot and Wendy Dean, "Physicians Aren't 'Burning out.' They're Suffering from Moral Injury," *STAT*, June 23, 2021, accessed 1/2023, https://www.statnews.com/2018/07/26/physicians-not-burning-out-they-are-suffering-moral-injury/.

57 Mian Amir et al., "Medical Student and Resident Burnout: A Review of Causes, Effects, and Prevention," *Journal of Family Medicine and Disease Prevention* 4, no. 4 (December 31, 2018), https://doi.org/10.23937/2469-5793/1510094.

58 Thomas Bodenheimer and Christine A. Sinsky, "From Triple to Quadruple Aim: Care of the Patient Requires Care of the Provider," *Annals of Family Medicine* 12, no. 6 (November 1, 2014): 573–76, https://doi.org/10.1370/afm.1713.

59 Simon G. Talbot and Wendy Dean, "Physicians Aren't 'Burning out.' They'Re Suffering from Moral Injury," *STAT*, June 23, 2021, accessed 1/2023, https://www.statnews.com/2018/07/26/physicians-not-burning-out-they-are-suffering-moral-injury/.

60 Dike Drummond, *Stop Physician Burnout: What to Do When Working Harder Isn't Working* (Heritage Press Publications, LLC, 2014), page 45.

61 Dike Drummond, *Stop Physician Burnout: What to Do When Working Harder Isn't Working* (Heritage Press Publications, LLC, 2014), page 49.

Chapter 7—Rarity and Grace

62 "What's in a Name? Compassion, Generosity Helped to Build Key Michigan," *University of Michigan Medical School*, June 16, 2017, accessed 2/2023, https://medicine.umich.edu/medschool/news/what%E2%80%99s-name-compassion-generosity-helped-build-key-michigan-medicine-facilities.

63 Yong Zeng et al., "*RS-1*Gene Delivery to an Adult*Rs1h*Knockout Mouse Model Restores ERG b-Wave with Reversal of the Electronegative Waveform of X-Linked Retinoschisis," *Investigative Ophthalmology & Visual Science* 45, no. 9 (September 1, 2004): 3279, https://doi.org/10.1167/iovs.04-0576.

64 National Organization for Rare Disorders, "X-Linked Retinoschisis—Symptoms, Causes, Treatment | NORD," *National Organization for Rare Disorders*, January 12, 2023, https://rarediseases.org/rare-diseases/x-linked-juvenile-retinoschisis/.

65 Paul A Sieving, "X-Linked Congenital Retinoschisis," GeneReviews®—NCBI Bookshelf, November 5, 2020, accessed 6/2022, https://www.ncbi.nlm.nih.gov/books/NBK1222/#retinoschisis.Summary.

66 the Associated Press, "Michigan Highway Shooter Who 'terrorized a Community' Sentenced—Los Angeles Times," Los Angeles Times, February 4, 2014, https://www.latimes.com/nation/nationnow/la-na-nn-michigan-shooter-sentenced-20140204-story.html.

67 Lisa Roose-Church Usa Today, "USA TODAY," USA TODAY, March 4, 2014, https://www.usatoday.com/story/news/nation/2014/03/03/michigan-highway-shooter-sentencing-terrorism/5982455/.

68 Suzanne E. Tomasi et al., "Suicide among Veterinarians in the United States from 1979 through 2015," *Javma-Journal of the American Veterinary Medical Association* 254, no. 1 (January 1, 2019): 104–12, https://doi.org/10.2460/javma.254.1.104.

Chapter 8—It's Bigger Than Me

69 Xiang-Qing Wang et al., "Risk of a Lamotrigine-Related Skin Rash: Current Meta-Analysis and Postmarketing Cohort Analysis," *Seizure-European Journal of Epilepsy* 25 (February 1, 2015): 52–61, https://doi.org/10.1016/j.seizure.2014.12.001.

70 "Stevens-Johnson Syndrome—Symptoms and Causes—Mayo Clinic," Mayo Clinic, January 7, 2023, accessed 6/2022, https://www.mayoclinic.org/diseases-conditions/stevens-johnson-syndrome/symptoms-causes/syc-20355936#:~:text=Stevens%2DJohnson%20syndrome%20(SJS),to%20heal%20after%20several%20days.

Chapter 9—Ripple of Change

71 Institute Of Medicine and Committee on Quality of Health Care In America, *Crossing the Quality Chasm: A New Health System for the 21st Century* (National Academies Press, 2001), 8.

72 ZDoggMD, "The Great Resignation, Or The Great Awakening?," November 19, 2021, , accessed 11/2021, https://www.youtube.com/watch?v=C7udJn4qBYw.

73 Airiodion Global Services, "Resolving Barriers to Change in Healthcare & Physicians—2021 Guide," accessed 1/2022, https://www.airiodion.com/barriers-to-change-in-healthcare/.

74 Airiodion Global Services, "Resolving Barriers to Change in Healthcare & Physicians—2021 Guide," accessed 1/2022, https://www.airiodion.com/barriers-to-change-in-healthcare/.

75 Matthew Kelly, *Perfectly Yourself: Discovering God's Dream for You* (Beacon Publishing, 2017), 60.

Chapter 10—The Tapers and the Abyss

76 Nelson Vergel, Excelmale.com, accessed 06/2022, https://www.excelmale.com/forum/.

77 Matthew M. Zack and Rosemarie Kobau, "National and State Estimates of the Numbers of Adults and Children with Active Epilepsy—United States, 2015," *Morbidity and Mortality Weekly Report* 66, no. 31 (August 11, 2017): 821–25, https://doi.org/10.15585/mmwr.mm6631a1.

78 Haidong Wang et al., "Global, Regional, and National Life Expectancy, All-Cause Mortality, and Cause-Specific Mortality for 249 Causes of Death, 1980–2015: A Systematic Analysis for the Global Burden of Disease Study 2015," *The Lancet* 388, no. 10053 (October 8, 2016): 1459–1544, https://doi.org/10.1016/s0140-6736(16)31012-1.

79 Sheel J. Pathak, "Sudden Unexpected Death in Epilepsy," StatPearls—NCBI Bookshelf, September 21, 2022, accessed 3/2023, https://www.ncbi.nlm.nih.gov/books/NBK559104/.

80 Drugwatch, "Cymbalta Lawsuit—Settlements, Withdrawal & Suicide Claims," *Drugwatch.Com*, November 4, 2022, accessed December, 2022, https://www.drugwatch.com/cymbalta/lawsuits/.

Chapter 11—Of Little Faith

81 "Do Astronauts Carry Suicide Pills? | RealClearScience," accessed 6/2022, https://www.realclearscience.com/blog/2013/10/astronauts-acnd-suicide-pills.html.

Chapter 12—Provider Wellness

82 Bryan Bohman et al., "Physician Well-Being: The Reciprocity of Practice Efficiency, Culture of Wellness, and Personal Resilience," *NEJM Catalyst*, August 7, 2017, http://catalyst.nejm.org/doi/full/10.1056/CAT.17.0429.

83 "Definition of Wellness," In *Www.Dictionary.Com*, accessed 3/2023, https://www.dictionary.com/browse/wellness.

84 Wikipedia contributors, "Wellness (Alternative Medicine)," Wikipedia, accessed 2/2019, https://en.wikipedia.org/wiki/Wellness_(alternative_medicine).

85 Dike Drummond, *Stop Physician Burnout: What to Do When Working Harder Isn't Working* (Heritage Press Publications, LLC, 2014), chapter 3.

86 "10 Tricks For Developing A Great Mindset," *Can Too Foundation*, accessed 3/2019, https://www.cantoo.org.au/blog/10-tricks-for-developing-a-great-mindset.

87 Catherine Florio Pipas, *A Doctor's Dozen: Twelve Strategies for Personal Health and a Culture of Wellness* (Dartmouth College Press, 2018), 17.

Chapter 13—Wellness = Balance = Thriving

88 John Throop, Don Powell, and Bradley Slywka, "A Successful Sabbatical Program to Reduce Burnout in Emergency Medicine Physicians," *NEJM Catalyst Innovations in Care Delivery* 3, no. 12 (November 16, 2022), https://doi.org/10.1056/cat.22.0209.

89 John Throop, Don Powell, and Bradley Slywka, "A Successful Sabbatical Program to Reduce Burnout in Emergency Medicine Physicians," *NEJM Catalyst Innovations in Care Delivery* 3, no. 12 (November 16, 2022), https://doi.org/10.1056/cat.22.0209.

90 John Throop, Don Powell, and Bradley Slywka, "A Successful Sabbatical Program to Reduce Burnout in Emergency Medicine Physicians," *NEJM Catalyst Innovations in Care Delivery* 3, no. 12 (November 16, 2022), https://doi.org/10.1056/cat.22.0209.

91 John Throop, Don Powell, and Bradley Slywka, "A Successful Sabbatical Program to Reduce Burnout in Emergency Medicine Physicians," *NEJM Catalyst Innovations in Care Delivery* 3, no. 12 (November 16, 2022), https://doi.org/10.1056/cat.22.0209.

92 John Throop, Don Powell, and Bradley Slywka, "A Successful Sabbatical Program to Reduce Burnout in Emergency Medicine Physicians," *NEJM Catalyst Innovations in Care Delivery* 3, no. 12 (November 16, 2022), https://doi.org/10.1056/cat.22.0209.

93 John Throop, Don Powell, and Bradlcy Slywka, "A Successful Sabbatical Program to Reduce Burnout in Emergency Medicine Physicians," *NEJM Catalyst Innovations in Care Delivery* 3, no. 12 (November 16, 2022), https://doi.org/10.1056/cat.22.0209.

94 Eric Reinhart, "Opinion | Doctors Aren't Burned Out From Overwork. We're Demoralized by Our Health System.," *The New York Times*, February 7, 2023, https://www.nytimes.com/2023/02/05/opinion/doctors-universal-health-care.html.

95 Eric Reinhart, "Opinion | Doctors Aren't Burned Out From Overwork. We're Demoralized by Our Health System.," *The New York Times*, February 7, 2023, https://www.nytimes.com/2023/02/05/opinion/doctors-universal-health-care.html.

96 Simon G. Talbot and Wendy Dean, "Physicians Aren't 'Burning out.' They'Re Suffering from Moral Injury," *STAT*, June 23, 2021, accessed 1/2023, https://www.statnews.com/2018/07/26/physicians-not-burning-out-they-are-suffering-moral-injury/.

97 Sonya Norman and Shira Maguen, "Moral Injury," accessed 2/2023, https://www.ptsd.va.gov/professional/treat/cooccurring/moral_injury.asp#:~:text=Moral%20injury%20is%20the%20distressing,individual's%20values%20and%20moral%20beliefs.

98 Simon G. Talbot and Wendy Dean, "Physicians Aren't 'Burning out.' They'Re Suffering from Moral Injury," *STAT*, June 23, 2021, accessed 1/2023, https://www.statnews.com/2018/07/26/physicians-not-burning-out-they-are-suffering-moral-injury/.

99 Matthew Kelly, *Perfectly Yourself: Discovering God's Dream for You* (Beacon Publishing, 2017), 21.

100 Bryan Bohman et al., "Physician Well-Being: The Reciprocity of Practice Efficiency, Culture of Wellness, and Personal Resilience," *NEJM Catalyst*, August 7, 2017, http://catalyst.nejm.org/doi/full/10.1056/CAT.17.0429.

101 Bryan Bohman et al., "Physician Well-Being: The Reciprocity of Practice Efficiency, Culture of Wellness, and Personal Resilience," *NEJM Catalyst*, August 7, 2017, http://catalyst.nejm.org/doi/full/10.1056/CAT.17.0429.

102 Bryan Bohman et al., "Physician Well-Being: The Reciprocity of Practice Efficiency, Culture of Wellness, and Personal Resilience," *NEJM Catalyst*, August 7, 2017, http://catalyst.nejm.org/doi/full/10.1056/CAT.17.0429.

103 Bryan Bohman et al., "Physician Well-Being: The Reciprocity of Practice Efficiency, Culture of Wellness, and Personal Resilience," *NEJM Catalyst*, August 7, 2017, http://catalyst.nejm.org/doi/full/10.1056/CAT.17.0429.

104 Bryan Bohman et al., "Physician Well-Being: The Reciprocity of Practice Efficiency, Culture of Wellness, and Personal Resilience," *NEJM Catalyst*, August 7, 2017, http://catalyst.nejm.org/doi/full/10.1056/CAT.17.0429..

105 American Board of Physician Specialties, "Physician Thriving: Financial Wellbeing and Burnout—Where Do You Stand?," May 21, 2020, https://www.abpsus.org/physician-thriving-financial-wellbeing-and-burnout-where-do-you-stand/.

Chapter 14—Role Reversal

106 "Laboratory of Neuroendocrinology | Dipartimento Di Scienze Farmacologiche e Biomolecolari—DISFEB," accessed 8/2020, https://eng.disfeb.unimi.it/ecm/home/research/research-labs/laboratory-of-neuroendocrinology.

107 "Laboratory of Neuroendocrinology | Dipartimento Di Scienze Farmacologiche e Biomolecolari—DISFEB," accessed 8/2020, https://eng.disfeb.unimi.it/ecm/home/research/research-labs/laboratory-of-neuroendocrinology.

108 "Laboratory of Neuroendocrinology | Dipartimento Di Scienze Farmacologiche e Biomolecolari—DISFEB," accessed 8/2020, https://eng.disfeb.unimi.it/ecm/home/research/research-labs/laboratory-of-neuroendocrinology.

109 BBC News, "The Extraordinary Case of the Guevedoces," BBC News, September 20, 2015, accessed 6/2022, https://www.bbc.com/news/magazine-34290981.

110 BBC News, "The Extraordinary Case of the Guevedoces," BBC News, September 20, 2015, accessed 6/2022, https://www.bbc.com/news/magazine-34290981.

111 BBC News, "The Extraordinary Case of the Guevedoces," BBC News, September 20, 2015, accessed 6/2022, https://www.bbc.com/news/magazine-34290981.

112 David Healy et al., "Diagnostic Criteria for Enduring Sexual Dysfunction after Treatment with Antidepressants, Finasteride and Isotretinoin," *The International Journal of Risk and Safety in Medicine* 33, no. 1 (January 1, 2022): 65–76, https://doi.org/10.3233/jrs-210023.

113 Silvia Giatti et al., "Effects of Paroxetine Treatment and Its Withdrawal on Neurosteroidogenesis," *Psychoneuroendocrinology* 132 (July 21, 2021): 105364, https://doi.org/10.1016/j.psyneuen.2021.105364.

114 Silvia Giatti et al., "Post-Finasteride Syndrome and Post-SSRI Sexual Dysfunction: Two Sides of the Same Coin?," *Endocrine* 61, no. 2 (April 19, 2018): 180–93, https://doi.org/10.1007/s12020-018-1593-5.

115 Roberto Cosimo Melcangi and Giancarlo Panzica, "Neuroactive Steroids and Metabolic Axis," *Frontiers in Neuroendocrinology*, November 13, 2017, https://doi.org/10.1016/j.yfrne.2017.11.002.

Chapter 15—Office Utopia

116 Greg Hiebert, *You can't give what you don't have* (Grayline Publishing, 2018), page 53.

117 Jason E. Marker, "Leadership Development, Well-Being, and Performance Improvement: Achieving the Quadruple Aim in Your Practice," *Brand*, accessed 10/2022, https://www.aafp.org/pubs/fpm/issues/2022/0900/leadership-wellbeing.html.

118 Jason E. Marker, "Leadership Development, Well-Being, and Performance Improvement: Achieving the Quadruple Aim in Your Practice," *Brand*, accessed 10/2022, https://www.aafp.org/pubs/fpm/issues/2022/0900/leadership-wellbeing.html.

119 Jason E. Marker, "Leadership Development, Well-Being, and Performance Improvement: Achieving the Quadruple Aim in Your Practice," *Brand*, accessed 10/2022, https://www.aafp.org/pubs/fpm/issues/2022/0900/leadership-wellbeing.html.

120 Hidden Brain Staff, "Humor Us | Hidden Brain Media," January 18, 2022, accessed 6/2022, https://hiddenbrain.org/podcast/humor-us/.

121 Bryan Bohman et al., "Physician Well-Being: The Reciprocity of Practice Efficiency, Culture of Wellness, and Personal Resilience," *NEJM Catalyst*, August 7, 2017, http://catalyst.nejm.org/doi/full/10.1056/CAT.17.0429.

122 Pragya Agarwal, "How To Create A Positive Workplace Culture," *Forbes*, August 30, 2018, accessed 9/2022, https://www.forbes.com/sites/pragyaagarwaleurope/2018/08/29/how-to-create-a-positive-work-place-culture/?sh=3e01d40c4272.

123 Pragya Agarwal, "How To Create A Positive Workplace Culture," *Forbes*, August 30, 2018, accessed 9/2022, https://www.forbes.com/sites/pragyaagarwaleurope/2018/08/29/how-to-create-a-positive-work-place-culture/?sh=3e01d40c4272.

124 Robert W. Yeh et al., "Parachute Use to Prevent Death and Major Trauma When Jumping from Aircraft: Randomized Controlled Trial," *BMJ*, December 13, 2018, k5094, https://doi.org/10.1136/bmj.k5094.

125 Robert W. Yeh et al., "Parachute Use to Prevent Death and Major Trauma When Jumping from Aircraft: Randomized Controlled Trial," *BMJ*, December 13, 2018, k5094, https://doi.org/10.1136/bmj.k5094.

126 Robert W. Yeh et al., "Parachute Use to Prevent Death and Major Trauma When Jumping from Aircraft: Randomized Controlled Trial," *BMJ*, December 13, 2018, k5094, https://doi.org/10.1136/bmj.k5094.

127 Jill Jin et al., "Simplified Outpatient Documentation and Coding Reduce Workload With Recent Updates To E/M Coding and Team Documentation," accessed 12/2022, https://www.ama-assn.org/system/files/steps-forward-documentation-coding-toolkit.pdf.

128 Melissa Walton-Shirley, "What Will It Take to Cure EHR Note Bloat?," *Medscape*, May 24, 2022, , accessed 8/2022, https://www.medscape.com/viewarticle/974420.

129 Jill Jin et al., "Simplified Outpatient Documentation and Coding Reduce Workload With Recent Updates To E/M Coding and Team Documentation," accessed 12/2022, https://www.ama-assn.org/system/files/steps-forward-documentation-coding-toolkit.pdf.

130 Melissa Walton-Shirley, "What Will It Take to Cure EHR Note Bloat?," *Medscape*, May 24, 2022, , accessed 8/2022, https://www.medscape.com/viewarticle/974420.

131 Jill Jin et al., "Simplified Outpatient Documentation and Coding Reduce Workload With Recent Updates To E/M Coding and Team Documentation," accessed 12/2022, https://www.ama-assn.org/system/files/steps-forward-documentation-coding-toolkit.pdf.

Chapter 16—Role Reversal Cont

132 Adele Framer, "What I Have Learnt from Helping Thousands of People Taper off Antidepressants and Other Psychotropic Medications," *Therapeutic Advances in Psychopharmacology* 11 (March 16, 2021): 204512532199127, https://doi.org/10.1177/2045125321991274.

133 Michael Pascal Hengartner et al., "Protracted Withdrawal Syndrome after Stopping Antidepressants: A Descriptive Quantitative Analysis of Consumer Narratives from a Large Internet Forum," *Therapeutic Advances in Psychopharmacology* 10 (December 24, 2020): 204512532098057, https://doi.org/10.1177/2045125320980573.

134 Michael Pascal Hengartner et al., "Protracted Withdrawal Syndrome after Stopping Antidepressants: A Descriptive Quantitative Analysis of Consumer Narratives from a Large Internet Forum," *Therapeutic Advances in Psychopharmacology* 10 (December 24, 2020): 204512532098057, https://doi.org/10.1177/2045125320980573.

135 Tim Newman, "Understanding Anhedonia: What Happens in the Brain?," *Www.Medicalnewstoday.Com*, January 31, 2018, accessed 6/2022, https://www.medicalnewstoday.com/articles/320737.

136 "Depersonalization-Derealization Disorder—Symptoms and Causes—Mayo Clinic," Mayo Clinic, May 16, 2017, accessed 6/2022, https://www.mayoclinic.org/diseases-conditions/depersonalization-derealization-disorder/symptoms-causes/syc-20352911.

137 Adele Framer, "What I Have Learnt from Helping Thousands of People Taper off Antidepressants and Other Psychotropic Medications," *Therapeutic Advances in Psychopharmacology* 11 (March 16, 2021): 204512532199127, https://doi.org/10.1177/2045125321991274.

138 B.J. Oddens and A. Vermeulen, *Androgens and the Aging Male* (CRC Press, 1996), 3-14.

139 Thomas G. Travison et al., "Harmonized Reference Ranges for Circulating Testosterone Levels in Men of Four Cohort Studies in the United States and Europe," *The Journal of Clinical Endocrinology and Metabolism* 102, no. 4 (April 1, 2017): 1161–73, https://doi.org/10.1210/jc.2016-2935.

140 J.A. García-Arnés and N. García-Casares, "Doping and Sports Endocrinology: Anabolic-Androgenic Steroids," *Revista Clínica Española,* November 1, 2022, accessed 12/2022, https://doi.org/10.1016/j.rceng.2022.09.003.

141 Miki Bloch et al., "Monoamines and Neurosteroids in Sexual Function During Induced Hypogonadism in Healthy Men," *Archives of General Psychiatry* 63, no. 4 (April 1, 2006): 450, https://doi.org/10.1001/archpsyc.63.4.450.

142 "Antidepressant Discontinuation Syndrome," GlobalRPH, accessed 11/2022, https://globalrph.com/drugs/antidepressant-discontinuation-syndrome-guide/.

Chapter 18—ROI for a Health System

143 Dike Drummond, "The Battle for the Quadruple Aim—Its 3 on 1 and the Outcome is UnClear", accessed 11/2021, https://www.thehappymd.com/blog/the-quadruple-aim-vs-physician-burnout.

144 Allen P Anandarajah, Timothy E. Quill, and Michael R. Privitera, "Adopting the Quadruple Aim: The University of Rochester Medical Center Experience," *The American Journal of Medicine* 131, no. 8 (August 1, 2018): 979–86, https://doi.org/10.1016/j.amjmed.2018.04.034.

145 John Noseworthy et al, "Physician Burnout Is A Public Health Crisis: A Message To Our Fellow Health Care CEOs," accessed 1/2022, https://www.healthaffairs.org/do/10.1377/forefront.20170328.059397/full/.

146 "Sir William Osler and Internal Medicine | ACP Online," accessed 4/2022, https://www.acponline.org/about-acp/about-internal-medicine/sir-william-osler-and-internal-medicine.

147 Diana K Sugg, "Show-and-tell for doctors Making the rounds: In a tradition that began at Hopkins Hospital, doctors learn from patients and each other," accessed 4/2022, https://www.baltimoresun.com/news/bs-xpm-1995-09-23-1995266001-story.html.

148 "Compassion Rounds | Physician Wellness and Resilience," Wellness, accessed 4/2022, https://www.orlandohealth.com/physicianwellness/services/compassion-rounds.

149 Bryant Adibe, "Rush Hospital Wellness: Creating Wellness in a Pandemic," accessed 7/2022, https://www.rush.edu/sites/default/files/2020-07/creating-wellness-pandemic-toolkit.pdf.

150 Bryant Adibe, "Rush Hospital Wellness: Creating Wellness in a Pandemic," accessed 7/2022, https://www.rush.edu/sites/default/files/2020-07/creating-wellness-pandemic-toolkit.pdf.

151 Bryant Adibe, "Rush Hospital Wellness: Creating Wellness in a Pandemic," accessed 7/2022, https://www.rush.edu/sites/default/files/2020-07/creating-wellness-pandemic-toolkit.pdf.

152 John Noseworthy et al, "Physician Burnout Is A Public Health Crisis: A Message To Our Fellow Health Care CEOs," accessed 1/2022, https://www.healthaffairs.org/do/10.1377/forefront.20170328.059397/full/.

153 Alexi A. Wright and Ingrid T. Katz, "Beyond Burnout—Redesigning Care to Restore Meaning and Sanity for Physicians," *The New England Journal of Medicine* 378, no. 4 (January 24, 2018): 309–11, https://doi.org/10.1056/nejmp1716845.

154 Dike Drummond, "Quadruple Aim Blueprint," accessed 2/2022, https://www.thehappymd.com/hubfs/Documents/4A%20Blueprint%20Documents/QuadrupleAimBlueprintStrategy.pdf.

155 "Chief Wellness Officer (CWO) Course," WellMD & WellPhD, accessed 3/2022, https://wellmd.stanford.edu/knowledge-hub/courses-conferences/cwo-course.html.

156 "Physician Health & Well-Being Conference," accessed 3/2022, https://www.aafp.org/events/physician-health-and-well-being-conference.html.

157 Dike Drummond, "The Battle for the Quadruple Aim—Its 3 on 1 and the Outcome is UnClear", accessed 11/2021, https://www.thehappymd.com/blog/the-quadruple-aim-vs-physician-burnout.

158 Tracy Brower, "6 Ways To Reinvent Your Wellness Strategy—According To Experts," , accessed 3/2022, https://urldefense.com/v3/__https://www.forbes.com/sites/tracybrower/2021/03/21/6-ways-to-reinvent-your-wellness-strategy-according-to-experts/__;!!Kyqyl2UCiGo4!ggAzDoeIZYxZftqGzSCYtoZyIt84cT1WNsEDSV8LMXgXnCqK5AvmI2e8PN1om5bwbA$.

Chapter 19—The Sack

159 Rex A. Hess, "Estrogen in the Adult Male Reproductive Tract: A Review," *Reproductive Biology and Endocrinology* 1, no. 1 (July 9, 2003): 52, https://doi.org/10.1186/1477-7827-1-52.

160 Tommaso Aversa et al., "Five-Year Prospective Evaluation of Thyroid Function Test Evolution in Children with Hashimoto's Thyroiditis Presenting with Either Euthyroidism or Subclinical Hypothyroidism.," *Thyroid* 26, no. 10 (October 1, 2016): 1450 56, https://doi.org/10.1089/thy.2016.0080.

161 "T3 (Triiodothyronine), Total, Serum—Mayo Clinic Laboratories | Endocrinology Catalog," accessed 3/2023, https://endocrinology.testcatalog.org/show/T3.

162 Leonard Wartofsky, "Levothyroxine: Therapeutic Use and Regulatory Issues Related to Bioequivalence," *Expert Opinion on Pharmacotherapy* 3, no. 6 (June 1, 2002): 727–32, https://doi.org/10.1517/14656566.3.6.727.

163 Leonard Wartofsky and Richard P. Dickey, "The Evidence for a Narrower Thyrotropin Reference Range Is Compelling," *The Journal of Clinical Endocrinology and Metabolism* 90, no. 9 (September 1, 2005): 5483–88, https://doi.org/10.1210/jc.2005-0455.

164 "T3 (Triiodothyronine), Total, Serum—Mayo Clinic Laboratories | Endocrinology Catalog," accessed 3/2023, https://endocrinology.testcatalog.org/show/T3.

165 Leonard Wartofsky, "Levothyroxine: Therapeutic Use and Regulatory Issues Related to Bioequivalence," *Expert Opinion on Pharmacotherapy* 3, no. 6 (June 1, 2002): 727–32, https://doi.org/10.1517/14656566.3.6.727.

166 Leonard Wartofsky and Richard P. Dickey, "The Evidence for a Narrower Thyrotropin Reference Range Is Compelling," *The Journal of Clinical Endocrinology and Metabolism* 90, no. 9 (September 1, 2005): 5483–88, https://doi.org/10.1210/jc.2005-0455.

167 "T3 (Triiodothyronine), Total, Serum—Mayo Clinic Laboratories | Endocrinology Catalog," accessed 3/2023, https://endocrinology.testcatalog.org/show/T3.

168 Leonard Wartofsky, "Levothyroxine: Therapeutic Use and Regulatory Issues Related to Bioequivalence," *Expert Opinion on Pharmacotherapy* 3, no. 6 (June 1, 2002): 727–32, https://doi.org/10.1517/14656566.3.6.727.

169 Leonard Wartofsky and Richard P. Dickey, "The Evidence for a Narrower Thyrotropin Reference Range Is Compelling," *The Journal of Clinical Endocrinology and Metabolism* 90, no. 9 (September 1, 2005): 5483–88, https://doi.org/10.1210/jc.2005-0455.

170 "T3 (Triiodothyronine), Total, Serum—Mayo Clinic Laboratories | Endocrinology Catalog," accessed 3/2023, https://endocrinology.testcatalog.org/show/T3.

171 Leonard Wartofsky, "Levothyroxine: Therapeutic Use and Regulatory Issues Related to Bioequivalence," *Expert Opinion on Pharmacotherapy* 3, no. 6 (June 1, 2002): 727–32, https://doi.org/10.1517/14656566.3.6.727.

172 Leonard Wartofsky and Richard P. Dickey, "The Evidence for a Narrower Thyrotropin Reference Range Is Compelling," *The Journal of Clinical Endocrinology and Metabolism* 90, no. 9 (September 1, 2005): 5483–88, https://doi.org/10.1210/jc.2005-0455.

173 Eva Bianconi et al., "An Estimation of the Number of Cells in the Human Body," *Annals of Human Biology* 40, no. 6 (November 14, 2013): 463–71, https://doi.org/10.3109/03014460.2013.807878.

174 Rundsarah Tahboub and Baha M. Arafah, "Sex Steroids and the Thyroid," *Best Practice & Research Clinical Endocrinology & Metabolism* 23, no. 6 (December 1, 2009): 769–80, https://doi.org/10.1016/j.beem.2009.06.005.

175 Adele Framer, "What I Have Learnt from Helping Thousands of People Taper off Antidepressants and Other Psychotropic Medications," *Therapeutic Advances in Psychopharmacology* 11 (March 16, 2021): 204512532199127, https://doi.org/10.1177/2045125321991274.

Chapter 20—Higher Quality

176 Van Overloop et al., *The Impact of Standardized Use of Head CT Decision Rules on Computed Tomography Imaging Utilization in Adult Minor Head Trauma*, Michigan Emergency Department Improvement Collaborative Annual Conference, Traverse City, MI, October 2022, permission granted from ECS for use.

177 Van Overloop et al., *The Impact of Standardized Use of Head CT Decision Rules on Computed Tomography Imaging Utilization in Adult Minor Head Trauma*, Michigan Emergency Department Improvement Collaborative Annual Conference, Traverse City, MI, October 2022, permission granted from ECS for use.

178 Van Overloop et al., *The Impact of Standardized Use of Head CT Decision Rules on Computed Tomography Imaging Utilization in Adult Minor Head Trauma*, Michigan Emergency Department Improvement Collaborative Annual Conference, Traverse City, MI, October 2022, permission granted from ECS for use.

179 David A. Kindig and Greg L. Stoddart, "What Is Population Health?," *American Journal of Public Health* 93, no. 3 (March 1, 2003): 380–83, https://doi.org/10.2105/ajph.93.3.380.

180 Coursera, "What Is Population Health? (+ Why It Matters)," Coursera, November 4, 2022, accessed 12/2022, https://www.coursera.org/articles/what-is-population-health.

181 Farzon A Nahvi, *Code Gray: Death, Life, and Uncertainty in the ER* (Simon and Schuster, 2023), 46.

182 Benjamin Schwartz, "Aligned Incentives," *Www.Linkedin.Com*, accessed January 2023, https://www.linkedin.com/pulse/aligned-incentives-benjamin-schwartz-md?trk=portfolio_article-card_title.

183 Benjamin Schwartz, "Aligned Incentives," *Www.Linkedin.Com*, accessed January 2023, https://www.linkedin.com/pulse/aligned-incentives-benjamin-schwartz-md?trk=portfolio_article-card_title.

184 Amanda Loudin, "'Only a Sociopath Could Work for a Large Health System,' Doc Says Sardonically," *Medscape*, February 24, 2023, accessed 3/2023, https://www.medscape.com/viewarticle/988422.

185 Tait D. Shanafelt, Joel Goh, and Christine A. Sinsky, "The Business Case for Investing in Physician Well-Being," *JAMA Internal Medicine* 177, no. 12 (December 1, 2017): 1826, https://doi.org/10.1001/jamainternmed.2017.4340.

186 American Medical Association and American Medical Association, "How Much Physician Burnout Is Costing Your Organization," American Medical Association, October 12, 2018, accessed, 3/2023, https://www.ama-assn.org/practice-management/physician-health/how-much-physician-burnout-costing-your-organization.

Chapter 21—Perspective and Set Points

187 Bruno Aouizerate, Corinne Martin-Guehl, and Jean Tignol, "Neurobiologie et Pharmacothérapie de La Phobie Sociale," *L'Encéphale* 30, no. 4 (September 1, 2004): 301–13, https://doi.org/10.1016/s0013-7006(04)95442-5.

188 Jamie Ducharme, "Tim Kaine Refuses to Let Long COVID Be an Afterthought," accessed 6/2022, https://www.yahoo.com/news/tim-kaine-refuses-let-long-110038029.html.

189 Michael Marshall, "COVID and Smell Loss: Answers Begin to Emerge," *Nature* 606, no. 7915 (June 1, 2022): 631–32, https://doi.org/10.1038/d41586-022-01589-z.

Chapter 22—Patient Experience

190 www.bamfhealth.com, "What is Theranostics?," accessed 1/2023, https://www.bamfhealth.com/.

191 Lindsey Bever, "She Listened to Her Doctors—and Her Baby Died. Now She's Warning Others about Breast-Feeding.," *Washington Post*, March 8, 2017, accessed 6/2022, https://www.washingtonpost.com/news/parenting/wp/2017/03/08/she-listened-to-her-doctors-and-her-baby-died-now-shes-warning-others-about-breast-feeding/.

192 Elisabeth Rosenthal, *An American Sickness: How Healthcare Became Big Business and How You Can Take It Back* (Penguin, 2018), 255.

193 Elisabeth Rosenthal, *An American Sickness: How Healthcare Became Big Business and How You Can Take It Back* (Penguin, 2018), 246-247.

194 Mms Analytics, "A Real Market in Medical Care? Singapore Shows the Way—TALON," TALON, November 22, 2021, accessed 11/2022, https://talonhealthtech.com/a-real-market-in-medical-care-singapore-shows-the-way/.

195 Lee Chien Earn, "Health System Overview: Singapore," accessed 11/2022, https://www.commonwealthfund.org/sites/default/files/2020-12/2020_IntlOverview_SING.pdf. .

196 "Life Expectancy by Country and in the World (2023)—Worldometer," accessed 11/2022, https://www.worldometers.info/demographics/life-expectancy/.

197 "How Does Health Spending in the U.S. Compare to Other Countries?—Peterson-KFF Health System Tracker," Peterson-KFF Health System Tracker, February 15, 2023, https://www.healthsystemtracker.org/chart-collection/health-spending-u-s-compare-countries/#GDP%20per%20capita%20and%20health%20consumption%20spending%20per%20capita,%202021%20(U.S.%20dollars,%20PPP%20adjusted).

198 Elisabeth Rosenthal, *An American Sickness: How Healthcare Became Big Business and How You Can Take It Back* (Penguin, 2018), 246-247.

199 Mms Analytics, "A Real Market in Medical Care? Singapore Shows the Way—TALON," TALON, November 22, 2021, accessed 11/2022, https://talonhealthtech.com/a-real-market-in-medical-care-singapore-shows-the-way/.

200 Lee Chien Earn, "Health System Overview: Singapore," accessed 11/2022, https://www.commonwealthfund.org/sites/default/files/2020-12/2020_IntlOverview_SING.pdf. .

201 "Life Expectancy by Country and in the World (2023)—Worldometer," accessed 11/2022, https://www.worldometers.info/demographics/life-expectancy/.

202 "How Does Health Spending in the U.S. Compare to Other Countries?—Peterson-KFF Health System Tracker," Peterson-KFF Health System Tracker, February 15, 2023, https://www.healthsystemtracker.org/chart-collection/health-spending-u-s-compare-countries/#GDP%20per%20capita%20and%20health%20consumption%20spending%20per%20capita,%202021%20(U.S.%20dollars,%20PPP%20adjusted).

203 "Out-of-Pocket Spending—Peterson-KFF Health System Tracker," Peterson-KFF Health System Tracker, December 22, 2022, https://www.healthsystemtracker.org/indicator/access-affordability/out-of-pocket-spending/#Average%20out-of-pocket%20health%20spending%20per%20capita,%20US%20dollars,%202021%20or%20nearest%20year%C2%A0%C2%A0.

204 "Ending Surprise Medical Bills | CMS," accessed 11/2022, https://www.cms.gov/nosurprises/Ending-Surprise-Medical-Bills.

205 "Ending Surprise Medical Bills | CMS," accessed 11/2022, https://www.cms.gov/nosurprises/Ending-Surprise-Medical-Bills.

206 American Hospital Association, "Detailed Summary of Health Provisions in Consolidated Appropriations Act, 2021," accessed 11/2022, https://www.aha.org/system/files/media/file/2020/12/detailed-summary-health-provisions-consolidated-appropriations-act-2021-bulletin-12-22-20.pdf.

207 American Hospital Association, "Detailed Summary of Health Provisions in Consolidated Appropriations Act, 2021," accessed 11/2022, https://www.aha.org/system/files/media/file/2020/12/detailed-summary-health-provisions-consolidated-appropriations-act-2021-bulletin-12-22-20.pdf.

208 Elisabeth Rosenthal, *An American Sickness: How Healthcare Became Big Business and How You Can Take It Back* (Penguin, 2018).

209 Emily Rodgers, "Healthcare Mystery Shopping: Improving Patient Experience (PX)," , accessed 11/2022, https://www.driveresearch.com/market-research-company-blog/healthcare-mystery-shopping-improving-patient-experience-px/.

Chapter 23—Horrible v Helpful

210 Laurent Lebreton et al., "Evidence That the Great Pacific Garbage Patch Is Rapidly Accumulating Plastic," *Scientific Reports* 8, no. 1 (March 22, 2018), https://doi.org/10.1038/s41598-018-22939-w.

Chapter 24—Prevention, Procedures and Profits

211 Elisabeth Rosenthal, *An American Sickness: How Healthcare Became Big Business and How You Can Take It Back* (Penguin, 2018), 190.

212 J. Nwando Olayiwola and Mark Rastetter, "Aiming for Health Equity: The Bullseye of the Quadruple Aim," *Journal of Hospital Management and Health Policy* 5 (June 25, 2021): 11, https://doi.org/10.21037/jhmhp-20-101.

213 Timothy Snyder, "It's Time We Fixed Our Hospitals," The Saturday Evening Post, January 10, 2022, accessed 2/2022, https://www.saturdayeveningpost.com/2022/01/its-time-we-fixed-our-hospitals/.

214 Timothy Snyder, "It's Time We Fixed Our Hospitals," The Saturday Evening Post, January 10, 2022, accessed 2/2022, https://www.saturdayeveningpost.com/2022/01/its-time-we-fixed-our-hospitals/.

215 Marty Makary, *The Price We Pay: What Broke American Health Care—and How to Fix It* (Bloomsbury Publishing USA, 2019).

216 Patrick Taylor, *An Irish Country Doctor* (St. Martin's Press, 2011), 101.

217 Marty Makary, *The Price We Pay: What Broke American Health Care—and How to Fix It* (Bloomsbury Publishing USA, 2019), 213.

218 Marty Makary, *The Price We Pay: What Broke American Health Care—and How to Fix It* (Bloomsbury Publishing USA, 2019), chapter 14.

219 National Association of Insurance Commissioners, "Pharmacy Benefit Managers," accessed 6/2022, https://content.naic.org/cipr-topics/pharmacy-benefit-managers.

220 Marty Makary, *The Price We Pay: What Broke American Health Care—and How to Fix It* (Bloomsbury Publishing USA, 2019), chapter 14.

221 National Association of Insurance Commissioners, "Pharmacy Benefit Managers," accessed 6/2022, https://content.naic.org/cipr-topics/pharmacy-benefit-managers.

222 Marty Makary, *The Price We Pay: What Broke American Health Care—and How to Fix It* (Bloomsbury Publishing USA, 2019), chapter 14.

223 pbmaccountability.org, "PBM Accountability Project," accessed 6/2022 https://b11210f4-9a71-4e4c-a08f-cf43a83bc1df.usrfiles.com/ugd/b11210_264612f6b98e47b3a8502054f66bb2a1.pdf.

224 commerce.senate.gov, "Pharmacy Benefit Manager Transparency Act of 2022," accessed 6/2022, https://www.commerce.senate.gov/services/files/4E353950-DB5D-409F-A6D7-1FA12B996843.

225 Elisabeth Rosenthal, *An American Sickness: How Healthcare Became Big Business and How You Can Take It Back* (Penguin, 2018), chapter 4.

226 Elisabeth Rosenthal, *An American Sickness: How Healthcare Became Big Business and How You Can Take It Back* (Penguin, 2018), chapter 4.

227 Dena Bunis, "Landmark Changes: New Drug price law could save older Americans billions in cost," *AARP Bulletin*, Volume 63, Issue 1, September 2022, pages 6-8.

228 Dena Bunis, "Landmark Changes: New Drug price law could save older Americans billions in cost," *AARP Bulletin*, Volume 63, Issue 1, September 2022, pages 6-8.

229 Steve Cohen, "Instead of Prior Authorization, Insurers Should Go Back to the Old 'Pay-and-Chase' Model," STAT, March 10, 2021, accessed 7/2022, https://www.statnews.com/2021/03/11/instead-of-prior-authorization-insurers-should-go-back-to-the-old-pay-and-chase-model/.

230 "Five Ways Commercial Insurer Policies Drive Up Costs and Hurt Patients | AHA News," American Hospital Association | AHA News, May 2, 2022, accessed 7/2022, https://www.aha.org/news/blog/2022-05-02-five-ways-commercial-insurer-policies-drive-costs-and-hurt-patients.

231 Elisabeth Rosenthal, *An American Sickness: How Healthcare Became Big Business and How You Can Take It Back* (Penguin, 2018), 179.

232 Steve Cohen, "Instead of Prior Authorization, Insurers Should Go Back to the Old 'Pay-and-Chase' Model," STAT, March 10, 2021, accessed 7/2022, https://www.statnews.com/2021/03/11/instead-of-prior-authorization-insurers-should-go-back-to-the-old-pay-and-chase-model/.

233 Steve Cohen, "Instead of Prior Authorization, Insurers Should Go Back to the Old 'Pay-and-Chase' Model," STAT, March 10, 2021, accessed 7/2022, https://www.statnews.com/2021/03/11/instead-of-prior-authorization-insurers-should-go-back-to-the-old-pay-and-chase-model/.

234 edihc.org, "Considerations for Improving Prior Authorization in Healthcare An eHealth Initiative Collaborative Project | 2019," accessed 7/2022, https://www.ehidc.org/sites/default/files/resources/files/Considerations%20for%20PA%202.26.19.pdf.

235 edihc.org, "Considerations for Improving Prior Authorization in Healthcare An eHealth Initiative Collaborative Project | 2019," accessed 7/2022, https://www.ehidc.org/sites/default/files/resources/files/Considerations%20for%20PA%202.26.19.pdf.

236 Dana Lawrence, "Passage of SB 247—a Win for Patients, Communities, Physicians," Michigan Family Physician: Summer 2022, pages 12-13.

237 Gretchen Morgenson, "Private Equity Firms Increasingly Going into Health Care," *NBC News*, March 28, 2022, accessed 4/2022, https://www.nbcnews.com/health/health-care/doctor-fired-er-warns-effect-profit-firms-us-health-care-rcna19975.

238 Vinayak K. Prasad, *Malignant: How Bad Policy and Bad Evidence Harm People with Cancer* (Johns Hopkins University Press, 2020), 104.

239 Vinayak K. Prasad, *Malignant: How Bad Policy and Bad Evidence Harm People with Cancer* (Johns Hopkins University Press, 2020), chapter 7.

240 Department of Justice, U.S. Attorney's Office, Western District of Michigan, "Muskegon Doctor Pleads Guilty To Billing For Office Visits She Never Performed And Agrees To Settle Civil Claims For Half A Million Dollars," accessed 6/2022, https://urldefense.com/v3/__https://www.justice.gov/usao-wdmi/pr/2022_0608_peterson__;!!Kyqyl2UCiG04!zSs2Xovte7z2nnTIvmnSdLwQswC03639tMJifVNN1Q2h_afusgcgu4vKq_Gf6xWMwOObp4CBieaV75wQbZC_Wyfq$.

241 Elisabeth Rosenthal, *An American Sickness: How Healthcare Became Big Business and How You Can Take It Back* (Penguin, 2018), 97.

Chapter 26—Who Are the Incentives Aligned For?

242 Benjamin Schwartz, "Aligned Incentives," *Www.Linkedin.Com*, accessed January 2023, https://www.linkedin.com/pulse/aligned-incentives-benjamin-schwartz-md?trk=portfolio_article-card_title.

243 Wikipedia contributors, "Great Resignation," Wikipedia, March 27, 2023, https://en.wikipedia.org/wiki/Great_Resignation.

244 Dylan Scott, "What the NYC Nurses Strike Reveals about US Health Care," Vox, January 11, 2023, accessed 1/2023, https://www.vox.com/health-care/2023/1/11/23548236/nyc-nurses-strike-2023-mount-sinai-montefiore-hospitals.

245 Dylan Scott, "What the NYC Nurses Strike Reveals about US Health Care," Vox, January 11, 2023, accessed 1/2023, https://www.vox.com/health-care/2023/1/11/23548236/nyc-nurses-strike-2023-mount-sinai-montefiore-hospitals.

246 Tait D. Shanafelt, Joel Goh, and Christine A. Sinsky, "The Business Case for Investing in Physician Well-Being," *JAMA Internal Medicine* 177, no. 12 (December 1, 2017): 1826, https://doi.org/10.1001/jamainternmed.2017.4340.

247 Ida Boysen, "Just Culture: A Foundation for Balanced Accountability and Patient Safety.," *The Ochsner Journal*, Volume 13, Issue 3, September 21, 2013, 400–406, https://www.ncbi.nlm.nih.gov/pmc/articles/PMC3776518/.

248 Ida Boysen, "Just Culture: A Foundation for Balanced Accountability and Patient Safety.," *The Ochsner Journal*, Volume 13, Issue 3, September 21, 2013, 400–406, https://www.ncbi.nlm.nih.gov/pmc/articles/PMC3776518/.

249 Vinayak K. Prasad, *Malignant: How Bad Policy and Bad Evidence Harm People with Cancer* (Johns Hopkins University Press, 2020), 195.

250 Liz Kwo, "Contributed: Top 10 Use Cases for AI in Healthcare," MobiHealthNews, July 2, 2021, accessed 11/2022, https://www.mobihealthnews.com/news/contributed-top-10-use-cases-ai-healthcare.

251 Sam Daley, "Artificial Intelligence in Healthcare: 38 Examples Improving the Future of Medicine," Built In, June 10, 2022, accessed 11/2022, https://builtin.com/artificial-intelligence/artificial-intelligence-healthcare.

252 Jared Kaltwasser, "Healthcare's Journey into the Metaverse," *Managed Healthcare Executive*, Volume 32, Number 10, Oct 2022, 30-31.

253 Jared Kaltwasser, "Healthcare's Journey into the Metaverse," *Managed Healthcare Executive*, Volume 32, Number 10, Oct 2022, 30-31.

254 Adam Hayes, "Blockchain Facts: What Is It, How It Works, and How It Can Be Used," Investopedia, September 27, 2022, accessed 11/2022, https://www.investopedia.com/terms/b/blockchain.asp.

255 Adam Hayes, "Blockchain Facts: What Is It, How It Works, and How It Can Be Used," Investopedia, September 27, 2022, accessed 11/2022, https://www.investopedia.com/terms/b/blockchain.asp.

256 Sam Daley, "Blockchain in Healthcare: 17 Examples to Know," Built In, August 9, 2022, accessed 11/2022, https://builtin.com/blockchain/blockchain-healthcare-applications-companies.

257 Mackenzie Bean, "7 Stats on Physician Burnout amid COVID-19," *Www.Beckershospitalreview.Com*, accessed on 1/2022, https://www.beckershospitalreview.com/hospital-physician-relationships/7-stats-on-physician-burnout-2.html#:~:text=Sixty%2Done%20percent%20of%20physicians,the%20Physicians%20Foundation%20released%20Aug.&text=The%20survey%20is%20based%20on,May%2026%20and%20June%209.

258 Maria Clark, "50+ Shocking Physician Burnout Statistics You'll Never Believe—Etactics," *Etactics | Revenue Cycle Software*, December 3, 2021, accessed 1/2022, https://etactics.com/blog/physician-burnout-statistics.

259 Farzon A Nahvi, *Code Gray: Death, Life, and Uncertainty in the ER* (Simon and Schuster, 2023), 68.

260 Eric Grosse, "'Pajama Time': Unraveling The 'Whys' Behind Physician Burnout," Forbes, December 5, 2022, accessed 1/2023, https://www.forbes.com/sites/forbestechcouncil/2022/12/05/pajama-time-unraveling-the-whys-behind-physician-burnout/?sh=35cc59a15cb6.

261 John Hammergren and Phil Harkins, *Skin in the Game: How Putting Yourself First Today Will Revolutionize Health Care Tomorrow* (John Wiley & Sons, 2008), 136.

262 John Hammergren and Phil Harkins, *Skin in the Game: How Putting Yourself First Today Will Revolutionize Health Care Tomorrow* (John Wiley & Sons, 2008), 137-139.

263 Sarah Kliff, Josh Katz, and Rumsey Taylor, "Why Hospitals and Health Insurers Didn't Want You to See Their Prices," The New York Times, August 23, 2021, accessed 1/2023, https://www.nytimes.com/interactive/2021/08/22/upshot/hospital-prices.html.

264 Sarah Kliff, Josh Katz, and Rumsey Taylor, "Why Hospitals and Health Insurers Didn't Want You to See Their Prices," The New York Times, August 23, 2021, accessed 1/2023, https://www.nytimes.com/interactive/2021/08/22/upshot/hospital-prices.html.

265 Sarah Kliff, Josh Katz, and Rumsey Taylor, "Why Hospitals and Health Insurers Didn't Want You to See Their Prices," The New York Times, August 23, 2021, accessed 1/2023, https://www.nytimes.com/interactive/2021/08/22/upshot/hospital-prices.html.

266 Regulations.gov, "Non-Compete Clause Rule (NPRM)," accessed 1/2023, https://www.regulations.gov/document/FTC-2023-0007-0001/comment.

267 Carl Schuessler, "Health Rosetta Case Study: Gasparilla Inn & Club, Mitigate Partners," accessed 1/2023, https://mitigatepartners.com/wp-content/uploads/2021/03/Health-Rosetta-Case-Study-Gasparilla-Inn-Club-by-Carl-Schuessler-of-Mitigate-Partners-2-22-20.pdf.

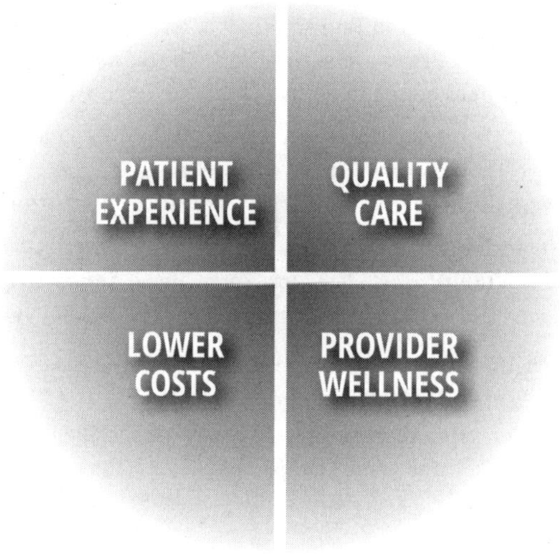
PATIENT EXPERIENCE
QUALITY CARE
LOWER COSTS
PROVIDER WELLNESS